ALEXANDRU NEAGOE is Lecturer at the
Areopagus Centre for Christian Education
and Contemporary Culture, and Pastor of the
First Baptist Church, Timisoara, Romania.

THE TRIAL OF THE GOSPEL

For many years Luke–Acts has been studied as a work of history and theology. *The Trial of the Gospel* sets out to examine Luke's writings as an apologetic work, by focusing on those parts of Luke's story where the apologetic overtones seem most prominent – the trial narratives. By analysing the trials of all major Lukan characters – Jesus, Peter, Stephen, and Paul – Alexandru Neagoe argues that the narratives are best understood when viewed as part of Luke's *apologia pro evangelio*, a purpose which is in keeping with the author's declared aim to give his readers 'assurance' about the 'matters' in which they had been instructed (Luke 1.4). Neagoe concludes that the specific role of the trial narratives is to provide the framework within which important tenets of the Christian faith are themselves put 'on trial' before the reader, with the intended result of the gospel's confirmation.

ALEXANDRU NEAGOE is Lecturer at the Areopagus Centre for Christian Education and Contemporary Culture and Pastor of the First Baptist Church, Timişoara, Romania.

SOCIETY FOR NEW TESTAMENT STUDIES

MONOGRAPH SERIES

General Editor: Richard Bauckham

116

THE TRIAL OF THE GOSPEL

The Trial of the Gospel

*An Apologetic Reading of
Luke's Trial Narratives*

ALEXANDRU NEAGOE

PUBLISHED BY THE PRESS SYNDICATE OF THE UNIVERSITY OF CAMBRIDGE
The Pitt Building, Trumpington Street, Cambridge, United Kingdom

CAMBRIDGE UNIVERSITY PRESS
The Edinburgh Building, Cambridge CB2 2RU, UK
40 West 20th Street, New York, NY 10011-4211, USA
477 Williamstown Road, Port Melbourne, VIC 3207, Australia
Ruiz de Alarcón 13, 28014 Madrid, Spain
Dock House, The Waterfront, Cape Town 8001, South Africa

http://www.cambridge.org

First published 2002

Printed in the United Kingdom at the University Press, Cambridge

Typeface Times/10/12   *System* LAT_EX 2_ε   [TB]

A catalogue record for this book is available from the British Library.

Library of Congress cataloguing in publication data

Neagoe, Alexandru, 1968–
The trial of the gospel: an apologetic reading of Luke's trial narratives / Alexandru Neagoe.
    p.   cm. – (Monograph series / Society for New Testament Studies; 116)
Includes bibliographical references and indexes.
ISBN 0 521 80948 7 (hardback)
1. Trials in the Bible.   2. Bible. N.T. Luke – Criticism, interpretation, etc.   3. Bible. N.T.
Acts – Criticism, interpretation, etc.   4. Apologetics – History – Early church, ca. 30-600.
I. Title.   II. Monograph series (Society for New Testament Studies); 116.
BS2589.6.T73 N43   2002
226.4′06 – dc21   2001037392 CIP

ISBN 0 521 80948 7 hardback

To Nuți, my love

CONTENTS

PREFACE

I cannot hope here to do justice to all those who have made possible the completion of this book, but special mention must be made of the following: I am honoured to express my special gratitude to Professor Max Turner, for his sharp yet constructive advice, and for the model of scholarly competence combined with Christian commitment which I saw in him as supervisor of my PhD dissertation on which the book is based. (The dissertation was supervised at London Bible College and submitted to Brunel University in the spring of 1998.) Thanks are also due to my second supervisor, Dr Conrad Gempf, for his willingness to offer critical evaluation on certain areas of my research and to my friend James McGrath, who undertook the tedious task of proofreading the thesis.

Throughout the period of my research, the Romanian Missionary Society fully covered my tuition fees and several other costs – special thanks are due to Les and Dottie Tidball and Alan and Ann Penrose. Most of my living expenses were covered by the Emmanuel Church, Northwood; I shall never know all those who contributed, but Ann Bailey and Keith and Joan Alsop must be singled out for their constant help and affection. Generous gifts also came from the Keswick Convention, the Jerusalem Trust, and the Castle Street Church, Tredegar. To all these, I can only say a heartfelt 'Thank you.'

I am also deeply grateful to my parents and to my sister's family for their ceaseless prayers on my behalf during the period of my studies. Last but not least, special thanks are due to my precious wife Nuți, who kindly accepted to put up with a very busy husband during the first few months of our marriage, while the preparations for publication were being made.

ABBREVIATIONS

ABD	D. N. Freedman *et alii* (eds.), *The Anchor Bible Dictionary*, 6 vols., New York: Doubleday, 1992
ANQ	*Andover Newton Quarterly*
AV	Authorized Version
BAFCS	*The Book of Acts in Its First Century Setting*
BETL	Bibliotheca ephemeridum theologicarum lovaniensium
BHPT	*Bibliotheca historico-philologico-theologica*
Bib	*Biblica*
BK	*Bibel und Kirche*
BR	*Biblical Research*
BTB	*Biblical Theology Bulletin*
BWANT	Beiträge zur Wissenschaft vom Alten und Neuen Testament
BZ	*Biblische Zeitschrift*
CBQ	*Catholic Biblical Quarterly*
ETL	*Ephemerides theologicae lovanienses*
EvQ	*Evangelical Quarterly*
Exp	*The Expositor*
ExpT	*The Expository Times*
FRLANT	Forschungen zur Religion und Literatur des Alten und Neuen Testaments
GELNT	J. P. Louw and E. A. Nida (eds.), *Greek–English Lexicon of the New Testament Based on Semantic Domains*, 2 vols., United Bible Societies, 1988
HTR	*Harvard Theological Review*
ICC	International Critical Commentary
Int	*Interpretation*
JBL	*Journal of Biblical Literature*
JOTT	*Journal of Translation and Textlinguistics*
JSNT	*Journal for the Study of the New Testament*

JSNTSup	*Journal for the Study of the New Testament*, Supplement Series
JTS	*Journal of Theological Studies*
LXX	The Septuagint
MT	The Masoretic Text (of the Old Testament)
n.d.	not dated
NEB	New English Bible
Neot	*Neotestamentica*
NIDNTT	C. Brown (ed.), *New International Dictionary of New Testament Theology*, 4 vols., revised edition, Carlisle: Paternoster, 1992
NIGTC	New International Greek Testament Commentary
NIV	New International Version
NovT	*Novum Testamentum*
NTG	New Testament Guides
NTS	*New Testament Studies*
RB	*Revue biblique*
RHPR	*Revue d'histoire et de philosophie religieuses*
RQ	*Restoration Quarterly*
RSR	*Recherches de science religieuse*
RSV	Revised Standard Version
SBL	Society of Biblical Literature
SBLDS	SBL Dissertation Series
SBLMS	SBL Monograph Series
SBT	Studies in Biblical Theology
SC	*The Second Century*
ScEsp	*Science et esprit*
SNTSMS	Society for New Testament Studies Monograph Series
ST	*Studia theologica*
StudBT	*Studia biblica et theologica*
TDNT	G. Kittel and K. Friedrich (eds.), *Theological Dictionary of the New Testament*, translated from German by G. W. Bromiley, 9 vols., Grand Rapids: Eerdmans, 1964–76
TLZ	*Teologische Literaturzeitung*
TNTC	*Tyndale New Testament Commentary*
TQ	*Teologische Quartalschrift*
TU	*Texte und Untersuchungen*

TynB	*Tyndale Bulletin*
WTJ	*Westminster Theological Journal*
WUNT	Wissenschaftliche Untersuchungen zum Neuen Testament
ZNW	*Zeitschrift für die neutestamentliche Wissenschaft*
ZTK	*Zeitschrift für Theologie und Kirche*

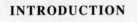

INTRODUCTION

1

INTRODUCTION

Trials and apologetics in Luke–Acts: setting the scene

Luke's[1] special interest in forensic trials has often been recognised in Lukan scholarship.[2] The textual evidence for such a concern on Luke's part abounds.[3] While in the Gospels[4] of Matthew and Mark Jesus predicts the disciples' trials only once (Matt. 10.17–20; Mark 13.9–11), in the Third Gospel he does so twice (12.11–12; 21.12–15). Similarly, whereas for the other two Synoptics Jesus' trial includes only two episodes (one before the Sanhedrin and one before Pilate), in Luke's Gospel four trial scenes are recorded: one before the Sanhedrin (22.66–71), a preliminary hearing before Pilate (23.1–5), a peculiarly Lukan episode before Herod (23.6–12), and a second session before Pilate (23.13–25). As one turns to Acts, the evidence is even more ample. After a brief presentation of the origins and lifestyle of the early Christian community in Jerusalem, the reader encounters two extensive trial scenes involving Peter (4.1–31;

---

[1] The author of both the Third Gospel and Acts will be referred to throughout as Luke. The common authorship (as well as narrative unity) of the two books is advocated or assumed by numerous recent Lukan studies: so, for example, W. S. Kurz, *Reading Luke–Acts: Dynamics of Biblical Narrative*, Louisville: Westminster/John Knox, 1993; I. H. Marshall, 'Acts and the "Former Treatise"', in B. W. Winter and A. D. Clarke (eds.), *The Book of Acts in its Ancient Literary Setting*, BAFCS, vol. I, Grand Rapids: Eerdmans; Carlisle: Paternoster, 1993, pp. 163–82; R. Pesch, *Die Apostelgeschichte*, Evangelisch-Katholischer Kommentar zum Neuen Testament 5:1–2, Zürich and Neukirchen-Vluyn: Benzinger, 1986, especially pp. 24–5; R. C. Tannehill, *The Narrative Unity of Luke–Acts: A Literary Interpretation*, 2 vols., Minneapolis: Fortress, 1986, 1990. Even when the generic, narrative, and theological unity has been called into question (M. C. Parsons and R. I. Pervo, *Rethinking the Unity of Luke and Acts*, Minneapolis: Fortress, 1993), the authorial unity has remained largely unchallenged.

[2] See, for instance: J. H. Neyrey, *The Passion According to Luke: A Redaction Study of Luke's Soteriology*, New York: Paulist Press, 1985, pp. 84–5; A. A. Trites, 'The Importance of Legal Scenes and Language in the Book of Acts', *NovT* 16 (1974), 278–84.

[3] For more detail on the evidence listed here, see the relevant sections below.

[4] To help distinguish between 'Gospel(s)' as New Testament literary documents and 'gospel' as the content of the Christian belief and proclamation, I shall write the former with an initial capital and the latter without.

5.17–42). These are soon followed by an even lengthier account of the trial and martyrdom of Stephen (6.9–7.60). Finally, Paul's whole missionary activity is scattered with conflicts and challenges which are often cast in a trial form, culminating, undoubtedly, with Paul's judicial history between his arrest in Jerusalem (21.27) and his two-year stay in Rome (28.30–1). It is not without justification, then, that Neyrey can write: 'Forensic trials in Acts have an incredible scope: (a) *all of the major figures* of Acts (Peter, Stephen, and Paul) are tried, (b) in *all of the significant places* where the Gospel was preached (Judea, Jerusalem, Achaia, and Rome); (c) the trials take place *before Jewish courts as well as Roman tribunals*.'[5]

It is somewhat intriguing, in view of such a significant Lukan emphasis, that there is to date not a single monograph specifically exploring Luke's use of the trial motif. The attention has tended to focus instead on individual trial scenes or, at most, on the trial(s) of a single Lukan character – mainly Jesus or Paul.[6] To the extent to which the question of authorial intent has been raised with regard to the trial material in larger sections of Luke–Acts, this has been done only indirectly, mainly in connection with the representation of Luke–Acts as some form of apologia. It is important, therefore, to introduce this discussion of Luke's trial motif with a more general survey of previous research on apologetics in Luke–Acts and thus acquire a better grasp of the angles from which Lukan trials have been interpreted in the past. This survey is at the same time necessary in view of the fact that the present study itself proposes an apologetic reading of Luke's trial motif.

Previous research on apologetics in Luke–Acts

The present survey[7] aims to include both works which have explicitly applied 'apologetic' terminology to aspects of Luke–Acts and works which have noted in Luke's writing tendencies which would naturally belong

---

[5] Neyrey, *Passion*, p. 85.

[6] For bibliographical information relating to individual Lukan characters, see the relevant chapters below.

[7] A partly similar survey of Lukan apologetics to the one presented here can be found in S. E. Pattison, 'A Study of the Apologetic Function of the Summaries of Acts', unpublished PhD dissertation, Emory University, 1990, pp. 10–35. Several observations justify my own review. First, the number and importance of the works which have been produced since Pattison's thesis are indicative of the need for a more up-to-date survey. Second, Pattison's survey is limited to Acts; this one includes Luke's Gospel. Third, only very limited attention is given by Pattison to works which I shall list under the heading 'An apologia for the gospel' (see pp. 12–21) – his survey does not in fact include such a category.

to what we regard as 'Christian apologetics'.[8] Due to the fluidity of the term in its contemporary use, its meaning within the present work needs to be defined here. When used with reference to a first-century context, I take 'Christian apologetic' (which I use interchangeably with 'Christian apologia') to mean *the exercise of advocating the reliability of the Christian faith, or aspects of it.*[9] The term 'advocating' is preferred to the more commonly used 'defending' because I take apologetics to include not only defence against specific objections but also the positive presentation of a case on behalf of the Christian faith.

The major sections in the survey below are based on the purported *object* of Luke's apologetic (i.e. on whose behalf Luke is arguing), while the subsections describe the specific *nature* of Luke's purported apologetic. It should also be noted that due to the broad scope of this survey I shall limit the discussion to works which view Luke's apologetic agenda as having some relation to Luke's entire work, or at least to the whole of Luke's second volume (which, generally speaking, has been the more closely associated with apologetics). More in-depth discussion of previous research on individual trial accounts will be offered at the beginning of relevant sections – in fact even some of the works which are presented here in an overview will be analysed in more detail later. As for the authors whose works are surveyed here, although most of them would insist that Luke has more than one purpose in mind, I shall discuss their suggestions only in the areas in which their work has made a distinctive contribution.

---

[8] One possibly surprising omission from the present survey is P. F. Esler's *Community and Gospel in Luke–Acts: The Social and Political Motivations of Lucan Theology* (Cambridge University Press, 1987). For those who view 'apologetics' and 'legitimation' as two closely related notions, Esler's repeated designation of Luke's task as one of socio-political legitimation may of itself provide sufficient grounds for including his monograph in the category of works dealing with Lukan apologetics. The reason for which I have refrained from including it is the author's specific dissociation of his thesis from interpretations which regard Luke's goal as apologetic (Esler, *Community*, pp. 205–19).

[9] In modern times, 'Christian apologetics' has also come to include the *study* (as well as the actual exercise) of advocating the Christian faith. For a definition of 'apologetics', as a modern theological discipline and as distinct from 'apology' ('the defence of Christian truth'), see A. Richardson, *Christian Apologetics*, London: SCM Press, 1947, p. 19. Nevertheless, such a linguistic distinction is typically ignored in contemporary literature. Among the numerous works which use the term 'apologetics' to include not only the study but also the exercise of defending Christian truth, see D. K. Clark and N. L. Geisler, *Apologetics in the New Age: A Christian Critique of Pantheism*, Grand Rapids: Baker, 1990; A. Dulles, *A History of Apologetics*, London: Hutchinson, 1971; N. L. Geisler, *Christian Apologetics*, Grand Rapids: Baker, 1978; P. J. Griffiths, *An Apology for Apologetics: A Study in the Logic of Interreligious Dialogue,* Maryknoll, NY: Orbis, 1991; P. Kreeft and R. K. Tacelli, *Handbook of Christian Apologetics*, Downers Grove, IL: Inter-Varsity Press, 1994.

An apologia for Paul

M. Schneckenburger, whose *Über den Zweck der Apostelgeschichte*[10] was the first thorough examination of Luke's purpose,[11] has argued that Acts was designed as an apology for Paul, addressed to Jewish Christians, with the intention of defending Paul's position in the church against the attacks of the Judaizers.[12]

In a similar vein, E. Trocmé has maintained that towards the end of the first century there were two rival branches of the church: the Pauline churches of Asia Minor, Macedonia, and Achaia, and the Judaizing churches, rooted especially in Alexandria. In this context, Trocmé suggests, Acts was written as 'une apologie intrachrétienne' ('an inter-Christian apologia'),[13] which through its commendation of Paul was meant to show that the Pauline churches were in no way inferior to the churches of Alexandria which were proud to trace their origins back to the Jerusalem church and the twelve apostles. In order to achieve this, Luke presented Paul as 'le *seul continuateur de l'oeuvre entreprise par les Douze*' ('the only continuator of the work performed by the Twelve').[14]

More recently, this general trend has been revitalised by the works of J. Jervell and R. L. Brawley. According to Jervell, Luke's extensive account of Paul's trial, and especially of his apologetic speeches in this context (22.1–21; 23.1; 24.10–21; 26.1–23), is a device which enables the author to put forward an apologia for Paul's Jewish orthodoxy, in the context of the apostle's controversial reputation in Luke's ecclesiastic milieu.[15] Brawley's contribution,[16] on the other hand, is to a large

---

[10] Bern, 1841.

[11] See W. W. Gasque, *A History of the Interpretation of the Acts of the Apostles*, Peabody, MA: Hendrickson, 1989, pp. 32–3.

[12] For a useful summary of Schneckenburger's position, see A. J. Mattill, 'The Purpose of Acts: Schneckenburger Reconsidered', in W. W. Gasque and R. P. Martin (eds.), *Apostolic History and the Gospel: Biblical and Historical Essays Presented to F. F. Bruce*, Exeter: Paternoster, 1970, pp. 108–12. See also Gasque, *History*, pp. 32–9.

[13] E. Trocmé *Le 'Livre des Actes' et l'histoire*, Paris: Presses Universitaires de France, 1957, pp. 54–5.

[14] Ibid., p. 67.

[15] J. Jervell, 'Paul: The Teacher of Israel: The Apologetic Speeches of Paul in Acts', in J. Jervell, *Luke and the People of God: A New Look at Luke–Acts*, Minneapolis: Augsburg Publishing House, 1972, pp. 153–83 (previously published in German as 'Paulus – Der Lehrer Israels. Zu den apologetischen Paulusreden in der Apostelgeschichte', *NovT* 10 (1968), 164–90). The Jewishness of the Lukan Paul, with its apologetic function, is also advocated in several other works of J. Jervell: 'James: The Defender of Paul', in Jervell, *Luke and the People of God*, pp. 185–207; 'Paul in the Acts of the Apostles: Tradition, History, Theology', in J. Kremer (ed.), *Les Actes des Apôtres*, BETL 48, Gembloux: J. Duculot; Leuven University Press, 1979, pp. 297–306; *The Unknown Paul: Essays on Luke–Acts and Early Christian History*, Minneapolis: Augsburg Publishing House, 1984.

[16] R. L. Brawley, *Luke–Acts and the Jews: Conflict, Apology, and Conciliation*, Atlanta: Scholars Press, 1987, esp. ch. 9.

extent a contemporary reading of Luke's writings through the spectacles of F. C. Baur,[17] according to whom the early church was torn between the Judaizing tendencies of the Petrine Christianity and the universalistic orientations of the Pauline churches (in welcoming Gentiles without requiring them first to become Jewish proselytes).[18] As the conflict from Jewish quarters was increasing, Brawley argues, Luke decided to compose his writings, which he aimed at the anti-Paulinist groups (Jews, Jewish Christians, converts from among God-fearers). Luke's purpose is partly apologetic, as he shows how even the Jewish opposition plays a legitimating role by establishing Jesus' identity (especially and programatically in the Nazareth incident) and by prompting Paul's Gentile mission. At the same time, Brawley argues, Luke's purpose is also conciliatory: Paul undergoes Jewish rituals; through the apostolic decree Gentiles are required to make concessions to Jewish Christians; the Pharisees are portrayed predominantly positively.[19]

Finally, a more solitary voice among the well-populated camp of those who view Paul's defence as central to the purpose of Acts is that of A. J. Mattill.[20] In his view, although Luke had already been gathering material for his story of the early church, the decisive factor in the final shaping of Acts was Luke's realisation of the indifference, or even hostility, of the Jewish Christians towards Paul, as he came under Jewish attack in Jerusalem (Acts 21). Luke's specific aim is, therefore, to deal with the objections of the Jewish Christians against Paul and thus to cause them to side with him, in the context of his still forthcoming trial in Rome.[21]

---

[17] Brawley himself (ibid., p. 3) acknowledges antecedents for his approach in the work of Baur.

[18] See Gasque, *History*, pp. 27–30.

[19] Brawley, *Luke–Acts*, pp. 157–8.

[20] Mattill, 'Purpose'. The same proposal finds confirmation for Mattill as he later studies the concepts of *Naherwartung and Fernerwartung* in the book of Acts, and as he 'reconsiders' H. H. Evans' Jesus–Paul parallels in Luke–Acts and R. B. Rackham's early dating of Luke's writings (A. J. Mattill, '*Naherwartung, Fernerwartung* and the Purpose of Luke–Acts: Weymouth Reconsidered', *CBQ* 34 (1972), 276–93, especially p. 293; 'The Jesus–Paul Parallels and the Purpose of Luke–Acts: H. H. Evans Reconsidered', *NovT* 17 (1975), 15–46, especially p. 46; 'The Date and Purpose of Luke–Acts: Rackham Reconsidered', *CBQ* 40 (1978), 335–50, especially p. 348).

[21] Somewhat similar to Mattill's position is that advocated by a number of scholars before him and according to which the book of Acts, or Luke–Acts as a whole, was written in order to provide material which could be used at Paul's trial before Nero: M. V. Aberle, 'Exegetische Studien. 2. Über den Zweck der Apostelgeschichte', *TQ* 37 (1855), 173–236; G. S. Duncan, *St. Paul's Ephesian Ministry: A Reconstruction (With Special Reference to the Ephesian Origin of the Imprisonment Epistles)*, New York: Charles Scribner's Sons, 1930, pp. 96–100; D. Plooij, 'The Work of St Luke', *Exp* 8:8 (1914), 511–23; and 'Again: The Work of St Luke', *Exp* 8:13 (1917), 108–24; J. I. Still, *St Paul on Trial*, London: SCM Press, 1923.

(*continued on next page*)

A few observations regarding the contention that Luke aimed to present an apologia for Paul are in place. The works advocating this position have the undisputed merit of having made Lukan scholarship aware of the unique significance which Paul – and particularly the accusations and defences surrounding his character in the final chapters of Acts – has for any analysis of Luke's aims. Equally valid is their special emphasis on Paul's relationship to Judaism, as a major dimension of the Pauline conflicts in Acts. Notwithstanding such positive contributions, certain severe limitations of this position cannot be overlooked. Thus, in its earlier forms, at least, this suggestion has been too much dependent on the nineteenth-century Tübingen representation of early Christianity, a representation which has often been criticised for building on Hegelian dialectic more than on textual evidence.[22] This criticism is further strengthened by the observation that Paul is not the only Lukan character whom Luke legitimates in relation to Judaism – one only needs to think of Jesus' rootedness in Judaism by means of the infancy narratives, of his general conformity to Jewish practices during his ministry, and of the close association of the early Christian community in Jerusalem with the Jewish temple. This is not to deny, of course, that Paul has a unique place in Luke's apologetic to Judaism, and the reasons for this will be discussed in chapter 7. For now, it suffices to say that Paul's Jewishness is for Luke part and parcel of his concern with the continuity between the new Christian movement and Israel's hopes, a concern within which Paul has an important, but not exclusive, place. Finally, and most significantly, whatever importance one is to attribute to Paul and his defence in Luke's scheme, it remains notoriously difficult to stretch it so that it can account for the whole of Acts,[23] let alone for the Third Gospel.[24]

Little else has been written after Mattill in support of his specific understanding of Luke's purpose, except for a short article by V. E. Vine ('The Purpose and Date of Acts', *ExpT* 96 (1984), 45–8), which states that Acts 'is to be seen as an appeal to the Judaizers for peace and reconciliation as Paul draws near to his trial. The hope is that they will close ranks behind Paul and not disown so faithful a witness to Christ' ('Purpose', 48).

[22] See, for example, Gasque, *History*, especially pp. 52–4; Pattison, 'Study', pp. 12–17. For a more sympathetic critique, cf. T. V. Smith, *Petrine Controversies in Early Christianity: Attitudes towards Peter in Christian Writings of the First Two Centuries*, WUNT 2:15, Tübingen: J. C. B. Mohr, 1985, pp. 24–33, 211–12. A recent version of the Tübingen reconstruction of Early Christianity is M. D. Goulder's *A Tale of Two Missions*, London: SCM Press, 1994.

[23] See, however, Brawley, *Luke–Acts*, pp. 28–50, who attempts to show that 'the story of Paul not only dominates the literary structure of the second half of Acts but also rests on major preparation for Paul in the first half of Acts' (p. 28).

[24] See also R. Maddox, *The Purpose of Luke–Acts*, ed. J. Riches, Edinburgh: T. & T. Clark, 1982, p. 21.

A political apologia pro ecclesia

The suggestion that Luke–Acts was written as a political apologetic directed to the Roman authorities with the purpose of acquiring or maintaining religious freedom for Christians has a particularly long history. In an article published in 1720, C. A. Heumann argued that Luke dedicated his writing to the Roman magistrate Theophilus so that it would serve as an apologia against the false accusations which were being brought against Christianity.[25] A similar position was taken by E. Zeller in his commentary, published in 1854. He suggested that Luke intended both to refute the charges of pagans against Christianity and at the same time to give Christian readers material which they in turn could use in their own defences against such charges.[26] Again, in a short book published in 1897, J. Weiss insisted that Acts is an apology addressed to pagans with the purpose of refuting Jewish accusations against Christians.[27]

(a) *A case for Christianity's* religio licita *status*

During the twentieth century the interpretation of Luke–Acts as a political *apologia pro ecclesia* has continued in several forms. One major variant started with the claim that at the time when Luke–Acts was written every religion in the Roman world had to be specially licensed by Rome in order to be allowed to function. Judaism, it was argued, enjoyed such a status of *religio licita*, and consequently the purpose of Luke–Acts was to present Christianity as a genuine branch of Judaism in order to enjoy its privileges.[28]

[25] C. A. Heumann, 'Dissertatio de Theophilo cui Lucas Historiam Sacram Inscripsit', *BHPT*, classis IV, Bremen, 1720, pp. 483–505.

[26] E. Zeller, *The Contents and Origin of the Acts of the Apostles Critically Investigated by Dr Edward Zeller*, London: Williams and Norgate, 1876 (original German edition, 1854), p. 164.

[27] J. Weiss, *Über die Absicht und den literarischen Charakter der Apostelgeschichte*, Marburg and Göttingen, 1897.

[28] Among the most notable statements of this position are: F. J. Foakes-Jackson and K. Lake (eds.), *The Beginnings of Christianity*, part 1, vol. II, London: Macmillan, 1922, pp. 177–87; H. J. Cadbury, *The Making of Luke–Acts*, London: SPCK, 1968 (first published New York: Macmillan, 1927), esp. pp. 299–316; and B. S. Easton, *The Purpose of Acts*, London, 1936, reprinted as *Early Christianity: The Purpose of Acts and Other Papers*, ed. F. C. Grant, London: SPCK, 1955, pp. 33–57. More minor contributions from similar angles can be found in: F. F. Bruce, *The Acts of the Apostles: The Greek Text with Introduction and Commentary*, third revised and enlarged edition, Leicester: Apollos, 1990, p. 23; G. B. Caird, *The Gospel of St Luke*, London: A. & C. Black, 1968, pp. 13–15; F. V. Filson, *Three Crucial Decades*, Richmond, VA: John Knox, 1963, pp. 17–18; J. A. Fitzmyer, *The Gospel According to Luke*, New York: Doubleday, 1981, vol. I, p. 10. E. Haenchen also speaks repeatedly of Luke's concern to gain political toleration for Christianity by emphasising

Undoubtedly the single most significant contribution of the proponents of the *religio licita* interpretation is their search for a reading of Luke's purpose which is able to do justice both to the author's emphasis on the continuity between Christianity and Judaism and to the political dimension of the narrative. Yet several observations make their solution very difficult to accept. First, few Roman officials would have been able to appreciate the weight of Luke's (mainly theological) case for Christianity's continuity with Judaism, even were they interested in it. Second, recent research has thrown serious doubts on the premise that the category *religio licita* even existed at the time of Luke's writing.[29] Third, if, according to the great majority of contemporary scholarship,[30] Luke's work is to be dated after the Jewish revolt of 66–74 CE,[31] it is difficult to imagine that Luke could have hoped to do Christianity a political favour by tying it to Judaism.

(b) *A case for Christianity's political harmlessness*

Not impressed by the arguments of those who saw Luke striving to acquire a *religio licita* status for Christianity, H. Conzelmann proposed a different understanding of Luke's defence of Christianity in relation to the Roman system.[32] According to Conzelmann, Luke's apologetic is prompted by the realisation that the church was likely to continue in the world and that it therefore needed to define its position in relation to both Judaism and the Roman Empire.[33] Accordingly, he sees in Luke–Acts a twofold apologetic concern, one related to Judaism and the other to the state. Nevertheless, he

---

its kinship with Judaism (*The Acts of the Apostles*, Oxford: Basil Blackwell, 1971, pp. 102, 630–1, 691–4), but does not condition this interpretation on the existence of a formal *religio licita* category at the time of Luke's writing. He prefers, therefore, to speak in terms of a 'religio quasi licita', a more general form of tolerance which Judaism enjoyed within the empire (*Acts*, pp. 630–1). Cf. also Haenchen's 'Judentum und Christentum in der Apostelgeschichte', *ZNW* 54 (1963), 155–87.

[29] See, for example, Maddox, *Purpose*, pp. 91–3.

[30] For a useful classification of scholarly opinion on the matter, see G. E. Sterling, *Historiography and Self-Definition: Josephos, Luke–Acts and Apologetic Historiography*, Leiden: E. J. Brill, 1992, pp. 329–30.

[31] On the dating of the Jewish revolt, see E. P. Sanders, *Judaism: Practice and Belief 63BCE–66CE*, London: SCM Press, 1992, p. 33.

[32] H. Conzelmann, *The Theology of St Luke*, London: Faber and Faber, 1960, pp. 137–49. See also H. Flender (*St Luke, Theologian of Redemptive History*, London: SPCK, 1967, pp. 56–62), who adopts Conzelmann's position and illustrates it in relation to the nativity story (Luke 2), the introduction to the parable of the pounds (Luke 19.11), and Jesus' examination before the Sanhedrin (Luke 22.66–23.1).

[33] Conzelmann, *Theology*, p. 137.

challenges the assumption of his predecessors, according to which Luke's apologetic to the state is to be understood in terms of Christianity's relation to Judaism.[34] For Conzelmann, Luke's political apologetic runs through Luke–Acts quite independently of his Jewish apologetic. In essence, it is said to consist of Luke's emphasis on the non-politicality of the Christian story, starting from John the Baptist and continuing into the ministry of Jesus and the early church.[35] Particular attention is paid, however, to the Lukan account of Jesus' passion[36] and to a number of incidents connected with Paul's trial.[37] Luke is allegedly at pains to show in these passages that 'to confess oneself to be a Christian implies no crime against Roman law'.[38]

Conzelmann has succeeded in bypassing most of the criticism associated with the *religio licita* theories. Nonetheless, numerous subsequent studies have shown that a political apologetic such as that proposed by him can in no sense be indicative of Luke's governing concern.[39] One sentence from C. K. Barrett, in particular, has posed a daunting obstacle to any study which would attempt to argue for the dominance of a political apologetic: 'No Roman official would ever have filtered out so much of what to him would be theological and ecclesiastical rubbish in order to reach so tiny a grain of relevant apology.'[40] Nevertheless, the criticism levelled against the work of Conzelmann and his companions should not be used to exclude every form of political apologetic.[41] Its significance is rather to indicate that such a Lukan concern, to the degree to which it is identifiable, is likely to be subject to a higher authorial agenda. The precise nature of this agenda remains the subject of our further exploration.

---

[34] Ibid., pp. 138, 148. See also H. Conzelmann, 'Geschichte, Geschichtsbild und Geschichtsdarstellung bei Lukas', *TLZ* 85 (1960), 244.

[35] Conzelmann, *Theology*, pp. 138–44.

[36] Special reference is made to the non-political character of Jesus' royal title, Jesus' death as a prophet, the portrayal of the Jewish political accusations as lies, and Pilate's triple declaration of Jesus' innocence (ibid., pp. 139–41).

[37] Ibid., pp. 141–4.   [38] Ibid., p. 140.

[39] In addition to the critiques mentioned below, see Maddox, *Purpose*, pp. 96–7; P. W. Walaskay, *'And so we came to Rome': The Political Perspective of St Luke*, Cambridge University Press, 1983, pp. 15–22.

[40] C. K. Barrett, *Luke the Historian in Recent Study*, London: Epworth, 1961, p. 63. See also the detailed criticism of Conzelmann's position in the works of R. J. Cassidy: *Society and Politics in the Acts of the Apostles*, Maryknoll, NY: Orbis, 1987, pp. 148–55; *Jesus, Politics, and Society: A Study of Luke's Gospel*, Maryknoll, NY: Orbis, 1978, pp. 7–9, 128–30.

[41] Cassidy rather overstates his case at times (see also Sterling's evaluation of Cassidy's position in Sterling, *Historiography*, p. 382).

An *apologia pro imperio*

In 1983 P. W. Walaskay published what he calls an 'upside-down' representation of the traditional understanding of Luke's political apologetic:[42] 'Far from supporting the view that Luke was defending the church to a Roman magistrate, the evidence points us in the other direction. Throughout his writings Luke has carefully, consistently, and consciously presented an *apologia pro imperio* to his church.'[43] According to this representation, Luke aims to persuade his readers that 'the institutions of the church and empire are coeval and complementary' and that 'the Christian church and the Roman Empire need not fear nor suspect each other, for God stands behind both institutions giving to each the power and the authority to carry out his will'.[44] Luke's account of the trials of Jesus and Paul, in particular, are said to bring the author's pro-Roman stance to the fore.[45]

The innovative character of Walaskay's work and its effort to reconcile the political dimension of Luke–Acts with the fact that Luke was probably addressing a Christian audience can only be admired. It may also be conceded that Luke appears to be in favour of a degree of openness towards Rome. Nonetheless, this cannot be taken as more than a secondary and sporadic concern – such a view faces the same problems as those noted in relation to readings of Luke–Acts as *apologia pro ecclesia*. There is for too much material in Luke–Acts which would be made redundant on such a view – Rome features in only a relatively small part of Luke–Acts. In addition to this, Luke's depiction of the Roman system and its representatives is not as uniformly favourable as Walaskay would have it; after all, Jesus dies with Pilate's consent,[46] while Roman governors, one after another, fail to release Paul, even when the evidence compels them to recognise his innocence.

An apologia for the gospel

The latter half of the twentieth century witnessed a steady increase in the number of works which speak of Luke's apologetic efforts as focusing specifically on the Christian message. I shall mention now some of the more notable contributions from this angle.[47]

---

[42] Walaskay, *Rome*.   [43] Ibid., p. 64.   [44] Ibid., pp. ix–x.   [45] Ibid.

[46] See J. A. Weatherly, *Jewish Responsibility for the Death of Jesus in Luke–Acts*, JSNTSup 106, Sheffield Academic Press, 1994, pp. 92–7.

[47] In addition to the contributions discussed below, attention may be called to a recent article: L. Alexander, 'The Acts of the Apostles as an Apologetic Text', in M. Edwards,

(a) *Luke–Acts as a defence against Gnosticism*

The existence of anti-Gnostic overtones in parts of Luke–Acts has often been suggested by New Testament scholarship.[48] It was, however, only through the work of C. H. Talbert that a detailed case was put forward that 'Luke–Acts was written for the express purpose of serving as a defence against Gnosticism.'[49]

Predictably, Talbert's thesis has been criticised for going a long way beyond what the evidence allows, when it argues that the whole Lukan narrative should be read as an anti-Gnostic defence; yet it is commonly granted that certain features of Luke–Acts could be understood along these lines.[50] For present purposes it suffices to say that, to the extent to which there is any value in Talbert's thesis, its findings have revealed one dimension of Luke's preoccupation with the apologia for the gospel.

(b) *Luke–Acts as the first fully fledged Christian apologia*

F. F. Bruce has argued that the author of Acts deserves to be called not only 'the first Christian historian',[51] but also 'the first Christian apologist'.[52] Bruce substantiates his assertion by pointing out that for Luke the new Christian faith is 'everywhere spoken against' (Ac. 28.22) and that 'of the three main types of defence represented among the second-century Christian apologists Luke provides first-century prototypes: defence against pagan religion (Christianity is true; paganism is false), defence against Judaism (Christianity is the fulfilment of true Judaism), defence against political accusations (Christianity is innocent of any offence against Roman law).'[53] The specific way in which Bruce explains each of

---

M. Goodman, and S. Price (eds.), *Apologetics in the Roman Empire: Pagans, Jews, and Christians*, Oxford University Press, 1999, pp. 15–43. In Alexander's view, Acts is built around a number of apologetic scenarios (pp. 28–38), the role of which is not to provide a direct defence against specific charges (pp. 20, 25), but rather to address an implied audience (which may well have been different from Luke's actual audience), defending the Christian world-view as a whole, which in Lukan terms is 'the Word of the Lord' (pp. 20–1, 38).

[48] Useful reviews of such contributions are available in Pattison, 'Study', pp. 17–21; C. H. Talbert, *Luke and the Gnostics: An Examination of the Lucan Purpose*, Nashville: Abingdon, 1966, pp. 13–4.

[49] Talbert, *Gnostics*, p. 15.

[50] Maddox, *Purpose*, pp. 21–2; Pattison, 'Study', pp.20–1.

[51] As already claimed by M. Dibelius (*Studies in the Acts of the Apostles*, ed. H. Greeven, London: SCM Press, 1956, p. 123).

[52] Bruce, *Acts*, p. 22. Caird speaks of Luke in similar terms, when he refers to Luke–Acts as 'the first great apologia for the Christian faith' (*Luke*, p. 14), but the nature of the apologia which Caird has in mind is exclusively political (*Luke*, pp. 13–5).

[53] Bruce, *Acts*, p. 22. In addition to these three types of defence, Bruce also speaks of a Lukan apologetic in relation to the church, by which he means an apologetic related to

these types of defence is not particularly innovative: the first type is exemplified by the two familiar Pauline incidents in Lystra and Athens;[54] the second by Stephen's speech and by Paul's defence addresses and loyalty to Judaism; the third by Luke's portrayal of Christianity as Israel's fulfilment and politically innocent.[55] Instead, Bruce's contribution to the study of Lukan apologetics consists precisely in his emphasis on the diversity of apologetic goals and strategies identifiable in Luke's writing and of his implicit assertion that these various apologetic dimensions must not be pursued at the expense of each other. It is not clear, however, that he has said enough to define the way in which they can be accommodated and correlated.

(c) *Luke–Acts as the confirmation of the gospel*

Fresh light was thrown on Luke's work by an article published in 1960 by W. C. van Unnik.[56] His suggestion is that Acts as a whole is to be understood as the confirmation of the Gospel, that is, Acts assures the readers (people who for various reasons were in need of certainty concerning the Christian message[57]) that the central message of Luke's Gospel, and therefore of the Christian *kerygma*[58] – that 'Jesus' activity is saving'[59] – is and remains valid for them.

That van Unnik's understanding of Acts is of an apologetic nature (according to my definition of the term) needs little argument. His explanation of the motif of witness in Acts makes this particularly clear: the Old Testament prophets, the eye-witnesses, and, most importantly, God himself (through signs and wonders and through the gift of the Holy

---

Jewish Christians, focusing largely on the legitimacy of the Gentile mission (pp. 25–7). For convenience, this aspect of Luke's apologetic will be discussed in the present study under the wider rubric of Luke's apologetic in relation to Judaism.

A lengthier discussion of the early Christian defence of the gospel against Judaism, paganism, the Roman empire, and 'pseudo-Christianity' is offered by Bruce in his *The Apostolic Defence of the Gospel: Christian Apologetics in the New Testament*, London: Inter-Varsity Fellowship, 1959. This, however, is not specifically related to Luke's work, although a significant part of Bruce's discussion focuses on material from Acts.

[54] The same incidents are used as evidence of Luke's apologetic to Gentile hearers by H. C. Kee, *Good News to the Ends of the Earth*, London: SCM Press, 1990, pp. 91–2.

[55] Bruce, *Acts*, pp. 22–5.

[56] W. C. van Unnik, 'The "Book of Acts": The Confirmation of the Gospel', *NovT* 4 (1960), 26–59.

[57] Ibid., 59.

[58] Van Unnik makes it clear that the message of the Gospels in general, and of Luke's Gospel in particular, is the Christian *kerygma* (ibid., 27–8).

[59] Ibid., 49.

Spirit, who is the real author of the Christian mission) all bear witness to the reliability of the Christian gospel.[60]

The line taken by van Unnik's article found subsequent confirmation in the work of several other authors. Chronologically, the first among these was E. Franklin.[61] To a large extent Franklin's study is a response to the Vielhauer, Conzelmann, and Haenchen consensus, according to which Luke's interest in salvation history is the sign that he had given up the eschatological hopes of the early church.[62] Franklin's contention is that 'Luke stood . . . within the main eschatological stream of the early Christian expectations, and that salvation history in his two volumes, though present, is used in the service of his eschatology rather than as a replacement of it.'[63] If Luke did not abandon the hope of Christ's early return, Franklin adds, the implication is that he wanted his readers to be 'ready to meet their Lord when he appears'.[64] Apparently, however, the readers were far from being ready, so Luke set out to reconfirm their belief in Christ

> by pointing out the necessity of the delay and by reasserting the belief in the immediacy of the return; . . . by describing the sheer rebellious nature of the disobedience which the Jewish rejection entailed; [and] by showing that the life of Jesus was of one piece with the whole saving work of God of which it was the climax.[65]

A second advocate of the trend initiated by van Unnik was D. P. Fuller.[66] His overall concern was the relationship between the Christian faith and knowledge through the historical method, with special reference to the resurrection of Christ.[67] According to Fuller, the participants in the modern discussion on this topic would have a great deal to learn from the way Luke combined the two. He believes Acts was written to provide verification for the Christian claims related to the Christ event, to which Luke's readers had no personal access.[68]

Finally, van Unnik's proposal has been further developed in the works of I. H. Marshall.[69] Both in his discussion of the purpose of Luke's Gospel

---

[60] Ibid., 53–7.

[61] *Christ the Lord: A Study in the Purpose and Theology of Luke–Acts*, London: SPCK, 1965.

[62] Ibid., pp. 3–6, 173.   [63] Ibid., p. 6. He elaborates on this in ch. 1.

[64] Ibid., p. 7; see also ch. 5.   [65] Ibid., p. 174.

[66] *Easter Faith and History*, London: Tyndale Press, 1968.

[67] Ibid., p. 25; see also pp. 13–26.   [68] Ibid., p. 223.

[69] Marshall's contribution comes in the form of several books and articles: *The Gospel of Luke: A Commentary on the Greek Text*, NIGTC 3, Exeter: Paternoster, 1978, pp. 35–6; *Luke – Historian and Theologian*, third edition, Exeter: Paternoster, 1988, pp. 158–9; *The*

and in that of the purpose of Acts, Marshall notes Luke's preoccupation with the confirmation of the Christian message: 'Luke wished to present the events in such a way that they would seem to confirm the reliability of the catechesis.'[70] Marshall dissociates himself, however, from those who believe that such a confirmation was necessary because the faith of Luke's readers was becoming shaky.[71] Rather, the need was simply for a fuller presentation of the story of the Christian *kerygma*, which Luke's readers had known only in general terms.[72]

As a general evaluation of the contributions in this section, it may be said that, despite a certain degree of disagreement on issues such as the occasion of Luke's writing (e.g. whether it is the readers' wavering faith or their insufficient information) or the relative importance of the various Lukan themes in the author's construction, the principal contention that Luke's governing concern is the confirmation of the gospel is undoubtedly a pointer in the right direction, not least because of its coherence with Luke's declared goal in Luke 1.4. There is, however, strategic ground still to be conquered before this proposal can be established as a wholly legitimate understanding of Luke's dominant purpose. Part of this still unconquered ground, I suggest, is Luke's intriguing preoccupation with judicial trials.

(d) *Luke–Acts as an exponent of a literary apologetic tradition*

In his study entitled *The Theology of Acts in Its Historical Setting*,[73] J. C. O'Neill has argued that 'Luke–Acts was primarily an attempt to persuade an educated reading public to become Christians; it was an "apology" in outward form but, like all true apologies, it had the burning inner purpose of bringing men to the faith.'[74] O'Neill insists that his understanding of the apologetic character of Luke–Acts is not in the narrow political sense, nor in the sense of a defensive stance.[75] Rather, his contention is that Luke's approach is moulded by the apologetic writings of Hellenistic Judaism which 'had for at least three centuries been confronted with the sort of missionary problem which the Church faced in the first century of

---

Acts of the Apostles: An Introduction and Commentary, TNTC, Leicester: Inter-Varsity Press; Grand Rapids: Eerdmans, 1980, pp. 17–22; *The Acts of the Apostles*, NTG, Sheffield: JSOT, 1992, pp. 31–46; 'Luke and his "Gospel" ', in P. Stuhlmacher (ed.), *Das Evangelium und die Evangelien*, Tübingen: J. C. B. Mohr, 1983, pp. 289–308. For his references to van Unnik's work see his *Historian*, pp. 93, 158 and *Acts* (1992), p. 44.

[70] Marshall, 'Luke', 305; see also Marshall, *Acts* (1992), p. 45.
[71] Marshall, 'Luke', 303–4.   [72] Ibid., 307. see more generally, 304–7.
[73] London: SPCK , 1970.   [74] O'Neill, *Theology*, p. 176.
[75] Ibid., pp. 176–7.

its life'[76] and which 'had produced a large body of missionary literature written in Greek which employed a developed apologetic to convince its Gentile readers of the truth of the Jewish faith'.[77] Accordingly, O'Neill says, Luke's writing as a whole is 'an argument for the faith'.[78] Luke's indebtedness to the apologetic methods of Hellenistic Judaism is said to be evident in the preface to his Gospel, in the historiographic form of his writing, and in a number of details of Acts, such as the commendation of the heroes of faith, the appeal to the state, the use of accepted philosophy, and the theology of conversion/repentance.[79]

Similar to O'Neill's position is that advocated more recently by G. Sterling, in his study on the genre of Luke–Acts. According to Sterling, Luke's work is to be understood as a 'self-definition' of Christianity in relation to the world, after the model of 'apologetic historiography', which he defines as *'the story of a subgroup of people in an extended prose narrative written by a member of the group who follows the group's own traditions but Hellenizes them in an effort to establish the identity of the group within the setting of the larger world'*.[80] As part of this tradition, Luke–Acts also offers a self-definition of Christianity by Hellenizing the *traditio apostolica* and in this way builds an effective apologetic for the beliefs which this *traditio apostolica* comprises. The function of this definition, Sterling suggests, can be best analysed from three different perspectives: Christianity, Israel, and Rome.[81] In relation to the first, Luke saw the need for a definition of Christianity at a time when contact with the eye-witnesses of the Christian story was coming to an end; Luke's case therefore is said to be that Christian identity means belonging to the *traditio apostolica* which he reliably relates. In relation to Israel, Luke addresses the problem of Christianity's branching away from Judaism by showing that Christianity is no novelty, but the continuation of Israel. In relation to Rome, Sterling's explanation is very much along the lines of the *religio licita* theories, with the only notable difference that for him Luke offers his apologia for Christianity only indirectly: rather than addressing the Roman authorities, Luke is simply giving to Christian readers examples of how they could make their own apologia, should that be necessary. It is these three perspectives that define Luke's specific apologetic for the *traditio apostolica* and the beliefs associated with it.

Thus, from the angles of historical setting and literary genre alike, Luke's endeavour has been viewed as a historiographic apologia for Christianity and its beliefs, in a world context. O'Neill's evangelistic

---

[76] Ibid., p. 139.   [77] Ibid., pp. 139–40.   [78] Ibid., p. 140.   [79] Ibid., pp. 140–59.
[80] Sterling, *Historiography*, p. 17.   [81] Ibid., pp. 378–86.

representation of this apologia suffers from dependence on the shaky premise of a non-Christian readership for Luke–Acts. Luke's 'argument for the faith' can make equally good sense when viewed as a 'confirmation of the gospel', addressed predominantly to Christians, and perhaps through their mediation to non-Christians as well. Sterling's explanation, on the other hand, is problematic in its representation of Luke's political agenda. In claiming that Luke's 'defence is that Christianity is simply the extension of the Old Testament and *therefore politically innocent*',[82] Sterling repeats one of the major fallacies of the *religio licita* interpretations (despite his dissociation from them in the matter of Luke's addressees). All in all, however, O'Neill and Sterling have successfully showed that when Luke–Acts is viewed against the background of Hellenism, and particularly Hellenistic Judaism, its apologetic presentation of the Christian faith comes to the fore. It remains for other studies on the Lukan narrative (the present one included) to demonstrate and detail this observation in relation to the contents of Luke's work.

(e) *Luke–Acts as apologia by virtue of its use of 'the plan of God' motif*

In the same vein as O'Neill and Sterling, J. T. Squires has recently spoken of Luke–Acts as 'a kind of cultural "translation", an attempt to tell a story to people who are in a context somewhat different from the context in which the story originally took place'.[83] In this process of translation, Squires adds, apologetics is a very appropriate task. But what vehicle would Luke use for his apologetics? Squires' answer is the theme of providence, or 'the plan of God', which, together with other related themes (such as portents, epiphanies, prophecy, and fate), is used 'to assert and expound the central features of the story of Jesus and the early church'.[84] His motivation in doing this is said to be threefold: first, to confirm the faith of his Christian readers; second, to encourage and equip them to present the gospel to the Hellenistic world in an already 'translated' form; third, to enable them to defend their beliefs in the face of possible objections. Methodologically, Luke's apologetic, far from being restricted to a political or defensive stance, includes, like Hellenistic historiography, elements of defence,

---

[82] Ibid., p. 385; italics mine.

[83] J. T. Squires, *The Plan of God in Luke–Acts*, Cambridge University Press, 1993, p. 190. The new context into which Luke is translating his story is, as would be expected, the Hellenistic one.

[84] Ibid., p. 53; see also p. 186.

assertion, polemic, and exposition, and is an important part of missionary preaching.[85]

Thus, Squires' monograph has highlighted Luke's use of one specific theme as part of his apologia for the gospel within the Hellenistic milieu. As such, his contribution has provided a convenient precedent for the study of other Lukan themes which might serve a similar purpose.

(f) *Luke–Acts as a Christian apologia related to Judaism*

In the earlier discussion of the reading of Luke–Acts as a work aimed to acquire for Christianity the status of *religio licita*, I noted that one of the major arguments on which the advocates of this theory have built their case is Luke's emphasis on the continuity between Christianity and Judaism. While the theory has often met with justified criticism, the assertion that Luke is at pains to show the fundamental agreement between the new Christian movement and the hopes of Israel has continued to gain support among students of the Lukan narrative.

Among the various apologetic devices which Luke employs in order to establish the legitimacy of Christianity and its beliefs in relation to Judaism, one which has commonly been noted by Lukan scholarship is the use of the Jewish Scriptures in Luke–Acts.[86]

A more indirect Lukan apologetic in relation to Judaism has been noted by L. T. Johnson.[87] According to his analysis, Luke's preoccupation is with God's dealings with the Jews and the implications of this for the validity of the Christian message. It is suggested that Luke's implied readers were mainly Gentile Christians, whose confidence in 'the things in which [they] have been instructed' (Luke 1.4) was being undermined by two historical events of which they had been a part: the Jewish rejection of the gospel and the Gentiles' acceptance of it. If those to whom God had

---

[85] Ibid., pp. 40, 191, 193–4.

[86] J. Dupont, 'Apologetic Use of the Old Testament in the Speeches of Acts', in J. Dupont, *The Salvation of the Gentiles: Studies in the Acts of the Apostles*, New York: Paulist Press, 1979, pp. 129–59; C. A. Evans, 'Prophecy and Polemic: Jews in Luke's Scriptural Apologetic', in C. A. Evans and J. A. Sanders (eds.), *Luke and Scripture: The Function of Sacred Tradition in Luke–Acts*, Minneapolis: Fortress, 1993, pp. 171–211, esp. p. 210.

[87] L. T. Johnson, *The Gospel of Luke*, Collegeville, MN: Liturgical, 1991, pp. 3–10. See also his article, 'Luke–Acts', published one year later in the *ABD*, vol. IV, pp. 405–8. A more embryonic form of his explanation can also be found in his earlier work *The Writings of the New Testament*, London: SCM Press, 1986. Johnson builds partly on the work of R. J. Karris ('Missionary Communities: A New Paradigm for the Study of Luke–Acts', *CBQ* 41 (1979), 80–97; *What Are They Saying about Luke and Acts: A Theology of the Faithful God*, New York: Paulist Press, 1979).

made his promises were now no longer sharing in them, while others were taking the benefits, what did that have to say about the faithfulness of the God in whom they had trusted? It is in response to this situation that Luke set out to give his readers ἀσφάλεια regarding the Christian teaching by addressing an issue of theodicy: 'By telling how events happened "in order" (*kathexes*), Luke shows how God first fulfilled his promises to Israel, and only then extended these blessings to the Gentiles. Because God had shown himself faithful to the Jews, therefore, the Word that reached the Gentiles was also trustworthy.'[88]

Finally, another major Lukan theme which has recently been portrayed as contributing to Luke's apologetic for the gospel in relation to Judaism is that of the Davidic Messiah.[89] M. L. Strauss' thesis does not aim to provide an analysis of Luke's apologetics; yet the results of his investigation into the Christology of Luke–Acts are repeatedly said to indicate that Luke is engaged apologetically with Judaism.[90] What Luke ultimately aims to achieve through his apologetic, Strauss suggests, is to reassure his Christian readers (presumably Jews and Gentiles alike, whose faith is being threatened by the ongoing debate with unbelieving Jews) that they truly are the eschatological people of God, the heirs of God's promises to Israel.[91]

Not everything that has been written on Luke's apologia for the gospel in relation to Judaism has done full justice to the Lukan text. Johnson's suggestion, in particular, seems problematic in so far as it views Luke–Acts as revolving around a question of theodicy. Throughout Luke's account of Jesus' ministry and the church's history, God is the one who legitimates (through miracles, inspired speeches, pneumatic experiences, etc.), not the one to be legitimated. This is particularly true with regard to the twin problems of Jewish rejection and Gentile acceptance of the gospel, to which Johnson points. The specific angle(s) from which they test the validity of the Christian message is not theodicy ('Can God's promises still be trusted?') but Christology and ecclesiology. Christologically, the challenge is: can the church claim that God's promises to Israel have been fulfilled in Jesus, since the Jews, who should be the most competent to judge, have largely rejected this interpretation and, instead, the church seems to find its adherents mainly in the Gentile world? Ecclesiologically, the concern is: can the church have any part in God's promises to Israel, since it has parted ways with the Jewish leadership and is now

---

[88] L. T. Johnson, *Gospel*, p. 10.
[89] M. L. Strauss, *The Davidic Messiah in Luke–Acts: The Promise and Its Fulfilment in Lukan Christology*, Sheffield Academic Press, 1995, especially pp. 345–6.
[90] Ibid., pp. 125, 259–60.   [91] Ibid., p. 348.

in the process of becoming an increasingly Gentile movement? A central argument in Luke's response is the reference to God's explicit verdict, which settles both the issue of Christology (by raising and exalting Jesus) and that of ecclesiology (the unbelieving Jews fulfil God's Isaianic pronouncement, while the Gentiles are brought in at God's own initiative). God's dealings with his people are thus not the object but the foundation of Luke's apologetic.

Such shortcomings aside, the trend of interpretations discussed in this section has shed light on what can confidently be regarded as a central area of Lukan apologetics, especially notable results being achieved in connection with Lukan topics such as the continuity between Israel and Christianity, the Jewish rejection of the gospel, the legitimacy of the Gentile mission, Jesus' Messianic identity (specifically established in relation to his passion-resurrection), and the witness of the Jewish Scriptures.

Conclusion

The present chapter commenced with a general statement of the significant place which Luke has allocated in his work to judicial trials. In view of the fact that the only context within which the function of Luke's trial material has been discussed in relation to Luke–Acts as a whole was that of apologetics, it was then necessary to carry out a survey of the major formulations of the apologetic character of Luke's work. The strategic place which Luke's trial accounts have played in most of these formulations has in this way become evident. It was the accusations and defences connected with Paul's trials in Acts that have provided, to a large extent, the basis for the contention that Luke's whole work, or at least his second volume, was written as a defence of Paul, most probably in relation to Judaism or Jewish-oriented Christians. It was the repeated exculpations of Jesus and Paul at the hands of Roman officials that gave rise to the understanding of Luke–Acts as a political apologetic for the church. It was the depiction of the Roman system and its representatives, mostly in connection with the trials of Jesus and Paul, that led Walaskay to find in Luke's work an *apologia pro imperio*. Notwithstanding the legitimacy of some of these interpretations with regard to specific parts or features of Luke's narrative, it has not been possible to take any of them as indicative of Luke's overall concern. Quite apart from any additional deficiencies which have been noted in their arguments, they display the common limitation of not being able to account for very much material in Luke–Acts.

The final major section of the survey has indicated, however, a fast-growing trend of interpretations which, although diverse and not always entirely convincing in their specific outlook, seem to point unanimously towards a much more plausible apologetic understanding of Luke's overall purpose, namely, as an apologia for the gospel. Intriguingly, though, despite the impressive number of works which have pointed in this direction and the equally numerous aspects of Luke's writing which have been portrayed from this angle, it is this camp that appears to have drawn the least systematic support from Luke's trial narratives. The immediate question is then: is Luke's striking interest in trials in any sense coherent with what appears to preoccupy him in so many other aspects of his work, or do the lengthy trial narratives have to be viewed as political or pro-Pauline excursuses which supplement the author's main agenda? Furthermore, are there sufficiently strong reasons to think of Paul's relationship to Judaism, Christianity's political harmlessness, or Rome's benevolence towards Christianity as the controlling emphases of the trial narratives themselves? These are questions to which answers can be attempted only after the actual analysis of Luke's trial narratives.

The present approach: thesis, plan of work, and method

The overall contention of the present study is that the trial narratives[92] of Luke–Acts function as an important part of Luke's *apologia pro evangelio* – a purpose which is in keeping with the author's declared wish to give his readers 'assurance' about the 'matters' in which they had been instructed (Luke 1.4). Within this overall agenda, the specific role of the trial narratives is to provide the means whereby important tenets of the Christian faith are put 'on trial' before the reader, with the intended result of the gospel's confirmation.

The first trial narrative under consideration in what follows (part one) is Luke's account of Jesus' trial. Due to the fact that this narrative is not a self-contained literary unit, since it comes as part of a larger 'story' (the Third Gospel), its study cannot be undertaken in isolation from the foregoing narrative. Consequently, the examination of Jesus' trial begins with a discussion of two of its major 'narrative precedents' – the Gospel plot and the passion predictions – as a way of defining the hermeneutical framework from which the reader is expected to approach the trial

---

[92] Unless specified otherwise, by the 'trial narratives' of Luke–Acts I shall mean parts of Luke's writing which depict 'trials' not in the general sense of 'testing', but in a forensic sense, allowing, however, for the fact that many of the 'trial' incidents are not *regular* forensic trials, that is, the litigants do not necessarily play a formal legal role.

narrative (chapter 2). Building on the results of this preliminary investigation, chapter 3 continues to discuss the role of Jesus' trial in Luke's Gospel by means of an analysis of the author's emphases in each of the four episodes of which the trial story is composed. Yet even the ending of the trial account is not the end of all that Luke has to say concerning Jesus' trial. Important indications exist that the issues which are at stake in Jesus' trial are only adequately settled beyond the account of the trial itself. Moreover, retrospective references to Jesus' trial continue to appear in the remaining part of Luke's Gospel and at various points in Acts. Under these considerations, chapter 4 focuses on the way Jesus' trial is represented by Luke retrospectively, specific attention being paid to the continuation of the trial conflict in the remaining part of Luke's passion narrative, to the outcome of this conflict in the resurrection narratives, and to the references to Jesus' trial in Acts. Thus, the examination of the function of Jesus' trial in Luke–Acts requires the analysis of much Lukan material outside the trial narrative itself and will inevitably lead to the account of Jesus' trial receiving a more extensive treatment in the present study than any other Lukan trial narrative.

In part two, under scrutiny is Luke's representation of the judicial or quasi-judicial encounters between Jesus' followers and their opponents. After a brief consideration of Jesus' predictions of the disciples' trials and of the significance of these predictions for one's subsequent understanding of the trial narratives, chapter 5 turns to the two trial episodes involving Peter (first accompanied by John and next by a larger apostolic group). The (apologetic) function of these accounts is explored by concentrating specifically on Luke's characterisation of the participants in the conflict, the specific object of his apologetic agenda, and the apologetic devices employed towards this goal. A similar investigation is then undertaken in chapter 6 in relation to the 'trial' of Stephen – this time by concentrating on the participants in the conflict, the nature of the conflict, the charges against Stephen, his defence speech, and the outcome of the trial. Finally, in chapter 7 attention is paid to the numerous trials of Paul in Acts, by focusing on three major groups of passages, dealing respectively with summary statements on Paul's trials (by the risen Christ and by Paul himself), Paul's mission trials (between Philippi and Ephesus), and Paul's custody trials (between Jerusalem and Rome). The specific search this time is for an interpretation of Paul's trials in Acts which does best justice to these stories in their entirety and diversity.

A concluding chapter (chapter 8) brings together the results of the investigation, indicates the implications of these results for a few other areas of Lukan study, and points out some related areas in which further research would seem profitable.

Methodologically, the book follows a thematic approach, drawing on insights from both redaction criticism and narrative criticism (without, however, making loyalty to a specific method the governing aim of any part of the investigation). In connection with the narrative criticism, use will also be made, when necessary, of aspects of rhetorical criticism and reader-response criticism, due to the particular relevance of these approaches for the study of Luke's apologetics (an enterprise inseparably connected with the implied author's *persuasion* of his implied *readers*). As far as the use of redaction and narrative criticism is concerned, a change of approach seems appropriate between passages from Luke's Gospel and passages from Acts. As far as the Gospel is concerned, although there is no generally accepted solution to the Synoptic problem, the most widely held (and probably correct) explanation continues to be the 'two-document' hypothesis, according to which Luke used Mark (or a document very much like Mark as we know it) and another source, Q,[93] which he independently shared with Matthew.[94] The implication of this is that redaction criticism remains a feasible tool in the study of the Gospel material. The situation is, however, different when one turns to Acts. The high degree of uncertainty about Luke's sources here[95] makes redaction criticism rather more speculative,[96] and therefore the examination of passages from Acts will be limited to observations related to the text in its extant form.[97]

---

[93] The precise nature of Q (written or oral; one or several documents) is of little consequence for the purposes of this study.

[94] The classic statement of this explanation is B. H. Streeter's *The Four Gospels: A Study of Origins*, London: Macmillan, 1924. The main alternative explanation, known as the Griesbach hypothesis, has found only relatively limited support. The most influential recent advocate of a modified version of this hypothesis has been W. R. Farmer: 'Modern Developments of Griesbach's Hypothesis', *NTS* 23 (1976–7), 275–95; 'A "Skeleton in the Closet" of Gospel Research', *BR* 9 (1961), 18–42; and *The Synoptic Problem: A Critical Analysis*, Macon, GA: Mercer University, 1976. For critical evaluation, see C. M. Tuckett, *The Revival of the Griesbach Hypothesis*, SNTSMS 44, Cambridge University Press, 1983; S. E. Johnson, *The Griesbach Hypothesis and Redaction Criticism*, Atlanta: Scholars Press, 1990.

[95] See, for example, C. K. Barrett, *The Acts of the Apostles*, ICC, Edinburgh: T. & T. Clark, 1994, vol. I, pp. 149–56; J. Dupont, *The Sources of the Book of Acts: The Present Position*, London: Darton, Longman, & Todd, 1964, pp. 88, 166–7.

[96] This is not to deny that significant results have been produced in the past through the redactional study of Acts (or of Mark's Gospel, for that matter).

[97] In support of such a change of methodology between Luke's Gospel and Acts, see J. T. Carroll, *Response to the End of History: Eschatology and Situation in Luke–Acts*, Atlanta: Scholars Press, 1988, p. 32; Strauss, *Davidic*, pp. 31–3.

Part one

JESUS ON TRIAL

2

NARRATIVE PRECEDENTS OF JESUS' TRIAL

Introduction

Having surveyed in the last chapter the major scholarly representations of Luke's apologetic motives and having outlined their merits and limitations in relation to the interpretation of Luke's trial narratives in general, we may now turn to the individual Lukan trial passages. The first narrative for consideration is Luke's account of Jesus' trial (Luke 22.66–23.25). As the next chapter will reveal, Luke's version of this event exhibits a considerable degree of independence from the Synoptic tradition. Which motives best explain the distinctiveness of Luke's story? Before embarking on the present analysis of the material, it seems appropriate to begin again by summarising some of the major contributions to the study of Jesus' trial in the Third Gospel and thus to set the stage for part one of the investigation (chapters 2–4). With this survey completed, we shall appear to be in a position to turn to the actual trial account. A look at the text soon reveals, however, that something important is still missing. We shall find ourselves at a significant loss in the appreciation of the event through joining the unfolding of a story almost at its end. To this problem there is but one remedy: an acquaintance with the foregoing part of the story, with a specific regard for those aspects of it which would seem to facilitate preparation for the encounter with the episode under consideration. This is precisely the purpose of the present chapter. But how should one go about such a 'preparation'? A detailed discussion of the whole Gospel narrative is certainly not an option here. The only feasible solution seems to be a *via media* between the complete overlooking of the foregoing story and a commentary on the whole Gospel. I shall attempt such a *via media* approach by means of a sketchy analysis of the Gospel plot (with greater emphasis on the introductory and programmatic sections towards the beginning of the story), supplemented by a more careful examination of three short passages in which the Lukan Jesus predicts, and to some degree explains, the events associated with his passion.

Previous studies on the trial of Jesus in the Third Gospel

Four decades ago, J. Blinzler opened his study on *The Trial of Jesus* with the observation that '[t]here is hardly a part of the life of Jesus which is receiving closer and more widespread study today than His trial'.[1] The number of publications on this subject since Blinzler's day shows that the trial of Jesus has continued to remain a topic of major preoccupation for those interested in Jesus' life and ministry.[2]

Probably the one aspect of Luke's account of Jesus' trial which has received the most scholarly attention (and indeed, which has been by far the most emotional topic) is the issue of responsibility for Jesus' death, or, more specifically, the Jewish involvement in the events leading to his execution. Discussions of this topic have taken place both at the narrative level (i.e. whom does Luke regard as responsible for Jesus' death?)[3] and at the historical level (i.e. what can be known about the 'facts' behind Luke's – or any other evangelist's – account of Jesus' trial?).[4] Inevitably,

---

[1] J. Blinzler, *The Trial of Jesus*, Cork: Mercier Press, 1959, p. 3.

[2] For a recent and relatively comprehensive bibliography on the subject, see R. E. Brown, *The Death of the Messiah*, London: Geoffrey Chapman, 1994, vol. I, pp. 315–27, 563–7, 665–75.

[3] Most often such discussions are not limited to Jesus' trial narrative proper, but, quite rightly, attempt to take into account other passages of Luke–Acts which throw light on Luke's view of the *Jewish* involvement in Jesus' condemnation. The most recent and detailed treatment of the subject is to be found in Weatherly's *Jewish*, which, building on a suggestion of J. Dupont, argues that 'among Jews Luke regards only the leaders of Jerusalem and the people of Jerusalem as responsible for the crucifixion of Jesus' and that 'both the Gospel and Acts affirm a measure of responsibility for various non-Jews, namely Pilate, Herod and the Roman soldiers. Neither book indicates any consistent attempt to ameliorate Gentile responsibility in order to accentuate Jewish responsibility' (p. 271). Weatherly's study, as he sees it, comes to correct a consensus which has been developing since World War II, according to which 'Luke writes for a church profoundly separate from, if not outright hostile to, Jews and Judaism' (p. 49). Particularly representative of the side which Weatherly opposes is the work of J. T. Sanders (*The Jews in Luke–Acts*, London: SCM Press, 1987, especially pp. 8–16, 37–83), which regards the account of Jesus' trials as part of Luke's systematic hostility to all Jews (i.e. leaders and people). Other works dealing with Luke's view of the Jewish involvement in Jesus' trial and death include: Brawley, *Luke–Acts*; O'Neill, *Theology*, ch. 2 (esp. pp. 79–81); J. B. Tyson, *The Death of Jesus in Luke–Acts*, Columbia, SC: University of South Carolina Press, 1986; E. J. Via, 'According to Luke, Who Put Jesus to Death?', in R. J. Cassidy and P. J. Scharper (eds.), *Political Issues in Luke–Acts*, Maryknoll, NY: Orbis, 1983, pp. 122–40; S. G. Wilson, 'The Jews and the Death of Jesus in Acts', in P. Richardson and D. Granskou (eds.), *Anti-Judaism in Early Christianity*, Studies in Christianity and Judaism, 2, Waterloo, Ontario: Wilfrid Laurier University Press, 1986, pp. 155–64. For further bibliography on anti-Jewish tones in Luke's passion narrative, see Brown, *Death*, vol. I, p. 389, n. 140.

[4] Blinzler, *Trial*; D. R. Catchpole, *The Trial of Jesus: A Study in the Gospels and Jewish Historiography from 1770 to the Present Day*, Leiden: E. J. Brill, 1971; S. Légasse, *The Trial of Jesus*, London: SCM Press, 1997; E. P. Sanders, *Jesus and Judaism*, London: SCM Press, 1985 (esp. ch. 11); P. Winter, *On the Trial of Jesus*, second edition, Berlin: Walter

this latter level has also brought into discussion a whole range of issues related to the Jewish and Roman legal proceedings which were considered to have some bearing on Jesus' trial.[5] At both levels attention has also been paid to the other canonical accounts of Jesus' trial.

Secondly, and closely related to the quest for the 'facts' behind the story, extensive work has been done on identifying the sources on which Luke may have drawn in this part of his writing[6] – the question being

de Gruyter, 1974. Although not specifically concerned with the issue of responsibility for Jesus' death, the recent work of A. Watson on *The Trial of Jesus* (Athens, GA: University of Georgia Press, 1995, esp. pp. 150–75) makes some rather novel claims in this regard. Its contention is that Jesus deliberately sought his own death, with the intention of fulfilling scriptural prophecy; yet he badly missed his goal, when instead of being stoned under the authority of the Sanhedrin, as he would have wished, he ended up being condemned and executed for sedition at the hands of the Romans, for whom he did not care – which is why the Gospels are said to try to place the primary responsibility on the Jews.

[5] Among the works which are specifically designed to investigate the socio-juridical background of Jesus' trial, the standard contribution still remains A. N. Sherwin-White's *Roman Society and Roman Law in the New Testament*, Oxford: Clarendon, 1963, pp. 1–47.

[6] As in the case of the Gospel as a whole, the prevailing position is that one of Luke's sources was Mark's Gospel (albeit that here Luke appears to follow Mark less closely than elsewhere). J. B. Green claims 'virtual certainty that the Third Evangelist made use of the Markan passion account ...' (*The Death of Jesus: Tradition and Interpretation in the Passion Narrative*, Tübingen: J. C. B. Mohr, 1988, p. 102). Cf. also A. Barr, 'The Use and Disposal of the Marcan Source in Luke's Passion Narrative', *ExpT* 55 (1943–4), 227–31; Brown, *Death*, vol. I, pp. 42–6.

More controversial has been the suggestion that in addition to Mark, Luke may have made use of another passion narrative, possibly part of a 'proto-Luke'. In support of the general idea of a 'proto-Luke', see especially V. Taylor, *Behind the Third Gospel: A Study of the Proto-Luke Hypothesis*, Oxford: Clarendon, 1926; V. Taylor, *The Passion Narrative of St Luke: A Critical and Historical Investigation*, ed. O. E. Evans, Cambridge University Press, 1972, esp. pp. vii–ix, 125. Advocating specifically Luke's use of this source in the passion narrative, see: Marshall, *Gospel*, p. 785; Marshall, *Historian*, esp. p. 62; F. Rehkopf, *Die lukanische Sonderquelle: Ihr Umfang und Sprachgebrauch*, WUNT 5, Tübingen: J. C. B. Mohr, 1959; H. Schürmann, *Der Paschamahlbericht*, Münster im Westphalia: Aschendorff, 1953; H. Schürmann, *Der Einsetzungsbericht*, Münster im Westphalia: Aschendorff, 1955; H. Schürmann, *Jesu Abschiedsrede*, Münster im Westphalia: Aschendorff, 1957; E. Schweizer, 'Zur Frage der Quellenbenutzung durch Lukas', in his *Neues Testament und Christologie im Werden: Aufsätze*, Göttingen: Vandenhoeck & Ruprecht, 1982, pp. 33–85; Taylor, *Passion*; P. Winter, 'The Treatment of His Sources by the Third Evangelist in Luke XXI–XXIV', *ST* 8 (1955), 138–72; P. Winter, 'Luke XXII 66b–71', *ST* 9 (1956), 112–5.

Against this hypothesis, with nuances ranging from mere scepticism about a *continuous* source to the dismissal of any non-Markan source (written or oral), see: J. Blinzler, 'Passionsgeschehen und Passionsbericht des Lukasevangeliums', *BK* 24 (1969), 1–4; Brown, *Death*, pp. 64–75; A. Büchele, *Der Tod Jesu im Lukasevangelium. Eine redaktionsgeschichtliche Untersuchung zu Lk* 23, Frankfurt: Josef Knecht, 1978; M. Dibelius, *From Tradition to Gospel*, London: Nicholson & Watson, 1934 (German original, 1919, 1933), esp. pp. 178–217, and 'Das historische Problem der Leidensgeschichte', *ZNW* 30 (1931), 193–201; Fitzmyer, *Luke*, vol. II, pp. 1359–62; F. J. Matera, 'Luke 22:66–71: Jesus Before the Πρεσβυτεριον' and 'Luke 23:1–25: Jesus Before Pilate, Herod, and Israel', in F. Neirynck (ed.), *L'Evangile de Luc*, revised edition, Leuven University Press, 1989, customarily raised with reference to the whole passion narrative (Luke 22–3).[7]

Thirdly, a broad variety of works has been produced under the general concern of discovering the function of Jesus' trial narrative within the overall scheme of Luke–Acts. Since it is here that our interests also lie, it is necessary to review briefly the main contributions in this area.[8]

Jesus' trial as an apologia related to Rome and Judaism

Although neither of the influential works of Cadbury and Conzelmann, to which reference has been made in the last chapter, deals at any length with the subject of Jesus' trial, the textual evidence with which they substantiate their representations of Luke's apologetics is customarily drawn from the account of Jesus' (and Paul's) trial. Thus, Pilate's declaration of Jesus' innocence, the initiative of Jews (rather than Romans) in Jesus' crucifixion, the non-politicality of Jesus' titles and death, the depiction of the Jewish accusations as lies, are all interpreted as indicating that a major goal of Luke's account of the trials of Jesus was to persuade the Roman state that Christianity, like its founder, was not politically subversive.[9]

Moreover, Cadbury and Conzelmann agree on the existence of a second level of apologetic – one directed at Judaism. At this level, the input which they bring from the account of Jesus' trial is more limited, but significant nonetheless. For Cadbury this input consists of the Scriptures' prediction of Jesus' suffering,[10] while Conzelmann points on the one hand to Luke's polemical stress on the Jewish involvement in

---

pp. 517–33 and 535–51 respectively; D. Senior, *The Passion of Jesus in the Gospel of Luke*, Collegeville, MN: Liturgical, 1989; G. Schneider *Die Passion Jesu nach den drei ältern Evangelien*, Munich: Kösel, 1973; M. L. Soards, *The Passion According to Luke: The Special Material of Luke 22*, Sheffield Academic Press, 1987.

[7] That Luke 22–3 should be regarded as the Lukan passion narrative is in keeping with Synoptic studies in general, which customarily understand Jesus' passion as starting with the reference to the plot to kill Jesus, during the Jewish festival of Unleaven Bread, and ending with Jesus' burial. With specific reference to Luke's Gospel, see Brown, *Death*, vol. I, p. 39; Senior, *Passion of Jesus*, especially p. 40.

[8] I do not discuss here the outstanding work of R. E. Brown (*Death*) for two reasons. First, the commentary format of the work makes interaction with it more meaningful on specific passages. Second, where Brown does summarise his views on the distinctiveness of Luke's account of Jesus' *passion* (as distinct from trial) – once in terms of Luke's theology (vol. I, pp. 30–3) and once with regard to the sources (vol. I, pp. 64–75) – there is very little to indicate that he is advocating any specific understanding of the Lukan account of Jesus' trial.

[9] Cadbury, *Making*, pp. 308–12; Conzelmann, *Theology*, pp. 83–8, 138–44.

[10] Cadbury, *Making*, p. 304.

Jesus' death, an involvement which calls them now to repentance, and on the other hand to the point of contact which Luke establishes with the Jews by saying that they acted in ignorance and to fulfil God's plan.[11] The only major disagreement between the perspectives of Cadbury and Conzelmann is on the relationship between these two levels of Lukan apologetics: is the Jewish apologetic subordinated to the Roman one (as suggested by Cadbury) or are the two running independently of each other (as Conzelmann insists)?[12] It is hoped that the present analysis of the Lukan text will enable us to evaluate the areas of both convergence and divergence between the perspectives of their works.[13]

A more thorough and nuanced interpretation of Jesus' Lukan trial along the lines of a political apologetic and Jewish polemic has been proposed more recently by J. B. Tyson, in his literary investigation on *The Death of Jesus in Luke–Acts*. What gives particular force to Tyson's analysis of Jesus' trial in the Third Gospel is the fact that he does not examine it as an isolated fragment of Luke's writing, but attempts to read it in the light of the plot which precedes it (the Jewish leaders, the Jewish public, Jerusalem, and the temple representing major factors in this). What is disappointing in his study, however, is that having surveyed the plot of such a richly Christological document,[14] and having paid specific attention (in connection with the Sanhedrin hearing) to Conzelmann's remark that 'Luke makes out of the trial a compendium of Christology for his readers',[15] Tyson is prepared to limit Luke's distinctive presentation of Jesus' trial to pro-Roman politics and anti-Jewish polemics.[16] A redress of this situation is therefore needed.

---

[11] Conzelmann, *Theology*, pp. 145–6.

[12] See chapter 8 for a more detailed statement of Cadbury's and Conzelmann's contributions.

[13] For a detailed critique of the political-apologetic interpretation in relation to Luke's presentation of Jesus' trial and death, see Cassidy, *Jesus,* pp. 63–76; R. J. Cassidy, 'Luke's Audience, the Chief Priests, and the Motive for Jesus' Death', in Cassidy and Scharper (eds.), *Political Issues*, pp. 146–67. For Cassidy's explicit criticism of Conzelmann's position, see. Cassidy, *Jesus*, pp. 128–30. In Cassidy's view, 'Luke's concern is not to establish Jesus' loyalty and submissiveness to the Roman empire, but rather to indicate in unmistakable terms that the chief priests and their allies were the ones primarily responsible for Jesus' ultimate fate' (*Jesus*, p. 69).

[14] Tyson himself notes the weaving together of three Christological titles in the account of the Sanhedrin trial (*Death*, p. 126).

[15] Tyson, *Death*, p. 127; cf. Conzelmann, *Theology*, p. 85, n. 3.

[16] Cassidy also limits his discussion of Jesus' trial in Luke's Gospel to the political element (*Jesus*, esp. ch. 5), but in his case this is less surprising, since his stated purpose is to investigate the socio-political dimension of Luke–Acts.

Jesus' trial as an *apologia pro imperio*

As noted in the last chapter, the trial of Jesus in Luke's Gospel is one of the two major foci[17] around which Walaskay builds his case that Luke–Acts ought to be understood as an *apologia pro imperio*.[18] Walaskay's twofold conclusion on Luke's account of Jesus trial is that (i) far from trying to impress the Romans with Jesus' political innocence, (ii) 'there is much in the Lucan narrative which commends the Roman government to the Christian community'.[19] What is intriguing with regard to these statements is the degree to which Walaskay is ready to overlook both the 'double-edged-ness' of their implications and the extent of mutual undermining between the two parts of the conclusion. To begin with their implications for the theory which Walaskay opposes, in his zeal for showing that Luke is not particularly keen to stress Jesus' political innocence, Walaskay points out that Pilate is both 'superficial in his investigation' and willing to 'allow this trial to degenerate to the point of an unjust execution'.[20] Surprisingly, however, Walaskay shows no concern about the implications of such a conclusion for his own emphasis on the positive portrayal of the Roman government. Similarly, his second conclusion, that Jesus received from Pilate a comparably gentle and fair treatment,[21] offers to the rival *apologia pro ecclesia* approach as much support as it does to his own. Moving to the mutual undermining between the two parts of Walaskay's conclusion, it is remarkable that he can have two consecutive paragraphs, one emphasising Pilate's superficiality and cowardice and the next one his gentleness and justice.[22]

But perhaps one ought to see also the positive side of Walaskay's (at least seeming) inconsistency. Perhaps the text itself is not meant to portray the Roman state in either an exclusively negative or an exclusively positive light (our analysis of the Lukan episodes of Jesus' trial should help to clarify whether this is the case). If so, Walaskay's overall exegesis may be correct but his thesis not proven.

Jesus' trial as the trial of the faithful God

The year 1985 saw the publication of two significant monographs on Luke's passion narrative – one by R. J. Karris[23] and the other by

---

[17] The second one, the trial of Paul in Acts, will be discussed in chapter 7.
[18] Walaskay, *Rome*, ch. 3.   [19] Ibid., p. 48.   [20] Ibid.   [21] Ibid., pp. 48–9.
[22] Ibid.
[23] *Luke: Artist and Theologian. Luke's Passion Account as Literature*, New York: Paulist Press.

J. Neyrey[24] – both of which pay considerable attention to Luke's account of Jesus' trials.[25]

According to Karris, Luke 23 brings together a whole strand of themes which had been running throughout the Gospel. Most significant among them are said to be the themes of the faithful God, justice, and food. The respective function of these themes is (a) to depict Jesus' trial as the trial of God's faithfulness to him;[26] (b) to show that Jesus' righteousness was one main cause of his crucifixion;[27] and (c) to portray Jesus' behaviour and teaching at meals as the second explanation of his death.[28]

Karris is certainly correct to note that according to Luke, Jesus' trial unfolds at more than one level. Indeed, it is not merely Jesus, as a historical figure, who goes on trial: Luke is not writing merely to inform the readers of the events associated with Jesus' trial. But what is the second level of the trial? My contention is that far from being himself on trial, God is portrayed as being the supreme Judge, the giver of the ultimate verdict with regard to Jesus. God's faithfulness is not 'tried' but it is assumed throughout Luke–Acts.[29] The resurrection accounts at the end of the Gospel come as the vindication not of God but of Jesus.

Also, while it is true that the immediate causes of the conflict which eventually ended in Jesus' crucifixion are often connected in Luke's Gospel to Jesus' lifestyle of justice and his eating habits, the primary 'conflict' in the unfolding of the Gospel is one relating to Jesus' Messianic identity – a conflict between what Jesus' words and deeds (expressions of a lifestyle of justice and particularly visible at the table, to use Karris' categories) seem to affirm about him on the one hand and what the religious authorities contend on the other.[30] It is this conflict that the reader will explicitly encounter in the double question of Jesus' opponents, at the beginning of the trial narrative: 'if you are the Christ . . . Are you then the Son of God?' (Luke 22.67, 70).

---

[24] *The Passion According to Luke: A Redaction Study of Luke's Soteriology*, New York: Paulist Press.

[25] Of importance for our purposes is also the fact that both of them make the additional step of trying to establish bridges between the narrative of Jesus' trial and the trial narratives of Acts.

[26] Karris, *Luke*, pp. 82–3, 91–2.   [27] Ibid., p. 37.   [28] Ibid., p. 70.

[29] *Pace* also L.T. Johnson, who similarly regards God's faithfulness (to Israel) as something which Luke labours to prove (see chapter 1 above).

[30] On this understanding of the conflict of Luke's Gospel, see the discussion of the plot leading to Jesus' trial, below.

Jesus' trial as the trial of Israel

Similar to the concerns of Karris' work are those expressed by Neyrey in the third chapter of his monograph.[31] He, too, enquires about the significance (or, more exactly in his case, the particularity) of Luke's account of Jesus' trial. Two major ideas seem to govern Neyrey's approach. First, he emphasises the Jewish rejection of Jesus, which is said to indicate that '*[t]he trial of Jesus becomes the trial of Israel*, for in unjustly condemning Jesus they bring down God's judgement on themselves'.[32]

Secondly, under the heading of 'Prophecy-Fulfilment', Neyrey investigates the formal connection between the trial of Jesus in Luke's Gospel and the trials of the church in Acts.[33] The significance which Neyrey attaches to this formal link is that the apostles' trials in Acts are said to be in fact continuations of Jesus' trial in Luke's Gospel. Consequently, similar to Jesus' own trial, their trials are also trials of Israel.[34]

Both of these Lukan emphases to which Neyrey points (the Jewish rejection of Jesus and the parallels between the trials of Jesus and those of the church) are crucial for a correct reading of Luke's trial narratives. Yet the way Neyrey explains them needs some revision. With regard to the former, it is doubtful that speaking of the Jewish leaders as being themselves on trial is the most helpful way of defining their role in the trial story, and even less certain that this is a dominant emphasis of the passage. To be sure, it is entirely legitimate to infer, on the basis of Luke's wider story, that in judging Jesus, Israel is *indirectly* passing judgement on itself, but this needs to be substantiated largely from other passages. The burden of proof is still with Neyrey to show that this is what Luke wishes to convey *here*. As for Neyrey's latter suggestion (that there is a pattern of Israel on trial throughout the trial narratives of Luke–Acts), this is particularly problematic in view of the fact that often (especially in the case of Paul) the ultimate verdict rests not with Jews but with Romans.

Concluding observations

The present state of research on the trial of Jesus may be summarised as follows:

(a) Much of the work in this area has been governed by concerns (historical, source-critical, judicial) which, by their nature, pay

---

[31] Neyrey, *Passion*, pp. 69–107.

[32] Ibid., p. 83. Neyrey finds evidence for the theme of Jesus' rejection by Israel in each of the four Lukan trial episodes (pp. 75, 76, 80, and 83–4, respectively).

[33] Ibid., pp. 84–8.   [34] Ibid., p. 89.

little attention to the distinctive emphases of Luke's account of Jesus' trial.

(b) Among the works which have attempted to uncover Luke's emphases, readings which may be qualified as 'apologetic' have exercised a particularly significant influence. Yet little agreement has been reached on how exactly Luke's apologetic motives ought to be understood: Cadbury, Conzelmann, and Walaskay have offered conflicting explanations. Their lack of agreement, together with the additional criticism (itself questionable at certain points) to which they have been subjected by works such as Cassidy's, suggests the need for a further consideration of Luke's apologetic in this part of his Gospel.

(c) Some of the more recent works (especially those of Karris and Neyrey), drawing on the benefits of narrative criticism, have been able to make more explicit an observation which earlier works had only indirectly expressed – the recognition of a second level of meaning to Luke's presentation of Jesus' trial. According to this understanding, together with Jesus, someone or something else goes 'on trial'.[35] For Cadbury, Conzelmann, and Tyson this 'co-defendant' of Jesus is largely the political innocence of Christianity (although Judaism's attitude to Jesus is also under scrutiny). For Walaskay, it is the friendly image of the Roman system. For Karris, it is God's faithfulness. For Neyrey, it is Israel. On closer scrutiny, however, none of these readings have been able to stand as satisfactory explanations of the Lukan account. The search is, therefore, still on for an understanding of Luke's concerns which does better justice to his version of Jesus' trial, and which is at the same time able to explain the variety of insights which previous studies have produced.

The plot leading to Jesus' trial

Before any attempt is made to understand Luke's narrative of Jesus' trial, it is important to see how this event relates to Luke's overall story. Accordingly, the specific concern of this section is with the plot which leads to Jesus' trial,[36] particular attention being paid to the notion of

[35] In more conventional language, this is in effect a way of saying that in addition to Luke's historical interest in this part of Jesus' life, a more specific issue is at stake ('on trial') as he writes.

[36] For some specialised discussions of plot see P. Brooks, *Reading for the Plot: Design and Interpretation in Narrative*, New York: Knopf, 1984, pp. 3–38; E. Dipple, *Plot*, London: Methuen, 1970. Among the works which employ the notion of plot in the study of the Gospels, see especially R. A. Culpepper, *Anatomy of the Fourth Gospel: A Study of Literary Design*, NT Foundations and Facets, Philadelphia: Fortress, 1983, pp. 77–98; R. A. Edwards, *Matthew's Story of Jesus*, Philadelphia: Fortress, 1985; J. D. Kingsbury, 'The Plot of Luke's

conflict, both because trials are *par excellence* scenes of conflict, and because of the significant role which conflict plays in the development of the Gospel's plot.[37] The specific areas on which I hope to shed light through this investigation are (i) what, according to Luke, appear to be the causes of Jesus' trial and (ii) what the readers are led to expect as they approach the trial narrative.

Among the most notable contributions to the study of conflict in Luke's Gospel[38] are undoubtedly the works of J. D. Kingsbury[39] and J. B.Tyson.[40] Central to both Kingsbury's and Tyson's approaches is the focus on the participants in the conflict (Jesus, the disciples, the people, the various authorities, Satan, etc.), with a view to clarifying who these participants are, what their Lukan image is, and what role each of them plays. This may seem an obvious route to take, since any conflict implies interaction between a number of participants. Moreover, such a focus may also yield useful results in the study of conflict at any individual point in the narrative. The approach becomes problematic, however, when one aims to see how the various scenes of conflict further the plot of the narrative. Any plot development presupposes some degree of coherence in the

---

Story of Jesus', *Int* 48 (1994), 369–78; F. J. Matera, 'The Plot of Matthew's Gospel', *CBQ* 49 (1987), 235–40.

[37] J. D. Kingsbury writes: 'At the heart of this gospel plot is the element of conflict' (*Conflict in Luke: Jesus, Authorities, Disciples*, Minneapolis: Fortress, 1991, p. 34) and '[a]s with the other canonical Gospels, the plot of Luke revolves around conflict' ('Plot', 369). Similarly, B. J. Malina and J. H. Neyrey: 'At every turn, Luke's story of Jesus and his disciples narrates scenes of conflict' ('Conflict in Luke–Acts: Labelling and Deviance Theory', in J. H. Neyrey (ed)., *The Social World of Luke–Acts: Models for Interpretation*, Peabody: Hendrickson, 1991, p. 97). Moreover, J. B. Tyson correctly stresses that the notion of conflict is central not only to Luke's Gospel, but to all narrative literature: 'I have chosen the general theme of conflict or opposition, which I take to be a fundamental theme in narrative literature. It is difficult to imagine a story without a plot line that operates around some kind of opposition ...' ('Conflict as a Literary Theme in the Gospel of Luke', in W. R. Farmer, (ed)., *New Synoptic Studies: The Cambridge Gospel Conference and Beyond*, Macon, GA: Mercer, 1983, p. 313).

[38] A word needs to be said about several works which are not discussed here in any detail and which may appear to deserve such a place. First, Brawley's *Luke–Acts* is meant to show 'how Luke views conflict arising from Jewish sources and what his response to it is' (p. 155), but a careful reading of this work soon reveals that Brawley's end-product is not any systematic analysis of conflict in Luke–Acts (and certainly not of the way this conflict contributes to the development of the plot), but rather the contention that far from giving up on the Jews (as some of Brawley's predecessors had argued), Luke appeals to them apologetically, seeking conciliation. Two other studies consider Lukan conflict from the angle of social theory (H. Moxnes, *The Economy of the Kingdom: Social Conflict and Economic Relations in Luke's Gospel*, Philadelphia: Fortress, 1988; and Malina and Neyrey, 'Conflict'), but again, both of them offer rather limited insights into the role of conflict in the development of Luke's plot.

[39] Kingsbury, *Conflict*; Kingsbury, 'Plot'.

[40] Tyson, 'Conflict'; Tyson, *Death*, chs. 2–4, pp. 29–113.

way events and characters are placed in the story.[41] In the case of Luke's
Gospel, however, the degree of such coherence is far from impressive in
so far as the participants in the conflict are concerned. Not only are they
not sufficiently black or white to allow one to pigeon-hole them according
to their role in the conflict, but often and (it would seem) rather randomly
they can be found on the 'wrong side'. Those who are 'meant' to be Jesus'
opponents function at times as his friends while his allies can play the
role of rivals. A few examples may be brought to illustrate this:

(1) For much of Luke's Gospel, the Pharisees play the role of
     Jesus' opponents. Tyson usefully places this material into three
     groups. The first one includes 'some thirteen pericopae that tell
     of the controversies between Jesus and the Pharisaic block of
     opponents'.[42] In most of them, Tyson concludes, 'Pharisees and
     their associates are cast in the role of Jesus' critical opponents.'[43]
     In the second group there are a number of passages where Jesus is
     the only speaker and he 'specifically criticizes' the Pharisees.[44]
     The third group includes three editorial notes, where once again
     a clearly negative image of the Pharisees emerges.[45]

     But this is hardly the full Lukan picture of the Pharisees. More
     positive images of Pharisees in Luke–Acts are also familiar.[46]
     Tyson shows clear awareness of this ambivalence,[47] but despite
     his reference to some relatively positive images of Pharisees,[48]
     his discussion of Lukan conflict has to play down such material,
     since it would seem evident that when the Pharisees are friendly
     to Jesus or in agreement with him no conflict is there to be ana-
     lysed. Moreover, one is left wondering what coherence Luke's

[41] See for instance Matera's references to authors both ancient and modern who regard
the notions of time and causality as necessary for any plot development ('Plot', 235–6).

[42] Tyson, *Death*, p. 64. The list of passages includes: Luke 5.17–26, 29–32, 33–5; 6.1–5,
6–11; 7.36–50; 10.25–8; 11.37–41; 13.31–3; 14.1–6; 15.1–2; 17.20–1; 19.28–40 (ibid.,
p. 65).

[43] Ibid., p. 68.

[44] Ibid. Tyson's examples include: Luke 11.42–4, 45–52; 12.1; 16.14–15; 18.9–14 (ibid.
p. 69).

[45] Luke 7.29–30; 11.53–4; 16.14 (ibid., p. 69).

[46] See Brawley, *Luke–Acts*, pp. 85–8; J. J. Sanders, *Jews*, pp. 85–8, despite Sanders'
other arguments for a negative Lukan image of Jewish groups.

[47] Tyson, *Death*, p. 68.

[48] He specifically calls attention to one occasion when Jesus appears to converse peace-
fully with the Pharisees (17.20–1), one when they warn Jesus of Herod's evil intentions
(13.31), and three where Jesus dines with them (7.36–50; 11.37–41; 14.1–6), a setting which
denotes some degree of mutual acceptance, despite the typically controversial tone of the
meal conversation (ibid., pp. 66–7).

plot can still have, if it unfolds around a conflict which is intense in one pericope and disappears or is completely reversed in the next one, often without editorial warning or explanation.[49]

(2)   The Jewish public is another example of a group whose conflict with Jesus is supposed to be a major factor in the development of the Lukan plot,[50] but whose attitude to him can at times display a striking lack of coherence.[51] For most of the Gospel the crowds appear favourable towards Jesus. Yet during Jesus' Roman trial they (ὁ λαός) join the chief priests and the rulers in demanding Jesus' death (23.13),[52] while only hours later, as Jesus is led to be crucified, they are associated with the women who lamented over Jesus (23.27).[53] True, there is no need to assume that the sympathetic crowds are the same as the ones asking for his crucifixion, but Luke displays no concern to differentiate between them or to indicate a coherent pattern in their attitude.[54]

(3)   Jesus' conflict with the disciples is also regarded by Kingsbury as contributing to the Gospel plot.[55] While Kingsbury is probably correct to state that the cause of this 'conflict' is typically the disciples' immaturity and incomprehension, it is much less clear that any coherent progression can be noted in the relationship

[49] Most intriguingly, perhaps, even where a pattern seems plausible – for example, that the conflict intensifies towards the end of the Gospel – the Pharisees do not conform to it, for it is precisely there that they, the customary troublemakers, disappear from the scene.

[50] One is reminded of Kingsbury's words: 'Luke's story of Jesus is primarily a story of conflict between Jesus and Israel, made up of the religious authorities and the people' (*Conflict*, p. 71).

[51] Among the recent attempts at making sense of the variety of ways in which the Jewish people in Luke's Gospel relate to Jesus, see especially Brawley, *Luke–Acts*, ch. 8 and Weatherly, Jewish, ch. 2, with the former arguing that the Jewish people are divided by Jesus and the gospel into believers and unbelievers (esp. p. 153), while the latter suggests a distinction between the people of Jerusalem and other Jewish people.

[52] *Pace* Weatherly's efforts to demonstrate that Luke means a gathering which is composed exclusively of Jewish leadership (*Jewish*, pp. 63–4). Such a reading would make Luke's τοὺς ἀρχιερεῖς καὶ τοὺς ἄρχοντας καὶ τὸν λαόν (23.13) nonsensical (see., e.g., D. L. Bock, *Luke*, Baker Exegetical Commentary on the New Testament 3, vol. II, Grand Rapids: Baker, 1996, p. 1827).

[53] See further discussion on these two verses in chapters 3 and 4 respectively.

[54] According to Tyson, there is a pattern of initial acceptance followed by final rejection and this withdrawal of the public support ultimately makes Jesus' death possible (*Death*, p. 44), but see Brawley's criticism of this pattern (*Luke–Acts*, pp. 51–3). Moreover, it is particularly hard to substantiate the claim that according to Luke Jesus' death was made possible by a decrease in his popular support. On the contrary, Luke's repeated references to the efforts of the Jewish leaders and Judas to find a way to deal with Jesus without the people knowing about it (19.47–8; 22.2, 6) make sense only if according to the evangelist Jesus was still enjoying considerable popular support.

[55] Kingsbury, *Conflict*, pp. 109–39.

between Jesus and the disciples. If anything, the disciples seem to display more confusion and failure in the latter part of the Gospel than during the earlier days of Jesus' Galilean ministry.[56]

(4) Both Kingsbury and Tyson note the existence of a cosmic dimension to the Lukan conflict – one involving Satan and demons as opponents of Jesus.[57] It is this group, at least, that one would expect to see consistently playing negative roles. There is at least one matter, however, in which even they can perform what in effect is a laudable job – declaring Jesus' identity. Not only do they know for themselves who Jesus is (4.3, 9), but they also declare it publicly (4.34, 41).[58]

All these observations (and the list of examples could continue) would seem to feed the suspicion that a focus on the participants in the conflict may not be the best way of defining how the theme of conflict contributes to the development of the Gospel plot. Had Luke intended this to be the primary focus of his narrative he would surely have made his characters play a more consistent part in the conflict. At the same time, blaming such incoherence on Luke's literary shortcomings is not a particularly easy explanation to accept, in view of Luke's recognised abilities as a storyteller,[59] and it should only be accepted as a last resort, if no better explanation is available. It is my contention in what follows that a more appropriate way of looking at Luke's story is to view it as a conflict surrounding certain 'matters' (the λόγοι about which Luke intends to give Theophilus certainty).[60] Probably the term which most helpfully qualifies the content of these 'matters', at least in so far as Luke's Gospel (as distinct from Acts) is concerned, is 'Christological' (especially if one avoids too sharp a distinction between Christology and soteriology, since

---

[56] Jesus' passion and death, in particular, seem to be their major points of incomprehension (9.44–5; 18.34; 24.26) and failure (22.3–4; 22.34, 45–6, 54–61).

[57] Kingsbury, *Conflict*, pp. 13–14; Tyson, *Death*, p. 57.

[58] G. Twelftree has argued that the titles which the demons applied to Jesus need not have carried the fully fledged Messianic content which they did in the early church and that their probable role, when used by demons, was self-defence, since in ancient magical practice 'to know the name or identity of an adversary was to score a point over them' (*Christ Triumphant: Exorcism Then and Now*, London: Hodder & Stoughton, 1985, p. 62; see pp. 60–3). This interpretation is plausible (even if based on textual silence, since the Gospels do not elaborate on the demons' motives), but it must not obscure the fact that in the economy of Luke's Gospel the demons' application of Christological titles to Jesus is part of the Gospel's positive statement of Jesus' identity.

[59] For some helpful discussions of Luke's literary abilities, see Karris, *Luke*; W. C. van Unnik, 'Eléments artistiques dans l'évangile de Luc', in Neirynck (ed.), *L'Evangile*, pp. 39–50.

[60] Luke 1.4.

for Luke to speak of Christ includes speaking of the salvation which God has made available through Christ).[61] I shall suggest, therefore, that a plausible way of making sense of the Gospel plot as a whole is by viewing it as unfolding around Luke's Christological assertions (which, no doubt, the author would have regarded as the Christological claims of the Christian gospel). Such a shift of emphasis from the participants in the conflict to the author's Christological claims is not meant to suggest that the Gospel's characters have little significance in the development of the plot, but rather that since the image of the participants is not Luke's primary focus (Jesus' image being the obvious exception), they continue to make sense even when on the 'wrong side' of the conflict, as long as their position at any moment helps the author's Christological case. To substantiate and clarify this, however, a brief representation of Luke's story according to such an understanding of conflict is necessary.

The preface to Luke's Gospel (1.1–4)

The preface to the Gospel serves to introduce the reader to the subsequent story and therefore its importance for the understanding of the Gospel plot should not be overlooked.[62] Luke begins by stating that the 'things' (πράγματα) which some of Luke's predecessors had written about and which now Luke himself is about to narrate in his story are to be regarded as belonging to a period of fulfilment (τὰ πεπληροφορημένα, 1.1).[63] The information about these matters, he continues, comes from reliable sources (1.2) or has been acquired through the author's personal thorough investigations (1.3). As such, this information is meant to provide Theophilus (and presumably others too) with 'certainty' (ἀσφάλειαν) concerning some 'matters'/'teachings' (λόγοι) about which he had been 'informed'/'instructed' (περὶ ὧν κατηχήθης).[64] It is these 'matters'

---

[61] It is not my intention here to debate which idiom is most distinctive of Luke's theology. For a helpful discussion on that, see Marshall, *Historian*, especially pp. 77–102.

[62] On the literary background of Luke's preface, see the following works and their bibliographical information: L. Alexander, 'Luke's Preface in the Context of Greek Preface-Writing', *NovT* 28 (1986), 48–74 and *The Preface to Luke's Gospel: Literary Convention and Social Context in Luke 1.1–4 and Acts 1.1*, SNTSMS 78, Cambridge University Press, 1993; Sterling, *Historiography*, pp. 339–46.

[63] Sterling, *Historiography*, p. 346. On understanding πληροφορέω here as 'to fulfil', rather than 'to accomplish' (H. J. Cadbury, 'Commentary on the Preface of Luke', in Foakes-Jackson and Lake (eds)., *Beginnings*, vol. II, pp. 495–6) or 'fully assure' (K. H. Rengstorf, *Das Evangelium nach Lukas*, ninth edition, Göttingen: Vandenhoeck & Ruprecht, 1968, p. 14), see Bock, *Luke*, vol. I, pp. 56–7; Fitzmyer, *Luke*, vol. I, p. 293.

[64] Bock, *Luke*, vol. I, pp. 64–5; Fitzmyer, *Luke*, vol. I, pp. 300–1; Marshall, *Gospel*, p. 44.

then, that according to Luke's own declaration of purpose are to be regarded as the primary focus of Luke's narrative.

The infancy narratives (1.5–2.52)

The first major section of Luke's story (1.5–2.52) introduces the reader to
the meaning of the time of fulfilment to which the preface has alluded.[65]
In a thoroughly Jewish environment, heavenly messengers come to bring
the good news of the birth of two boys – John and Jesus. Through the
announcements of these births, as well as through the various receptions
of the infants, the reader discovers the importance of the two: 'John is
the forerunner who announces fulfillment's approach, but Jesus is the
fulfillment.'[66] Together they represent the actualisation of the Jewish
hopes for a time when God would come to bring salvation to his people (1. 32–3, 35, 54–5, 68–79; 2.10–11, 28–34). The parallelism between
the two birth stories is intriguing, yet for Luke the boys are no peers.
While John may be 'great before the Lord' (1.15), 'filled with the Holy
Spirit' (1.16), 'prophet of the Most High' (1.76), Jesus' status is incom-
parably higher, for he is 'Son of the Most High' (1.32), 'Son of God'
(1.35), 'Saviour' (2.11), 'Christ the Lord' (2.11), 'your [God's] salvation' (2.30), 'a light for revelation to the Gentiles, and for the glory of
your people Israel' (2.32). It is no surprise, then, that Coleridge can speak
of Luke's first two chapters as 'preparing for the birth of a distinctively
Lukan Christology'.[67]

The ministry of John the Baptist (3.1–20)

Reflecting on John's role in Luke's theological scheme, Conzelmann has
argued that Luke has deliberately separated John from Jesus, both geographically and historically, in order to indicate that John belongs to
the epoch of promise, rather than, with Jesus, to that of fulfilment.[68]

---

[65] On the centrality of the fulfilment motif in the infancy narratives, see, for example,
M. Coleridge's monograph, which argues that 'the infancy narrative offers an account of
the divine visitation which has at its heart a dynamic of promise-fulfilment' (*The Birth of
the Lukan Narrative: Narrative as Christology in Luke 1–2*, JSNTSup 88, Sheffield: JSOT,
1993, p. 23). See also R. Laurentin, *The Truth of Christmas. Beyond the Myths. The Gospels
of the Infancy of Christ*, Petersham, MA: St Bede's, 1982, pp. 62–89.

[66] Bock, *Luke*, vol. I, p. 68; see also R. E. Brown, *The Birth of the Messiah: A Commentary
on the Infancy Narratives in the Gospels of Matthew and Luke*, new updated edition, London:
Geoffrey Chapman, 1993, pp. 282–5.

[67] Coleridge, *Birth*, p. 23; cf. pp. 226–7. On the profile of the Christology which the
infancy narratives introduce, see also Strauss, *Davidic*, pp. 76–125.

[68] Conzelmann, *Theology*, pp. 18–27.

Conzelmann's position has, however, been subjected to sharp criticism by W. Wink and I. H. Marshall, according to whom the Lukan John belongs to both the old and the new eras, thus functioning as a bridge between the two.[69] The close association between Jesus and John in the infancy narratives (which Conzelmann leaves out of his study of Lukan theology) represents a particularly persuasive argument for the latter interpretation.

Such a recognition of John's close association with Jesus in Luke's theology (following the Synoptic tradition), together with the climactic words of 3.16–17, indicates that Luke 3.1–20 is a passage of strategic Christological significance in Luke's work, since at its centre stands someone whose *raison d'être* in the narrative is, to a large extent, to assure the reader that Jesus is the actualisation of God's promises to Israel.

Jesus' baptism and genealogy (3.21–38)

The Christological importance of Jesus' baptism in the Third Gospel is correctly underlined by Bock when he characterises this event as 'one of the most christologically significant in the entire Gospel, because it presents one of two divine testimonies given during Jesus' ministry (the transfiguration account, 9.28–36, is the second such event)'.[70] Indeed, the effect of Luke's restructuring of the Markan account (1.9–11), placing the actual baptism statement in a subordinate position to the account of the Spirit's descent and of the heavenly voice, is that God's confirmation of Jesus' divine sonship becomes the primary emphasis of the pericope.[71]

Similar, albeit much more subtle, statements about Jesus' identity and mission are made through Luke's version of Jesus' genealogy. The most distinguishing feature of the Lukan genealogy compared with Matthew's is its extension beyond Abraham, to Adam, who is in turn described as '[son] of God' (τοῦ θεοῦ, 3.38). While it is difficult to be certain about the theological purpose(s) of a section which (especially in Luke's version) records nothing more than a list of names, two emphases can be noted with some confidence. First, the ending of the list with God has been taken as indicative of Luke's concern to portray Jesus as the Son of God.[72] What gives particular weight to this proposal is the position of the genealogy, between two sections which focus on Jesus' divine

[69] W. Wink, *John the Baptist in the Gospel Tradition*, Cambridge University Press, 1968, pp. 42–86; Marshall, *Historian*, pp. 145–7.

[70] Bock, *Luke*, vol. I, p. 332.   [71] Marshall, *Gospel*, p. 150.

[72] M. D. Johnson, *The Purpose of the Biblical Genealogies, With Special Reference to the Setting of the Genealogies of Jesus*, SNTSMS 8, second edition, Cambridge University Press, 1988, pp. 235–9.

sonship (3.22; 4.3, 9).[73] Second, the conclusion of his human genealogy in Adam has been regarded as a portrayal of Jesus as an exponent of the humanity created by God, a Second Adam figure.[74] Despite the absence of an explicit Second Adam Christology in Luke's writing, a reading of the genealogy along these lines is in keeping with the well-known fact that the Lukan Jesus and his movement do go beyond Judaism (Abraham's offspring), to all the nations (Adam's descendants).[75]

Jesus' temptation by the devil (4.1–13)

Despite the existence of certain 'anticipations of conflict' in the infancy narratives (1.52–4, 71, 74; 2.34–5),[76] Luke's overall emphasis up to this point in the story has undoubtedly been on a positive presentation of Jesus' identity and mission. However, this radically changes in Luke 4, where the element of conflict becomes explicit in two pericopae, both of which are programmatic for the subsequent conflict of Luke's story (4.1–13 and 4.16–30).[77]

---

[73] Marshall has argued against Johnson's suggestion, insisting that '[t]o regard all the names from Joseph to Adam as one gigantic parenthesis . . . misses the point of the genealogy, and to regard divine sonship as mediated to Jesus through his ancestors conflicts with the birth story' (Marshall, *Gospel*, p. 161). In answer to the first objection it may be said that focusing on the last element in the genealogical chain need not render the intermediary section as a parenthesis any more than this would be the case when speaking of Jesus as a descendant/son of Abraham on the basis of the Matthean genealogy. Similarly, in response to the second observation, one could argue that a genealogical description of Jesus' divine sonship is no more incompatible with the idea of divine conception than Jesus' genealogical portrayal as an exponent of humanity (for which, we shall see, Marshall finds grounds in Luke's text) is at odds with his partaking of this status by virtue of his birth of a woman.

[74] Ibid., p. 16 (partly following J. Weiss, J. Jeremias, and E. E. Ellis); J. Nolland, *Luke*, Dallas, TX: Word, 1989, vol. I, p. 167; Bock, *Luke*, vol. I, pp. 348–9.

[75] One other emphasis of the Lukan genealogy has been advocated by Johnson (Jesus as prophet), but his line of argumentation for this is somewhat dubious (M. D. Johnson, *Purpose*, pp. 240–52; against it see Marshall, *Gospel*, p. 161; Nolland, *Luke*, vol. I, p. 172).

[76] Tyson, *Death*, pp. 49–51.

[77] The programmatic role of Jesus' encounter with Satan for the Lukan plot is suggested by the end of the pericope, where the reader learns that Satan left Jesus 'until an opportune time' (ἄχρι καιροῦ – the clear implication is that the devil will renew his efforts). This is substantiated at various stages in the Gospel through passages which speak of demonic activity, but most importantly during the 'dark hour' of Jesus' passion.
As for the Nazareth story, J. T. Sanders correctly summarises the scholarly opinion, when he writes: 'This scene is "programmatic" for Luke–Acts, as one grows almost tired of reading in the literature on the passage' (*Jews*, p. 165). Equally suggestive is E. Samain's title: 'Le discours-programme de Jésus à la synagogue de Nazareth. Luc 4,16–30', *Foi et Vie* 11 (1971), 25–43. For further bibliography substantiating this assertion, see M. M. B. Turner, *Power from on High: The Spirit in Israel's Restoration and Witness in Luke–Acts*, Sheffield Academic Press, 1996, p. 213, n. 1.

The first pericope relates a conflict between Jesus and the devil. What establishes the continuity between this passage and the previous chapters is the unfolding of the conflict around the devil's repeated approach of Jesus with the words 'if you are the Son of God...' (4.3, 9).[78] The devil's challenge strikes at the root of the Christological claims of the earlier chapters (esp. 1.32, 35; 3.22, 23–38). It entices Jesus to a selfish misuse of his filial prerogative and thus to a compromise of his Messianic vocation.[79] Instead, however, Jesus' obedience to God precisely at the points where God's son Israel (Exod. 4.22–3) had failed (i.e. in respect to hunger, worship, and the testing of God) provides the reader with the assurance that Jesus is the one through whom the 'new exodus' and the eschatological restoration of Israel are now being brought about.[80]

Jesus' ministry outside Jerusalem (4.14–19.44)

The Lukan account of Jesus' ministry before his final entrance into Jerusalem is much too vast to allow a sequential discussion of the text. Instead, I shall focus first on the strategic section dealing with Jesus' preaching in Nazareth, and secondly a few general observations will be made about the nature of the conflict which permeates this whole section of Jesus' ministry.

(a) *Jesus in his home town (4.16–30)*

If the temptation episode introduces the Gospel conflict at a cosmic level, the Nazareth one does the same at a human level.[81] The first half of

---

[78] Nolland correctly notes: ' υἱός ... τοῦ θεοῦ, "Son of God", takes up 3:22, ὁ υἱός μου, "my Son", and relates also to the genealogy which concludes (at 3:38) with [υἱὸς] τοῦ θεοῦ "son of God"' (*Luke*, vol. I, p. 179). See, however, S. R. Garrett's interpretation of the passage in terms of a 'struggle for authority' (*The Demise of the Devil: Magic and the Demonic in Luke–Acts*, Minneapolis: Fortress, 1989, pp. 37–43).

[79] See Marshall, *Gospel*, pp. 170–1 and Nolland, *Luke*, vol. I, p. 179, for the preference of this interpretation of the temptation over against alternative understandings.

[80] Marshall, *Gospel*, p. 166; Strauss, *Davidic*, pp. 215–17; Turner, *Power*, pp. 204–8. Cf. B. Gerhardsson, *The Testing of God's Son*, Lund: Gleerup, 1966, *passim*; C. A. Kimball, *Jesus' Exposition of the Old Testament in Luke's Gospel*, Sheffield: JSOT, 1994, pp. 80–97; J. B. Gibson, *The Temptation of Jesus in Early Christianity*, Sheffield: JSOT, 1995, pp. 85–7. The existence of an Adam–Christ typology has also been argued by some (Nolland, *Luke*, vol. I, p. 182; E. E. Ellis, *The Gospel of Luke*, revised edition, Grand Rapids; Eerdmans; London: Marshall, Morgan & Scott, 1974, p. 94; Bock, *Luke*, vol. I, p. 363) and challenged by others (e.g. Fitzmyer, *Luke*, vol. I, p. 512).

[81] For the vast literature on this passage, see especially the bibliographies in U. Busse, *Das Nazareth-Manifest Jesu: Eine Einführung in das lukanische Jesusbild nach Lk.*

the Nazareth account concentrates on Jesus' positive presentation of his ministry as fulfilment of an Isaianic prophecy (4.18–21; cf. Isa. 61.1–2), while the second half focuses on his conflict with the Nazarenes and the Old Testament precedent for it.[82] Not surprisingly, these two emphases have created two rival ways of interpreting the episode and its relationship to the rest of Luke–Acts. The more broadly accepted of the two interpretations focuses on the aftermath of Jesus' preaching, which it regards as indicative of Luke's tendency to give up on the Jews and turn towards the Gentiles.[83] The second reading, made explicit by Brawley, denies that the passage acts programmatically in the sense described by the first approach, and instead places the greater weight on Jesus' presentation of his identity.[84] I suggest that such a polarity is unnecessary as long as the programmatic character of the second half is not seen in terms of the priority of Gentiles over Jews,[85] but rather in the broader sense that those who appear to be the least entitled to taste of the benefits of 'the year of the Lord's favour' are the most likely to do so. Such a reading would not only explain the connection between the two major thrusts of the pericope (i.e. in the first half the underprivileged are the poor, the captives, the blind, and the oppressed; in the second half they are the foreigners – those outside Jesus' home town and those outside Israel) but also be understandable in the light of Luke's general interest in the underprivileged, the marginalised, and the lost, – those with no claim before God. Consequently, the conflict which ties this pericope both to the previous material and to what is to come is not so much one between Jesus and the Nazarenes (or Jesus and the Jews for that matter) but one dealing with the legitimacy of Jesus' ministry: can he truly be the divinely appointed agent for the restoration and salvation of God's people[86] when he appears to bypass those who 'deserve' attention and to focus on those who cannot even hope for it? Prophetic oracles (4.18–19) and scriptural precedents (4.25–7) are brought in response to such objections.

4.16–30, Stuttgart: Katholisches Bibelwerk, 1978 and G. K. Shin, *Die Ausrufung des endgültigen Jubeljahres durch Jesus in Nazareth: Eine historisch-kritische Studie zu Lk. 4,16–30*, Bern: Lang, 1989.

[82] See Conzelmann, *Theology*, p. 34.

[83] Among the particularly influential proponents of this position see R. H. Lightfoot, *History and Interpretation in the Gospels*, London: Hodder & Stoughton, 1935, pp. 196–205; Haenchen, *Acts*, pp. 101, 414, 417–18, 535, 729–30; J. T. Sanders, *Jews*, pp. 165–8. A milder version of this approach has been proposed by Conzelmann, *Theology*, pp. 34–7, 194.

[84] Brawley, *Luke–Acts*, ch. 2.   [85] After all, Capernaum is no Gentile place.

[86] For a more thorough examination of the specific Christology which operates in the passage, see, among many others, Turner, *Power*, pp. 213–66 and the bibliographical material cited there.

(b) *The nature of the conflict in Luke 4.14–19.44*

The story of Jesus' ministry in Galilee (4.14–9.50) and on the way to Jerusalem (9.51–19.44)[87] can be viewed as consisting of two types of material. On the one hand one finds material in which the dominant tone is that of a positive presentation of Jesus' identity and mission, whether this be done by excerpts of his teaching, or by stories of healings, exorcisms, resuscitations, nature miracles, or by editorial notes (often inserted at the end of the pericopae). On the other hand, Luke includes stories and statements which present Jesus by contrasting his teaching and way of life with those of the Pharisees, scribes, and teachers of the law. It is only this second kind of material that, strictly speaking, would appear to bear the mark of conflict, for it is here that all the disputes between Jesus and his various opponents take place. Yet the conflict which is delineated by this material alone is hardly sufficient to indicate the overall profile of Luke's plot, since it leaves out so much of the story. Even more importantly, the points of dispute in the various scenes of overt conflict usually tie in very closely with the message of the 'conflictless' episodes. A few examples should be enough to illustrate this.

(1)   On two occasions the dispute between Jesus and certain Jewish groups is over Jesus' authority to forgive sins (5.17–26 and less acutely in 7.48–50). Jesus validates his authority to forgive with a healing miracle (5.22–5), but Luke's reader already knows (i) of other instances where Jesus proved his power to heal or exorcise (4.31–41; 5.12–15) and (ii) of the exceptional character of Jesus' relationship to God (as revealed in the birth narratives, at Jesus' baptism, etc.).

(2)   Several times conflict arises because of Jesus' fellowship with 'sinners' (5.30–2; 7.39; 15.1–2). Jesus explains his actions with words such as: 'Those who are well have no need of a physician, but those who are sick; I have not come to call the righteous, but sinners to repentance' (5.31–2; cf. 8.40–8; 15.3–32), but in

---

[87] While a broad consensus exists that the 'journey' section begins at 9.51, opinions vary about where it ends. 18.14, 31, 34; 19.10, 27, 28, 44, 46, 48; 20.18 have all been suggested. I take it as ending at 19.44 because in 19.45 Jesus has already arrived in Jerusalem and the temple and has begun his ministry there. For more on this question see D. P. Moessner, *Lord of the Banquet: The Literary and Theological Significance of the Lukan Travel Narrative*, Minneapolis: Fortress, 1989, pp. 33–4, nn. 1, 3; Nolland, *Luke*, vol. II, p. 529 and J. L. Resseguie, 'Interpretation of Luke's Central Section (Luke 9:51–19:44) since 1856', *StudBT* 5 (1975), 3, n. 2.

addition to Jesus' deliberately explanatory words, the reader knows that, from the outset of his ministry, Jesus had specifically described his mission in terms of outreach to the sick, the captives, those who can make no claim before God, and that the Scriptures had legitimated Jesus in taking this approach (4.18–19, 25–7).

(3) Jesus is repeatedly accused of breaking the Sabbath, for instance by allowing his disciples to pluck, rub, and eat grain (6.1–2) or by healing the sick (6.6–11; 13.10–17; 14.1–6). He justifies his actions by reference to his status (6.5), to the fact that God's saving activity cannot be limited to the six days (6.9; 13.14–16), or to the urgency of the people's needs (14.5). In addition to his explicit responses, however, numerous other sections of the narrative have already made abundantly clear both Jesus' exalted status and his legitimate concern with the needy.

(4) One of the sharpest types of conflict in the Gospel is that caused by the unsparing words with which Jesus attacks the way of life of the religious elite (e.g. 11.37–12.1; 16.14–15).[88] Yet Luke's confidence that the reader will side with Jesus and will see the validity of his criticism is partially based on the many other instances where the lifestyle and concerns of these people have already been described in a way which justifies Jesus' criticism (5.21–2, 30, 33; 6.2, 7, 11; 7.39; 15.1–32).

The effect of such connections between passages which explicitly speak of conflict and passages which appear to make only positive statements, is that they establish the coherence of the Lukan story by bringing together its various components into one major plot-line: a plot which focuses not so much on the participants in the conflict, but rather on the reliability of the (mainly Christological) claims of the gospel. This is not to say, of course, that the 'Christological' conflict is always overtly so. Very often it appears to take a purely 'praxiological' form, focusing (from the point of view of the Lukan characters) on how a Jewish teacher ought to behave and speak. Yet as far as the *readers* are concerned, enough information is provided in the course of the narrative (especially the opening four chapters) inevitably to load this 'praxiological' conflict with

---

[88] That such words were a major cause of conflict is particularly emphasised by Luke through his redactional summary in 11.53–4 (absent in Mark and Matthew; note also Luke's use of similar language in 20.20).

Christological significance and, indeed, to subordinate the former to the latter.

Jesus' ministry in Jerusalem (19.45–21.38)

Throughout Jesus' Galilean ministry and his long 'journey' to Jerusalem, the Lukan conflict boils down to the inability of the would-be experts in the law to accommodate aspects of Jesus' teaching and ministry, aspects which Luke's readers nevertheless know to be appropriate in virtue of their privileged overview of Jesus' life and of his place in the plan of God. This gap between Luke's Christology (as exhibited in his account of Jesus' ministry) and what the religious authorities are willing to accept continues to provide the logic for the conflict which guides the plot of Luke's story into the next major section – Jesus' ministry in Jerusalem and the temple.

It has become customary for students of the conflict in the Third Gospel to focus on the differences between how Luke describes this conflict before and after Jesus' arrival in Jerusalem. Thus, it has been noted that Jesus' opponents are no longer the Pharisees and their associates but rather the priestly group (the 'chief priests' in particular).[89] Also, a change has been noted in the intensity of the conflict, which, in the words of Kingsbury, abruptly loses its 'conversational' tone and becomes instead 'acutely confrontational'.[90] As for the issues between Jesus and his opponents, they are said to be no longer related to Torah observance, but rather to the question of authority and, more specifically, the issue of control over the temple.[91]

Despite the importance of these changes in Luke's presentation of conflict outside and inside Jerusalem, they must not be allowed to obscure for the reader the degree of continuity which also exists between these different phases of Jesus' ministry – after all, Luke must have intended his Gospel to be read as a single story. A closer look at these changes shows that they are primarily ones of degree, rather than qualitative ones, and that the Christological conflict of the Gospel continues along much the same lines as up to this point. Thus, for instance, it is not entirely correct to say that the conflict ceases to be 'conversational' and becomes 'acutely confrontational', for some 'conversation' can still be found even during Jesus' ministry in the temple (20.1–8, 21–5, 27–39).[92] True, it may now

---

[89] E. P. Sanders, *Jesus*, pp. 59–60; Tyson, *Death*, ch. 3.

[90] Kingsbury, *Conflict*, pp. 97–99.

[91] Ibid., p. 98; Tyson, *Death*, pp. 64–79 and ch. 4, *passim*.

[92] There is certainly no less 'conversation' in these three passages than in the earlier controversies over Sabbath observance and forgiveness pronouncements.

be a more heated conversation and often prompted by wrong motives,[93] but this is hardly sufficient to deny its 'conversational' character. Also, the change of focus from Torah to the temple may indeed add new dimensions to the Christological conflict of the Gospel – namely, the claim of Jesus' lordship over the Jewish centre of worship[94] and of his right to transform the temple effectually into the premises of his teaching ministry – but in so far as the Gospel plot is concerned, these dimensions are still in line with the foregoing material through which Jesus' portrait has been fashioned and legitimated. Thus, what ensures the continuity and coherence of the Gospel plot before and after Jesus' arrival in Jerusalem is the Christological focus of the conflict.

Of special significance is the fact that with the beginning of Jesus' ministry in Jerusalem a major new step has been taken towards Jesus' trial. The clear indication of this is Luke's repeated reference to the resolution of the Jewish leaders to have Jesus killed and to their search for a fitting opportunity to achieve this goal (19.47–8; 20.19–20; 22.2). The crucial question here is what, according to Luke, appears to be the specific cause of this resolution. Without going too much into the details of this issue, it would appear that Luke has provided important clues in this respect (i) by recording the first statement of this resolution (19.47–8) immediately following Jesus' twofold Messianic act of quasi-royal approach of the Holy City and subsequent 'cleansing' of the temple,[95] (ii) by repeatedly associating the authorities' resolution with the popular support enjoyed by Jesus' teaching in the temple,[96] and (iii) by having the authorities probe Jesus regarding the nature and source of his authority in doing 'these things' (20.2, 8).[97] It would appear, then, that the immediate precedent of the Jewish leaders' decision to have Jesus killed (and, correspondingly, the specific cause of Jesus' trial) is their repudiation of the legitimacy of Jesus' role as Israel's Messiah and teacher – a scenario which is in evident harmony with our understanding of the Gospel conflict in general.

---

[93] Note especially 20.20.

[94] As noted by Tyson, 'Jesus' cleansing of the temple constitutes a claim that he is the temple's lord' (*Death*, p. 109).

[95] For a recent discussion of Luke's presentation of these two combined episodes, with particular focus on Luke's political apologetic, see B. Kinman, *Jesus' Entry into Jerusalem in the Context of Lukan Theology and the Politics of His Day*, Leiden: E. J. Brill, 1995.

[96] Twice within the space of three verses Luke mentions that as Jesus was teaching the people in the temple the Jewish leaders were conspiring against him (19.47–20.1). See also 20.19–20; 22.2.

[97] For an evaluation of the possible antecedents of the rather obscure ὺ·ὺῦ·, see Marshall, *Gospel*, pp. 724–5.

Concluding remarks on the Lukan plot

The two major goals of this section have been to understand how, according to Luke, Jesus' trial came about and to approximate the concerns and expectations with which Luke's implied reader was likely to approach the account of Jesus' trial. The results may be summarised as follows: first, with regard to the course of events which has led to Jesus' trial it has been found that the inability of the religious authorities of Jesus' day to tolerate certain aspects of Jesus' teaching and lifestyle is the direct cause of conflict for most of the Gospel, and their contention that Jesus had no 'authority' to act as Israel's Messiah and teacher in the way he did (especially from the point of his entrance into Jerusalem and the temple) led to their decision to do away with him.

Second, the Lukan accounts of Jesus' birth, his introduction and baptism by John, his genealogy, his confrontation with the devil, and his whole ministry in Galilee, on the way to Jerusalem, and in Jerusalem itself have all revealed Luke's concern to assure his readers (often in rather subtle and indirect ways) that, contrary to the claims of many, Israel's hopes have come to fruition in the person of Jesus of Nazareth. As Jesus' trial draws near, then, the readers' attention is focused on a conflict surrounding Jesus' identity and mission. Is he truly Israel's Messiah? Can the readers still have assurance that the narrator's claims on Jesus' behalf are right, even after learning of the Jewish authorities' contention to the contrary? Which way will the events go in the remaining part of the story?

Jesus' prediction and explanation of his trial
Luke 9.22

Luke 9.22 is the first of the three instances in which the author has Jesus make formal reference to his forthcoming passion-resurrection[98] (and, implicitly, to his trials). Luke's redactional activity is minimal at this point. His wording of Jesus' saying follows almost verbatim Mark 8.31. One notable modification which Luke introduces is a closer connection

---

[98] There are also a number of other Lukan passages where Jesus refers more indirectly to his death and (to a lesser degree) resurrection. Fitzmyer notes three such groups of passages. First, the 'veiled' references (a term which Fitzmyer borrows from H. Schürmann and V. Howard): Luke 5.33–5; 11.29–32; 13.31–5; 20.9–18. Second, a group of passages where Jesus comments on the salvific nature of his death: Luke 22.19–20; 22.28. Third, some other 'minor announcements': Luke 12.50; 17.25; 22.22; 24.7 (Fitzmyer, *Luke*, vol. I, p. 778). For a brief analysis of three distinctively Lukan allusions to Jesus' passion (13.33; 17.25; 22.37), see B. C. Frein, 'Narrative Predictions, Old Testament Prophecies and Luke's Sense of Fulfilment', *NTS* 40 (1994), 29–30.

between Jesus' saying and the paragraph dealing with Peter's confession of Jesus as the Christ. Luke achieves this in two ways. First, he eliminates the introductory Καὶ ἤρξατο διδάσκειν αὐτούς, which in Mark 8.31 announces the beginning of a new sentence. Second, he makes the passion saying part of the closing sentence of the account of Peter's confession by means of the aorist participle εἰπών. One significance of this modification is the stronger connection between Jesus' Christological identity and his forthcoming passion. Luke does not give any explicit indication here of the exact nature of this relationship, but the difficulty of believing in an apparently failed Messiah together with the emphasis of the prediction on the divine necessity of Jesus' rejection and vindication would seem to indicate that Luke's concern was to stress the fact that there is no contradiction between Jesus being the awaited Messiah and his rejection and death.

Despite this, it remains customary, even for commentators who are fully aware of the close connection in Luke's narrative between Peter's confession and Jesus' prediction, to treat them as two separate units.[99] What compels them to accept this separation is, in the words of Nolland, 'the way in which vv 18–20 form the climax of a whole development and thus have their major links with what precedes, while vv 21–22 start a new development and should, therefore, be read primarily in connection with what is yet to come'.[100] Yet such systematic arrangements, necessary as they may be in the writing of a commentary, should not be allowed to undo what Luke has done when he deliberately brought together the themes of Jesus' identity and his passion. Linking Jesus' prediction of his trial with the foregoing question of who he is, or linking it to the subsequent 'journey' to Jerusalem, is not an either-or for Luke, since Jesus' 'going-up' to Jerusalem to face trials is for Luke part and parcel of the divine plan for the Messiah.

The second significant modification which Luke introduces is the omission of any mention of Peter's reaction to the passion announcement and of Jesus' response to Peter's reaction (Mark 8.32–3). While it is possible

---

[99] So, for example, Marshall, *Gospel*, p. 367; Fitzmyer, *Luke*, vol. I, p. 777; Nolland, *Luke*, vol. II, p. 458; Bock, *Luke*, vol. I, p. 844. One notable exception is H. F. Bayer, *Jesus' Predictions of Vindication and Resurrection: The Provenance, Meaning and Correlation of the Synoptic Predictions*, WUNT 2:20, Tübingen: J. C. B. Mohr, 1986, pp. 190–3.

[100] Nolland, *Luke*, vol. II, p. 458. Fitzmyer also feels some unease about the separation, so needs to justify it: 'We have separated it [the passion announcement] here from the foregoing, not only because of the problems that the interpretation of the announcement creates, but also because of the Lucan curtailment of the Peter-scene. It also deserves separate treatment because of its relation to further announcements in the Lucan Gospel' (Fitzmyer, *Luke*, vol. I, p. 777).

that one of Luke's reasons for this deletion is his general tendency to avoid negative portrayals of the disciples,[101] the effect of this (at least from the point of view of Luke's reader) is again that a closer unity is established, this time with the immediately following section,[102] where Jesus explains that his followers must be prepared to go with him all the way to the point of losing (ἀπόλλυμι) their lives in order that they may bear testimony to the Son of Man (Mark 8.34–8; cf. Luke 9.23–6).

I have concentrated thus far on Luke's modification of the Markan material. A few observations must now be made about Luke's positive use of his source, since, as noted above, that is reflected to a very large degree in the present form of the Lukan prediction of Jesus' passion. The major point of relevance to the present discussion is the strongly apologetic tone of Jesus' statement. Two aspects need special mention in this respect. First, there is the reference to the divine necessity of Jesus' passion and exaltation, expressed through the verb δεῖ. Although the term is present in the Markan form of the passion prediction too, it is particularly at home in the Lukan narrative. W. Grundmann observes that 'Of the 102 occurrences of δεῖ or δέον ἐστί [in the NT], 41 are to be found in the Lukan writings.'[103] Among the many aspects of the history of Jesus and the early church which Luke regards as the outcome of divine necessity, expressed through δεῖ,[104] the events surrounding Jesus' passion and exaltation occupy a leading position (Luke 9.22; 17.25; 24.7, 26; Acts 1.16; 3.21; 17.3).[105] But what exactly is the role which this motif of divine necessity plays in Luke's account of Jesus' passion? In his monograph dealing with the Lukan theme of the plan of God, J. T. Squires ends the chapter on 'Fate: the Necessity of the Plan of God' with the following remarks:

> An apologetic purpose is evident in the various ways that the plan of God is described as necessary and foreordained. This is especially so in the two 'test case' incidents of the passion of

[101] So Fitzmyer, *Luke*, vol. I, p. 777. This suggestion, however, needs to reckon with the fact that in the same chapter the disciples are going to be characterised by failure to stay awake during Jesus' transfiguration (9.32a), inability to comprehend Jesus' words (9.37–45), desire to be great (9.46–8), and selfishness (9.49–50).

[102] Referring to this omission, Marshall states that it 'enables Luke to link together more closely the prediction of Jesus' own suffering and his call to the disciples to take up the cross and follow him' (*Gospel*, p. 367).

[103] W. Grundmann, 'δεῖ', *TDNT*, vol. II, p. 22. See also E. Fascher, 'Theologische Beobachtungen zu δεῖ im A.T.', *ZNW* 45 (1954), 244–52.

[104] For a list of such events, see again Grundmann, 'δεῖ', 22–3.

[105] Frein ('Narrative', 29) notes that the term occurs in each of the three peculiarly Lukan predictions of Jesus' passion (13.33; 17.25; 22.37).

Jesus and the mission to the Gentiles, which are apologetically asserted by this means. The theme of the necessary plan of God is a significant theological factor in Luke–Acts, providing a defence of Christian beliefs as well as functioning as apologetic assertion and exposition of those beliefs.[106]

Such an understanding of Luke's use of necessity language accounts very satisfactorily for the emphatic position of δεῖ[107] in the Lukan account of Jesus' prediction of his trials. Far from being incompatible with his identity as 'the Christ of God' (to use Peter's words), Jesus' passion (as well as his resurrection) is precisely what the Scriptures had predicted of the Messiah and what, therefore, 'must' come true.[108] In this way Luke provides his readers with the 'hermeneutical key' for the understanding of Jesus' trial narratives in a way which upholds the church's belief that he is the Messiah.[109]

But there is a second aspect of Jesus' trials which Luke needs to deal with apologetically at this point. His readers are presumably very familiar with the fact that this Jesus whom the Christians proclaim as the Messiah has not been recognised as such by those who were in the most privileged position to do so – the Jewish leaders of Jesus' day. If they said 'No', on what basis can the less informed enquirer, living some decades after the events, say otherwise? Luke recognises the seriousness of the challenge, as he borrows Mark's three terms (πρεσβύτεροι, ἀρχιερεῖς and γραμματεῖς) to indicate the extensiveness of the Jewish leadership. He eliminates the definite articles preceding the second and third term, thus indicating more forcefully the unity of their decision in rejecting Jesus.[110] Finally, however, he ends his account of the trial prediction with an emphatic reference to Jesus' resurrection (ἐγερθῆναι is the last word in the sentence), a reference which he changes from an active to a passive mood, thus placing additional emphasis on God as the implied author of Jesus' resurrection. By contrasting so dramatically the decision of God

---

[106] Squires, *Plan*, p. 185.

[107] Note that δεῖ controls the four infinitive verbs which describe respectively Jesus' suffering (παθεῖν), rejection (ἀποδοκιμασθῆναι), death (ἀποκτανθῆναι), and resurrection (ἐγερθῆναι).

[108] Although δεῖ is an impersonal verb and therefore it is impossible to establish with certainty who or what is the cause of the necessity expressed through it, there is no reason to doubt Marshall's observation that '[t]he parallel passages 18:31; 24:46; Mk. 9:12; 14:21 indicate that for Luke and the early church this "must" lay in the necessity to fulfil what was laid down in the Scriptures' (*Gospel*, p. 369). See. also W. J. Bennett, 'The Son of Man Must. . .', *NovT* 17 (1975), 113–29.

[109] See the similar role of Luke 24.26–7, 46.   [110] Marshall, *Gospel*, p. 370.

with the decision of Jewish leaders,[111] Luke provides his readers with the strongest possible assurance (ἀσφάλεια, Luke 1.4) that the Christian proclamation of Jesus as the Messiah is valid: God has confirmed it.

To sum up, Jesus' first prediction of his passion in the Lukan narrative indicates a strong connection between Jesus' passion-resurrection and his Messianic identity, and also between the trials of Jesus and the trials which his disciples will undergo in the process of bearing witness to him. The claim that he is the awaited Messiah cannot be falsified by the religious authorities' rejection of him, for it is God who ultimately vindicates him through the Scriptures (which bear witness to what he 'must' undergo) and through the resurrection.

Luke 9.43b–45

With regard to the order of pericopae, Luke clearly continues to follow the Markan narrative – Jesus' second passion prediction is placed between the healing of a demon-possessed boy and the disciples' argument about who will be the greatest (Mark 9.14–37). The same is not true, however, with regard to the actual content of the prediction, where several significant changes can be noted between the Markan and Lukan accounts. First, Luke omits Mark's geographical details and Jesus' pre-occupation with the Messianic secret (Mark 9.30). Second, he adds an introductory note about everyone's marvelling (θαυμαζόντων) at Jesus' deeds (Luke 9.43b) and a reference to Jesus' request for a particularly attentive hearing from his disciples (θέσθε ὑμεῖς εἰς τὰ ὦτα ὑμῶν τοὺς λόγους τούτους, Luke 9.44a). Thirdly, he drastically reduces Jesus' actual passion prediction to a statement about him being 'delivered into the hands of men' (thus excluding all reference to his death and resurrection) and moves this action from the Markan present tense (παραδίδοται) into the (more appropriate) future (μέλλει παραδίδοσθαι) (Luke 9.44b; cf. Mark 9.31b). Finally, he greatly elaborates on the disciples' incomprehension of Jesus' words. What is the result of these changes?

The absence in Luke's text of the Markan geographical details and Messianic secret enables Luke to introduce the passion prediction with a

---

[111] Recognising Luke's deliberate contrast between the action of God and that of the Jewish leaders, F. Neirynck and T. A. Friedrichsen write: 'The change of Mark's intransitive ἀναστῆναι to the passive ἐγερθῆναι fits in with Luke's general usage. Lk. 9,22 can be seen in light of the active ἤγειρεν in Acts: They put him to death, but God raised him. Luke stresses here the action of the Sanhedrin . . . and, in contrast to their activities, emphasizes God's action in raising up Jesus. The passive ἐγερθῆναι in Lk. 9,22 is a real theological passive' (F. Neirynck and T. A. Friedrichsen, 'Note on Luke 9,22. A Response to M. D. Goulder', in Neirynck (ed.), *L'Evangile*, p. 398).

summary statement, Πάντων δὲ θαυμαζόντων ἐπὶ πᾶσιν οἷς ἐποίει (9.43b), which looks back over Jesus' mighty works[112] and thus offers the readers a background for the correct understanding of the prediction: it comes '*while* they were all marvelling at everything he did'.[113] As in the case of the first passion prediction, which Luke ties to Peter's confession, here again he places the reality of Jesus' passion alongside a strongly Christological claim, in order to assure his readers that Jesus' passion and his Messiahship (this time attested by his works) are not mutually exclusive.

Jesus' request for attentive listening is most certainly meant to function as a rhetorical device whereby Luke's readers/hearers are summoned to be themselves the ones who pay special attention to what follows, very possibly because it deals with an issue which is of special concern to them. The hypothesis that his readers (or other people with whom the readers are in contact) are finding it hard to accommodate Jesus' passion alongside the belief in him as the Messiah finds further confirmation in the remaining two redactional changes, especially when these are taken together. Luke's shortening of the passion prediction to a statement about the handing over of Jesus into the hands of his opponents – παραδίδοσθαι εἰς χεῖρας ἀνθρώπων[114] – and the ample elaboration on the disciples' incomprehension strongly suggest that Luke's primary concern here is not to *list* the historical facts related to Jesus' passion (facts of which, at least in general terms, his readers are probably already aware, and on which he will anyway give more information towards the end of his first volume) but rather to deal at this point with the disciples' (and readers') *attitude* towards the reality of these events. The emphasis on the disciples' lack of comprehension should therefore also be understood as a rhetorical device meant to address (through the example of the disciples)

---

[112] πᾶσιν indicates that the statement does not refer simply to the preceding exorcism but more broadly to Jesus' activity in general.

[113] Note the use of the present participle θαυμαζόντων.

[114] It is very tempting to try to determine the exact reference of Luke's παραδίδοσθαι (cf. Nolland, *Luke*, vol. II, p. 514): does the word refer to Judas' betrayal (Luke 22.4, 6, 21, 22, 48), or to the Jewish handing over of Jesus to those who had the legal power to execute him (Luke 20.20; Ac. 3.13; 21.11), or to Satan's machinations (Luke 22.3; cf. 4.6), or to the divine purpose (see the discussion of the divine necessity in the first passion prediction above)? There is no indication that Luke would have wanted to separate these different levels of the 'handing over' of Jesus; rather, as the passages listed above suggest, for him Jesus was going to be 'delivered into the hands of men' at the prompting of Satan, through human agency, and according to the will of God. Rather than being concerned at this stage with *who* is responsible for Jesus' handing over, Luke's focus is on the fact *that* the Christ is going to be delivered into the hands of evil men (ἄνθρωποι here clearly carries a negative connotation, perhaps with the sense of a 'mob'), with all the implications which this entails.

any readers who might themselves have difficulties with accommodating Jesus' passion alongside his Messiahship (possibly because they are not making enough efforts to understand it)[115] or, more likely, to explain to the readers how it is that so many of their (Jewish or Jewish-oriented) contemporaries find in Jesus' passion a stumbling block (hence Luke's emphatic addition that 'it was concealed from them, that they should not perceive it').[116]

Luke 18. 31–4

In Mark's Gospel, the third prediction of Jesus' trial follows soon after the previous two. For Luke, however, it comes almost nine chapters later, as a result of an extensive insertion dealing with Jesus' journey to Jerusalem. In the course of this section Luke departs from his Markan source and draws instead on material from Q and L, but beginning with 18.15 he returns to the Markan material, following again the latter's order of pericopae. Yet, as in the case of the second passion prediction, so as the actual content of the pericope is concerned, Luke 18.31–4 reveals a significant amount of redaction.[117] The major redactional changes are:

(1) As in the first two passion predictions, Jesus' announcement is connected more closely to the preceding episode, which this time focuses on Jesus' conversation with a 'rich ruler' (18.18–30). While it is true that the passion prediction is separated from this pericope 'by a change of audience and theme',[118] it remains equally true that, compared with Mark's Gospel, the Lukan separation is considerably diminished[119] by the elimination of the ending of the preceding pericope (Mark 10.31) and much of the introduction to the present one (Mark 10.32; cf. Luke 18.31).[120] The

---

[115] Luke might be trying here to prevent the readers from following the example of the disciples who 'were afraid to ask him about this saying'.

[116] On several occasions Luke refers to groups of people (usually Jews) who fail to believe or understand because of some form of hardening or blinding process (Luke 8.10; 18.34; Ac. 28.26–7), a process which apparently can only be reversed by God's action (Luke 24.31).

[117] It has been suggested by B. S. Easton (*The Gospel according to Luke*, New York: Scribner, 1926, p. 275) and T. Schramm (*Der Markus-Stoff bei Lukas*, Cambridge University Press, 1971, p. 133) that Luke might have followed a non-Markan source, but the lack of convincing evidence in this respect makes the suggestion speculative at best (Marshall, *Gospel*, pp. 689–90; Bayer, *Jesus*, p. 195).

[118] Nolland, *Luke*, vol. II, p. 894.

[119] In the words of E. Schweizer, the Lukan prediction 'follows Mark but is linked more closely with what precedes' (*The Good News according to Luke*, trans. D. E. Green, London: SPCK, 1984, p. 288).

[120] Luke leaves out both the travelling details and the reference to the amazement and the fear of Jesus' companions.

exact connection between the two is not immediately obvious. According to Marshall, 'the pericope affords a commentary on the preceding saying of Jesus: although eternal life is promised, the path to it is by way of the suffering of Jesus'.[121] Yet the stress in the preceding pericope is not on how eternal life is made available from the point of view of God or his agent Jesus or both as Marshall's suggestion would require, but on how it is to be obtained by the seeker. Jesus' answer to this question had led to a call to follow him (18.22), a call which Peter and the other disciples had accepted (18.28). The connection with the passion prediction would then seem to be in terms of the cost of following someone who goes to Jerusalem to suffer. Jesus is going to 'obtain life' (through resurrection; 18.33) after being willing to pay the price of shame and death; for whoever follows him – Luke's connection warns – 'inheriting eternal life' (18.18) could also require a similar price. Such a connection between Jesus' passion and the cost of following him would then be similar to the link which we have seen Luke establishing between the first passion prediction and the verses following it.

(2) Of special redactional significance is Luke's addition of the explanatory statement καὶ τελεσθήσεται πάντα τὰ γεγραμμένα διὰ τῶν προφητῶν [τῷ υἱῷ τοῦ ἀνθρώπου] (18.31c). The reference to the divine necessity which in Luke's first account of Jesus' trial prediction is expressed simply through the impersonal verb δεῖ, thus leaving unclear what the cause of this necessity is, finds here a much fuller expression. Jesus 'must' go up to Jerusalem in order to 'accomplish' what the prophets had predicted of the Son of Man. It is not clear what passages Luke has in mind, although there is no reason to doubt Nolland's contention that 'Dan 7:13 is surely to be included'.[122] The thrust of Luke's statement, however, is not to point to any particular 'Son of Man' tradition, nor even to elaborate on the theological significance of the title, but rather to stress the correspondence between Jesus' passion and the Old Testament Messianic predictions. Once again, then, Luke's apologetic concerns take the form of a 'hermeneutical key' which Luke offers to his audience to help them read the subsequent passion and trial narratives in a way that enhances rather than hinders their belief in Jesus as the awaited Christ.

---

[121] Marshall, *Gospel*, p. 689.

[122] Nolland, *Luke*, vol. II, p. 895; see also his excursus on the pre-Lukan history of the 'Son of Man' phrase on pp. 468–74 and his discussion of Luke's use of the phrase in *Luke*, vol. I, pp. 254–5. Of interest also is Strauss' case for an Isaianic background to Luke's understanding of Jesus' 'new exodus' in Jerusalem and the representation of the present prediction along these lines (*Davidic*, pp. 333–4).

(3) It is also significant to note that Luke omits any reference to the chief priests and the scribes as the ones who will put Jesus to death (Mark 10.33; cf. Matt. 20.18). According to Luke, Jesus will be delivered (παραδοθήσεται) to 'the Gentiles' (τοῖς ἔθνεσιν), a term which in the light of Luke's subsequent passion narrative must mean 'the Romans'.[123] They are, apparently, the ones who, according to Luke, would inflict upon Jesus the actions described by the following five verbs (ἐμπαίζω, ὑβρίζω, ἐμπτύω, μαστιγόω, and ἀποκτείνω).

(4) With regard to the list of verbs which describe Jesus' passion and death, Luke includes all four verbs present in Mark's account and adds a fifth one, ὑβρισθήσεται ('will be insulted/shamefully treated'), thus enforcing the note of humiliation already present in the previous verb.[124]

(5) If after the second passion announcement Luke's reference to the disciples' lack of comprehension was an expansion of a shorter Markan statement to this effect, this time one encounters a peculiarly Lukan statement, and a forceful one for that matter: 'But they understood none of these things; this saying was hid from them, and they did not grasp what was said' (18.34, RSV).[125] Luke offers no explicit identification of the cause of this incomprehension. The wording of the phrase seems to allow for an understanding of the cause as to do with both the disciples themselves[126] (*they* did not 'understand' and did not 'grasp') and some process of veiling, the author of which appears to be God[127] (the saying 'was hid' from them) and which therefore can only be reversed by God (Luke 24.31, 45). There is no indication that Luke would have wished sharply to distinguish between the two. But why would Luke want to make so much of the disciples' failure to comprehend Jesus' words? 'It is almost inconceivable', Schweizer remarks, 'that anyone could fail to understand the plain words of vss. 32–33';[128] and the beginning of an answer is immediately indicated by him: 'this very fact reveals Luke's

---

[123] So, for example., Nolland, *Luke*, vol. II, p. 895; Schweizer, *Luke*, p. 288; contra J. T. Sanders, *Jews*, pp. 13, 206–7.

[124] Marshall, *Luke*, p. 690; Schweizer, *Luke*, 288.

[125] The statement is also paralleled by Luke's characterisation of Joseph and Mary in Luke 2.50.

[126] R. Summers, *Commentary on Luke*, Waco, TX: Word, 1972, p. 220. Summers exaggerates, however, when he attempts to interpret even the expression 'this saying was hidden from them' as solely to do with the disciples: 'It was not *hidden* in that Jesus did not want them to understand. It was *hidden* because of their reluctance to accept it and because there was nothing in their experience to help them to understand the reference to being raised from the dead.'

[127] F. W. Danker, *Jesus and the New Age. A Commentary on Luke's Gospel*, revised edition, Philadelphia: Fortress, 1988, p. 302;

[128] Schweizer, *Luke*, p. 288.

theological interest: here lies the real difficulty standing in the way of faith'.[129] Luke knows that Jesus' humiliation and death is a reality which many of his contemporaries are finding hard to reconcile with the belief in him as the Christ and therefore he makes the most of any opportunity to warn his audience to avoid making the same mistake, or to give his readers an explanation for the widespread rejection of the gospel by those familiar with the Scriptures.

Concluding remarks on the trial predictions

While the events predicted by the passages discussed above are not, strictly speaking, limited to Jesus' trials, the end of Luke's gospel makes it clear that Jesus' trials constitute an important part of his passion, with which the passages above are concerned. Yet the very fact that neither in the passion predictions, nor, as will be seen, anywhere else, does Luke ever refer to Jesus' trial in isolation from his sufferings, death, and resurrection raises the suspicion that perhaps Luke's understanding of Jesus' trials does not allow for such a separation.

The single most significant result which this enquiry into Jesus' passion predictions has afforded is the ample evidence for a special Lukan concern to show the compatibility of certain beliefs about Jesus (beliefs which are not revealed in the predictions themselves but which can be gleaned from their context) with the fact of his passion.[130] Several observations have converged in this direction. First, two of the three predictions are linked more closely than in Mark's gospel to the strongly Christological passages which precede them: the first one to a confession of Jesus' identity (9.20) and the second one to the equally revealing character of Jesus' ministry (9.43b). In both of these instances the predictions are introduced in such a way as to ensure that the readers have not lost sight of the powerful testimonies to Jesus' Christological identity. Second, the emphasis on the disciples' incomprehension after the second and third predictions warns the readers of the danger of not 'comprehending' the fact that the Son of Man *has* to suffer, and at the same time enables them to see that those who refuse to understand this do so not out of a more coherent reasoning but because they may in fact be subjects of a 'veiling' process (the exact nature and cause of which is not spelt out in detail). Third, the correspondence between the events related to Jesus' passion and the

---

[129] Ibid.

[130] While sporadic observations to this effect are by no means foreign to the literature with which we have interacted, the case does not appear to have been argued in a sufficiently systematic form.

Scriptures' predictions with regard to the Son of Man (hinted at through the δεῖ of 9.22 and mentioned more explicitly in 18.31) is meant to be a strong indication that Jesus' passion, far from being incompatible with the gospel's claims regarding him, actually contributes to the confirmation of these claims. Fourth, the implicit contrast between the opinions of people (Jewish leaders and Romans alike) with regard to Jesus and the verdict of God expressed in Jesus' resurrection prepares the reader to read the passion narrative (trial account included) with particular consideration of God's position in the matter.

To the extent that the Lukan accounts of Jesus' passion predictions can be seen to throw light on the character of the subsequent trial and passion narratives, the findings of this section strongly alert the reader to the author's apologetic concerns – an apologetic of which the object is certain beliefs about the person of Jesus and his role in Israel's salvation. Correspondingly, then, the four aspects mentioned above with regard to Luke's passion predictions would be understood as apologetic devices whereby Luke works towards his goal.

A final observation related to the passion predictions is that on two occasions (i.e. through the redactional links between the first prediction and the verses following it and between the third prediction and the preceding pericope) the readers are made aware of some correspondence between the experience of Jesus and that of his followers: in both cases the way ahead is going to involve a high cost.

Conclusion

In the first part of the present chapter, a survey of previous contributions to the study of Jesus' trial in Luke's Gospel has revealed the need for a more satisfactory explanation of Luke's version of this event. Consequently, the remaining part of the chapter has attempted two preliminary steps towards such an explanation. First, a consideration of the Gospel plot has indicated that the coherence of Luke's narrative is far from impressive as long as one focuses on the participants in the conflict (a practice which seems to have dominated Lukan studies in this area). An alternative reading has therefore been proposed, one which focuses on the issues which are at stake in the Gospel conflict. According to this reading, the Gospel plot begins in the first three chapters with a predominantly positive (albeit only embryonic) presentation of Jesus as the one in whom Israel's hopes have materialised. This tone radically changes in chapter 4, where a Christological conflict is introduced both at a cosmic and at a human level. For the whole of Jesus' ministry in Galilee and on the way to Jerusalem this conflict continues, as 'conflictless' portrayals of Jesus' identity and mission alternate with passages where such portrayals are challenged and defended. As Jesus reaches Jerusalem, the conflict becomes much more acute, and its Christological character increasingly overt, as the Jewish authorities base their new resolution to do away with Jesus on the refutation of his 'authority' to act and speak as Israel's Messiah and teacher. It is this conflict, I suggest, that forms an important part of the hermeneutical framework from which the attentive reader is expected to approach Luke's account of Jesus' trial.

The second step which this chapter has taken towards a new understanding of Jesus' trial in Luke's Gospel has been an analysis of the way in which the passion predictions prepare the reader for the trial narrative. This further substantiated the results of the plot analysis. Both in his version of the actual predictions and in his specific placement of the predictions within their immediate context Luke exhibits a deliberate concern to assure the reader that Jesus' passion, for all its awkwardness from the point of view of the disciples' comprehension, must not be regarded as incompatible with the confession of Jesus as the Christ. On the contrary, Jesus' passion comes to confirm his Messiahship, since it contributes to the fulfilment of God's plan for his chosen one, and provides the gateway to God's direct vindication of him through the resurrection.

3

LUKE'S ACCOUNT OF JESUS' TRIAL

Introduction

If, as noted at the beginning of the last chapter, the function of Jesus' trial in Luke's Gospel cannot be satisfactorily explained by any of the available interpretations – that is, as a political apologia for Christianity or Rome or as a 'trial' of Israel or of God – does this imply that the textual traits and emphases on which the proponents of these interpretations have built their cases are simply illusory? Or should the overall function of the trial narrative be understood as a combination of several of these emphases, perhaps in slightly modified forms? If a combination of motives is the solution, should one view them as independent of each other, or are they part of a unified goal which is yet to be established? It is the contention of the present chapter that such a unified purpose provides the most satisfactory solution and that, in continuity with the observations regarding the Lukan plot and the trial predictions, the nature of Luke's purpose can be best described in terms of a Christological apologetic. The route which will be taken in order to substantiate this suggestion is the analysis of Luke's emphases in each of the four episodes of which Jesus' trial in the Third Gospel is composed.

The hearing before the Sanhedrin (22.66–71)

According to Mark's Gospel, Jesus' hearing before the Sanhedrin[1] (Mark 14.53–64) takes place by night, at the high priest's house, with the

[1] A clarification of the use of the term 'Sanhedrin' henceforth is necessary. Traditionally it has been understood that the Sanhedrin which tried Jesus was a fixed judicial body, consisting of seventy or seventy-one members, and functioning in much the same way as the (Great) Sanhedrin of the Mishna (see, e.g., E. Lohse, 'συνέδριον', *TDNT*, vol. VII, pp. 863–4; E. Schürer, *The History of the Jewish People in the Age of Jesus Christ (175 B.C.–A.D. 135)*, revised and edited by G. Vermes et al., vol. II, Edinburgh: T. & T. Clark, 1979, pp. 210–18). This view has been seriously challenged in recent years on the grounds of insufficient, or even contrary, contemporary evidence (Brown, *Death*, vol. I, pp. 339–50; E. P. Sanders, *Judaism*, pp. 472–90). In line with these observations, the understanding

episodes of Jesus' mistreatment and Peter's denial immediately following (Mark 14.65 and 14.66–72 respectively). According to Luke, however, Jesus is first denied and mistreated (while still being at the high priest's house), and then, 'when day came', he is transferred to the Sanhedrin for a short and informal hearing. The relationship between these two chronologies and the actual historical sequence of events has often been discussed,[2] but this is of little consequence for present concerns.

From the narrative point of view, one significant outcome of these changes is that the various stages of Jesus' trial are brought together in what appears to be a much more unified trial narrative. Once the notion of trial is introduced with Jesus' hearing before the Sanhedrin, there is no more digression into side issues such as Peter's denial or even Jesus' mistreatment (these have already been dealt with before the trial started). Instead, the Sanhedrin hearing develops directly into the trials before Pilate and Herod.

The first stage of Jesus' trial is prompted by a gathering of 'the eldership of the people' (τὸ πρεσβυτέριον τοῦ λαοῦ), which is made up of 'both chief priests and scribes' (ἀρχιερεῖς τε καὶ γραμματεῖς). Neyrey correctly notes that 'Luke emphasizes that the broadest possible official representation of Israel was present.'[3] Moreover, the three terms used to describe the judicial assembly are almost identical to the ones used by Luke in the first passion prediction (Luke 9.22), with the sole difference that in the prediction 'the eldership' refers to a plurality of individuals (οἱ πρεσβύτεροι) who act in parallel to the other two groups (the terms are separated by the conjunction καί), while in the present context the elders are regarded as a unified body (τὸ πρεσβυτέριον) – hence its common designation as 'the Sanhedrin'[4] – which acts on behalf of the people (τοῦ λαοῦ) and includes the other two groups. This striking verbal similarity between the trial account and the passion predictions, a similarity which is also visible in the common emphasis on ὁ υἱὸς τοῦ ἀνθρώπου (9.22, 44; 18.31; cf. 22.69), alerts the reader to the fact that the fulfilment of those predictions is now beginning to unfold, and that, accordingly, the events which are going to be narrated

adopted here is that, rather than denoting a fixed number of known members of a formal body, meeting on a regular basis, the term 'Sanhedrin', when used with reference to first-century Judaea, should be understood as a relatively fluid group of chief priests, scribes, and influential citizens ('elders'), organised around the high priest and performing various administrative and judicial roles (Brown, *Death*, vol. I, pp. 340–3, 349).

[2] See, for example, Catchpole, *Trial*, pp. 153–220; E. P. Sanders, *Jesus*, pp. 309–17; Brown, *Death*, vol. I, 'Act II', *passim*.

[3] Neyrey, *Passion*, p. 71.

[4] E. g. Marshall, *Gospel*, p. 848; Nolland, *Luke*, vol. III, p. 1109.

are to be understood as the necessary (δεῖ, 9.22; cf. 18.31b) outworking of the divine plan. Conversely, the fulfilment of Jesus' words in his own trials adds weight to his prophetic vocation: not only does he follow in the prophetic line through his rejection (as we shall see), but he also delivers prophetic utterances which in their own right (i.e. quite apart from OT prediction) 'must' come true.

Following Luke's introduction of the judicial body, and the short reference to the place of the session (apparently the regular meeting place of the Sanhedrin: τὸ συνέδριον αὐτῶν),[5] Luke proceeds to relate the actual interrogation (22.67–71). What is striking is that he completely omits the rather lengthy Markan description of the Sanhedrin's search for (false) witnesses and the resolution of that search in the temple-related accusation (Mark 14.55–9).[6] One particularly easy explanation would be to say that Luke was following his non-Markan source (on the assumption, of course, that he had one),[7] but this still leaves one with the question of why Luke would have preferred, at this stage anyway, the source which omitted such apparently vital information to the one which included it. Equally inadequate is to state that Luke did not need this information here because he was going to include it in the account of Stephen's trial (Ac. 6.13–14):[8] it still remains to be explained why Luke found it relevant there but not here, not to mention the uncertainties about the time gap between the writing of the Gospel and of Acts or about how detailed Luke's planning of Acts was as he wrote the Gospel.

Whatever else the absence of false witnesses and accusations may mean, it certainly has the result of enabling Luke to shift the focus of the trial away from what according to Mark and Matthew are artificial (or at least misrepresented) issues,[9] towards a more explicitly Christological dispute. Statistically, if for Mark the Christological debate takes three and a half of the thirteen verses which narrate the Sanhedrin examination

---

[5] While it is possible that συνέδριον here means simply 'council' (C. F. Evans, *Saint Luke*, London: SCM Press, 1990, p. 834), it is more likely to be understood as 'council chamber' (Marshall, *Gospel*, p. 848; P. Winter, *Trial*, p. 28, n. 4; cf. J. T. Sanders, *Jews*, pp. 4–5).

[6] For a list of proposed explanations of this omission see Brown, *Death*, vol. I, pp. 436–67.

[7] Green, *Death*, p. 69; Marshall, *Gospel*, pp. 847–8; Nolland, *Luke*, vol. III, p. 1109.

[8] Brown, *Death*, vol. I, p. 436; P. Doble, 'The Son of Man Saying in Stephen's Witnessing: Acts 6.8–8.2', *NTS* 31 (1985), 68–84.

[9] Although it is very likely that temple-related issues (Mark 14.58; Matt. 26.61) will have been part of the Sanhedrin's actual concerns (resulting not least from the temple 'cleansing'), Mark and Matthew want their readers to understand that in the way in which they were formulated the complaints were 'false' and therefore could not have accurately represented the Sanhedrin's real concerns.

(14.61b–64 out of 14.53–65), for Luke it takes five out of six verses (22.67–71 out of 22.66–71).

A key device which has enabled Luke to cast the episode into the form of such a pregnantly Christological dialogue is his splitting of the single Markan question σὺ εἶ ὁ χριστὸς ὁ υἱὸς τοῦ εὐλογητοῦ; (14.61) into two parts: εἰ σὺ εἶ ὁ χριστός (22.67) and σὺ οὖν εἶ ὁ υἱὸς τοῦ θεοῦ; (22.70).[10] Thus, Luke's 'compendium of Christology' (to quote Conzelmann's description of the Sanhedrin interrogation[11]) opens by asking whether Jesus is ὁ χριστός. Throughout the Gospel, Luke had been providing ample evidence for his readers that this was so. Yet various Jewish groups had repeatedly attempted to cast doubt on this claim. Now, together with Jesus himself, Luke also climactically places this disputed contention 'on trial'. The most formal body of representatives of all those Jews who had been doubting Jesus' Messiahship now challenge Jesus, in an equally formal setting (albeit, as we shall see, not particularly formal from a judicial point of view), to tell them plainly whether he is the Christ. Jesus' reply (22.67b–69) appears to avoid a direct answer. Yet from the angle of Luke's 'interaction' with his readers Jesus' reply is of great significance. The first part of his response, 'If I tell you, you will not believe' – a statement not found in the other Synoptics – ironically changes the character of his answer from one which is meant to provide the grounds for his condemnation to one which raises the possibility of belief.[12] The Sanhedrin is implicitly told that their problem is not lack of evidence for his Messiahship but lack of openness to the possibility of belief. And if for them this attitude is a sad reality, for the readers it becomes both the challenge 'to supply the faith the Sanhedrin lacks'[13] and an explanation for the unbelief of many of their Jewish contemporaries. Moreover, it was precisely the same three Jewish groups (οἱ ἀρχιερεῖς καὶ οἱ γραμματεῖς σὺν τοῖς πρεσβυτέροις) that in 20.1–8 had been faced with the inescapable evidence of his divine anointing and had chosen not to give an answer (Luke 20.1–8). On the

---

[10] Walaskay's (and to a lesser degree Goulder's) suggestion that Luke split the question because of political concerns (Walaskay, *Rome*, p. 39; M. D. Goulder, *Luke, a New Paradigm*, Sheffield: JSOT, vol. II, 1989, p. 753) faces the difficulty that for Luke the Sanhedrin hearing revolves around theological and not political issues (Fitzmyer, *Luke*, vol. II, p. 1463).

[11] Conzelmann, *Theology*, p. 85.

[12] The irony of the Lukan account of the Sanhedrin hearing, with specific emphasis on the way the evidence for Jesus' condemnation turns out to be at the same time evidence for belief in him as the Messiah, has been creatively investigated by J. P. Heil in his article 'Reader-Response and the Irony of Jesus before the Sanhedrin in Luke 22:66–71', *CBQ* 51 (1989), 271–84.

[13] Ibid., 283.

basis of that incident, the Lukan Jesus can now add: 'and if I ask you, you will not answer' (22.68), a statement which to the readers suggests that, as in the case of the Jewish leaders in Luke 20.1–8, those of their contemporaries who deny Jesus' Christological vocation cannot produce any valid grounds for their position.[14]

Yet, for those who are open to the alternative of belief, the evidence for the validity of the claim that he is the Christ will certainly be there: 'from now on the Son of Man shall be seated at the right hand of the power of God' (22.69). The statement is a double allusion, partly to Daniel 7.13–14, where 'one like a son of man' comes to the Ancient of Days and receives kingly dominion, and partly to Psalm 110.1, where God tells someone who was about to be enthroned on David's throne, 'sit at my right hand until I make your enemies a footstool for your feet'. Thus, like Mark, Luke speaks of Jesus' future enthronement which would vindicate him over his opponents,[15] answering at the same time their challenge: 'if you are the Christ...' The new element introduced by Luke here is the time reference ἀπὸ τοῦ νῦν,[16] which indicates that Jesus' enthronement is about to begin. Although the enthronement would take place in heaven (Luke 19.12; Ac. 2.33–6), and although Jesus' vindication will be substantiated in his resurrection, ascension, and exaltation, as far as Luke is concerned Jesus is already moving towards that vindication through his passion (Luke 9.51; 24.26). There is, therefore, no need to take Luke's ἀπὸ τοῦ νῦν, or the omission of the reference to the visibility of Jesus' glorification (ὄψεσθε, Mark 14.62), as evidence that Luke had given up the hope of Jesus' physical return or that he had placed it in the indefinite future.[17] Rather, its force is that Luke was concerned to tell his readers that, by virtue of Jesus' glorification (of which they were soon going to read in Luke's narrative), God himself had pronounced the ultimate verdict on the Christological claim which is now on trial (Ac. 2.23–4; 3.13–15), and the evidence for this verdict is *already* available in the event of Jesus' resurrection-exaltation. One

[14] Luke's present statement has often been understood as a possible allusion to Jer. 45.15 (LXX), in which case his implicit rebuke of his interrogators acquires an additional prophetic flavour (J. Plevnik, 'Son of Man Seated at the Right Hand of God: Luke 22,69 in Lucan Christology', *Bib* 72 (1991), 337).

[15] Nolland, *Luke*, vol. III, p. 1110; cf. Brown, *Death*, vol. I, pp. 504–5.

[16] While it is difficult to establish with any certainty whether the expression is to be understood as originating independently of Matthew's ἀπ' ἄρτι, in Matt. 26.64 (E. Bammel, 'Erwartungen zur Eschatologie Jesu', *TU* 88 (1964), 3–32; Marshall, *Gospel*, p. 850) or as due to a time reference in a common non-Markan source (Catchpole, *Trial*, pp. 157–9; Nolland, *Luke*, vol. III, p. 1110), it certainly matches Luke's emphases here.

[17] *Pace* Conzelmann, *Theology*, pp. 84–5, n. 3.

need not wait until the parousia to obtain the 'assurance' which Luke wishes for his readers (Luke 1.4). For Luke and his readers Jesus is already glorified, and later in the narrative Luke will provide evidence for this, especially as he reminds them that it was as the ascended Christ that Jesus poured out the Holy Spirit (Ac. 2.33) and that at least one Christian martyr had actually seen 'the Son of Man standing at the right hand of God' (Ac. 7.56). Luke's 'from now on' becomes his way of saying that the evidence that God has given such a verdict is already available.[18]

As noted already, the second half of the Sanhedrin's Christological challenge (σύ οὖν εἶ ὁ υἱὸς τοῦ θεοῦ;) comes as a response to Jesus' first answer. This fusing of royal enthronement and divine sonship in the person of Jesus reminds the reader of the words of the angel Gabriel at the beginning of the Gospel, informing Mary that her child 'will be called the son of the Most High; and the Lord God will give to him the throne of his father David . . .' (Luke 1.32; cf. 1.35).[19] The development of these Christological motifs from the infancy narrative through the present passage and beyond is summarised by Fitzmyer in his characteristic style:

> What was foreshadowed in the infancy narrative, where the chords were first struck (1:32,35; 2:11,26), reaches with crescendo its climax in this scene, having been orchestrated in various ways in the Gospel up to this point (recall 3:15; 9:20; 20:41–3:22; 4:3,9,41; 8:28; 9:35). Faint echoes of it will again be heard in the Gospel's coda (23:2,35,39; 24:26) – and often in the Lucan second volume, where Jesus himself will become the preached one: not merely Messiah, and Son of God, but even the Son of Man standing at God's right hand (Acts 2:32–33,36; 7:55).[20]

Thus, one cannot escape the impression that we are dealing here with what in Luke's view is 'the foundational confession of Jesus by the

---

[18] In the light of this explanation, it could hardly be less true that through his departure from the Markan text here Luke is 'toning down the overtone of vindication' (Plevnik, 'Son', 338). His concern is precisely to make that vindication more accessible to the readers.

[19] Plevnik (ibid., 331–2) also draws attention to two differences between the use of these concepts in the two passages, but they hardly overshadow the similarities.

[20] Fitzmyer, *Luke*, vol. II, p. 1462. This resonance between the Christology of this episode and Luke's Christology elswhere in his two volumes casts doubt on Green's contention that there are signs in Luke 22.66–71 that Luke has 'introduced a christology at variance with what we would normally associate with the Third Evangelist' (Green, *Death*, p. 76).

Church'.[21] For the Jewish leaders, this confession is the logical implication (οὖν) of the Son of Man's session at the right hand of the power
of God. The problem for them was that they were in no position as yet to
verify the validity of such an apparently pretentious claim, since Jesus'
vindication was still to happen. As far as they are concerned, then, Luke,
through the mouths of his protagonists, can blame their rejection of Jesus
(tragic though this was), at least partly, on their ignorance (Ac. 3.17;
13.27). For Luke's readers, however, the reality of Jesus' glorification
and vindication *has* been made manifest, and therefore if they are to follow the (correct) logic of the Jewish leaders, they too ought to conclude
that Jesus is indeed the Son of God and that the Christian confession of
him is well founded.

It is no surprise then that Luke is so keen to place the weight of
this conclusion on the shoulders of the Jewish leaders: ὑμεῖς λέγετε
ὅτι ἐγώ εἰμι. It was they, Luke contends, who discovered the logical
connection between Jesus' glorification and the church's Christology![22]

The concluding verse of the Lukan Sanhedrin hearing makes Luke's
emphasis even clearer. There is here no tearing of mantle by the high
priest, no pronouncement of the blasphemy charge or of the death sentence, and an impersonal μαρτυρίας replaces the Markan μαρτύρων
(22.71; cf. Mark 14.63–4). The cumulative effect of these differences is
that the quasi-judicial tone of the event is played down[23] and, instead,
Luke is able to conclude with a rhetorical question which states the suf-
ficiency of the 'testimony': τί ἔτι ἔχομεν μαρτυρίας χρείαν; Moreover,
by associating this question with the Sanhedrin's query about Jesus' divine sonship (22.70), rather than referring to the redundancy of 'witnesses' in the context of Jesus' culpability (Mark 14.63–4), Luke has
once again skilfully turned the evidence which offered the Jewish leaders
the grounds for Jesus' crucifixion into evidence which offers the readers

---

[21] Neyrey, *Passion*, p. 72.

[22] The fact that Jesus' response 'is not a *direct* affirmation' (Marshall, *Gospel*, p. 851,
italics mine) has led most commentators to view it as indicating the need for some qualification of the Sanhedrin's words (Marshall, *Gospel*, p. 851; Fitzmyer, *Luke*, vol. II, pp. 1463,
1468; Bock, *Luke*, vol. II, p. 1802), while others have still insisted on a full affirmative, par-
alleling the 'I am' of Mark 14.62 (Brown, *Death*, vol. I, p. 493). However, Jesus' emphatic
ὑμεῖς λέγετε (lit. 'you yourselves are saying') need not be understood as suggesting any
reserve in Jesus' acceptance of the 'Son of God' title. Rather, the words strengthen the
Gospel's case for Jesus' divine sonship by representing it as the Sanhedrin's own inference.
This is in line with the foregoing narrative, where far from refraining from attributing to
Jesus divine sonship, the narrator has been deliberately advocating it (see my discussion of
Luke's plot).

[23] On the non-judicial tone of the Sanhedrin hearing see, among many others, Green,
Death, p. 69; Tyson, *Death*, p. 128.

reasons to believe in him.[24] As for the specification that the μαρτυρία came ἀπὸ τοῦ στόματος αὐτοῦ, its role is to remind the reader of the prophetic (and, for that matter, the *rejected prophet*) role of Jesus,[25] who in the present circumstances functions both as the object of the testimony and as its channel.

In conclusion, Jesus' examination before the Sanhedrin is presented in the Third Gospel in a way which clearly sets it apart from the other Synoptics. After a presentation of the quasi-judicial body Luke concentrates almost exclusively on the debate over Jesus' Christological identity (thus leaving out, most notably, any reference to the false witnesses and their accusations). By splitting Mark's single Christological question (Mark 14.61) into two parts, Luke has not only developed a fuller debate on this topic but also been able to represent the whole episode as flanked by the two resulting Christological queries – the former setting in motion the whole trial account (including the Roman part) and the latter representing the climax and conclusion of the Sanhedrin hearing. The effect is that what is for the other Synoptics an episode in which Jesus moves towards the cross (at least partly) because of false *witnesses* has become in Luke's report an event which establishes the adequacy of the *witness* to Jesus' divine sonship. Indeed, it is the Jewish leaders themselves (cf. ὑμεῖς λέγετε) who have represented this status as implied (οὖν, 22.70a) by the statement about the Son of Man's session 'at the right hand of the power of God' (22.69), a claim which for the readers has already been verified (since for them Jesus' ἀπὸ τοῦ νῦν is already in the past).

Such a Christological apologetic becomes all the more striking when the pericope is viewed against the Gospel's plot. As noted in the last chapter, the early chapters of Luke's story introduce Jesus as Israel's awaited Messiah. Particular emphasis is then given (through the baptism, genealogy, and temptation passages) to the characterisation of Jesus as the Son of God. His Messianic identity and mission continue to be (directly or indirectly) at the heart of the narrative conflict throughout the Gospel. Within this context, the Sanhedrin examination, with its focus on Jesus' Messiahship in general and his divine sonship in particular, comes to test and confirm precisely what the Gospel has set out to establish – the μαρτυρία (22.71) that Jesus is the Christ and the Son of God.

[24] Luke's use of μαρτυρίας in his overall shift from a judicial to a theological (Christological) emphasis makes superfluous Nolland's complaint that '[t]he reference to "testimony" comes slightly oddly into the Lukan narrative, which lacks the Markan calling of witnesses' (*Luke*, vol. III, p. 1111).

[25] Neyrey, *Passion*, p. 75.

The initial trial before Pilate (23.1–5)

More visibly than in the other Synoptics, Luke's account of the Roman trial of Jesus [26] develops naturally out of the Sanhedrin examination.[27] The passage opens with a brief reference to those who initiated the trial: Καὶ ἀναστὰν ἅπαν τὸ πλῆθος αὐτῶν ... (23.1). It is clear that αὐτῶν is to be understood as referring to the Jewish Sanhedrin, introduced in 22.66 as 'the eldership of the people', made up of 'both chief priests and scribes'. Luke's emphasis here, however, is not on the variety of the groups represented, but on their solidarity (ἅπαν τὸ πλῆθος) in what is to follow. By bringing Jesus for trial before the Roman prefect, the Jewish leaders are once again portrayed as fulfilling Jesus' prediction, according to which 'the Son of Man must suffer many things, and be rejected by the elders and chief priests and scribes' (Luke 9.22), and 'will be delivered to the Gentiles' (18.32).[28]

The content of their charge is unique to Luke: 'We have found this man perverting our nation, and forbidding us to give tribute to Caesar, and saying that he himself is Christ a king' (23.2). The division of the accusation into three clauses, introduced respectively by three participles (διαστρέφοντα, κωλύοντα, and λέγοντα) and separated from each other by the conjunction καί, may on the surface indicate that one is dealing here with three parallel charges.[29] The restatement of the charge as ἀνασείει τὸν λαόν (23.5), as well as Pilate's summary of it in the words ἀποστρέφοντα τὸν λαόν (23.14), suggests, however, that the first clause of the triple construction is to be regarded as the governing charge, with the latter two as explicative of it.[30]

It is entirely legitimate to enquire which of the two possible meanings of διαστρέφοντα ('to mislead' or 'to pervert')[31] does better justice to the

---

[26] Because of the dominance of the figure of Pilate in the whole of Luke 23.1–25, the passage is commonly referred to as the account of Jesus' Roman trial.

[27] Luke's transposition of the incidents of Peter's denial and Jesus' mockery enables him to move from the Sanhedrin examination directly to the Roman trial (compare the position of Luke 22.54–65 with Mark 14.65–72 in the respective passion accounts). Moreover, in Luke's account, the Sanhedrin trial ends without a proper declaration of the sentence (Luke 22.71; cf. Mark 14.64) – the 'sentence' is to bring him before Pilate (Luke 23.1).

[28] See also Fitzmyer, *Luke*, vol. II, p. 1473.

[29] Cassidy, for instance, comes close to such an understanding (*Jesus*, pp. 65, 167), although even he is open to seeing the three charges as 'interrelated' through the common claim that 'Jesus had adopted a stance similar to the Zealots' (p. 65).

[30] In favour of this interpretation see Brown, *Death*, vol. I, p. 738; Nolland, *Luke*, vol. III, pp. 1117–18; G. Schneider, 'The Political Charge against Jesus (Luke 23:2)', in E. Bammel and C. F. D. Moule (eds.), *Jesus and the Politics of His Day*, Cambridge University Press, 1984, 407–8. See also verse 5.

[31] See J. P. Louw and E. A. Nida (eds.), *Greek–English Lexicon of the New Testament, Based on Semantic Domains*, New York: UBS, 1988, vol. I, p. 61, and vol. II, pp. 375, 770.

text.[32] Yet the difference which the choice between these two makes to the major thrust of the passage is minimal.[33] Either way, it remains clear from the context that Jesus is being accused of leading the (Jewish) nation (τὸν λαόν) in a direction which is unacceptable to Rome. [34] Luke's readers will have undoubtedly appreciated the political tone of such a charge. Nevertheless, coming from Jewish lips, such a concern with loyalty to Rome can hardly look genuine – at least not as their *dominant* interest. Moreover, the Gospel story has not offered the readers grounds for seeing much substance in such a charge – Luke's picture of Jesus is not that of a political revolutionary.[35] Instead, a major Lukan *leitmotiv* has been the developing conflict between Jesus and Israel's official leaders, a conflict based on allegations (or at least suspicions) to the effect that Jesus is exercising a misleading influence upon people, in terms of their relationship, not to Rome, but to God (6.11; 7.39, 49; 11.38; 15.2; 19.47–8). In the words of Fitzmyer, 'Jesus may indeed have subverted the nation in warning the crowds against the "leaven of the Pharisees" (12.1), i.e. subverted it in a religious sense. But such action in a political sense has not been evident thus far in the Gospel.'[36]

On the basis of such information, the Sanhedrin's charges acquire for Luke's readers a second level of meaning (i.e. in addition to the political one), one to which Pilate could not have had access (without an account of Jesus' ministry before him): the religious authorities of Jesus' day are once again challenging the legitimacy of his influence in Israel – he had allegedly been leading the people away from God.[37]

---

[32] Brown (*Death*, vol. I, p. 739) insists that the former should be preferred.

[33] Nolland's interchangeable use of terminology illustrates this well: 'The explanation of the *"perversion"* follows: Jesus is being accused of *leading* the Jewish nation away from its proper loyalty to Caesar' (*Luke*, vol. III, p. 1117, italics mine).

[34] Fitzmyer, *Luke*, vol. II, p. 1473; Nolland, *Luke*, vol. III, p. 1117, et al.

[35] Even if one is to agree with Cassidy's contention that Jesus' refusal to defer to the political authorities of his day, alongside his revolutionary attitude towards certain groups of people (the poor, the infirm, women) posed, indirectly and in the long term, a threat to the Roman political structures (*Jesus*, esp. pp. 76–9), such associations would have been much too subtle for Luke's readers to find in them any substance for the Sanhedrin's charge. The only incident which may have raised some suspicions in this respect is Jesus' riding on a donkey upon his entry into Jerusalem, but even on this occasion Luke depicts a rather 'a-triumphal entry', with fewer political connotations than in the other Synoptics: it is, for instance, only the group of disciples, and not the general public, that join in the procession (Kinman, *Jesus*, pp. 91–122).

[36] Fitzmyer, *Luke*, vol. II, p. 1473.

[37] In his 'Reader-Response and the Irony of the Trial of Jesus in Luke 23:1–25' (*ScEsp* 43 (1991), 175–86), J. P. Heil takes a similar approach, by noting the 'irony' of a double meaning of the present passage: Jesus is being accused of leading the Jewish nation 'away from the Roman government', when in fact he had been leading it 'to God and away from its Jewish leadership' (p. 176).

The political side of the charge becomes even more explicit with what looks like a specific example of Jesus' alleged subversion. He is accused of 'forbidding us to give tribute to Caesar'. The readers are now in an even better position to see the falsity of the charge, for in 20.20–6 the evangelist has narrated an incident which deals specifically with that issue, and in which Jesus evidently does not oppose the payment of tribute to Caesar. That this incident is meant to be recalled at this point in the trial narrative is indicated by the explanation with which Luke had introduced it there: 'the scribes and the chief priests' (20.19) had initiated the plot in order 'that they might take hold of what he said, so as to deliver him up to the authority and jurisdiction of the governor' (20.20). Thus already the introduction to the incident serves to remind the readers that the present accusation is based on an artificial device of Jesus' opponents – the issue of paying taxes to Caesar had not emerged from anything that Jesus had said or done, but was simply a trap whereby his opponents were hoping to obtain some 'hard facts' which could eventually impress a Roman judge. However, the most likely and also the most vital item of that incident for Luke's readers to recall now is Jesus' answer: 'Then render to Caesar the things that are Caesar's, and to God the things that are God's' (20.25). These words, too, come to assure the readers of the falsity of the present political charge. But not only of that: as a preliminary answer[38] to the main charge of 'misleading the nation', they provide information both on how Jesus had (mis?)led the people with regard to the Roman state (when forced to take a stand on that) and also with regard to God. Once again, J. P. Heil has aptly noted the irony of the narrative: 'The irony . . . is that in falsely accusing Jesus of "misleading" the people by hindering the payment of taxes to Caesar, the Jewish leaders are reminding the reader that Jesus has been truly leading the people to God.'[39]

The second specific matter in which Jesus is accused of having misled the nation is the claim to Messianic kingship: καὶ λέγοντα ἑαυτὸν χριστὸν βασιλέα εἶναι. More visibly even than was the case with the previous charges, the present one shows signs of both falsity and plausibility, and it is precisely out of this apparent ambiguity that the double meaning of the statement once again emerges. On the one hand, Jesus' alleged claim to kingship is meant to be taken as tantamount to political rivalry to Rome. At this level the readers can be sure that the

[38] We can say only 'preliminary' because the definite answer will come only through the account of Jesus' exaltation.

[39] Heil, 'Luke 23:1–25', 178. A further example of irony in the present charge is the fact that Jesus 'was notorious for associating with tax collectors (Luke 5:27–30; 7:34; 15:1; 18:9–14)' (Brown, *Death*, vol. I, p. 740).

charge is untrue: the Gospel has provided no evidence that Jesus was in the business of setting up an alternative to Caesar's political power.[40] On the other hand, however, various items in the Gospel have provided grounds for the reader to believe that Jesus truly was a Messianic king (thus, most notably, 1.32–3; 2.10, 11; 19.38; 22.67). Most significant for the plausibility of the Jewish charge is the fact that in the last two of these instances Jesus clearly refuses to dismiss, if not positively entertains, the idea of Messianic kingship. The question which still remains to be settled for the reader is whether Jesus was entitled to assume, or at least not deny, such a status (as the more reliable voices of the narrative[41] seem to have indicated so far: e.g. heavenly messengers in the infancy narrative and the words and deeds of Jesus throughout his ministry), or whether, despite all these, the Jewish leaders may still be right in dismissing and opposing this claim.

Taken together, the Sanhedrin's charges set the stage for much of Luke's account of Jesus' Roman trial. Two issues seem to be at stake. The first one, which could be evaluated by both Pilate and the reader, is Jesus' political stance. The second, and apparently more important (since this gives the passage continuity with the rest of the Gospel's plot), is Jesus' Christological status (i.e., is he, or is he not, the legitimate ruler of God's people?), and this query is only accessible to Luke's readers.

In the light of these observations, Pilate does the readers a service by directing the question of kingship to Jesus: ὁ δὲ Πιλᾶτος ἠρώτησεν αὐτὸν λέγων· σὺ εἶ ὁ βασιλεὺς τῶν Ἰουδαίων; (23.3). Jesus' answer is related by all three Synoptics in the same wording: σὺ λέγεις. The answer reminds Luke's readers of Jesus' parallel response to the Sanhedrin (22.70), although, unlike the Sanhedrin, Pilate hears no ἐγώ εἰμι. The impression which one gets, in view of this parallelism, is certainly not that Jesus is more courteous to Pilate than to the Sanhedrin, or that Jesus' response to Pilate is in Luke more polite than in the other Synoptics (as any reading which emphasises Luke's pro-Roman stance would like to see).[42] Rather, in keeping with

---

[40] See again Kinman's discussion of Jesus' 'a-triumphal entry', indicating that not even this incident could have given the readers grounds to sympathise with the charge that Jesus was politically subversive (Kinman, *Jesus*).

[41] On the importance of the degree of reliability of various 'voices' within Luke's narrative, see J. A. Darr, *On Character Building: The Reader and the Rhetoric of Characterization in Luke–Acts*, Louisville: Westminster/John Knox, 1992, pp. 50–8.

[42] While Walaskay conveniently bypasses the implications of this fact for his *apologia pro imperio* theory, Conzelmann wants to gain even from here some support for his *apologia pro ecclesia*, by pointing out that '[a]ccording to Luke, Jesus does not refuse to answer the Roman authorities. He gives the information they require and so enables them to arrive at

the earlier announcement that Jesus' ultimate vindication is only going to come through his exaltation (22.69), it looks as if for the moment Luke deliberately chooses not to have the issue of Jesus' Messianic status explicitly settled,[43] and certainly not to have it settled by Jesus himself.[44]

Having narrated the content of the Sanhedrin's charges against Jesus (23.2), Luke sees no need to make any further mention of the *abundance* of the accusations or of Jesus' refusal to respond to them (Mark 15.3–5). Instead, he goes on to relate the first of three declarations of Jesus' innocence by Pilate: οὐδὲν εὑρίσκω αἴτιον ἐν τῷ ἀνθρώπῳ τούτῳ. Walaskay wonders how it is possible that, after Jesus' response which is an implicit 'yes' to the claim of kingship, Pilate should still 'find no crime in this man'.[45] Brown correctly explains: 'Jesus is transparently innocent to anyone whose eyes are not closed by prejudice . . . Pilate's instinct in 23:4 is equivalent to his perception in Mark 15:10 (Mat 27:18): "For he had knowledge that it was out of envy/zeal that the chief priests had given him over." '[46]

Not pleased with Pilate's initial verdict, Jesus' prosecutors continued to press their charges (23.5).[47] The main thrust of the 'revised edition' of their complaint is much along the lines of the original formulation: Jesus is accused of exercising a seditious influence upon people. What is different this time is the way they substantiate their charge. If originally they pointed out two specific matters in which he had allegedly 'misled' the nation (taxes and kingship), now their efforts concentrate on the method employed (by 'teaching': διδάσκων) and the geographical extent of his influence (καθ' ὅλης τῆς Ἰουδαίας, καὶ ἀρξάμενος ἀπὸ τῆς Γαλιλαίας ἕως ὧδε). Once again Luke's two-level construction of the Sanhedrin's accusations becomes

the objective legal decision, which is in fact immediately done officially. The answer he gives is no fuller than in Mark, but there is no refusal to answer' (Conzelmann, *Theology*, p. 86). There are two problems with this understanding of the passage. First, Jesus' non-committal σὺ λέγεις hardly gives Pilate the information he requires. Secondly, and more importantly, Conzelmann's stress on Luke's omission of Jesus' refusal to answer Pilate (cf. Mark 15.4–5) misreads the Markan account. It is not to Pilate that Jesus refuses to respond (that happens only in John 19.9), but to the chief priests' accusations, Pilate being instead the one who wonders at the fact that Jesus made no response to *their* charges. Moreover, Luke also omits Jesus' parallel silence during the Sanhedrin hearing (Mark 14.61).

[43] We shall see later in more detail how Jesus' resurrection settles the issue of his Messiahship. Suffice it now to note for comparison the explicitness of Jesus' post-resurrection utterances on the subject of his Messiahship (24.26, 46).

[44] It is God himself who will do this, by bringing Jesus back to life and exalting him (Ac. 2.24, 32–3, 36; 17.31; et al.).

[45] Walaskay, *Rome*, p. 40.   [46] Brown, *Death*, vol. I, p. 742.

[47] Note the use of the imperfect ἐπίσχυον, indicating repeated or continuous action.

evident. On the one hand the readers realise that Jesus' opponents are not prepared to abandon their political charge (the falsity of which Pilate's words have now confirmed); moreover, they also know from the Gospel's narrative that no crowds were ever 'stirred up' politically by Jesus. On the other hand, however, the readers also know from the Gospel that Jesus had indeed 'stirred up' many a crowd, albeit for different reasons;[48] that the single most prominent method of his ministry was teaching;[49] and that the two provinces in which his ministry had unfolded were Judaea and Galilee,[50] with the latter being the starting point[51] (ἀρξάμενος ἀπὸ τῆς Γαλιλαίας) and Jerusalem (ἕως ὧδε) the place of completion.[52]

Thus, while at one level verse 5 emphasises the (artificially constructed) charges brought against Jesus, at another level it subtly reminds the reader that the real cause of his trial is his teaching, which had repeatedly 'stirred' the multitudes of people into enthusiasm for him and for God, and the religious leaders into rivalry against him. Once again then, as far as the reader is concerned, what goes on trial in Jesus' Roman trial is not merely Jesus' political stance, but also, and more importantly for the Gospel's plot, Jesus' right to be the teacher of Israel and, by implication, the validity of his teaching.

When seen as a unit, the present passage, with its distinctively Lukan elaboration on the charges against Jesus, promises to be of major significance for one's understanding of Jesus' Roman trial in the Third Gospel. The picture which we have seen consistently recurring is one which requires two levels of reading of the narrative. At one level, the readers note the overtly political character of the dispute. Thus, Pilate's verdict (23.4) comes to confirm what the readers themselves can infer on the basis of the Gospel's portrait of Jesus: Jesus is politically innocent. At a

---

[48] Luke 5.1, 15, 17–19; 6.17, 19; 8.4, 19, 40; 9.11, 37; 11.29; 12.1; 14.25; 19.3, 36. See D. Schmidt, 'Luke's "Innocent" Jesus. A Scriptural Apologetic', in Cassidy and Scharper (eds.), *Political Issues*, pp. 113–15.

[49] Luke 4.15, 31; 5.3, 17; 20.1; 21.37.

[50] Luke 4.44; 5.17; 6.17; 7.17. The term 'Judaea' may also be understood in its broader Lukan sense of 'Palestine', 'the land of the Jews' (1.5; 6.17; 7.17; 23.5), in which case Galilee becomes part of it.

[51] Luke 4.14; cf. Ac. 10.37;

[52] Tyson (*Death*, pp. 130–1) is probably correct to suggest that ἕως ὧδε makes implicit allusion to the scandal of Jesus' teaching in the temple. Yet, since the place of Jesus' Roman trial could not have been the temple, the actual referent of ὧδε can only be Jerusalem (on the location of Jesus' trial see Brown, *Death*, vol. I, pp. 705–10). This representation of Jerusalem as the place where Jesus' ministry concludes corresponds not only to the actual unfolding of the Gospel's events, but also to the distinctively Lukan emphasis on Jesus' journeying towards Jerusalem beginning with 9.51 (cf. 13.22; 17.11; 18.31).

second, Christological, level, the Jewish charges come to challenge Jesus' legitimacy as the ruler of God's people. Pilate cannot answer this question for he is not even aware of it. Instead, the readers, who are familiar with the Gospel's plot, can glimpse the answer for themselves. By fulfilling his own passion predictions (23.1) and by being the one who has been leading Israel *to* God (a reading of 23.2, 5 required by the foregoing narrative), Jesus is portrayed as the Messiah, the true ruler of Israel. Yet, through Jesus' non-committal response to Pilate's question (23.3), the readers are given a hint that the more substantial answer to the Christological issue is still on the way.

The trial before Herod (23.6–12)

The absence of this episode from the other Synoptics has, predictably, led to much scholarly effort being invested in the issues of Luke's sources[53] and, closely connected to this, the historicity of the trial.[54] My concern here, however, is with neither of these, but with how the present passage contributes to Luke's overall picture of the trial of Jesus.

The passage has often been regarded as of little significance not only from the point of view of its place in Luke's passion narrative,[55] but also in terms of its contribution to the Lukan account of Jesus' trial.[56] Among those who have attempted to explain Luke's inclusion of the passage are those who have paid special attention to the political side of Luke's apologetic in Luke 23. Walaskay, for instance, suggests that 'Luke has used this scene to portray the mocking of Jesus, thus lifting

---

[53] Two major solutions have been offered. First, the episode is understood as an entirely Lukan creation, possibly inspired by Ps. 2.1–2 (cf. Ac. 4.24–8), or as aimed to provide a parallel to Pilate's trial before a Herodian ruler in Ac. 25–6: M. Dibelius, 'Herodes und Pilatus', *ZNW* 16 (1915), 113–26; Légasse, *Trial*, p. 67; A. Loisy, *L'Evangile selon Luc*, Paris: E. Nourry, 1924, reprinted Frankfurt: Minerva, 1971, pp. 544–5; Walaskay, *Rome*, p. 43. Second, Luke wrote the account based on some earlier traditions or source which spoke of Herod's involvement in the death of Jesus: Brown, *Death*, vol. I, pp. 778–83; Fitzmyer, *Luke*, vol. I, pp. 1478–9; H. W. Hoehner, *Herod Antipas*, SNTSMS 17, Cambridge University Press, 1972, pp. 230–2; H. W. Hoehner, 'Why Did Pilate Hand Jesus over to Antipas?', in E. Bammel (ed.), *The Trial of Jesus – Cambridge Studies in Honour of C. F. D. Moule*, SBT 2:13, London: SCM Press, 1970, pp. 84–90; Marshall, *Gospel*, pp. 854–5; G. Schneider, *Das Evangelium nach Lukas*, Gütersloh: G. Mohn; Würzburg: Echter, 1977, p. 474.

[54] Naturally, the works mentioned above in the first category tend to argue against the historicity of the event, while those in the second group favour it.

[55] So Fitzmyer: 'In the Lucan passion narrative this scene is actually a minor one. It has no significance for the understanding of Jesus' person or fate' (*Luke*, vol. II, p. 1480). See also Dibelius, 'Herodes', p. 121.

[56] According to Hoehner, 'Herod is brought into the trial but adds nothing to the progress of the trial. It has been thought by some that since there has been no progress in the trial of Jesus, this pericope has no point...' (*Herod*, p. 249).

it away from the Marcan context, Pilate's court.'[57] The explanation for this transposition is that Luke was 'glad to transfer the outrage from the soldiery of Rome to the soldiery of the local tetrarch'.[58] Hoehner refuses to be persuaded by such explanations. In his view,

> It is difficult to see any apologetic purpose in Luke for the inclusion of Jesus' trial by Antipas. With this episode, Luke apparently does not attempt to exonerate Rome and blame the Jews. Since Antipas was not a Jew by birth, the Jews did not think of him or the Herodian family as representatives of the Jews.[59]

One wonders whether Hoehner may not be overly sceptical with regard to the feasibility of such explanations. After all, the political apologetic readings do not always require '*full* Jews' on the side of Jesus' opposition in order to 'exonerate Rome' or, for that matter, to exonerate the Christian protagonists before Rome (to use the *apologia pro ecclesia* categories). Any non-Romans will do. As Walaskay puts it, '[t]he half-Jew Herod and his soldiers serve Luke's purpose well'.[60]

Yet what one is certainly justified to question with regard to the political apologetic readings is whether they offer a full picture of Luke's emphases in the present passage.[61] To answer this question, it is important to survey briefly the main emphases of the passage.

Verses 6–7 represent a transitional phase in the trial account. Luke makes use of his previous reference to Galilee (23.5) to create a redactional bridge between the previous episode and the following one. In the course of this bridge section he also narrates the sending of Jesus to Herod, with a cursory explanation as to what prompted this act, namely, Pilate learning that Jesus belonged to the 'authority' (ἐξουσίας) of Herod.

[57] Walaskay, *Rome*, p. 43.

[58] J. M. Creed, *The Gospel according to St Luke: The Greek Text, with Introduction, Notes, and Indices*, London: Macmillan, 1930, 280; quoted and endorsed by Walaskay (*Rome*, p. 43).

[59] Hoehner, *Herod*, p. 227. If Luke had simply needed a non-Roman (and preferably Jewish) context within which to place the mistreatment of Jesus, then he should not have worried any further, for he had already achieved exactly that in 22.63–5.

[60] Walaskay, *Rome*, p. 43.

[61] One noteworthy attempt at demonstrating that such readings fail to do full justice to the passage is to be found in an article by E. Buck: 'The Function of the Pericope "Jesus Before Herod" in the Passion Narrative of Luke', in W. Haubeck and M. Bachmann (eds.), *Wort in der Zeit: Neutestamentliche Studien. Festgabe für Karl Heinrich Rengstorf zum 75. Geburtstag*, Leiden: E. J. Brill, 1980, pp. 165–78. According to Buck, the passage displays 'a very pronounced paradigmatic-parenetic orientation', whereby Christians who were being unjustly persecuted could 'observe and derive strength from the example of the Lord who faced the collusion of idle curiosity, apathy and mockery without a word' (p. 178).

This explanation has been the source of numerous intriguing, albeit somewhat speculative, investigations on Pilate's precise reasons for sending Jesus over to Herod.[62] Yet, with regared to the plot of Luke's story, the two verses must be recognised for what they are – a transitional section, Luke's primary emphases remaining therefore to be sought in the account of the actual trial.

The first noticeable feature of the trial is Jesus' apparent *lack of cooperation* with Herod: not only does he fail to satisfy the tetrarch's desire to see a sign (ἤλπιζέν τι σημεῖον ἰδεῖν ὑπ' αὐτοῦ γινόμενον, 23.8), but he also refuses to answer his questions (αὐτὸς δὲ οὐδὲν ἀπεκρίνατο αὐτῷ, 23.9). Cassidy's contention that according to Luke 'Jesus did not cooperate with or defer to the authorities who judged him'[63] is certainly justified as far as Jesus' Herodian trial is concerned. Second, the picture of the chief priests and the scribes standing by and 'vigorously' (εὐτόνως) accusing Jesus (23.10), is yet another depiction of Jesus being *rejected* by the representatives of Israel. Third, the theme of Jesus' *mockery* at the hands of 'Herod and his soldiers' is emphatically expressed through a series of three aorist participles (23.11): (i) Jesus is 'despised' or 'treated with contempt' (ἐξουθενήσας); (ii) 'mocked' (ἐμπαίξας); and (iii) dressed (περιβαλών) with a 'gorgeous garment' (ἐσθῆτα λαμπράν), as a further expression of mockery.[64] Fourth, the

---

[62] T. Mommsen (*Römisches Strafrecht*, Leipzig, 1899, pp. 356–7) has argued that at the time of Jesus' trial Roman law required that trials must be conducted by the authorities of the province to which the accused belonged (*forum domicilii*) and that consequently Pilate was judicially bound to send Jesus to Herod. Sherwin-White (*Roman Society*, pp. 28–31) has challenged this by insisting that the Roman practice of that period was instead of a *forum delicti* type, which meant that the crime needed to be judged in the province where it was committed, and *forum domicilii* was introduced only later (in support of Sherwin-White's position, see also Hoehner, *Herod*, pp. 235–6). If Sherwin-White is correct, then the implication is that Pilate *chose* to send Jesus to Herod, and this raises once again the question of why he would do so. Most scholars offer more than one answer. Among the most favoured explanations are: (i) Pilate wanted to get rid of an awkward case (Hoehner, *Herod*, p. 236, and in 'Why Did Pilate', 88); (ii) Pilate wanted an independent evaluation from someone legally connected with Jesus (Brown, *Death*, vol. I, p. 766); (iii) After the massacre mentioned by Luke in 13.1, Pilate was trying to avoid any further offence to Herod, or even positively to attempt a reconciliation by means of this act of courtesy (Brown, *Death*, vol. I, p. 767; Hoehner, *Herod*, pp. 236–7, 239, and in 'Why Did Pilate', 88; Sherwin-White, *Roman Society*, p. 31, n. 5).

[63] Cassidy, *Jesus*, p. 73.

[64] The interpretation of ἐσθῆτα λαμπράν has been the source of much speculation: what kind of garment is meant? What colour was it? (For a list of suggestions see Brown, *Death*, vol. I, pp. 774–6; Marshall, *Gospel*, pp. 856–7. A particularly thorough investigation is to be found in P. Joüon, 'Luke 23,11: ἐσθῆτα λαμπράν', *RSR* 26 (1936), 80–5.) According to the other two Synoptics, the clothing of Jesus is specifically linked to the mockery of his royal allegations (Mark 15.17–18; Matt. 27.28–9). In Luke's Gospel that is much less clear (Brown, *Death*, vol. I, p. 776; Fitzmyer, *Luke*, vol. II, p. 1482). Yet, while the specific

sending of Jesus back to Pilate is meant to be taken as a further indication of Jesus' *innocence* – Pilate will make that clear in verse 15. What exactly indicated to Pilate Herod's verdict is not clear.[65] Luke seems more interested to inform his readers about what the verdict actually was than about how it was communicated. Moreover, the verdict of innocence will become even more striking for Luke's readers in light of the fact that someone who had earlier tried to kill Jesus (13.31) now has the chance to do exactly that and does not do it.

The common denominator of these emphases begins to emerge when they are seen in the light of Jesus' passion predictions (9.22, 44; 18.31–3; cf. 17.25; 22.2; 24.44). As noted in the analysis of the predictions, their primary thrust was to make the reader aware that, far from being an embarrassment to the Christological claims implicit (or explicit) in the Gospel's plot, the (then) forthcoming passion of Jesus was to be seen as the necessary fulfilment of what the Scriptures had predicted about the Messiah. Consequently, as the trial and passion of Jesus unfold, the readers are not only justified in looking out for indications that the events of which they are learning come as the fulfilment of Old Testament prophecies but even expected to do so.

Reference has already been made to the suggestion that Luke's whole account of Jesus' trial before Herod was constructed on the basis of Psalm 2.1–2.[66] While as an explanation of the account's origins the suggestion is at best not proven, its merit lies in drawing attention to the connection between Psalm 2 and Luke's account of Jesus' trial, a connection which Luke himself validates in Acts 4.26–7. This much is clear: as far as Luke is concerned, Jesus' trial before Pilate *and Herod* should add to the reader's assurance that Jesus is God's χριστὸς (Ac. 4.26; the same term as in Ps. 2.2, LXX; cf. also the Hebrew equivalent מְשִׁיחוֹ in MT).

However, Psalm 2 does not constitute the only Old Testament prediction which, according to Luke, sees part of its fulfilment in Jesus' Herodian trial. The resemblances to Isaiah's fourth Servant Song (Isa. 52.13–53.12) seem particularly striking.[67] There are at least two reasons for Luke's reader to pay particular attention to these common elements. The first

matter to which the garment was meant to point may remain unclear, the context of the statement suggests that the act of clothing Jesus in this way is still to be taken as part of Jesus' mockery (Fitzmyer, *Luke*, vol. II, p. 1482, views the act as intended 'to mock his guiltlessness'; cf. also Nolland, *Luke*, vol. III, p. 1124).

[65] Brown finds in ἐσθῆτα λαμπράν the necessary indication (Brown, *Death*, vol. I, pp. 776–7).

[66] Cadbury, *Making*, p. 30; Dibelius, *Tradition*, p. 199; 'Herodes', 113–26.

[67] While sporadic references have been made to these connections (e.g. J. B. Green, 'The Death of Jesus, God's Servant', in D. D. Sylva (ed.), *Reimaging the Death of the Lukan*

one, of a more general kind, is to be found in Luke 22.37, a passage
which aims to prepare the readers to approach the subsequent passion
account with this Isaianic prophecy in mind. The second, and much more
specific reason, is offered retrospectively in Acts, when Philip explains
to the Ethiopian eunuch that Jesus is the suffering figure of Isaiah 53 who
'does not open his mouth' before those who put him to death, is humiliated
('Εν τῇ ταπεινώσει [αὐτοῦ]), and is deprived of justice (ἡ κρίσις αὐτοῦ
ἤρθη) (Ac. 8.32–3; cf. Isa. 53.7–8). However, one is probably meant to
assume that the Isaianic passage which Luke has in mind as he narrates
the eunuch episode is not limited to the two verses which are quoted, but
the whole of the fourth Servant Song.[68]

A useful window into the similarities between the two passages is offered by the emphases of the Lukan pericope (as noted above).[69] Thus,
Jesus' determination to remain silent when about to be put to death reflects the Isaianic Servant's attitude in a parallel situation: οὐκ ἀνοίγει
τὸ στόμα (Isa. 53.7; cf. Ac. 8.32). Jesus is rejected, just as the
Isaianic figure is 'rejected by people' (ἐκλεῖπον παρὰ τοὺς υἱοὺς τῶν
ἀνθρώπων, Isa. 53.3). Jesus is mocked and despised, just as the Isaianic Servant is despised (ἄτιμον, ... ἠτιμάσθη, καὶ οὐκ ἐλογίσθη,
Isa. 53.3) and humiliated ('Εν τῇ ταπεινώσει, Isa. 53.8; cf. Ac. 8.33).
Finally, the innocent Jesus resembles the one who for Isaiah is δίκαιος
par excellence (Isa. 53.11).

These resemblances need not be taken as indications that Luke must
have intended to establish a specific connection between Isaiah's fourth
Servant Song and Jesus' Herodian trial. Had he wanted to achieve this,
one might speculate, he could have presumably made it clearer by some
explicit references to or quotations from that passage. Rather, these allusions should be understood against a broader backdrop, namely that the
whole of Jesus' passion, of which the Herodian trial is a part, represent for
Luke the fulfilment of Isaiah's Servant prophecies,[70] of which the fourth
Song is likewise a part. As for the likelihood that Luke's readers would
have been able to spot such connections and appreciate their significance,
this may or may not have been the case at a first reading/hearing of the

---

Jesus, Bonner Biblische Beiträge 73, Frankfurt am Main: Hain, 1990, p. 21; Karris, *Luke*,
p. 85), they do not appear to have been adequately explored.

[68]   Barrett, *Acts*, vol. I, p. 429.

[69]   The Old Testament text with which Luke's account is to be compared is LXX, rather
than MT, since the almost verbatim LXX quotation of Ac. 8.32–3 indicates that it was this
text that Luke had in mind (Bruce, *Acts*, p. 227; Barrett, *Acts*, vol. I, p. 430).

[70]   For a notable attempt at demonstrating the centrality of the Isaianic Servant prophecies
to Luke's Christology in general and passion narrative in particular, see Green, 'Death',
19–24.

story (especially before having the interpretative help of Acts 8.32–3). Yet repeated contact with Luke's whole story will have significantly increased such a probability.

It may safely be concluded, then, that Luke 23.6–12 contributes to the Lukan story of Jesus' trial and that it does so in terms of a Christological apologetic based on prophetic fulfilment. While a simultaneous element of political apologetic is not excluded,[71] this would be far from sufficient to account for Luke's emphases. Luke's dominant concern is to further his case that Jesus' sufferings and subsequent death show him to be the suffering righteous one whose coming the Old Testament prophecies had long announced.

Yet even this is not quite the whole story. As Luke's readers begin to appreciate the case for Jesus' Messiahship which Luke puts forward through his account of Jesus' trial before Herod, they realise that, ironically, it is the opportunity of doing just this (giving evidence of his Messiahship) that Jesus himself appears to dismiss by his refusal to perform a sign and to answer Herod. The tendency has often been to classify Jesus' responses (or lack of them) to questions concerning his identity and mission according to the specific categories of people addressed (one is reminded again of the common representation of the Lukan Jesus as friendly towards the Romans and dismissive towards the Jews). While this approach may help to clarify the narrative function of such groups, its weakness is that it tends to be too static – it often overlooks the possibility of changes in Jesus' attitude, or in who is advancing the evidence for Jesus' Messianic status, as the narrative develops.

When attention is paid instead to the dynamics of Luke's Christological argument, Jesus' attitude here appears rather less surprising. Building on the Gospel's Christological conflict, the trial narrative opens with the Sanhedrin's explicit challenge, 'If you are the Christ, tell us' (22.67a) – thus making explicit the Christological question which until now has only indirectly guided the narrative. In a manner different from the other Synoptics, Jesus informs the readers that he will not put forward the case for his own Messiahship, for 'if *I* tell you, you will not believe' (22.67b). Instead, the answer will be given (by God) through his exaltation (22.69). From this point onwards, Jesus' answers become rather less elaborate (both to the Sanhedrin and to Pilate – 22.70; 23.3), and eventually, when the opponents begin to show more heat than light, by 'vigorously accusing

---

[71] *Pace* Schmidt ('Luke's "Innocent" Jesus', *passim*), who regards the 'scriptural apologetic' and the political apologetic as mutually exclusive.

him' (23.10),[72] Jesus stops answering altogether,[73] refusing at the same time to perform miracles. When his attitude is seen in this context, it seems that the Lukan Jesus has now reached the stage where he is no longer prepared to adduce further evidence for his Messiahship, whether through words (answers) or deeds (signs). Plenty of these had been offered so far throughout the Gospel. Herod himself could have benefited from them while both he and Jesus were in Galilee, but now for him the 'time of visitation' is over (and Luke's reader must learn the lesson from that). Now, when the atmosphere has become overly hostile and the audience bent upon disbelief, all that Jesus chooses to do is to await the vindication which is to come through the exaltation of the Son of Man – for the account of which Luke's readers still need to wait a little longer.

To summarise the results of this section: (i) the narrative function of the Herodian trial is much more than a display of Jesus' political innocence – the episode furthers the case for Jesus' Messiahship by portraying him as the suffering righteous one (one of Luke's favourite descriptions of Jesus, 23.47; Ac. 3.14; 7.52; 22.14),[74] whose coming the Scriptures had announced; (ii) the passage sharpens the Gospel's Christological conflict: Jesus' fulfilment of scriptural prophecy argues for his Messiahship, while the Jewish leaders continue to dismiss it; (iii) Jesus' refusal to provide further evidence for his status indicates that a resolution of the conflict is still awaited.

Again before Pilate (23.13–25)

The existence of apologetic tendencies in the present passage has become such a commonplace in New Testament scholarship that it needs no detailed argumentation here.[75] Whatever else the passage may be saying, one could hardly fail to note the Lukan emphasis on Pilate's declarations of Jesus' innocence and announced intentions of releasing Jesus, in contrast with the vehement Jewish mob calling for Jesus' death. It is

---

[72] For a description of the heated atmosphere, see Brown, *Death*, vol. I, pp. 770–1.

[73] There is no indication that Luke regards the vehement accusation or the mockery as subsequent to or resulting from Jesus' silence. On the contrary, the hostile atmosphere is already assumed, as the reader recalls Herod's earlier enmity towards Jesus (13.31). Brown also thinks that ἐν λόγοις ἱκανοῖς should be understood as emotional verbosity (ibid., pp. 771–3).

[74] For a brief survey of Luke's emphasis on Jesus' innocence as a scriptural apologetic, see Schmidt, 'Luke's "Innocent" Jesus', especially pp. 116–19.

[75] See, among others, R. Bultmann, *History of the Synoptic Tradition*, trans. by J. Marsh, Oxford: Basil Blackwell, 1963, p. 282; Conzelmann, *Theology*, pp. 85–8; Fitzmyer, *Luke*, vol. II., p. 1489; Walaskay, *Rome*, pp. 44–5.

hard to believe that anyone concerned with the political innocence or subversiveness of Jesus or, by extension, of Christians, or anyone interested in Rome's attitude towards Christianity, would not have been given cause for thought by reading such a passage. But however distinguished a history this particular reading of the passage may have, it needs to be asked once again whether it offers a full picture of the narrative emphases, and whether the danger may not exist for it to become an abnormally dominant paradigm which obscures, or even denies, other understandings of the text.

Nevertheless, if any new reading of the passage (apologetic or otherwise) is to be regarded as feasible, it must face up to the challenge of accounting satisfactorily for the strikingly polarised nature of the passage (Pilate's declaration of Jesus' innocence v. the Jews' call for his death), which the political-apologetic readings of the passage seem to have explained so successfully.[76] On the other hand, it is important to remember that, however convincing the political-apologetic interpretation of the passage may be, it also has two major limitations: (i) it explains only what Luke's narrative would have achieved for one particular group (those with a political interest), the size of which might not have been particularly significant, and (ii) it explains only what the passage would have achieved as part of Luke 23 (the only part of the Gospel to develop political motives at some length), but not as part of the whole Gospel, the major concerns of which lie elsewhere.

Much of what has been said so far has pointed to a conflict running throughout the Third Gospel, with one set of voices arguing in favour of Jesus being God's chosen agent for the salvation of his people, and another set (typically the Jewish leaders) doubting or denying such indications. The mere recollection of this fact should already throw new light on the present passage. What the reader finds here is the Gospel's most dramatic representation of this conflict,[77] albeit one which unfolds in terms of only one specific issue – Jesus as the (suffering) righteous one.[78]

Whether the reader was expected to be politically minded or not, a Jew or a Gentile, a committed Christian or someone merely showing interest in this apparently new religion, of one thing Luke could be reasonably

[76] For a particularly lucid statement of this position, see Conzelmann, *Theology*, pp. 85–8.

[77] Commenting also on the dramatic force of Luke 23.13–25, Karris states that 'Luke's drama of Jesus' passion is at a peak here' (*Passion*, p. 90). Hence, for Karris, this whole section can comprise a 'dramatic structure' (pp. 89–90).

[78] Here we come close to Schmidt's suggestion that 'Luke's "Innocent" Jesus' (to quote the title of his article) functions as a scriptural apologetic.

certain: there was going to be some degree of concern with regard to the question of how it was possible, if Jesus was indeed such an innocent, caring, and gifted person as the Gospel had portrayed him, that he was put to death (as the Christian kerygma openly declared). If the readers were not to find in Jesus' death a 'stumbling block', nothing was going to be more important for Luke at this stage than establishing that he *did not deserve* to die. Naturally, then, the Christological conflict of the Gospel concentrates here on the issue of Jesus' innocence. A brief survey of the passage should help us see more precisely how Luke develops this theme.

Source-critically, verses 13–16 raise the same kind of problems as the previous episode, since they function largely as 'the conclusion to the examination by Herod'.[79] The rest of the story is typical of the Lukan passion narrative, showing clear awareness of the Synoptic tradition, but at the same time abbreviating or supplementing it rather freely.

In terms of narrative development, the first four verses set the stage for this new phase of Jesus' trial. It is Pilate himself who this time takes the initiative (23.13; contrast 23.1–2), by calling together 'the chief priests and the rulers and the people' (τὸν λαόν) and making before them (and before the reader) a lengthy declaration of Jesus' innocence, according to which the results of both his own 'examination' (ἀνακρίνας) and that of Herod point in the same direction: the charges against him have not been substantiated (ἐγὼ ἐνώπιον ὑμῶν ἀνακρίνας οὐθὲν εὗρον ἐν τῷ ἀνθρώπῳ τούτῳ) and there is nothing that could justify a death sentence (οὐδὲν ἄξιον θανάτου ἐστὶν πεπραγμένον αὐτῷ). Yet, in an effort to appease them,[80] and perhaps also to warn Jesus against any further steps in the direction of his Messianic pretension,[81] Pilate is willing to have Jesus 'chastised' (23.16).

Pilate's articulate explanation stands in contrast to the mob-type response of the Jews (23.18), the intensity of which is distinctively Lukan.[82] Of significance is also the fact that the 'all' (παμπληθεί) who cried out

---

[79] Marshall, *Gospel*, p. 857. On the issue of tradition and redaction in these verses, see Fitzmyer, *Luke*, vol. II, pp. 1483–6; Green, *Death*, pp. 82–6; Marshall, *Gospel*, pp. 857–8; Taylor, *Passion*, pp. 88–9.

[80] On interpreting παιδεύειν here as an appeasement effort, see Brown, *Death*, vol. I, pp. 792–3; Marshall, *Gospel*, p. 859; Nolland, *Luke*, vol. III, p. 1127.

[81] Fitzmyer, *Luke*, vol. II, p. 1484.

[82] Both ἀνέκραγον, a second aorist form of ἀνακράζω, and παμπληθεί are not found anywhere else in the New Testament (J. H. Thayer, *Greek–English Lexicon of the New Testament*, Grand Rapids: Zondervan, n.d., pp. 39, 475; cf. Marshall, *Gospel*, p. 860; Nolland, *Luke*, vol. III, p. 1131).

this time clearly include the Jewish λαός of 23.16.[83] What makes this detail significant for the reader is the fact that up to this point the crowds have either been positively disposed towards Jesus (19.47–8; 20.6,19; 21.38; 22.2) or played a passive role (23.13; cf. the ὄχλοι of 23.5). Yet it would be wrong to assume that the friendly crowds of previous passages have been composed of the same individuals as the crowd which now calls for his crucifixion, and that consequently a radical decrease in the popular support of Jesus has taken place.[84] What Luke is keen to stress, rather, is that Jesus is now isolated from any human support (as his rivals had long wished – 19.47–8; 22.2) and that the opposition to him is stronger than ever in the Gospel. Yet, prominent as the opposition may be, its judgement is immediately revealed as being utterly unjust. In the same breath as their call for Jesus' condemnation, the Jews ask for the release (ἀπόλυσον) of Barabbas,[85] whom Luke next introduces (23.19)[86] as being guilty of two crimes:[87] insurrection (στάσις) and murder (φόνος). The former makes the perversity of the accusers' judgement particularly evident: they overlook in Barabbas precisely the same political crime as they attribute to Jesus.[88]

---

[83] According to Fitzmyer, 'it would be naive to think that he [Luke] refers merely to the leaders' (*Luke*, vol. II, p. 1489). For more detail see also Marshall, *Gospel*, p. 860; Nolland, *Luke*, vol. III, p. 1131.

[84] *Pace* Tyson, *Death*, p. 44. Not only had the crowds' high regard for Jesus been, according to Luke, the biggest hindrance to Jesus' arrest, but immediately after the trial, as Jesus is led to his execution and as he hangs on the cross, the multitudes are again portrayed as his sympathisers (23.27; in 23.35 they do not join in the mocking, as they do in the Synoptic parallels).

[85] Luke gives no explanation as to the basis of the Jews' call for the release of a prisoner. The Markan explanation, in terms of a Passover amnesty, is probably assumed, although this still leaves open the question of how Luke's readers would have known about this explanation. Their broader knowledge of such practices, whether in Palestine or in the wider Graeco-Roman world, might be the answer. (In favour of the historicity of such a practice in Palestine, see C. B. Chavel, 'The Releasing of a Prisoner on the Eve of Passover in Ancient Jerusalem', *JBL* 60 (1941), 273–8; Blinzler, *Trial*, pp. 218–21. Against it, see J. Jeremias, *The Eucharistic Words of Jesus*, third edition, London: SCM Press, 1966, p. 73, and in a more hesitant form Légasse, *Trial*, p. 68. For evidence of similar practices in the Graeco-Roman world, see R. L. Merritt, 'Jesus, Barabbas, and the Paschal Pardon', *JBL* 104 (1985), 57–68.)

[86] The other two Synoptics introduce Barabbas before referring to the Jewish call for his release, also adding a reference to a Passover custom of releasing a prisoner (Matt. 27.15–18; Mark 15.6–10), but no more significance should probably be attributed to the Lukan transposition and abbreviation of material than that it is the result of his Herodian inclusio prior to the present stage of the trial.

[87] It is possible that the two are to be regarded as referring to the same incident, as in the case of the Markan account (15.7), but Luke's wording does not require this.

[88] H. D. Buckwalter correctly refers to this incident as '*the irony of Barabbas' release*' (*The Character and Purpose of Luke's Christology*, SNTSMS 89, Cambridge University

The dramatic conflict around the issue of Jesus' innocence continues to intensify, as Pilate makes further efforts to release Jesus, efforts which are received by the crowd with hysterical shouts for Jesus' crucifixion (23.21). Once again the intensity of the conflict is distinctively Lukan, not only through the account of the repeated and alternating efforts for and against Jesus' innocence, but also through the double use of the imperative σταύρου (contrast Mark 15.13; Matt. 27.22).

Pilate's last effort on Jesus' behalf comes through a third declaration of his innocence (23.22). Pilate's rhetorical question – τί γὰρ κακὸν ἐποίησεν οὗτος; – is tantamount to the conclusion that the accusers are unable to prove that Jesus has done anything wrong. As for himself, Pilate can declare, οὐδὲν αἴτιον θανάτου εὗρον ἐν αὐτῷ. Yet, for the second time Pilate's declaration of Jesus' innocence comes combined with the offer to have Jesus chastised (cf. 23.16). While the primary meaning of the offer is, as in the first instance, that Pilate is attempting as a last resort a compromise solution (appeasing the Jews and cautioning Jesus), the repetition of the simultaneous stress on Jesus' innocence and his sufferings represents for the reader on a smaller scale the Christology of Luke 23, that is, Jesus as the suffering righteous one.[89] In the words of Büchele, 'Lk. will mit seiner Darstellung nicht nur auf die juristische Unschuld Jesu abheben. Vielmehr ist diese Hintergrund, [sic] Folie für seine Darstellung Jesu als des "leidenden Gerechten"' ('With his portrayal, Luke does not wish merely to uphold Jesus' judicial innocence. This background is much more a foil for his portrait of Jesus as "the righteous sufferer"').[90]

Parallel with the climactic intensification of the Christological conflict, one also notes a gradual increase in the contrast between the way Pilate

Press, 1996, p. 111). Neyrey goes too far, however, when he states that 'Luke clearly portrays the Jews as favoring rebellion in choosing a murderous rebel to Jesus' (*Passion*, p. 82). The fact that they ask for his release hardly means that they *approve* of his deeds. It simply indicates their use of double standards: they overlook in Barabbas the same charge that they are so eager to condemn in Jesus. It is, of course, possible to argue that the Jews' concomitant condemnation of Jesus and exemption of Barabbas is understandable. Barabbas was presumably a freedom fighter and therefore possibly a national hero. Jesus, by contrast, is for this (manipulated) crowd a false prophet, potentially dangerous for the people, and therefore a villain. Yet this is neither what Luke states (no reference is made to Barabbas' heroism), nor, more importantly, sufficient to obscure the injustice of the prosecutors' judgement in pressing a political charge against a prophet but not against a revolutionary.

[89] For the centrality of the concept of the suffering righteous one to Luke's understanding of Jesus' passion and death, see Büchele, *Tod*, pp. 76–92; R. J. Karris, 'Luke 23:47 and the Lucan View of Jesus' Death', *JBL* 105 (1986), 65–74, reprinted in Sylva (ed.), *Reimaging*, pp. 68–78.

[90] Büchele, *Tod*, p. 78.

and the Jews set forth their cases. Once again Pilate's reasonable attitude, challenging the Jews to give credible evidence of Jesus' culpability, repeating his conclusion on the basis of the evidence offered so far, and even being willing to go further than necessary by accepting a compromise solution, is sharply contrasted with their response, which is characterised by mob pressure (οἱ δὲ ἐπέκειντο) in the form of loud voices (φωναῖς μεγάλαις) (23.23).

The chapters-long Christological conflict of the Gospel, last expressed in the Roman trial in terms of Jesus' innocence, comes to an apparent end in a short but emphatic sentence, which appears to reveal the resolution of the conflict: καὶ κατίσχυον αἱ φωναὶ αὐτῶν. Two words establish the force of this sentence. The first one is κατίσχυον. Its role is to inform the readers that those denying Jesus' innocence, and thus playing a representative role for all those who throughout the Gospel have been (directly or indirectly) questioning or denying the narrator's Christological case on Jesus' behalf, have actually 'prevailed'. The rhetorical weight of this information can hardly be overstated. For a long time the reader has been waiting for a resolution of the conflicting 'voices' of the narrative. All kinds of evidence have been offered to suggest that the resolution would be in terms of Jesus' vindication. Despite all this, the resolution appears to have happened contrary to the Gospel's indications. The second key word, φωναὶ, indicates, however, that what has actually 'prevailed' is not their arguments but their 'voices'/'shouts'(NIV).[91] Thus this sentence becomes, in a nutshell, Luke's explanation of how it was historically possible that an innocent man should be put to death. It was not, Luke argues, because Jesus' opponents were able to produce any convincing evidence against him, but simply because the pressure of their persistent shouts caused Pilate to give in to their request.

In the remaining two verses (24–5) the Lukan account continues to show some degree of similarity with the other Synoptics (cf. Mark 15.15; Matt. 27.26). What is distinctively Lukan is the stress on the irregularity of the trial's outcome. On the one hand, Luke cannot refer to Pilate as 'wishing (βουλόμενος) to satisfy the crowd' (Mark 15.15), for this would mean that Pilate still had a choice. As far as Luke is concerned, Pilate has no longer been in control of the situation since the moment when the voices of the Jews 'prevailed'. Even

---

[91] Note Luke's use of the φωνή word group in describing the Jewish involvement in the last part of Jesus' trial: in 23.21 they 'shouted out' (ἐπεφώνουν); in 23.23a they 'insisted with loud voices/shouts' οἱ δὲ ἐπέκειντο φωναῖς μεγάλαις), until finally 'their voices (φωναί) prevailed'.

the 'verdict' which he gives (ἐπέκρινεν) is nothing more than the ratification of his own defeat, for what he pronounces is that '*their* request (αἴτημα αὐτῶν) should be granted', leading to the release of the man whom *they* asked for (ὃν ἠτοῦντο) and to Jesus being delivered up to *their* will (θέλημα αὐτῶν). All these, the reader knows, are against Pilate's own findings. On the other hand, it is only the Third Gospel which supplements the information about Barabbas' release with a rehearsal of his crimes, thus confirming to the reader the injustice of the present outcome of the conflict, and almost demanding that this not be the *final* outcome.

The results of this section can be summarised as follows:

(a) The passage furthers Luke's theme of Jesus' innocence. Pilate's judgement is shown to be right and the Jewish one misguided by the fact that (i) noise is all that Jesus' prosecutors are able to offer in substantiation of their request for his death (23.18, 21, 23), and that (ii) their desire to have Jesus crucified as a political instigator (23.2) is sandwiched between their concomitant calls for the release of someone whom the narrator has repeatedly characterised as an insurrectionist and murderer (23.19, 25).

(b) While Luke's emphasis on Jesus' innocence is expressed in predominantly political terms, its narrative function is much broader. Two major indications to this effect have been noted. First, the simultaneous emphasis on both innocence and condemnation (seen in Pilate's offer to have the innocent Jesus chastised, and even more clearly in the outcome of the trial) indicates that, just as in the rest of Luke 23, Jesus is for Luke not simply 'innocent' but 'the suffering innocent one' (a concept which implies a theological dimension). Second, one of Luke's major distinctives is the dramatic dialogue and contrast between Pilate and the Jews, portraying them as representatives of the conflicting voices which throughout the Gospel had been taking part in the Messianic conflict, with the pro-Jesus voice making responsible judgements, while the opposition is typically unable to give reasonable responses. This continuity between the episode and the Gospel's concern with offering assurance about Jesus' Messianic status shows the passage to be a major part of Luke's Christologically oriented *apologia pro evangelio*.

(c) The incongruity between the outcome of the trial and the kind of outcome which the reader has been led to expect suggests that although Jesus' judicial trial has now come to an end (and was proved to be a miscarriage of justice, since Pilate had been unable to put into practice his correct reasoning), his 'theological trial continues, for God's final verdict has not yet materialised.

Conclusion

In the present chapter I have sought to test and expand on the preliminary findings of the last chapter, in which I suggested that Luke's account of Jesus' trial ought to be understood as a continuation of the Gospel's Christological conflict, and that Luke's leading concern here is the apologetic presentation of Jesus' passion as confirmatory of, rather than contradictory to, the claim of his Messianic identity.

Before summarising my interpretation of Luke 22.66–23.25, it is important to note that although many of the insights of previous scholarship have been confirmed,[92] further evidence has been found that no single interpretation available to date has done sufficient justice to the function of the passage. First, evidence has been found for a political apologetic[93] in Luke's unparalleled emphasis on the illegitimacy of the political accusations against Jesus and on Pilate's repeated exculpation of him. While it may be argued that the refutation of the charges is not as explicit as the charges themselves, there is little doubt that Luke has offered the readers ample evidence against the credibility of the political accusations. The depiction of Jesus' political stance in the foregoing narrative, Pilate's repeated exculpation of Jesus, the unfavourable description of the accusers' attitude and judgement, are all arguments against the claims of the political charges. Yet the paucity of political language in the Sanhedrin episode and the fact that even in the Roman trial Jesus is not merely 'innocent' but '(the) suffering innocent (one)' indicate that the function of the trial story can by no means be reduced to that of a political apologia. Secondly, while it is true that during the Roman part of the trial Israel's representatives function as Jesus' prosecutors,[94] the emphasis in 22.66–71 is rather different. Their role there is expressed not in judicial but in Christological terms. They are the ones who initiate and fuel the Christological debate, who even establish part of its rationale,[95] but who, instead of finding in their conversation with Jesus sufficient grounds for belief in him (as the readers are expected to), dismiss the evidence (22.67–8) and instead take the Christological testimony as sufficient grounds for bringing Jesus before Pilate (22.71–23.1). Moreover, taking the role of the Jewish leaders as the hermeneutical key to the trial story would tend to place in

---

[92] See the review of research on Jesus' trial in chapter 2.

[93] As suggested by Cadbury, Conzelmann, and Tyson.

[94] As emphasised in various forms by the numerous works dealing with the issue of responsibility for Jesus' death, as well as by Neyrey's interpretation of the narrative as 'the trial of Israel'.

[95] For example, when they read divine sonship into Jesus' reference to his future glorification (22.69–70).

a secondary position Luke's characterisation of his protagonist. Thirdly, while it is beyond dispute that Luke portrays Pilate in a more positive light than the Jewish leaders, there is little justification for taking the positive portrayal of the Roman system as Luke's dominant concern: [96] the first trial episode does not even feature a representative of Rome, and when Pilate does come on the stage, his astute judgements are eclipsed by his inability to carry them out. Fourthly, even less justification exists for taking 'the trial of the faithful God' as the thrust of the narrative:[97] the one instance in which reference to God is made (22.69)[98] portrays him on the throne, not in the dock.

Instead, what gives coherence to the trial narrative both in its own right and as part of the Gospel's plot is the author's continuous preoccupation with the apologetic characterisation of Jesus as Christ (22.67), Son of God (22.70), legitimate ruler of Israel (23.2–3, 5), suffering righteous one (23.6–25). Against the framework of this Christological apologetic, textual emphases such as those highlighted by previous scholarship take more appropriate proportions, emerging at the same time no longer as disconnected (or even conflicting) agendas but as facets of one unifying intent: an apologetic presentation of Christianity's beliefs about Jesus. The Sanhedrin trial, with its distinctively Lukan elaboration on Jesus' Messianic attributes and their justification, is a carefully constructed Christological apologetic in relation to Judaism. The Roman trial, on the other hand, with its emphatic socio-political language, adds the further dimension of an equally effective Christological apologetic in relation to Rome – a particularly appropriate dimension in the context of a church which is seeking to update its identity for an imperial setting. It assures all those with imperial sensitivities that commitment to Jesus as Messiah, 'king of the Jews' (23.2–3), is not intrinsically incompatible with socio-political order (23.4, etc.).

---

[96] Contra Walaskay.   [97] Contra Karris.
[98] There is no need to discuss here the reference to God as part of the term 'son of God' (22.70).

4

THE TRIAL OF JESUS IN NARRATIVE
RETROSPECTION

Introduction

While, as indicated in chapter 2, it is customary for studies of the trial of
Jesus in the Third Gospel to pay some attention to the narrative *precedents* of this event, virtually no attempt has yet been made to investigate
the way in which subsequent elements of Luke's narrative may also (*retrospectively*) throw light on Luke's account of Jesus' trial.[1] The paucity
of such studies may appear understandable in view of the consideration
that what determines the nature of a trial is what has been happening up
to that point, rather than subsequent events. Nevertheless, a number of
factors (which will be further substantiated in the course of the chapter)
make the investigation of the present chapter necessary:

(1)   Luke's passion predictions (esp. 9.21; 18.31–3), as well as par-
      allel passages in the resurrection narrative (24.7, 46) and in Acts
      (e.g. 2.22–4), seem to indicate that Luke thinks of Jesus' trial as
      of one piece with his death, resurrection and glorification. Con-
      sequently, the emphases of the trial narrative might be expected
      to exhibit certain common elements with the latter accounts, and,
      accordingly, one's findings in the latter may have a confirmatory
      (or corrective) role for those in the former.

(2)   According to the last two chapters, although the Lukan account
      of Jesus' trial represents the climax of the Gospel's Christo-
      logical conflict (since it is here that Jesus' Messianic status

---

[1]   A minor exception is Blinzler's five-page discussion of the trial of Jesus in Acts (*Trial*,
pp. 280–5). More recently, F. J. Matera ('Responsibility for the Death of Jesus according to
the Acts of the Apostles', *JSNT* 39 (1990), 77–93) has investigated those trial passages in
Acts in which Luke 'explicitly places the responsibility for Jesus' death upon the shoulders
of the Jews' (p. 78), but both his choice of passages for discussion and the angle from which
they are studied are defined by his specific concern with responsibility for Jesus' death.
Also, J. Neyrey has entitled (somewhat misleadingly) a section of his monograph 'Jesus'
Trials in Acts' (*Passion*, pp. 89–107), but the section focuses on the trials of Peter, Stephen,
and Paul, rather than on passages which refer to the trial of Jesus.

is formally challenged by the highest Jewish authority – the Sanhedrin), the final outcome of this conflict has not yet been reached. The reader is still left with the question of how a death sentence can be the fitting end to what Jesus has come to accomplish. In this sense, then, 'the jury is still out' and the trial account is not yet complete. Consequently, while a *historical* study of the trial of Jesus may be justified in limiting its investigation to the actual trial account, an analysis of the place of Jesus' trial in Luke's *narrative* needs to take into consideration the resolution of the trial conflict in the subsequent accounts of Jesus' death and resurrection.

(3) Luke's retrospective references and allusions to Jesus' trial provide vital clues as to the author's understanding and representation of this event.

Thus, the specific questions which will guide the investigation of the present chapter are: (1) What are the major narrative emphases of the post-trial section of Luke's passion narrative and to what extent are they in continuity with the apologetic tendencies which have been noted in the analysis of the trial narrative? (2) In what way do the death-and-resurrection accounts develop the Gospel's plot beyond the point where the trial narrative left it, and how does this elucidate the place of Jesus' trial in the Gospel's story? (3) What picture of Jesus' trial is revealed by Luke's retrospective references to it, and what intended use for the trial account is suggested by the function of these references in their various contexts?

I shall attempt to answer these questions by looking first at the remaining part of Luke's passion narrative, next at the resurrection accounts, and finally at the various instances in Acts where reference is made to Jesus' trial.

The post-trial section of Luke's passion narrative (Luke 23.26–56)

For convenience, I shall divide Luke 23.26–56 into four parts, dealing respectively with the road to Jesus' execution (23.26–32), the crucifixion scene (23.33–43), his death and accompanying events (23.44–9), and his burial (23.50–6).[2] In each of these parts, major Lukan distinctives point back to the account of Jesus' trial.

---

[2] For this choice of textual divisions see Büchele, *Tod*, pp. 42–61. Nolland (*Luke*, vol. III, pp. 1142, 1150) and Bock (*Luke*, vol. II, p. 1840) divide further the second part into 23.33–8 and 23.39–43, although Nolland admits that '[w]hile divided here for convenience, the Lukan unit [beginning with 23.33] probably extends to v 43 ("with the criminals" in

The road to Jesus' execution (23.26–32)

Apart from 23.26 and 23.32, which have Gospel parallels (the former in Matt. 27.31–2/Mark 15.20–1 and the latter in Matt. 27.38/Mark 15.27/John 19.18), this section is uniquely Lukan. What one finds here is the account of Jesus walking towards the place of his execution, accompanied by crowds and lamenting women, and Jesus' rather extensive address to the latter group.

The thrust of the passage is determined by a number of factors, among which the identity of the crowds and of the lamenting women, their respective roles in the narrative, and the significance of Jesus' words are particularly important.[3]

It is impossible to determine with certainty whether πολὺ πλῆθος τοῦ λαοῦ (23.27) ought to be regarded as actual sympathisers of Jesus or as people (presumably both inhabitants of Jerusalem and visitors for the Passover) who were watching the events out of mere curiosity.[4] Very probably, a mixture of both is meant. What is clear, however, is that Luke distinguishes between these crowds and the αὐτοί of 23.25–6, who take charge of Jesus' execution (albeit no effort is made to explain the contrasting roles played by ὁ λαός here and in 23.13).[5] It appears, then, that the role of the crowds in the present context is in line with the many other instances in Luke–Acts, where Jesus or his disciples are followed by sympathetic or curious multitudes and where part of the narrative function of these multitudes is to enhance the positive image of Luke's protagonists and their

the opening verse prepares for the interaction with these criminals with which the unit concludes; the sympathetic but silent witness of the People and the turning of the repentant criminal to Jesus in his need frame the threefold mocking in between)' (p. 1142). Marshall (*Gospel*, p. 862) and Ellis (*Gospel of Luke*, pp. 265–6) include 23.32 in the second, rather than first, section, although according to Marshall 'the reference to the two criminals could be regarded as forming the end of the previous section, since it deals with the way to the cross. . .; it is a bridge passage' (p. 865). The fact that 23.26–34 belong together is also indicated by the notion of movement, present in the use of (ἀπ)άγω in 23.26 and 23.32, contrasting the indication of arrival (ὅτε ἀπῆλθον) in 23.33.

[3] Useful surveys of the many different angles from which this passage has been studied, together with the corresponding solutions which have been offered by various scholars, are given by Neyrey (*Passion*, pp. 108–9) and M. L. Soards ('Tradition, Composition, and Theology in Jesus' Speech to the "Daughters of Jerusalem" (Luke 23:26–32)', *Bib* 68 (1987), 221–4).

[4] Ancient sources indicate that the participation of crowds at executions out of curiosity was common (e.g., Lucian, 'The Passing of Peregrinus', in E. H. Warmington (ed.), *Lucian*, vol. V, London: William Heinemann; Harvard University Press, 1936, p. 34; cf. E. Klostermann, *Das Lukasevangelium*, Handbuch zum Neuen Testament 5, third edition, Tübingen: J. C. B. Mohr, 1975, p. 227; Marshall, *Gospel*, p. 863; Bock, *Luke*, vol. II, p. 1844).

[5] As noted earlier, the probable explanation is that different members of the public are meant, but Luke does not say so.

ministry (Luke 4.15, 42; 5.1; 7.11; 8.4, 19, 40, 45; 9.11, 37; 11.29; 12.1; 14.25; 19.48; 20.6, 19; 22.2; Ac. 2.47; 4.21; 5.13, 16; 13.42–5; 14.11).

Even more explicitly favourable is Luke's portrayal of the lamenting women.[6] Again, whether one takes the actions of these women as expressions of genuine concern for Jesus or simply as ritualistic,[7] their lament is certainly to be understood as some form of dissatisfaction with what is happening to Jesus. It is rather ironic, therefore, that some recent commentators have argued that these women function in Luke's narrative as representatives not of 'the people' of Israel, or Jerusalem, in general, but specifically of that section of Israel which has always opposed and killed God's messengers.[8] How could they be taken as representatives of those who kill the prophets precisely at the time when they lament the killing of a prophet?

True, Neyrey is correct to stress that these women are associated with Jerusalem, upon which words of doom are then pronounced, but their association with Jerusalem places them not among the villains of this city, but among its innocent victims. As they lament the fate of Jesus – an innocent victim himself – Jesus turns to tell them that they and their children will also become such victims, by virtue of their association with this city which 'kills the prophets' (13.34) and which, because of that, will soon be subject to God's judgement. As for the vivid doom imagery of 23.29–31, its main thrust is to emphasise the awfulness of these days of divine judgement – a judgement which Luke's readers could probably see fulfilled in the events of AD 70.

In broad strokes, then, Luke's presentation of Jesus' journey to execution emphasises much more than the other Gospels the degree of injustice which is being done in the execution of Jesus. The multitude of sympathetic people and particularly the lamenting women are the *human* witnesses to and deplorers of this injustice. The forthcoming judgement upon Jerusalem for its special role in the killing of his supreme prophet is on the other hand the indication of *God's* opinion in the matter.

But this is only the defensive part of Luke's apologetic. The continuity between Luke's concerns in the present passage and the trial narrative

---

[6] As shown below, there is very little justification for distinguishing between the way Luke views the people and the women (*pace* J. H. Neyrey, 'Jesus' Address to the Women of Jerusalem (Luke 23:27–31) – A Prophetic Judgment Oracle', *NTS* 29 (1983), 75–6; *Passion*, pp. 110–11; contrast Brown, *Death*, vol. II, p. 920; C. H. Giblin, *The Destruction of Jerusalem According to Luke's Gospel*, Analecta Biblica 107, Rome: The Pontifical Biblical Institute, 1985, p. 97; Nolland, *Luke*, vol. III, p. 1136; Soards, 'Tradition', 229).

[7] See Bock, *Luke*, vol. II, pp. 1844–5 for a discussion of alternative interpretations of their actions.

[8] So, for example, Neyrey, *Passion*, pp. 110–11.

is also evident in the way Luke positively sets his case on Jesus' behalf. The trial accounts, we have seen, display Luke's interest in setting forth his case for Jesus' Messiahship. The same concerns can be detected here, through the presentation of Jesus as a prophet.[9] Even on the way to his death, Jesus makes prophetic predictions; resembling faithful prophets of the Old Testament, he announces the judgement which awaits Israel because of her disobedience to God and rejection of his messengers.[10]

The crucifixion scene (23.33–43)

Luke's Christological apologia continues in the account of Jesus' crucifixion. The following elements seem to contribute to the author's positive statement of his case: (1) Luke's transposition of Isaiah 53.12 from the crucifixion account (cf. Mark 15.28) to an earlier point in the narrative (22.37), where it is placed on Jesus' (rather than the narrator's) lips, enables the reader to view Jesus' crucifixion between the two criminals as a fulfilment not only of the Scriptures but also of Jesus' own prophetic prediction. Once again, in this way, Jesus is confirmed as belonging to Israel's line of true, albeit rejected, prophets (cf. Luke 13.33; Ac. 7.52). (2) As in the other Synoptics (Matt. 27.35; Mark 15.24), the reference to the casting of lots (Luke 23.34b) points to Psalm 22.19 (LXX; 22.18 MT), thus representing Jesus' ordeal as fulfilment of scriptural prophecy. (3) Like the account of the Sanhedrin trial, the Lukan crucifixion narrative poses the question of Jesus' identity more emphatically than the other Gospels. For both Mark and Matthew this challenge comes in the form of two Christological titles ('the Christ' and 'the king of Israel' in Mark 15.32; 'the Son of God' in Matt. 27.40, 43 and 'the king of Israel' in Matt. 27.42), while Luke has three ('the Christ of God' and [God's] 'Chosen One'; 'the king of the Jews' in 23.36–7[11]), with the notion of his kingship again being present in the words of the believing criminal (23.42). (4) Although the term 'Saviour' is never applied to Jesus in the present passage, this is one of the most central components of his (ironical)[12]

---

[9] J. T. Carroll, 'Luke's Crucifixion Scene', in Sylva (ed.), *Reimaging*, pp. 113–14.

[10] Parallels between Jesus' address to the women and Old Testament prophetic oracles (especially Isa. 54.1; Hos. 10.8; also the parallel use of ἰδοὺ ἔρχονται ἡμέραι between 23.29 and Jer. 7.32; 16.14; 38.31, LXX) have often been noted (e.g. Neyrey, *Passion*, p. 113; Nolland, *Luke*, vol. III, p. 1137).

[11] Luke's transposition of the inscription on the cross from its place in Mark (15.26) to the mockery scene adds force to the rejection of Jesus as king of the Jews.

[12] Neyrey has correctly argued that the passage makes deliberate use of irony in order to highlight the theme of 'salvation' (and, implicitly, Jesus as 'Saviour'): "'Salvation" is the ironical subject of the triple mockery: "He *saved* others, let him *save* himself"

characterisation here.[13] If according to Mark and Matthew Jesus' saving power is challenged twice (once by the people, in Mark 15.30/Matt. 27.40, and once by the Jewish leaders, in Mark 15.31/Matt. 27.42), according to Luke this happens three times (by the leaders, in 23.35, by the soldiers, in 23.37, and by one of the criminals, in 23.39). Even more importantly, it is only in Luke's account that this challenge receives an answer, as Jesus gives the assurance of salvation to one of the criminals (23.43).[14]

A more defensive stance of Luke's apologetic is also present: (1) Jesus' prayer, "Father, forgive them; for they know not what they do" (23.34a) has no parallel in the other Gospels, and, quite apart from the textual uncertainties which it entails,[15] it appears to fit rather awkwardly in this context. How could those responsible for Jesus' death[16] be regarded as ignorant of their deed? A similar Lukan 'ignorance motif' has often been noted in Acts 3.17 and 13.27 (and very probably this is what makes the balance tip in favour of the authenticity of the text),[17] but it seems that the precise meaning of this ignorance has not been adequately explained. It is clear that Luke did not conceive of those responsible for Jesus' death as acting out of *judicial* ignorance. They knew that they were condemning a man who was not 'worthy of death' (23.22). Rather, I suggest, in view of Luke's indication that Jesus' Messianic vocation was ultimately vindicated only through his resurrection-exaltation (22.69; Ac. 2.36; 17.31; etc.), the Jewish leaders and their allies could, to some degree, be regarded as acting out of *Christological* ignorance. In both Acts 3.17 and 13.27 this

---

(23:35) ... "*save* yourself" (23:37) ... "*save* yourself and us" (23:39). This mockery of Jesus as Saviour is in stark contrast with the heavenly proclamation of Jesus as "the Saviour, Christ the Lord" at his birth (2:11). The mocking remarks at the crucifixion are ironic for, while the mockers deny that he is Saviour, God affirms that he is. And "salvation" becomes the substance of Jesus' proclamation to the repentant criminal (23:43) and the hope of the repentant crowd in 23:48' (*Passion*, p. 132). Neyrey's case is, however, much weaker when he goes on to state that Jesus' 'own salvation by God is highlighted by Luke in 23:46', with the result that 'Jesus becomes the Saved Saviour' (p. 132).

[13] In the words of Fitzmyer, Jesus 'is crucified precisely as "saviour", a major theme in Lucan theology' (*Luke*, vol. II, p. 1501). On the centrality of 'salvation' to Lukan theology, see especially Marshall, *Historian*, pp. 92–214.

[14] It is remarkable, in the light of these observations, that Luke should have come to be understood so often as having no *theologia crucis*. For a list of advocates of this position, see W. G. Kümmel, 'Current Theological Accusations against Luke', *ANQ* 16 (1975), 134, n. 18. Against it, see especially P. Doble, *The Paradox of Salvation: Luke's Theology of the Cross*, SNTSMS 87, Cambridge University Press, 1996, *passim*.

[15] For a list of arguments for and against the Lukan authenticity of the statement, see Marshall, *Gospel*, pp. 867–8.

[16] On viewing αὐτοῖς as referring not merely to the actual executioners (who *may* have been ignorant of Jesus' innocence), but also to all those responsible for his crucifixion, see Fitzmyer, *Luke*, vol. II, pp. 1503–4; Nolland, *Luke*, vol. III, p. 1146.

[17] See, for example, Fitzmyer, *Luke*, vol. II, p. 1503; Marshall, *Gospel*, p. 867.

ignorance motif is used by Luke's protagonists to emphasise the privileged vantage point of the audience, living *after* God's exaltation of Jesus, and the challenge for them to 'know' better who Jesus was than his executioners did. Correspondingly, Jesus' prayer is meant by Luke, apart from anything else, as an apologetic explanation (Jesus was crucified because his executioners did not know who he was), as well as a challenge (the readers are challenged to supply the Christological 'knowledge' which Jesus' executioners lacked). (2) In contrast to Mark 15.29 and Matthew 27.39, where they join in the mockery, Luke 23.35 depicts the multitudes as standing and watching, but not deriding Jesus.[18] The significance of this for Luke's readers is that, far from being on the side of those who delight in Jesus' execution, the bystanders are closer to those who testify to the injustice of what is being done to Jesus. (3) Certainly the most significant difference between the respective portrayals of Jesus' crucifixion by Luke and his Markan source is in terms of the interaction between the two criminals and Jesus (23.39–43). All that Mark's readers learn about the criminals' attitude to Jesus is that they, too, joined in reviling him (Mark 15.32b). In Luke, we have already noted, the episode turns out to be a testimony to Jesus' ability to save. But this is not all. Just as much, it is a testimony to Jesus' innocence. Unlike the criminals, who receive what they deserve, Jesus has done 'nothing wrong' and, therefore, his crucifixion is what he does *not* deserve (23.41).

The relevance of these observations for the present purposes is twofold. First, they show that the crucifixion narrative is guided by similar apologetic concerns to those uncovered in the trial account. On the one hand, Luke continues his case for Jesus' Messiahship. He does so (i) by showing how Jesus' crucifixion fulfils both the Scriptures and Jesus' own prophetic words (23.33, 34b), (ii) by sharpening the Christological focus of the narrative (through the use of Christological titles), and (iii) by supplying grounds for the Christological assertions (through the salvation of one criminal – even if the answer to the Christological challenges of the mockery account is probably meant to be further supplied by the reader on the basis of the Gospel's story so far and, even more, through the subsequent resurrection narratives). On the other hand, Luke continues to refute any possible objections associated with the stigma of Jesus' crucifixion. He explains to his readers that Jesus' crucifixion was possible only because those responsible for it failed to recognise who he was (23.34a). Moreover, Luke contends, not everyone consented to this deed: the (less biased) bystanders took no delight in the event (23.35a), and one of those

---

[18] See Carroll, 'Crucifixion', 111–12.

crucified with Jesus positively took notice of the injustice done to Jesus (23.41).

Second, although no explicit reference to Jesus' trial is made, certain aspects of the crucifixion account have a clear bearing in this regard: (i) the Sanhedrin's formal request, 'If you are the Christ, tell us' (22.67), continues to be answered for the reader through the Christological emphasis of the crucifixion narrative; (ii) Pilate's triple declaration of Jesus' judicial innocence finds new support (implicitly from the crowds and explicitly from one of the criminals).

The death of Jesus (23.44–9)

The specifics of Luke's account of Jesus' death can be conveniently studied by focusing on four Lukan departures from his Markan source: his transposition of the reference to the tearing of the temple curtain, as he places it before the account of Jesus' last words and death (23.45b), rather than after it (Mark 15.38; cf. Matt. 27.51); the replacement of Jesus' cry of abandonment by God (Mark 15.34; cf. Matt. 27.46), as well as his last inarticulate cry (Mark 15.37; cf. Matt. 27.50), with a cry whereby Jesus entrusts his spirit to God (23.46); the substitution of δίκαιος for υἱὸς θεοῦ in the centurion's reaction to the events surrounding Jesus' death (23.47; Mark 15.39; cf. Matt. 27.54); and the addition of the multitudes' response to the same events (23.48).

Judging by the range of alternative explanations offered to date, the first of these changes raises by far the most exegetical difficulties, and therefore requires some special attention. D. Sylva notes that the scholars who have paid some attention to the meaning of the tearing of the curtain in the Third Gospel tend to attribute to it one or more of three meanings: (a) a portent of forthcoming destruction of the temple; (b) a sign of the abrogation of the temple and the worship associated with it; and (c) a sign expressing an idea similar to that of Hebrews 10.19–20, according to which Jesus' death opened for humanity the way to God.[19] Sylva limits his criticism of these interpretations to the observation that very little effort has been made to substantiate any of them.[20] More significant than this observation based on silence is the fact that the first two of these suggestions do not square easily with Luke's predominantly positive image of the temple, and in

[19] D. D. Sylva, 'The Temple Curtain and Jesus' Death in the Gospel of Luke', *JBL* 105 (1986), 240–1 (for bibliographical information related to each of the three positions see p. 241, n. 7).

[20] Ibid., 240–1.

particular with the positive role which the temple plays in Acts.[21] As for the third proposal, its major weakness is that there is no convincing evidence in Luke–Acts to suggest that the tearing of the curtain was understood by Luke in this way.

In addition to these three interpretations mentioned by Sylva, those offered by F. Matera, Sylva himself, and J. Green are worth noting.[22] Matera argues that Luke aims to avoid any connotation of the temple's final destruction in this event, by placing it alongside the sun's failure to give light (23.45a). He wishes rather to represent it as a portent that the 'last days' predicted by Joel 2.30 (with their 'wonders in the heavens and on earth') have been set in motion by Jesus' death.[23] The difficulty with the first part of Matera's understanding has been helpfully formulated by Green:

> If Luke has been motivated by the desire to avoid the impression that the death of Jesus is the end of the temple and its cult, why include *any* mention of the rending of the temple veil in this context? Just as Luke excised the threat of temple destruction from the account of Jesus before the Jewish council (Mark 14.57–8; Luke 22.66–71; cf. Acts 6.13–4), could he not have chosen to delete this detail here? By simply transposing the order of these two events, Jesus' death and the rending of the temple veil, has Luke really succeeded in disassociating them?[24]

As for Matera's suggestion that the torn curtain is for Luke a specific fulfilment of Joel's prophecy, a clearer allusion or reference to this passage (so Acts 2.17; cf. Joel 2.28–9) would seem necessary.

According to Sylva's interpretation, 'Luke 23:45b is primarily connected with 23:46a and ... the image that 23:45b, 46a presents is that of Jesus' communion at the last moment before his death with the Father, who is present in the temple.'[25] It is virtually impossible to prove or

---

[21] This observation has been developed most notably by F. J. Matera ('The Death of Jesus according to Luke: A Question of Sources', *CBQ* 47 (1985), 475). On Luke's view of the temple see, among others, M. Bachmann, *Jerusalem und der Tempel: Die geographischtheologischen Elemente in der lukanische Sicht des judischen Kultzentrums*, Stuttgart: Kohlhammer, 1980, *passim*; Tyson, *Death*, ch. 4; F. D. Weinert, 'The Meaning of the Temple in Luke–Acts', *BTB* 11 (1981), 85–9.

[22] For further possibilities of interpretation, see Nolland (*Luke*, vol. III, p. 1157). Additional bibliographical information in J. B. Green, 'The Demise of the Temple as "Culture Center" in Luke–Acts: An Exploration of the Rending of the Temple Veil', *RB* 101 (1994), 497–9; Sylva, 'Temple Curtain', 241, n. 7.

[23] Matera, 'Death', 475. A similar position is adopted by Brown (*Death*, vol. II, pp. 1102–6).

[24] Green, 'Demise', 498.   [25] Sylva, 'Temple Curtain', 243.

disprove the validity of Sylva's choice of punctuation of the text (inserting a full stop after 23.45a and a comma after 23.45b) and thus of his contention that the reference to the tearing of the curtain is *primarily* connected with that to Jesus' address to God. Yet he is certainly correct to note that Luke's repositioning of the curtain report associates this information with Jesus' last words in a way which is not true for the other Synoptics. We shall return to this observation later. Sylva's second remark, that 23.45b, 46a present Jesus' communion with God, is something of a truism so far as Jesus' prayer is concerned, but it is rather hard to make sense of with regard to the torn veil. Sylva substantiates and explains this by means of Stephen's parallel prayer in Acts 7.59, which happens after an opening of the heaven (7.56), but Luke gives no indication that Jesus' communion with God is made possible by the 'opening' of the veil in the same way that, it may be inferred, Stephen's communion with the enthroned Jesus is made possible by the opening of the heavens. For Stephen the heaven is open so that he can 'see' the Son of Man; for Jesus, by contrast, no such 'seeing', or any other form of access, is said to have been made possible by the torn veil. No indication is given that Jesus' communion with God is now in any way different from what it had been previously.[26]

Not satisfied with the solutions offered by source and redaction critics to this Lukan riddle, Green takes an alternative approach by paying special attention to the socio-cultural significance of the temple in Luke–Acts, and thereby argues that 'Luke portrays the rending of the temple veil as symbolic of the destruction of the symbolic world surrounding and emanating from the temple, and not as symbolic of the destruction of the temple itself.'[27] Green's approach is commendable for its efforts to integrate the reference to the torn veil with Luke's broader theology of the temple, but unfortunately it still leaves one wondering why the transposition was necessary, if Luke's concern was merely along the lines described by Green.

This leaves us, therefore, in need of a more plausible explanation of the passage. For this, I shall begin by looking for clues in the Lukan plot which has led up to the present event of Jesus' death. As noted in chapter 2, Jesus' trial and death happen as a result of his conflicts with the Jewish leaders over Torah interpretation (mainly outside Jerusalem) and

---

[26] Green makes a similar objection to Sylva's explanation, when he states that 'in the case of Jesus, access to God is available in the passion before the tearing of the curtain (cf. also 22:39–46). Already, then, Jesus was communing with "the God of the temple"' (Green, 'Demise', 503). Cf. also Brown's critique of Sylva's position (Brown, *Death*, vol. II, pp. 1104–6).

[27] Green, 'Demise', 514.

temple control (mainly in Jerusalem). Of these two, the latter is the more immediate cause of his death. His disruption of temple affairs (19.45), his bold statement of the temple's *raison d'être* (19.46), and his use of the temple as his teaching premises (19.47a; 20.1a) amount to him effectively taking possession of the temple – a right which the Jewish authorities were not willing to grant him and, therefore, decided to have him killed (19.7b; 20.19). The probable question on the readers' minds, as they encounter these accounts, is whether Jesus did or did not have the right to act in this way. This question, the evangelist must have foreseen, was likely to come into focus once again if he was to follow Mark at all in associating Jesus' death with a new temple-related incident – the torn curtain. It must have been regarded as important, therefore, how this incident was going to influence the readers' decision regarding the legitimacy of Jesus' actions in the temple.

It is along these lines, I suggest, that a solution to the riddle of the torn veil can be found. By moving this report to before the account of Jesus' death, Luke has been able to place it alongside Jesus' dying prayer (as noted by Sylva) and in this way build a twofold argument in favour of the legitimacy of Jesus' temple ministry. First, the tearing of the curtain takes the form of a symbolic act, whereby now, at Jesus' death, God himself repeats on Jesus' behalf the action which set in motion the events which brought Jesus to this point of death – Jesus was condemned for a temple disturbance (19.45), but now God himself causes an even greater temple 'disorder'. Jesus is thereby vindicated and his opponents are proved wrong. Secondly, a parallel argument is provided through Jesus' dying prayer. The temple – the readers had learnt in the controversial incident of 19.45–6 – was designed to be a 'house of prayer', so Jesus' authority in the temple is substantiated because even in his dying moments he is what he has always been (Luke 5.16; 21.37; 22.39–46) – a man of prayer. To sum up, whatever else the tearing of the temple curtain may mean in its Lukan position, one of its central functions is that of a symbol whereby God is portrayed as sanctioning Jesus' authority to transform (or, rather, reform) the temple into a house of prayer and gospel-proclamation. In the context of Luke 23, this information ties in closely with the broader theme of Jesus' innocence: far from dying as a wrongdoer, Jesus dies under the sign of divine favour. One final confirmation that this reading of the Lukan veil reference is along the right lines comes from the fact that the last verse of Luke's Gospel, as well as numerous passages in Acts (2.46; 3.1; 5.21, 25, 42), reveal Luke's concern to show how Jesus' followers did their best to preserve Jesus' correct use of the temple – as a house of prayer and as a place where God's word was correctly taught – and how this transformed use of the temple always enjoyed God's favour.[28]

The remaining three Lukan digressions from Mark have been less controversial in Lukan scholarship and therefore can be analysed more cursorily. Luke's omission of the Markan 'my God, my God, why have you forsaken me?' (Mark 15.34; cf. Ps. 22.1), as well as the subsequent 'loud cry' (Mark 15.37), in favour of 'Father, into your hands I commit my spirit!' should be understood, as indicated above, as part of Luke's emphasis on Jesus' intimacy with God through prayer. The more distant term 'God' is replaced by the much more intimate one 'Father'. Instead of the Markan words of despair, addressing a now distant 'God', one finds the tone of a confident trust in a benevolent and intimate 'Father'. Thus, the potentially unfavourable account of Jesus' death (i.e. unfavourable for the readers' perception of Jesus), becomes a (re)statement of his intimacy and favour with God.[29]

Next, Luke replaces the Markan words of the centurion, ἀληθῶς οὗτος ὁ ἄνθρωπος υἱὸς θεοῦ ἦν (Mark 15.39), with ὄντως ὁ ἄνθρωπος οὗτος δίκαιος ἦν (23.47). This apparently minor change proves to be in fact rather significant, for the presentation of Jesus as δίκαιος has long been recognised as one of the major distinctives of Luke 23.[30] G. D. Kilpatrick has been one of the first interpreters to argue that, in view of Luke's interest in Jesus' political innocence, the term should be translated as 'innocent'.[31] More recently, however, the tendency has been to argue that 'righteous' is more in line with the Lukan usage of the term (especially as in 23.50).[32] My contention is that such a mutually

---

[28] The disciples' presence in the temple is typically accompanied by God's favourable actions on their behalf (Ac. 2.47b; 5.12–16, 19–21). They are even sent by God's heavenly messengers to exercise their ministry there (Ac. 5.20). Gamaliel's words, on one occasion, are also significant in this respect (Ac. 5.38–9).

[29] Note the similar combination of prayer, Father–Son relationship, and divine favour in the baptism story (Luke 3.22).

[30] The theme has been particularly emphasised in recent years by R. J. Karris in *Luke*, ch. 5; and 'Luke 23:47' 65–74, reprinted in Sylva (ed.), *Reimaging*, pp. 68–78. There is more bibliography on this in Carroll, 'Crucifixion', 200, n. 45.

[31] G. D. Kilpatrick, 'A Theme of the Lucan Passion Story and Luke xxiii. 47', *JTS* 43 (1942), 65–74.

[32] Karris, 'Luke 23:47', in Sylva (ed.), *Reimaging*, pp. 68–71; Nolland, *Luke*, vol. III, pp. 1158–59. Particularly notable is Doble's recent argumentation at length in favour of a theological interpretation of the term, against the background of the book of Wisdom: 'Wisdom's model offered a scriptural matrix around which Luke was able to rework the passion story as a defence of Jesus' death: it was one element in God's plan of salvation. Consequently, an interpreter needs to produce very good reasons for *not* rendering δίκαιος at Luke 23.47 in a way which reflects Luke's normative twofold use, that is, a general case of God's loyal saints, within which Jesus was a special case' (*Paradox*, p. 159). For a detailed history of the interpretation of this term, see Doble, *Paradox*, pp. 70–92.

exclusive choice between these two meanings becomes redundant[33] when one takes into account Luke's common apologetic concerns in his presentation of Jesus' trial and death. As has been seen, throughout the trial narrative Luke puts forward his case for Jesus' Messiahship both through his positive presentation of his case and through his subtle refutation of possible objections. At the first level, he contends that Jesus truly is the Christ, the Son of Man, the Son of God. At the latter level, the evangelist addresses the potential objection that Jesus' condemnation may have been due to him being found guilty by the Jewish or Roman authorities or both. Correspondingly, I suggest, a major Lukan concern in the death narrative is to add weight to these apologetic emphases of the trial account. The concepts of 'righteous' and 'innocent' are, on this reading, both present in the term δίκαιος, corresponding respectively to the two levels of Lukan apologetics – the former consisting of a further statement of Jesus' Messiahship (he dies as the suffering righteous one) and the latter of a second Roman witness (following Pilate) to the fact that Jesus' death (and, implicitly, his trial) was an affront to justice.

Luke's final innovation concerns the multitudes' response to the death of Jesus. It is only Luke, of all the evangelists, who informs his readers that 'all the multitudes who assembled to see the sight, when they saw what had taken place, returned home beating their breasts' (23.48). What on two occasions has been a silent non-participation of the crowds in Jesus' crucifixion (23.27, 35) turns now into a public display of their response to Jesus' death. The exegetical discussions associated with this passage have customarily focused on what the action of the multitudes says about *themselves*, that is, whether it should be taken as indicating actual repentance or something less than that.[34] This choice of focus is understandable in the light of the openness of the passage to alternative interpretations in this area. Yet this must not be allowed to obscure what for Luke is probably the primary thrust of the passage, namely, what their response has to say about *Jesus*. It is clear that the verse is part of the long series of

[33] R. Karris' shift of position in this respect is particularly noteworthy. In his earlier monograph, his position is very similar to mine: 'Rather than get trapped in an either-or dead-end discussion, let us say that the Greek adjective *dikaios* means both "innocent" and "righteous" in 23:47' (Karris, *Luke*, p. 110). Yet, in his article, published one year later, he insists that '<u>dikaios</u> does not mean innocent, but means righteous' ('Luke 23:47', in Sylva (ed.), *Reimaging*, p. 68).

[34] In favour of the notion of repentance see Matera, 'Death', 484; Brown, *Death*, vol. II, p. 1168 (Brown is careful, however, to distinguish between their 'repentance' and the centurion's 'conversion'). Marshall, on the other hand considers it 'more likely that the action is a simple expression of grief at the death of a victim of execution, perhaps grief at his undeserved death; to read repentance into it is unjustified' (*Gospel*, p. 877). Green finds insufficient grounds to hold firmly to either position ('Demise', 500–1).

Lukan declarations of Jesus' innocence, declarations coming from Pilate, arguably Herod, the women of Jerusalem, the centurion, and, indirectly (through their non-involvement thus far), the crowds themselves. Once again, then, Luke's readers can find in the crowds new witnesses that Jesus did not deserve to die. What is much harder to decide on the basis of 23.48 alone is whether their displeasure with Jesus' death should be understood as springing merely out of the perception that this man did 'nothing worthy of death' (to use Pilate's words in 23.15) or also out of certain insights into the identity of this victim. In the light of the broader context of the passage, it can be confidently inferred that a distinction should be made between what, at a historical level, the multitudes could have meant by their action, on the basis of their limited knowledge of who Jesus was, and the reaction which is expected at this point from the readers, on the basis of the Gospel's overall characterisation of him. Thus, while from the limited perspective of the multitudes Jesus may have been simply someone who did not deserve to die because of his innocence, from the privileged perspective of the readers his death is all the more a cause for remorse (even if 'necessary' at the same time), for he is the Christ of God. The centurion's response, as discussed above, provides a useful parallel in this respect.[35]

The burial of Jesus (23.50–6)

Luke's account of Jesus' burial continues to show both Luke's dependence on Mark and his substantial reworking of the latter's material.[36] Among the various differences between the two Gospels, most significant for our purposes is Luke's characterisation of Joseph of Arimathea, both because through it one meets the most lengthy Lukan addition (23.50b–51a) and because of the explicit allusion which it makes to the earlier trial narratives.

By means of two typically Lukan formulae,[37] Joseph is brought on the scene (23.50). His place of origin is said, just as in the other Synoptics, to be Arimathea (23.51). Luke adds, however, that this is a 'town of the Jews' (i.e. belonging to Judaea). The addition is probably meant to

[35] On the literary parallel between the reaction of the centurion and that of the multitudes, see Brown, *Death*, vol. II, p. 1167.

[36] On source- and redaction-critical issues associated with this passage, see Brown, *Death*, vol. II, pp. 1226–8; Büchele, *Tod*, pp. 59–60; Fitzmyer, *Luke*, vol. II, pp. 1523–4; Marshall, *Gospel*, pp. 878–81; Nolland, *Luke*, vol. III, pp. 1162–6.

[37] Καὶ ἰδού and ἀνὴρ ὀνόματι ... (Fitzmyer, *Luke*, vol. I, p. 121; Brown, *Death*, vol. II, p. 1227).

provide geographical help for Gentile readers,[38] although a simultaneous reminder that not all Jews have rejected their Messianic king (cf. 23.3, 37–8) may also be intended.[39] Following Mark 15.43 (but this time different from Matt. 27.57 and John 19.38), Joseph is said to be 'a member of the council' (βουλευτής), that is, most certainly of the συνέδριον (22.66) which has been directly responsible for Jesus' condemnation and death.[40]

Luke's most notable change is the replacement of two terms denoting Joseph as an honourable (εὐσχήμων, Mark 15.43a) and courageous (τολμήσας, Mark 15.43b) man with a considerably lengthier description: 'a good and righteous man, who had not consented to their purpose and deed' (23.50b–51a). As often noted,[41] the first part of this description recalls the pious Jews of Luke's early chapters, such as Zechariah and Elizabeth, who were 'righteous before God' (1.6), or Simeon, who was both 'righteous and devout' (2.25) and 'looking for the consolation of Israel' (2.25; just as Joseph was 'looking for the Kingdom of God', 23.51b). The second part of Luke's addition raises the question of narrative referents for the Sanhedrin's 'purpose and deed' (τῇ βουλῇ καὶ τῇ πράξει). According to Fitzmyer, '[t]he "decision" may refer either to the plot of the chief priests and Temple officers with Judas (22.4–5) or to the sentence implied in the Council's assertion that no further testimony was needed (22:71). The "action" is the handing of Jesus over to Pilate (23:1).'[42]

There is no reason to assume that either the 'purpose' or the 'deed' must refer to such singular events. Since Jesus began his temple ministry, the 'purpose' of the Jewish leaders has been that of having Jesus killed (19.47; 20.19–20; 22.2, 4). Repeated 'action' was also taken in order to see this intention materialise (19.47–8; 20.1–8, 19–26; 22.2–6, 52–4, 66–71; 23.1–25). Correspondingly, throughout this period, or at any point(s) during it, the Lukan Joseph can be understood as having voiced his disagreement with the Sanhedrin's intentions and actions. Yet out of this long process whereby the Sanhedrin's 'purpose and deed' were geared towards Jesus' death, one can perhaps single out the time of Jesus' trial as a time when the Sanhedrin's intention of having Jesus killed was openly expressed and when formal action (especially by twisting Pilate's arm) was taken. Thus, while it would be incorrect to say that Luke's words here point *exclusively* to Jesus' trial (or any single incident), it is safe to say that they point *especially* in that direction.

---

[38] Marshall, *Gospel*, p. 880.
[39] Brown, *Death*, vol. II, p. 1228; Fitzmyer, *Luke*, vol. II, p. 1526.
[40] Fitzmyer, *Luke*, vol. II, p. 1526.   [41] E.g. Brown, *Death*, vol. II, pp. 1127–8.
[42] Fitzmyer, *Luke*, vol. II, p. 1526.

The apologetic significance of 23.51b and 23.52a now becomes clear. Through his characterisation of Joseph of Arimathea, Luke states that (i) not all Israel, not even all Jewish leaders, found Jesus worthy of death; those who bore the characteristics of godly Israelites ('good and righteous', 'looking for the Kingdom of God') showed a positive disposition towards him; (ii) the decision to have Jesus put to death (a decision which was formally reached at his trial)[43] was unjust, since the one member of the Sanhedrin who was 'just' (δίκαιος) did not consent to this decision.

Jesus' resurrection: the final vindication of the Messiah

A systematic analysis of the Lukan resurrection narrative is impossible within the limits of the present section and unnecessary for its goals.[44] I shall focus therefore on three short passages from Luke 24 (24.7, 24.20, and 24.44–7), where some reference is made to the trial of Jesus. This focus will allow, however, for considerable interaction with the rest of the resurrection account, since a reference to Jesus' trial can (notably) be found in each of the three major sections of the chapter – the resurrection morning (24.1–12), the walk to Emmaus (24.13–35), and Jesus' appearance to the group of disciples (24.36–49). Once again it is hoped that further light can be thrown on Luke's understanding of Jesus' trial, this time specifically in so far as the evangelist sees it related to Jesus' resurrection.

Luke 24.7 and the resurrection morning

Luke's reference to the angelic reminder of Jesus' passion prediction (24.7; absent in Mark) has commonly been viewed by Lukan scholarship as displaying distinctively Lukan tendencies.[45] It is thus significant for

---

[43] Although, as has been seen in the trial narrative, Luke does not record a formal death verdict being reached by the Sanhedrin (22.71; contrast Mark 14.64), their decision to hand Jesus over to Pilate is tantamount to a formal resolution that he is worthy of death.

[44] For such analyses, see especially R. J. Dillon, *From Eye-Witnesses to Ministers of the Word: Tradition and Composition in Luke 24*, Rome: Biblical Institute Press, 1978; C. F. Evans, *Resurrection and the New Testament*, SBT 2:12, London: SCM Press, 1970, pp. 92–115; C. Hickling, 'The Emmaus Story and its Sequel', in S. Barton and G. Stanton (eds.), *Resurrection: Essays in Honour of Leslie Houlden*, London: SPCK, 1994, pp. 21–33; I. H. Marshall, 'The Resurrection of Jesus in Luke', *TynB* 24 (1973), 55–68; J. I. McDonald, *The Resurrection: Narrative and Belief*, London: SPCK, 1989, pp. 95–116; J. H. Neyrey, *The Resurrection Stories*, Wilmington, DE: M. Glazier, 1987, pp. 38–60; J. Plevnik, 'The Eyewitnesses of the Risen Jesus in Luke 24', *CBQ* 49 (1987), 90–103 and 'The Origin of Easter Faith according to Luke', *Bib* 61 (1980), 492–508.

[45] In the words of Bock, 24.7 is 'one of the most important passages in the chapter' (*Luke*, vol. II, p. 1893) and '[its] uniqueness to Luke and its multiple Lucan traits lead many to regard it as a particularly Lucan summary of events' (p. 1895).

present purposes that an implicit reference to Jesus' trial can be found here.

The passage clearly recalls the Gospel's earlier passion predictions, both through the remembrance motif of 24.6, 8 and through the verbal similarities between 24.7 and the earlier predictions (9.22, 44; 18.31–3). As they are recorded here, Jesus' words focus on three events, expressed respectively through three aorist infinitives (παραδοθῆναι, σταυρωθῆναι, ἀναστῆναι), all subordinated to the impersonal δεῖ. Just as in 9.44, however, it is virtually impossible to define the specific narrative referent of Luke's παραδίδωμι[46] and, consequently, whether the present passage can be taken as a direct reference to Jesus' trial. It seems more adequate to regard the term as a broader reference to Jesus' passion, of which, of course, Jesus' trial is a major part. As for the remaining two infinitives, their referents are evidently Jesus' crucifixion and resurrection, respectively.

The question which concerns us here then becomes: to the extent that παραδοθῆναι can be taken as referring to Jesus' trial, what does the present passage have to say about Luke's understanding of this event and of its relation to Jesus' resurrection?

On the one hand, Jesus' trial, crucifixion, and resurrection are portrayed as functioning *in parallel* to each other: they all serve to confirm Jesus' Messianic identity, (i) by showing that Jesus' prophetic predictions have been fulfilled, and (ii) by indicating that God's plan (δεῖ) for 'the Son of Man' has been realised in him. On the other hand they are presented as a *progression*. The angels' gentle rebuke of the women for seeking 'the living among the dead' (24.5), as well as the sequence of the three infinitives, indicates that, according to the evangelist, Jesus' passion, just as much as his death, could not have been the fitting finale of God's plan for Jesus. The resurrection is their necessary sequel. The corollary of this observation is that the correct meaning of any of the events which had unfolded as part of Jesus' passion and death (Jesus' trial included) can only be defined in the context of a progression which ends with Jesus' resurrection.

Thus, what the Lukan account of the resurrection morning says about the earlier trial narrative is (a) that the events associated with Jesus' trial are part of a wider complex of events (spanning Jesus' passion, death, and resurrection) which represent the actualisation of God's plan for 'the Son of man', and (b) that the progressive relation between the trial and the resurrection accounts is fundamental for a correct understanding of the

---

[46] See the note on παρ αδίδοσθαι at Luke 9.44 (chapter 2).

former. Why exactly this relationship is so important and what the nature of the implied progression is (i.e. in what way the resurrection accounts take the plot of the trial narrative further) is not evident from this passage alone.

Luke 24.20 and the journey to Emmaus

The relevance of the Emmaus story for the study of Jesus' Lukan trial is established particularly by 24.20. The verse has much in common with the passion predictions (especially 9.44 and 18.32) and also with the angelic reminder of these predictions in 24.7. Unlike in 24.7, however, where παραδίδωμι lacks specificity, in 24.20 the action is undertaken by 'our chief priests and rulers'. They are those who delivered Jesus up εἰς κρίμα θανάτου (lit. 'to the verdict of death').

The use of παραδίδωμι in connection with the Jewish leaders' treatment of Jesus has often been understood as an allusion to the leaders' 'handing over' of Jesus to Pilate for judgement (23.1).[47] This reading correctly connects the verb to the account of Jesus' trial, but does not do full justice to the indirect object of the verb, which is specifically said to be 'the judgement of death', rather than the Roman authorities. As such, the sentence appears to call attention rather to the would-be 'verdict of death' of 22.71 and, even more specifically, to 23.13, 18, 21, 24–5,[48] where 'the chief priests and the rulers' (23.13; i.e. the same two groups of 24.20) repeatedly pronounce their death sentence upon Jesus – a verdict which, ironically, comes to overrule even Pilate's judgement to the contrary. In the light of these observations, it is no exaggeration to say that 24.20 is the most explicit reference to Jesus' trial to be found in the Lukan resurrection narrative. Once again, then, we are led to the question of how Luke represents Jesus' trial and its connection to Jesus' resurrection.

It has often been noted that according to 24.20 it is only the Jewish leaders,[49] and not Pilate or the Roman soldiers, who are held responsible for Jesus' death.[50] To explain this, recourse has typically been made to

---

[47] So Bock, *Luke*, vol. II, p. 1913. Marshall also sees in it 'a hint of Jesus being handed over to the Romans' (*Gospel*, p. 895).

[48] So Fitzmyer, who notes that 24.20 alludes to 22.71 and 23.24–33 (*Luke*, vol. II, p. 1564).

[49] Despite the disciples' identification of the initiators of Jesus' death as 'our' leaders, a distinction between them and the Jewish people (Weatherly, *Jewish*, pp. 68–9) is legitimate at this point, not least in view of the disciples' remorseful attitude.

[50] Bock, *Luke*, vol. II, p. 1913; Fitzmyer, *Luke*, vol. II, p. 1564; Marshall, *Gospel*, p. 895. This is not to deny Bock's and Marshall's detection of a 'hint' at the Roman involvement through the use of παραδίδωμι.

Luke's alleged pro-Roman or anti-Jewish stance or both.[51] Yet what establishes the place of 24.20 in the Emmaus story is the poignant reference to the disciples' dilemma regarding Jesus' place in salvation history. This dilemma, Luke explains, consisted of the apparently conflicting implications of Jesus' ministry on the one hand and of his trial and crucifixion on the other. Jesus' ministry, as attested by the double witness of God and 'the whole people' (24.19c), showed him to be 'a prophet mighty in deed and word' (24.19b). His trial, with the Jewish leadership as prosecutors and with crucifixion as outcome, seemed on the other hand to suggest the opposite. Thus, the disciples' dilemma is: how can they, after the events of Jesus' trial and crucifixion, continue to hold on to the belief that Israel's hopes for someone through whom God would redeem Israel have been fulfilled in the person of Jesus (24.21)? When the relationship between 24.20 and its immediate context is understood in this way, Luke's focus on the Jewish, rather than Roman, involvement in Jesus' death is understandable without resorting to political apologetic or antisemitism for an explanation: it is Jesus' rejection by Jewish, rather than Roman, authorities that poses the real Messianic dilemma for Luke's characters: not only has Jesus died, but he has died at the initiative of those who should have the been most competent to recognise his Messianic vocation.

As far as Luke's readers are concerned, this dilemma ceases to exist precisely at the point when it has been exposed. Once again they are in a more privileged position than the Lukan characters, for while the disciples' eyes were for the time being 'kept from recognising' the risen Lord (24.16), the readers know all along who the enigmatic traveller is. Unlike the disciples, who have to rely on some hard-to-believe rumours (24.22–4), they already know that the story of Jesus did not finish with the 'verdict of death', but that a dramatic reversal of this verdict has been introduced through Jesus' resurrection and that this reversal has no small significance for the question of his identity and his role in salvation history. Thus the memory of Jesus' trial and its aftermath, which for the two disciples is a question mark on their previous beliefs about him, for the Lukan readers becomes a pointer to the ultimate confirmation of Jesus as the Messiah. Verse 26 usefully summarises Luke's solution to the dilemma of verse 20: far from contradicting the testimony of his ministry, Jesus' trial and crucifixion confirm him as 'the Christ', for they (i) represent the fulfilment of what, according to the divine plan, the Christ had to suffer (24.26a) and (ii) point forward to the reversal of the death sentence in Jesus' glorification (24.26b). Thus the element of progression

---

[51] J. T. Sanders, *Jews*, p. 10.

in the way Jesus' trial and his resurrection function in relation to each other[52] becomes much clearer at this point: Jesus' resurrection-exaltation comes *after his trial and therefore as a reversal of it.*

In summary, the Emmaus episode portrays Jesus' trial as a major challenge to the evidence of Jesus' ministry (24.19) and to its Christological implications (24.21), and as the springboard for the final confirmation of these assertions in Jesus' resurrection (24.26).

Luke 24.44–7 and Jesus' appearance to the group of disciples

In words which are without parallel in the other Gospels, 24.44–7[53] relates Jesus' address to the group of disciples in Jerusalem (24.33), given after his appearance in their midst and his dealing with their doubts regarding the physicality of his resurrection (24.36–43). The message of these verses is evidently similar to that of 24.7, 26 and continues to build on the earlier passion predictions. A few brief observations should therefore suffice.

Once again Luke places great emphasis on the prophecy-fulfilment relationship which exists between the Jewish Scriptures[54] and certain aspects of Jesus' story (24.44). Which parts of the story are particularly on the author's mind at the time becomes clear only in 24.46, through the specification of his passion (παθεῖν, 'to suffer') and resurrection (ἀναστῆναι ἐκ νεκρῶν). As in 22.7, only indirect reference to Jesus' trial is made – this time by virtue of the trials being part of his πάθημα. Again, as in 22.7, Jesus' passion and his resurrection are represented as affirmative of his Messianic status (specifically expressed now through the use of 'the Christ') by virtue of their confirmation of Jesus' prophetic predictions (24.44a), and by their correspondence with the Scriptures' predictions of the Messiah (24.46).

---

[52] See the comments on 24.7 above.

[53] Although it is possible to argue for the existence of chronological breaks both before and after verse 44 (Creed, *Luke*, p. 300; Marshall, *Gospel*, p. 904; A. Plummer, *A Critical and Exegetical Commentary on the Gospel according to St Luke*, ICC, Edinburgh: T. & T. Clark; New York: Scribner, 1896, p. 561), Luke has so connected the various incidents of this part of the narrative that 24.36–53 functions as a literary unit (Fitzmyer, *Luke*, vol. II, pp. 1572–3, 1578).

[54] Although it is doubtful that for Luke the Psalms stand for the whole of the Jewish *Kĕtûbîm* (Fitzmyer, *Luke*, vol. II, p. 1583), the reference to 'the law of Moses and the prophets and the psalms' (24.44) most certainly reflects the Jewish tripartite division of the Scriptures and thus it is meant to indicate their *entirety*, which is said to bear witness to Jesus (Bock, *Luke*, vol. II, pp. 1936–7).

The new element here is that to the two items – Jesus' passion and resurrection – which are said to have been predicted by the Scriptures and to which repeated reference has been made through the various passion predictions, a third one is now added: 'and that repentance and forgiveness of sins should be preached in his name to all nations, beginning from Jerusalem' (24.47). This is a rather intriguing addition, since it is clear that this element cannot function in Luke's argument in exactly the same way as the first two. If it is true that the function of these two is, like in all the passion predictions, to confirm Jesus' Messiahship through a prophecy-fulfilment argumentation, it becomes evident that the third element cannot be used in the same way, for it simply has not happened yet. Rather, its function becomes evident if the logic of Luke's argumentation in 24.46–7 runs roughly as follows:

(1)   Jesus' passion and resurrection show him to be the Christ, for the Scriptures had predicted these things about the Christ.
(2)   If Jesus is indeed the Christ, then whatever else the Scriptures have predicted about the Christ must also come to fulfilment *in the person of Jesus* and will inevitably do so under divine approval.
(3)   As it is, the Scriptures have also predicted that 'repentance and forgiveness of sins [would] be preached in his [Christ's] name to all the nations, beginning from Jerusalem'.
(4)   Therefore, one must expect and accept (i) that 'repentance and forgiveness of sins' will be preached *in the name of Jesus*; (ii) that this preaching will go 'to all the nations'; and (iii) that this mission to the nations will not be a breach with the Jewish tradition but some kind of extension of it.

If this representation of Luke's argument in these verses is along the right lines, the role of 24.47 is to prepare the reader to see and accept the legitimacy of the Christian witness (about to be narrated in Acts) both in its content (proclaiming repentance and forgiveness in the name of Jesus) and in its geographical or ethnical target (beyond the boundaries of Judaism, albeit in continuity with it). Accordingly, Jesus' trial, as part of the more general passion–resurrection series of events, has the twofold apologetic function of confirming Jesus' Christological status (24.44, 46) and, by extension, of attesting the validity of the Christian witness (24.47).

The trial of Jesus in Acts
Jesus' trial and Peter's Pentecost address (2.22–4, 36)

The first reference to Jesus' trial in Acts comes as part of Peter's Pentecost address to the multitude of Jews[55] who had gathered to see the unusual manifestations[56] amongst the group of disciples.[57] The first half of Peter's speech (2.14–21) is an explanation of the Pentecost events as the fulfilment of Joel's prophecy (Joel 3.1–5, LXX). With verse 22, however, Peter's speech takes an abrupt Christological turn, so that the whole of the second half (2.22–36) becomes an extended argument that 'God has made [this Jesus] both Lord and Christ' (2.36). Jesus' resurrection (2.24–32), his exaltation to/by[58] the right hand of God (2.33a, 34–5) and his outpouring of the Holy Spirit (2.33b; cf. 2.16–18) are all proofs of this reality. The outcome of this whole argumentation is that the hearers were 'cut to the heart' (2.37) and a great number of them became disciples (2.41).

It is in the context of this Christological argument in the second half of Peter's speech, that reference to Jesus' trial is made. Jesus is said to have been 'handed over (ἔκδοτον) by the definite plan and foreknowledge of God' (2.23a). The use of the verbal adjective ἔκδοτος has commonly been understood as a possible reference to Jesus being handed over by the Jews to the Romans for trial.[59] At a *prima facie* reading this suggestion does not appear particularly convincing, since τῇ ὡρισμένῃ βουλῇ καὶ προγνώσει τοῦ θεοῦ indicates that what is in view here is the cosmic,

---

[55] It is difficult to decide whether εἰς Ἰερουσαλὴμ κατοικοῦντες Ἰουδαῖοι of 2.5 (cf. 2.9–11) refers to permanent residents of Jerusalem and its surroundings (Haenchen, *Acts*, p. 168, n. 7; Matera, 'Responsibility', 79) or to pilgrims gathered in Jerusalem for the feast (Bruce, *Acts*, p. 115; Marshall, *Acts* (1980), p. 70; J. T. Sanders, *Jews*, p. 233).

[56] Acts 2.6.

[57] Quite possibly πάντες of 2.1 refers to the larger group of one hundred and twenty (1.15), not just to the (now) twelve apostles (1.26) (so Marshall, *Acts* (1980), p. 68; more tentatively Barrett, *Acts*, vol. I, p. 112).

[58] Opinion is divided on whether τῇ δεξιᾷ should be viewed as a dative of instrument or of place. For the former position, see: Barrett, *Acts*, vol. I, p. 149; Bruce, *Acts*, p. 126; J. Dupont, *Etudes sur les Actes des Apôtres*, Paris: Cerf, 1984, pp. 302–4. For the latter, see: D. M. Hay, *Glory at the Right Hand: Psalm 110 in Early Christianity*, Nashville: Abingdon, 1973, pp. 70–3; M. Gourges, *A la droite de Dieu. Résurrection de Jésus et actualisation du psaume 110:1 dans le Nouveau Testament*, Paris: Gabalda, 1978, pp. 164–9; Turner, *Power*, p. 275.

[59] So Barrett, who is 'uncertain whether this word refers to the betrayal of Jesus to the Jews by Judas or to the Jews' treachery to their fellow countryman in handing him over to the Romans' (*Acts*, vol. I, p. 142). Similarly Bruce: 'The reference may be to Jesus' being "handed over" by the will of God to his enemies (cf. Rom. 8:22), or to his being handed over by the Jewish authorities to the Romans' (*Acts*, p. 123). Cf. also my earlier discussion of the similar function of παραδίδωμι in Luke 24.7, 20.

rather than the historical, level of events.[60] Yet 2.23b makes it clear that
the cosmic level corresponds to a historical one, and that the historical
event which is on the author's mind is precisely Jesus' Roman trial, for it
was there that the Jewish leaders twisted 'the hand/arm of lawless men',
and thus brought about Jesus' crucifixion.

Moving to the actual representation of Jesus' trial in Peter's address,
several points can be noted. First, at a historical level the trial runs counter
to the evidence of Jesus' ministry, during which God himself bore witness to Jesus' identity (2.22). The whole point of Peter's accusation in
2.23 is that the Jews had acted against God's explicit attestation[61] of
Jesus. Secondly, from God's perspective the trial was, however, nothing but the fulfilment of his plan for Jesus (2.23a). Thus, rather ironically, even as the trial posed its human challenge to Jesus' identity, God
continued to 'attest' him. Thirdly, the sentence of death, reached at Jesus' trial and carried out in his execution, was finally and definitively
reversed by God, as he resurrected and exalted Jesus, thereby establishing him as 'Lord and Christ' (2.24–36). Finally, the use of the second
person plural with reference to the Jewish involvement in Jesus' trial
(2.23b, 36) establishes the responsibility of Peter's audience for Jesus'
crucifixion.[62] The role of this is to highlight a contrast not between Jews
and Romans[63] (since it is through Roman 'hands'[64] that the Jews are said
to have achieved their purpose) but between Jesus' opponents and the God

---

[60] In the words of S. J. Kistemaker, 'God himself handed Jesus over to the Jews' (*Exposition of the Acts of the Apostles*, New Testament Commentary, Grand Rapids: Baker, 1990,
p. 94).

[61] Although translators disagree on how ἀποδεδειγμένον should be rendered ('accred-
ited' (NIV), 'attested' (RSV), 'singled out . . . and made known' (NEB)), the basic meaning
of the sentence remains reasonably clear: God, through various works of power, made it
plain that Jesus was the man of his choice.

[62] In view of Peter's address being located in Jerusalem (where Jesus' trial also took
place) and apparently being given not very long after the crucifixion-Pentecost (Barrett
regards the healing episode as 'a specific illustration of the τέρατα καὶ σημεῖα of 2:43'
(*Acts*, vol. I, p. 174)), it is not impossible that Luke's readers could have been expected
to understand that some of Peter's audience were among the λαός of Luke 23.13. More
probably, however, they are regarded as sharing a corporate responsibility by virtue of being
ἄνδρες 'Ισραηλῖται (2.22; cf. 3.12). Weatherly's efforts to show that Luke has in mind
here only the Jews of Jerusalem (*Jewish*, pp. 75, 83–4) are rather ambitious in view of
(i) the absence of such a distinction in these verses and (ii) the identification of the audience
as those among whom Jesus had performed 'mighty works and wonders and signs' (activities
which in Luke's Gospel happen only outside Jerusalem).

[63] The customary exegetical remarks about Jewish responsibility versus Roman instru-
mentality (e.g. Haenchen, *Acts*, p. 180; Kistemaker, *Acts*, p. 94; cf. J. T. Sanders, *Jews*,
p. 10) could easily be understood as suggesting that Luke intended to draw a comparison
between the attitude of the Jews and that of the Romans.

[64] Although ἄνομος ('lawless') was commonly used by Jews with reference to Gentiles
in general (see W. Gutbrod, 'νόμος', *TDNT*, vol. IV, pp. 1086–7), in its present context

who 'attested' Jesus as 'Lord and Christ' (2.22, 36).[65] The function of this
contrast, the passage further reveals, was not to condemn the listeners[66]
but to serve as the basis for their repentance, forgiveness, and salvation
(2.37–40).

Jesus' trial and Peter's explanation of a lame man's healing
(a) *Peter's address to the Jewish public (3.13–18)*

The healing of a lame man outside the temple gate (3.1–10) provided
Peter and John with the opportunity of offering to the amazed crowd an
explanation of the event (2.11–26). The core of Peter's explanation is that
the healing has not been performed by means of their personal qualities
(3.12), but rather through the name of Jesus (who is now glorified and
therefore has the authority to perform such miracles) and through faith
in his name (3.13a, 16). It is clear, however, that the Lukan Peter is not
content merely to clarify for the audience how the healing was possible.
Rather, just as in the case of the Pentecost address, he goes out of his
way to turn the explanation of a miraculous incident into a Christological
discourse.

At the centre of this discourse stands a rather detailed reminder of Jesus'
trial (3.13b–15, 17–18). The following features establish the character
and significance of the trial for Peter's audience and, in turn, for Luke's
readers:

(1)   Once again Peter's audience is held responsible for what hap-
      pened at Jesus' trial (3.13–15, 17; cf. 2.22, 36).[67]
(2)   The Jewish judgement with regard to Jesus was completely re-
      versed by God's action, as he 'glorified his servant Jesus'[68]

---

the term clearly denotes the Romans, for they were those 'without a/the law' who were
instrumental in Jesus' execution (cf. Barrett, *Acts*, vol. I, p. 142; Bruce, *Acts*, p. 123).

[65] So Matera, 'Responsibility', 78.

[66] As stressed by J. T. Sanders, *Jews*, pp. 10, 39, 51.

[67] Again Weatherly's insistence that it is only the Jerusalemites that are held responsible
has insufficient textual support (*Jewish*, pp. 82, 85), while J.T. Sanders' interpretation of
the passage as antisemitic (*Jews*, pp. 236–8) ignores the ample evidence that the notion of
Jewish responsibility is developed in the passage not for condemnation's sake but in order
to lead to the Jews' turning to Christ (3.19–26). See on this the discussion in sections (6)
and (8) below; cf., for example, Franklin, *Christ*, pp. 101–2.

[68] According to Haenchen, '[t]he glorification which Luke has in mind is not that of the
resurrection but that of the miracle peformed in Jesus' name', for it would be 'nonsense for
the statement "It is not we who have healed this man" to be followed by "but God raised
Jesus"' (*Acts*, p. 205, text and n. 3). This position is hardly convincing, since Luke's logic
is that '[t]he cripple had been cured *because* Jesus had been glorified' (F. F. Bruce, *Book of
Acts*, revised edition, Grand Rapids: Eerdmans, 1988, p. 80, italics mine). Thus, it seems

(3.13a; the statement clearly alludes to the Servant of Isaiah 52.13[69] and thus points to God's confirmation of Jesus' Messiahship) and 'raised [him] from the dead'(3.15).

(3)   Not only God, but even Pilate disagreed with the Jewish judgement about Jesus (3.13b). This information has the potential both for a political apologia and for adding weight to the more dominant contention of the speech: the inappropriateness of the Jewish rejection of Jesus (with its corollary, as we shall see, in the call for their acceptance of him).[70]

(4)   Their rejection of Jesus amounted to a denial of him as the 'holy and righteous one' (3.14a), terms which are not simply a reflection on his moral status and legal innocence but are also Christological categories.[71]

(5)   The fallacy of the Jewish judgement at Jesus' trial, as they 'denied' him, is once again revealed by their parallel call for a murderer's release (3.14b).

(6)   Yet their judgement was made 'in ignorance' (κατὰ ἄγνοιαν, 3.17) – an ignorance which against the backdrop of the passage and of Lukan thought would not have been total (in view of the revealing character of Jesus' ministry, 2.22), but would nonetheless have been significant, since the definite vindication of Jesus' identity only came through his resurrection-exaltation (2.36; 5.31), which has now been confirmed through events such as Pentecost or the healing of the lame man.[72] The remark has a double significance. On the one hand it suggests that Peter's aim, as he renders his audience responsible for Jesus' death (3.13b–15), is not to condemn them but to win them over for Jesus the Christ – a conciliatory approach which is also evident in Peter's address to them as 'brethren'. On the other hand, precisely the circumstances which attenuated the responsibility of the Jews at

best to understand the passage as referring to Jesus' exaltation as last described by Luke in Acts 2.33a, 36.

[69]   Barrett, *Acts*, vol. I, p. 194; Marshall, *Acts* (1980), p. 91; et al.

[70]   The thought might be similar to that of Paul in Romans 11.11: it is hoped that salvation may be brought to ethnic Israel by stirring them to jealousy as they see the positive response of the Gentiles.

[71]   Haenchen refers to τὸν ἅγιον καὶ δίκαιον as 'messianic epithets' (*Acts*, p. 206). Barrett is reluctant to regard them primarily as Christological categories, but still thinks it 'safe to say that the adjectives were chosen as conveying some hint of Messianic status...' (*Acts*, vol. I, p. 196).

[72]   Thus, there is no need to attribute the presence of 3.17 after 2.22 to Luke's poor assimilation of his sources (*pace* Haenchen, *Acts*, p. 207) (for further insights into Luke's notion of ignorance here, see Marshall, *Acts* (1980), p. 92).

the time of Jesus' trial enhance it at the time of Peter's preaching (and, for that matter, at the time of Luke's readers' acquaintance with these facts), for on this side of Jesus' resurrection-exaltation all excuses are gone.

(7) Once again Jesus' suffering (trial included) is portrayed as confirming Jesus' Messiahship by virtue of its fulfilment of God's plan for his Christ (3.18).

(8) The Jewish realisation of their role in Jesus' trial ought to lead them to repentance (3.19a; note the connection with the foregoing through οὖν) – both because they *must* (they sinned by rejecting Jesus) and because they *may* (they acted in ignorance) do so. The notion of repentance, emphatically expressed through the combination of μετανοεῖν and ἐπιστρέφειν,[73] should most certainly be understood here specifically as a reversal of their position with regard to Jesus – from rejection to acceptance of him as the Christ, the eschatological leader of the people of God (3.22a), allegiance to whom is now the condition for belonging to the people of God (3.22b–23). Such a repentance, the passage further reveals, would lead to the forgiveness of their sins (εἰς τὸ ἐξαλειφθῆναι ὑμῶν τὰς ἁμαρτίας, lit. 'for the wiping away of your sins', 3.19b) and, in turn, to 'times of refreshing' (καιροὶ ἀνα ψ ύξεως) and the sending of 'the Christ foreordained for you, Jesus' (3.19c, 20), with the former referring probably to moments of spiritual blessing, which would refresh God's people during the otherwise difficult period before the Parousia,[74] and the latter to the second coming of Christ,[75] when the Jews who

[73] Barrett helpfully summarises the relationship between the two: 'If there is a distinction between μετανοεῖν and ἐπιστρέφειν it will be that the former signifies a turning away from evil and the latter a turning towards good, or rather, in biblical usage, towards God. But the doubling of the verb . . . is probably no more than a means of emphasis' (*Acts*, vol. I, pp. 202–3).

[74] So C. K. Barrett, 'Faith and Eschatology in Acts 3', in E. Grüsser and O. Merk (eds.), *Glaube und Eschatologie: Festschrift für Werner Georg Kümmel zum 80. Geburtstag*, Tübingen: J. C. B. Mohr, 1985, pp. 10–13; C. K. Barrett, *Acts*, vol. I, p. 205; Turner, 'Acts 3 and the Christology of Luke–Acts', in 'Acts', unpublished papers for Open Theological College, n.d., 3–4; contra J. Calvin (*Commentary upon the Acts of the Apostles*, ed., H. Beveridge, vol. I, Grand Rapids: Eerdmans, 1949, p. 150), H. Conzelmann (*Acts of the Apostles*, translated by J. Limburg *et alii*, Philadelphia: Fortress, 1987, p.29), and others, who see καιρ οἱ ἀναψ ύξεως as referring to the final time of salvation, when Jesus will be sent as Messiah (3.20b). Barrett's valid objection to this interpretation is that '[i]t does not do justice to the plural καιροί (a number of specific points in time) or to the meaning of ἀνα ψ ύξις, which suggests temporary relief rather than finality (*Acts*, vol. I, p. 205).

[75] J. A. T. Robinson (*Twelve New Testament Studies*, SBT 34, London: SCM Press, 1962, pp. 139–53) has argued that τὸν προκεχειρισμένον ὑμῖν χριστόν means that Jesus was

believe will enjoy the final consummation of the long-awaited Messianic age.[76]

To summarise, Jesus' trial is portrayed as the event whereby Israel as a nation, through its representatives, formally rejected Jesus' Christological attributes, an event which now, in the light of God's explicit and contrary verdict in the matter, should become the basis for Israel's repentance and blessing through their acceptance of Jesus as the promised Messiah.

(b) *Peter's address to the Jewish authorities (4.10–11)*

For the second time Peter offers an explanation of the lame man's healing, but this time no longer at the prompting of a benevolent crowd but at the request of a hostile Jewish leadership, composed of 'rulers and elders and scribes' (τοὺς ἄρχοντας καὶ τοὺς πρεσβυτέρους καὶ τοὺς γραμματεῖς)[77] – the three groups most certainly denoting the Jewish Sanhedrin.[78] The Christological emphasis of Peter's explanation is this time made inevitable by the Sanhedrin's question: ἐν ποίᾳ δυμάμει ἢ ἐν ποίῳ ὀνόματι ἐποιήσατε τοῦτο ὑμεῖς; (4.7b; cf. 4.9b). Peter's response takes broadly the same form as in his earlier address to the crowds. As then, albeit this time following much more directly from their question, Peter affirms that the healing was performed ἐν τῷ ὀνόματι Ἰησοῦ Χριστοῦ τοῦ Ναζωραίου and ἐν τούτῳ (with the latter referring either to τῷ ὀνόματι or to Ἰησου; the choice between the two hardly affects the meaning). Two parallel pairs of contrasting statements are made about Jesus:

A1. ὃν ὑμεῖς ἐσταυρώσατε (4.10c)
B1. ὃν ὁ θεὸς ἤγειρεν ἐκ νεκρῶν (4.10d)
A2. ὁ ἐξουθενηθεὶς ὑφ᾽ ὑμῶν τῶν οἰκοδόμων (4.11b)
B2. ὁ γενόμενος εἰς κεφαλὴν γωνίας (4.11c)

---

yet to become the Messiah (at the Parousia). However, this interpretation not only is contrary to Lukan thought (both in the present passage and elsewhere) but also fails to do justice to the perfect tense of the verb which indicates that Jesus' appointment as the Messiah *has already* taken place (Barrett, *Acts*, vol. I, p. 204; Bruce, *Acts*, p. 144).

[76] Marshall, *Acts* (1980), pp. 93–4. It is possible, however, that this contains the additional thought that (the) repentance (of the Jews) would hasten the Parousia – a thought similar to that of 2 Peter 3.12 (so Conzelmann, *Acts*, p. 208; Kistemaker, *Acts*, p. 135).

[77] The genitive pronoun αὐτῶν in '*their* rulers' seems to refer to the (Jewish) converts of 4.4, but it can also be understood as referring to 'the Jews' in general (Barrett, *Acts*, vol. I, p. 223).

[78] Ibid.

Although the reference to Jesus' trial is here less explicit than in Acts 3, the statements about the Jewish crucifixion and rejection of Jesus could hardly point to anything else. First, despite occasional ambiguities,[79] it remains clear that elsewhere (e.g. 2.23b) Luke thinks of Jesus' actual crucifixion as being carried out by Romans and not by Jews, so the Jews' 'crucifixion' of Jesus must refer to the fact that *in effect* they produced it by taking Jesus to Pilate and pressing their case for Jesus' death – actions which were part of the trial.[80] Second, it was at the trial that the same Jewish Sanhedrin which now judges Peter and John formally and finally rejected Jesus as the Christ.

The representation of Jesus' trial in these verses is also similar to that in Acts 3. (1) The healing of the lame man 'in the name of Jesus' is a visible indication that God has exalted Jesus and thereby reversed the Jewish leaders' formal rejection of him in the context of his trial. This is the logic of the double contrast.[81] (2) The contrast between the Jewish leaders' position and that of God is not simply one between the condemnation and the exculpation of an innocent man, but one between the rejection and the affirmation of Jesus as the promised Messiah; there can be little doubt that Luke intends these events to be read as the fulfilment of a Messianic passage.[82] (3) The implication of Jesus' vindication by God (an implication much more likely to benefit Luke's readers than Peter's listeners) is that it is only in Jesus and through his name that salvation is now made available (4.12). Thus, in a briefer form than in Acts 3, Luke again portrays Jesus' trial as the event through which the Jewish leaders have rejected Jesus as their Messiah, but in spite of this and, from God's perspective, *because* of it[83] there is now salvation available to everyone in his 'name' (alone).

Jesus' trial and the prayer of a threatened community (4.27–8)

Peter and John's clash with the Jewish authorities is a cause for some concern among 'their own' (οἱ ἴδιοι, 4.23), who, as a result of this, turn

---

[79] Luke 23.25–6, for instance, appears to suggest that the Jews carried out the execution (as argued, among others, by J. T. Sanders, *Jews*, pp. 9–13), although the presence of the centurion in 23.47 eliminates the ambiguity.

[80] Weatherly, *Jewish*, p. 69.

[81] Although Luke (and Ps. 118.22, which he quotes) does not explain *how* the rejected stone 'has become the head of the corner', the parallelism noted above indicates that the 'becoming', just as much as the resurrection, is to be attributed to the action of God.

[82] The widespread use of Psalm 118.22 (117.22, LXX) as a Messianic 'proof-text' in the early church is indicated by its frequent occurrence in the New Testament (explicit quotations in Matt. 21.42; Mark 12.10; Luke 20.17; 1 Pet. 2.7; allusions in Mark 8.31; Luke 9.22; 17.25; 1 Pet. 2.4) and once in Barnabas 6.4 (Barrett, *Acts*, vol. I, pp. 229–30).

[83] This is how God's plan, revealed in Scriptures such as Psalm 118.22, has been fulfilled.

to God in prayer. It is as part of this prayer that explicit reference to Jesus' trial is once again made (4.27–8). The picture of the trial which emerges from these verses and their context is defined by the following features:

(1) Major emphasis is placed on the fact that Jesus' trial represents the fulfilment of God's will. This is done (a) by pointing out the correspondence between David's divinely inspired utterances about God's Anointed One (τοῦ χριστοῦ αὐτοῦ) and the events which have come to pass as part of Jesus' trial (4.25–7; Ps. 2.1–2), and (b) by stating that these events have accomplished precisely what God had predestined to happen (4.28).

(2) Somewhat differently from most Lukan accounts of Jesus' trial analysed so far (Luke 23.1–25; 24.20; Ac. 2.22–3, 36; 3.13–15; 4.10–11; a possible exception is Luke 24.7), where the responsibility (at a human level) for Jesus' condemnation appears to lie primarily, and sometimes exclusively, with Jewish groups, here the balance seems to swing to the Gentile side. It is the 'nations' (ἔθνη) who 'rage' and the 'peoples' (λαοί) who 'plot vain things' (4.25). It is the 'kings of the earth' and its rulers – soon identified as Herod and Pilate – who 'set themselves in array' and 'gather together against the Lord and his Anointed One' (4.26–7). By contrast, it is only once that the 'peoples of Israel' (λαοῖς Ἰσραήλ)[84] are also mentioned, alongside the 'Gentiles' (ἔθνεσιν), as Jesus' opponents (4.27b). Haenchen concludes in light of this that 'the verdict passed on Pilate by the psalm-exegesis [present in Luke's source] was at odds with [Luke's] own theology, which (as we have seen in connection with 3.13) sought to exculpate the governor'.[85] It is intriguing, however, that Haenchen should be happier to regard the text as a breach of the assumed Lukan 'theology' of an innocent Pilate than to question the existence or dominance of such a tenet of Lukan theology.[86] My analysis of Jesus' trial so far has suggested that while elements of such a 'theology' (or, more accurately, apologetic) can often be noted, they never seem to determine the main thrust of the trial account, but are subordinate to Luke's much more dominant apologia for Jesus' Messianic identity and role. On this reading, the present passage is a clear example of the latter type of apologia taking precedence over the former.

---

[84] The plural λαοῖς Ἰσραήλ probably makes best sense if understood in the sense of 'tribes of Israel' (so Haenchen, *Acts*, p. 227).

[85] Ibid., p. 228.

[86] Equally problematic are J. T. Sanders' attempts to obscure Luke's reference to Roman complicity (*Jews*, pp. 12–13). See Weatherly, *Jewish*, pp. 92–4 for a critique of Sanders' exegesis and for his own interpretation of the passage, according to which 'Luke throws the net of responsibility beyond the circle of the Jews in Jerusalem. Pilate, Herod and unnamed ἔθνη are among those who gathered in Jerusalem to accomplish God's purpose in the passion of Jesus' (p. 94).

(3) The remembrance of Jesus' trial serves as the basis for the Christian community's hope and prayer that the God who on that occasion reversed the evil intentions of Jesus' adversaries and used them to confirm (through their ironic fulfilment of God's plan) Jesus as his Christ (4.25b–28), will once again turn the present 'threats' – aimed at preventing further proclamation 'in the name of Jesus' (4.17b, 18) – into new occasions when the 'word' is proclaimed and its claims (especially those of a Christological nature) are attested by miracles in the name of Jesus (4.29–30).[87]

Jesus' trial and the apostles' determination to preach (5.28, 30–1)

Once again proclamation in the name of Jesus (5.28; cf. 4.18) leads to conflict between the apostles (this time not only Peter and John, but the whole apostolic group, 5.18) and the Jewish Sanhedrin (συνέδριον, 5.27). Two elements of the dialogue between the two groups call attention to Jesus' trial. First, the Sanhedrin's specific charge against the apostles is that, through their preaching, the apostles are said to 'intend to bring upon us this man's blood' (βούλεσθε ἐπαγαγεῖν ἐφ' ἡμᾶς τὸ αἷμα τοῦ ἀνθρώπου τούτου, 5.28b). Second, Peter, the apostles' spokesman, reiterates a very similar idea when he speaks of Jesus as the one 'whom you killed by hanging him on a tree' (ὃν ὑμεῖς διεχειρίσασθε κρεμάσαντες ἐπὶ ξύλου, 5.30b). In both of these instances attention is called to the fact that the Jewish authorities are those who killed Jesus. Yet since, as has been repeatedly noted, Luke shows clear awareness of the fact that the actual crucifixion was carried out by the Romans, the event to which the two present references to Jesus' death point cannot be other than Jesus' trial, namely, the decision of the Jewish Sanhedrin to hand Jesus over to Pilate and to press a death sentence against him.[88]

Two major statements are made about Jesus' trial. First, once again the Lukan Peter sets the Jewish treatment of Jesus in sharp contrast to God's

---

[87] In every instance in Acts so far, where miracles are said to have been performed by or in the name of Jesus, part of their function has been the implicit confirmation of the Christian claim that Jesus has been vindicated by God and, as such, is now the one through whom forgiveness and salvation are available (Ac. 2.33, 36; 3.13, 16; 4.10–12). It seems fair to assume, then, that here too the role of these hoped-for miracles 'in the name of [God's] holy servant Jesus' would be (partially at least) to affirm the believers' claims about Jesus.

[88] Agabus' prophecy (Ac. 21.11) provides an interesting parallel. The prophet speaks of the Jews delivering Paul into the hands of the Gentiles, when a few verses later Paul is rescued by Romans from the Jews (21.27–36). The meaning of the prophecy, most certainly, is that the Jewish opponents are ultimately responsible for Paul's Roman chains (Marshall, *Acts* (1980), p. 340).

action. While the Jews killed Jesus, God 'raised' (ἤγειρεν)[89] him and 'exalted him to/by[90] his right hand as leader and saviour' (ἀρχηγὸν καὶ σωτῆρ αὔψωσεν τῇ δεξιᾷ αὐτοῦ). Moreover, the specification that Jesus was exalted 'as leader and saviour' indicates that for Luke the contrast between the Jewish attitude and God's is not simply over the issue of Jesus' innocence, but, much more significantly, over the matter of Jesus' role for the people of God.[91]

Second, God's intention for the Jews in general and Jewish lead-ers in particular, as he reversed their verdict on Jesus, was not their condemnation, as the Sanhedrin took the apostolic preaching to imply (5.28b), but 'to give' (δοῦναι) in this way repentance and forgive-ness to Israel (5.31b).[92] True, the responsibility of the Jewish leaders (5.28b) remains (it is in fact reinforced by Peter in 5.30b), and yet the very purpose of the apostles' kerygma is that this responsibility may not turn into condemnation but will rather lead to repentance and forgiveness.

Jesus' trial and Stephen's discourse before the Sanhedrin (7.52)

The history of ethnic Israel, as told by Stephen, is a history of rejection of God's prophets (7.9, 25, 35, 39), so much so that prophetic identity and rejection by the Jewish nation have become two inseparable cat-egories: 'Which of the prophets did your fathers not persecute?' The last in this line of rejected prophets, the one of whose coming the other prophets had in fact spoken (5.52b), is Jesus, whom Stephen describes as ὁ δίκαιος, οὗ νῦν ὑμεῖς προδόται καὶ φονεῖς ἐγένεσθε (lit. 'the righteous one, whose betrayers and murderers you have now become', 5.52c). Thus, Jesus' trial is brought into view as the event where the

---

[89] It is not entirely clear whether ἤγειρεν should be understood as a reference to Jesus' resurrection (so Kistemaker, *Acts*, p. 205; Marshall, *Acts* (1980), p. 119; cf. Ac. 3.26; 13.33–4) or to him being 'raised up' on the scene of history in the same way as David was (Ac. 13.22; so Bruce, *Book*, p. 112). In view of the parallel passages in Luke, where the action of the Jews is contrasted to that of God (Ac. 2.23–4; 3.15; 4.10), the former is most certainly to be preferred, but the choice between the two alternatives is not particularly crucial for our argument. Either way, God's action towards Jesus is one of favour, and thus in contrast with that of the Jewish authorities.

[90] On the translation of τῇ δεξιᾷ αὐτου, see note 58 on Acts 2.32.

[91] Attention has often been called to the Mosaic typology as a context for the depic-tion of Jesus here (R. H. Fuller, *The Foundations of New Testament Christology*, London: Lutterworth, 1965, p. 48; Marshall, *Acts* (1980), p. 120; cf. Ac. 7.35).

[92] Following Plümacher, Barrett refers to this verse as 'an admirable summary of Lucan theology' (Barrett, *Acts*, vol. I, p. 290).

Jewish authorities had 'betrayed' Jesus by handing him over to Pilate and 'killed' him through their insistent calls for his crucifixion.[93]

The significance of the trial, according to this passage, consists of the following: (1) It was at Jesus' trial that Israel's habitual rejection of God's prophets was once again, and this time most notably, actualised. (2) What gives this event its unique character is not so much the condemnation of an innocent man (although that is inevitably implied in the depiction of Jesus as δίκαιος) – since that was true every time a prophet was rejected – but the fact that the rejection of *this* prophet had a decisively Christological character. By condemning Jesus, the Jewish authorities formally denied the claim that he was 'the Righteous One'[94] in whom Israel's prophetic oracles (the words of 'those who announced beforehand') were fulfilled. (3) Far from being incompatible with his Messianic status, the events of Jesus' trial – as Stephen's opponents ought to have recognised – in fact confirm it, for in the history of Israel this has always been the lot of God's messengers.

Jesus' trial and the Ethiopian eunuch (8.32–5)

In the discussion of Jesus' trial before Herod, several narrative emphases seemed to suggest that Isaiah's fourth Servant Song (Isa. 52.13–53.12) may have been specifically in the evangelist's mind as he wrote the account of this part of Jesus' trial. One Lukan passage to which I referred in support of this suggestion was Acts 8.32–5, where Luke explicitly points out the correspondence between a section of this Song and certain events of Jesus' passion.

Philip's conversation with the Ethiopian eunuch focuses on the prophecy-fulfilment relationship between Isaiah's fourth Servant Song (Isa. 52.13–53.12) and certain aspects of Jesus' passion. The discussion of Jesus' trial before Herod has drawn attention to a number of specific resemblances between Isaiah's prophecy and this particular part of Jesus' trial, resemblances to which attention is again called in Acts 8.32–5, namely, the Servant's silence (Isa. 53.7; Luke 23.9; Ac. 8.32) and his humiliation (Isa. 53.8; Luke 23.11; Ac. 8.33). To these, other parallels of a

---

[93] Barrett also finds in Jesus' trial the fitting referent for Luke's terms here: 'the Jews handed Jesus over to Pilate; such an action towards their fellow countryman could be described as betrayal. In this sense they were also his murderers' (*Acts*, vol. I, p. 377).

[94] Barrett finds it 'hard to avoid the conclusion that it [ὁ δίκαιος] is a title' (*Acts*, vol. I, p. 377), while Marshall believes that 'here *righteous* will have the sense of "innocent"..., but the phrase ["those who had prophesied *beforehand the coming of the Righteous One*" is undoubtedly meant to refer to Jesus as the Messiah' (*Acts* (1980), p. 147).

more general kind between the trial of Jesus in Luke 23 and Acts 8.32–5 can be added, such as the common emphasis on the Servant's innocence (Luke 23.4, 14, 15, 22, 47; implicitly in 'sheep' and 'lamb', Ac. 8.32) and the injustice of his treatment by his adversaries (Jesus' unfair condemnation in Luke 23; ἡ κρίσις αὐτοῦ ἤρθη in Ac. 8.33).

The immediate significance of these parallels between Jesus' trial in Luke 23 and the Isaianic quotation of Acts 8.32–3 is the indication that according to Luke the events of Jesus' trial show him to be the fulfilment of Isaiah's Suffering-Servant prophecy. Further, the correspondence between these events and Isaiah's prophecy is represented as the basis for Philip's proclamation of Jesus (8.35) and for the eunuch's belief in him as the Son of God (8.37).

Jesus' trial and Peter's address in the house of Cornelius (10.39–40)

This passage makes no explicit mention of Jesus' trial, but points to it only indirectly, by virtue of Peter's declaration that the Jews[95] 'killed [Jesus], having hanged him on a tree' (10.39), a statement which, as we have seen in connection with 5.30, only makes sense if taken as indicative of the Jewish part in Jesus' trial.

Peter's words here are thus a further instance in Acts where the Jewish involvement in Jesus' trial is placed alongside and contrasted with (i) the evidence of his ministry (10.35–40), which is affirmative of his unique status before God (Χριστός, πάντων κύριος, 10.36; ὁ θεὸς ἦν μετ' αὐτοῦ, 10.38) and (ii) God's final testimony in the matter, as he resurrected Jesus (5.40) and appointed him as 'judge of the living and the dead' (10.42). As such, the function of the trial-and-death reference in the story of Acts 10 is to serve as a warning to Peter's (this time) Gentile audience (and indirectly to Luke's redress) not to repeat the mistake of the Jews who rejected the one through whom God had visited them, but to accept the testimony of God, who appointed and confirmed him as Christ, Lord and judge.

Jesus' trial and Paul's Antiochian mission (13.27–29a)

This last reference to Jesus' trial in Acts occurs as part of Paul's address to the ἄνδρες Ἰσραηλῖται καὶ οἱ φοβούμενοι τὸν θεόν

---

[95] The subject(s) of ἀνεῖλαν can only be τῶν Ἰουδαίων and, possibly (the inhabitants of) Ἰερουσαλήμ (Barrett, *Acts*, vol. I, p. 526).

(13.16) in the Pisidian Antioch synagogue (13.14). Paul's cursory survey of Israel's history culminates with the appearance on the scene of Jesus as Israel's promised Saviour (σωτῆρα, 13.23; cf. also ὁ λόγος τῆς σωτηρίας ταύτης in 13.26), so that the thrust of the discourse is placed on the offer of forgiveness (ἄφεσις ἁμαρτιῶν, 13.38) and justification (δικαιωθῆναι, 13.38; δικαιοῦται, 13.39) through Jesus (διὰ τούτου, 13.38; ἐν τούτῳ, 13.39) to 'everyone who believes' (πᾶς ὁ πιστεύων, 13.39) and on the accompanying danger of forfeiting all these through disbelief (13.40–1).

The specific pointers to Jesus' trial in the passage are (i) the aorist participle κρίναντες ('having condemned', 13.27), through which the readers are reminded of the Sanhedrin's formal decision to hand Jesus over to Pilate and of their subsequent pressure on the governor to have Jesus sentenced to death, and (ii) the whole of 13.28, which calls specific attention to Jesus' Roman trial.

Luke's presentation of Jesus' trial resulting from these verses highlights the following features: (1) No responsibility for Jesus' condemnation is attributed to Paul's Antiochene audience; this rests rather with the people of Jerusalem, among whom the rulers form a distinctive group.[96] (2) The Jerusalemites' rejection of Jesus was possible only because of their double ignorance: they 'did not know him nor the words of the prophets which are read every Sabbath'[97] (τοῦτον ἀγνοήσαντες καὶ τὰς φωνὰς τῶν προφητῶν τὰς κατὰ πᾶν σάββατον ἀναγινωσκομένας. While this reference to ignorance evidently parallels that of 3.17, its significance here is slightly different. In 3.17 its role is primarily conciliatory (it assures the audience of the availability of forgiveness and blessing, 3.19–20); here it is mainly explanatory (it shows how it was possible for the Christ to be condemned by the Jewish leadership). Yet one significant element of continuity exists: in both cases the hearers and the readers are tacitly being challenged not to repeat the mistake of those who rejected Jesus – at the time of their acquaintance with the events it is no longer possible to plead ignorance of Jesus' identity, for God has now vindicated him (13.30–7). (3) The trial of Jesus brought about the fulfilment of prophetic oracles, thus confirming him as the promised Messiah. This is stated first in 13.27, where 'the words of the prophets which are read every Sabbath' are said to have been fulfilled[98] in Jesus' condemnation (lit. '[they] having condemned

---

[96] Ibid., p. 640; Marshall, *Acts* (1980), p. 225.

[97] The irony of their ignorance of the prophetic oracles is made particularly striking by the fact that the oracles 'are read every Sabbath'.

[98] 13.27b is rather awkward grammatically, with ἐπλήρωσαν lacking any referent (τῶν

[him]', κρίναντες) and again in 13.29, where πάντα τὰ περὶαὐτοῦ γεγραμμένα clearly points back to the events of 13.27–8. (4) The condemnation of Jesus was utterly unreasonable: Jesus' opponents asked for his death although nothing deserving of it was found in him (13.8). (5) The decision to condemn Jesus and its apparent resolution in Jesus' burial (13.29b) was reversed[99] by God's intervention in raising Jesus from the dead (13.30) – an act which cannot be denied, since both human witnesses (13.31) and scriptural testimony (13.32–7) confirm it.

Conclusion

In the introductory section of the present chapter, a number of specific questions were taken as guidelines for the subsequent investigation. It remains now to outline the findings in relation to these issues.

(1) *The emphases of the post-trial section of Luke's passion narrative and their continuity with the apologetic tendencies of the trial account.* Throughout Luke's account of Jesus' journey towards the place of his execution (23.26–32), his crucifixion (23.33–43), death (23.44–9), and burial (23.50–6) ample evidence has been found of apologetic concerns which closely resemble those discovered in the trial narrative. On the one hand, Luke's permanent concern is to further his case for Jesus' Messianic vocation. This is done (i) by prophecy-fulfilment argumentation, as Jesus is showed to fulfil both what the Scriptures had predicted of the Messiah and his own prophetic predictions, (ii) by Luke's characterisation of Jesus as (the) righteous (one), the one who saves (the criminal), the one whose authority to restore Israel's worship is attested by God through the torn curtain, and whose intimate relationship with God is once again made evident in his dying prayer, or (iii) simply by sharpening the Christological challenge posed by Jesus' crucifixion (through his emphatic use of Christological titles in the context of Jesus' mockery), a challenge which draws attention to the issue of Jesus' identity, which is to be decisively settled through the resurrection narrative. On the other hand, Luke deals with potential objections associated with Jesus' death by showing the utter injustice of this act (injustice to which the lamenting women, the

---

προφητῶν τὰς κατὰ πᾶν σάββατον ἀναγινωσκομένας is subordinated to the preceding participle ἀγνοήσαντες). Yet the fact that τὰς φωνὰς κτλ. is the immediate precedent of ἐπλήρωσαν suggests that it is these 'utterances' that ought to be regarded as the object of fulfilment. This is soon confirmed by the parallel statement in 13.29: ἐτέλεσαν πάντα τὰ περὶ αὐτοῦ γεγραμμένα ('they have completed/fulfilled *everything that has been written* about him').

[99] Note particularly the tone of contrast introduced by the particle δέ in 13.30.

repentant criminal, the Roman centurion, the remorseful multitudes, and Joseph of Arimathea bear witness) and by indicating that, at a human level, the implementation of this injustice is at least partially explained (and the guilt associated with it attenuated) by the ignorance of those involved (23.34).

(2) *The Gospel plot beyond the trial account and its significance for Luke's representation of Jesus' trial.* The Christological conflict of the Gospel, a conflict which had reached its most formal expression in the trial narrative, continues throughout the accounts of Jesus' crucifixion, death, and burial, as Luke weaves together the evidence for Jesus' Messiahship with challenges posed to it by mockers, crucifixion, and death. Finally, the resurrection is brought on the scene as the *necessary* resolution of this conflict (24.7, 26, 46) and therefore the irreversible attestation of Jesus' Messianic role. The significance of these findings for present purposes is their indication that a primary function of Jesus' trial in Luke's story is its contribution to the development of Luke's Christological apologia: through it attention is called to the diametrically opposed verdicts of the Jewish leaders and of God over the issue of Jesus' identity (with the former verdict being issued at the trial itself and implemented through the crucifixion, and the latter being indicated throughout the passion story but most importantly and visibly through the resurrection).

(3) *Jesus' trial – its representation and function in subsequent Lukan contexts.* In keeping with what has already been noted about Jesus' Lukan trial in the study of the actual trial narrative and also of the crucifixion, death, and burial accounts, the numerous references to Jesus' trial in the resurrection narratives and also in Acts continue to display Luke's interest in the confirmation of the gospel, as specifically embodied in certain Christological statements. Thus Jesus' trial is almost invariably described as the occasion when the formal rejection of Jesus amounts to the denial of the central claims which Luke's Gospel had set out to make on Jesus' behalf. Ironically, however, it is precisely these events, which carry with them this denial, that turn out in fact to provide part of the confirmation of what they are meant to disprove. By rejecting Jesus and giving him over 'to the verdict of death', Jesus comes to fulfil the divine plan for the Messiah, as this plan is revealed in the prophetic oracles. Moreover, the pronouncement and implementation of the verdict of death calls for and draws attention to God's own visible verdict in the matter, as this is given convincingly and definitively through Jesus' resurrection-exaltation.

The contexts in which these trial references occur is also revealing. In the resurrection narratives, all three trial references (24.7, 20, 44–7) come to assure the bewildered women and disciples that what had just happened to Jesus over the previous few days is entirely in keeping with God's plan for the Christ, and that rather than being a cause of confusion, these events ought to confirm the disciples' belief in him as the awaited Messiah. No less unanimous is the evidence of Acts. Out of the nine trial references which have been noted, seven come as parts of speeches which aim to persuade their (friendly or hostile, Jewish or Gentile) audiences that Jesus is the one through whom forgiveness and blessings are now available to all those who believe 'in his name' (regardless even of the degree of their responsibility for Jesus' death). An eighth reference (4.27–8) occurs as part of a prayer, in which the trial echo serves as the basis for the petition and hope that the God who has already vindicated Jesus through the passion events, will continue to vindicate Jesus' 'name' through the church's bold proclamation and through the performance of miracles (4.29–30). The ninth reference (8.32–3) is a quotation from Isaiah, which becomes the basis of Philip's proclamation of Jesus and the eunuch's belief in him as 'the Son of God'. The fact that virtually all these trial references come in contexts where their function is to provide assurance with regard to Jesus' identity and his role in the economy of God's salvation strongly suggests that the account of Jesus' trial is itself meant to have a similar function for Luke's readers.

In the light of these findings, it seems as if the long tradition of Lukan studies on the trial of Jesus, with its focus on issues such as political innocence, Roman benevolence, divine faithfulness, or Jewish culpability, has underestimated, if not bypassed, what appears so consistently to be at the heart of Luke's representation of Jesus' trial: the author's concern with the confirmation of the Christological tenets of the gospel.

Part two

THE CHURCH ON TRIAL

5

THE TRIALS OF PETER

Introduction

Although the trials of Jesus and Paul have long constituted important foci in the study of Luke–Acts in general and of Lukan apologetics in particular, very little attention has been paid to Luke's account of the trials of Peter and Stephen. This is not to say, of course, that Acts 4–7 has not been subject to scholarly investigation in any sense, but rather that the concerns which have guided the study of these chapters have almost completely bypassed the specific question of the role of Peter's and Stephen's trials in the narrative of Luke–Acts.[1]

The paucity of studies in this area is all the more notable when account is taken of the fact that (i) after Jesus and possibly Paul, Peter is the most dominant human[2] character of Luke–Acts; (ii) two chapters (4–5) at the beginning of Luke's second volume are dominated by the trials of Peter; (iii) Luke's incorporation in these chapters of two trial stories which have so much in common can only be explained by a special Lukan interest in the common elements of these incidents;[3] (iv) in the case of Stephen, virtually all his narrative life – occupying most of yet another two chapters of Acts – is taken up with aspects of his trial (proceedings, speech, and outcome).

---

[1] A detailed examination of the portrait of Peter in Luke–Acts, albeit with very little attention being paid to his trials, is available in the work of W. Dietrich, *Das Petrusbild der Lukanischen Schriften*, ed. K. H. Rengstorf and L. Rost, Stuttgart: W. Kohlhammer, 1972.

[2] The specification 'human' is necessary because of the important roles played by God and the Holy Spirit.

[3] Enquiring about Luke's possible reasons, Marshall notes that 'it has sometimes been suggested that [the two trial stories] are variant traditions of the same event' (Marshall, *Acts* (1980), p. 97). Marshall's observation that the two accounts may correspond to the prescriptions of the Jewish law, according to which a first offence may simply lead to a warning, and only a second one to punishment (p. 97) sheds light on the *historical* level, but is not sufficient to explain why Luke found it appropriate to include both incidents in his *narrative*. For a list of the major similarities between the two stories, see Tannehill, *Narrative*, vol. II, pp. 63–4.

For the concerns of the present study, probably the single most significant implication of the insufficient attention previously paid to the trials of Peter and Stephen is the underestimation of the undermining force of these chapters for the existing explanations of the apologetic tendencies which Luke's trial narratives are said to exhibit. Thus, after a discussion of Jesus' prediction of the disciples' trials, the present chapter goes on to argue first that the available interpretations of Lukan apologetics[4] have not, as a matter of fact, simply paid little attention to Peter's trials; they are, more importantly, unlikely to *be able* to account adequately for certain features of these narratives. Next, I shall outline some of the more notable contributions in the study of Acts 4–5, contributions which, although often not dealing with Peter's trial *per se*, offer helpful insights in this area. Finally, an interpretation of these chapters along the lines of an *apologia pro evangelio* will be proposed. The examination of Stephen's trial remains the object of the next chapter.

Jesus' prediction of the disciples' trials (Luke 12.11–12; 21.12–15)

Just as Jesus' predictions of *his own* trials, in their Lukan form, function as windows into the evangelist's understanding of the trials of Jesus, so also Jesus' predictions of *the disciples'* trials can be expected to throw light on Luke's understanding of these. While both Matthew and Mark have Jesus speaking only once to the disciples about their forthcoming trials (Matt. 10.17–20; Mark 13.9–11),[5] in the Third Gospel this happens twice – which itself may be suggestive of the importance which Luke attributes to the disciples' trials.

The first Lukan prediction comes as part of a larger section dealing with Jesus' exhortation to readiness for the coming judgement (12.1–13.9).[6] One major ingredient of this preparation is the courage to confess publicly one's allegiance to the Son of Man (12.1–12).[7] Thus the hypocrisy which the disciples are warned against (12.1) is defined specifically in terms of 'covering up' (συγκεκαλυμμένον), 'hiding' (κρυπτόν), 'saying in the dark' (ἐν τῇ σκοτίᾳ εἴπατε), and 'whispering in the ear'

---

[4] See for these the history of research on Lukan apologetics in chapter 1.

[5] Matthew comes close to a second reference in his would-be parallel of Mark 13.9/Luke 21.12 (Matt. 24.9), but he clearly plays down the trial imagery found in his (probable) Markan source.

[6] So Nolland, *Luke*, vol. II, p. 675; *pace* Marshall, *Gospel*, pp. 508–9, who sees this section as extending to 13.21.

[7] For a more detailed statement of the centrality of this theme to 12.1–12, see Marshall, *Gospel*, pp. 509–10.

(πρὸς τὸ οὖς ἐλαλήσατε – 12.2-3). Implicit in all such actions is some form of fear of people. The disciples, however, are not to fear 'those who kill the body' but are to fear God,[8] who has authority even beyond bodily destruction (12.5), and under whose control are even the smallest events in the world (12.6–7). Consequently, they must be ready to confess the Son of Man before people (12.8–9), lest they are (in certain extreme situations at least) in danger of excluding themselves from the possibility of God's forgiveness (12.10).[9]

It is against the background of this emphatic statement of the disciples' duty to confess Jesus even in hostile situations that the disciples are informed about the time when they will be brought 'before the synagogues and the rulers and the authorities' (12.11), that is, on trial before Jewish and Gentile courts.[10] According to the Lukan context of Jesus' words, then, the disciples' trials are events where bold confession of Jesus is to be expected.[11]

As for the wording of the prediction, much of it is similar to that of Matthew 10.19–20 and Mark 13.9, 11. One difference which is of interest for our purposes, however, is that while both Matthew and Mark use λαλέω to describe the disciples' response (Matt. 10.19; Mark 13.11), Luke prefers ἀπολογέομαι (12.11), thus calling specific attention to the element of defence (apologia) in the trial accounts to which this prediction points. Also, Luke prefers his Q source, where attention is called both to the form and to the content of the disciples' response (πῶς ἢ τί – Matt. 10.19; Luke 12.11), to Mark, where only the content is in view (τί – Mark 13.11) – a preference which is entirely in keeping with a more dominant apologetic agenda. As for the aim of such apologias, it is clear that their primary goal should not be the personal safety of the disciples; that is something of which the providence of God (12.6–7), and not the disciples' defence, takes care. Indeed, it is specifically against excessive concern with personal safety on the part of the disciples that much of 12.1–12 warns. Rather, it would seem that the Holy Spirit's role (12.12)

---

[8] For the alternative interpretations of the one who 'has the authority to cast in hell' (most of which have found little support in recent scholarship), see Fitzmyer, *Luke*, vol. II, p. 959.

[9] Useful classifications of the numerous alternative understandings of the 'unforgivable sin' are offered by Fitzmyer (ibid., p. 946) and Marshall (*Gospel*, pp. 517–18).

[10] τὰς συναγωγάς evidently refers to Jewish courts, while τὰς ἀρχὰς καὶ τὰς ἐξουσίας are commonly understood as denoting Gentile (esp. Roman) authorities (Marshall, *Gospel*, p. 520; Nolland, *Luke*, vol. II, p. 680).

[11] This is not to say that 12.8–10 and 12.11–12 refer to exactly the same incidents; rather, 12.11–12 denote situations of crisis, when the disciples may be particularly likely to be afraid (hence μὴ μεριμνήσητε, 12.11) and when it thus becomes especially important for them to remain faithful to the requirement of 12.8–11.

is going to be precisely that of 'teaching' the disciples to speak in a way which places loyalty and witness to the Son of Man above personal safety and which entrusts the latter to God's care.[12]

Jesus' second Lukan announcement of the disciples' trials (21.12–19)[13] belongs, as in the Markan parallel, to his eschatological discourse (Luke 21.5–36; Mark 13.1–37) and resembles many of the features of the Third Gospel's first such prediction. The following points seem to describe Luke's concerns here:

(1) Once again it is stated that the disciples can expect trials both before Jews (τὰς συναγωγάς; to this Luke adds φυλακάς, thus indicating the outcome of at least some of the trials) and before Gentiles (βασιλεῖς καὶ ἡγεμόνας).

(2) Just as in the cases of Matthew's and Mark's accounts, the 'crime' which is going to induce the disciples' trials is their allegiance to Jesus (ἕνεκεν ἐμοῦ in Matt. 10.18/Mark 13.9; ἕνεκεν τοῦ ὀνόματός μου in Luke 21.12; διὰ τὸ ὄνομά μου in Luke 21.17).

(3) Luke's ἀποβήσεται ὑμῖν εἰς μαρτύριον, where Matthew and Mark have the shorter εἰς μαρτύριον αὐτοῖς, places additional emphasis on the representation of these trials as settings in which the disciples are to bear *witness to Jesus*. Ironically, therefore, the disciples are not to be perceived as *defendants* but as *witnesses*, for they are not on trial on their own account but for Jesus' 'name's sake' (21.12b).

(4) Just as in the first prediction, the verb used to describe the disciples' response is ἀπολογέομαι, rather than Matthew's and Mark's λαλέω (Matt. 10.19; Mark 13.11), with the specification that the disciples' apologia must not rely on their preparations for it, but on Jesus' direct assistance of them.

(5) The announced outcome of the trials (constituting Luke's most substantial innovation in the present trial announcement)[14] is that the adversaries will 'not be able to withstand or contradict'

---

[12] In the words of Nolland, '"What is necessary to say" is centrally to confess one's allegiance to the Son of Man... The Holy Spirit will teach the disciple, in the hour of stress, the priority of confession over self-defense' (*Luke*, vol. II, p. 681).

[13] Although 21.16–19 appears to speak primarily of domestic opposition and general hatred, rather than judicial trials, its inclusion in the trial prediction is justified by the fact that in 21.16 Luke changes the account from the third to the second person (cf. Mark 13.12; also Matt. 10.21), thus strengthening the continuity between the foregoing and the subsequent verses.

[14] The promise of 21.18 is also found only in Luke as part of the trial prediction, but its content is partly paralleled by Luke 12.7a/Matthew 10.30.

(οὐ δυνήσονται ἀντιστῆναι ἤ ἀντειπεῖν) the 'mouth and wisdom' (στόμα καὶ σοφίαν) of the disciples (21.15).

(6) The trials will sometimes be initiated by those belonging to the disciples' closest circles – γονέων καὶ ἀδελφῶν καὶ συγγενῶν καὶ φίλων (21.16)[15] – terms which in the context of Luke–Acts may nevertheless allow for the looser meaning of 'fellow Jews', such as in the cases of Stephen and Paul, whose trials are prompted by those whom they specifically call Ἄνδρες ἀδελφοὶ καὶ πατέρες (Ac. 7.2; 22.1). It seems to be just as scandalous for Luke that Jewish believers should be 'delivered up' to the Roman authorities by their fellow Jews as if something of the sort happened within close domestic circles.

(7) The trials may at times result in disciples' deaths. Thus, what is guaranteed by Jesus' involvement in the disciples' trials (21.15) is not their personal safety but rather the success of their 'witness' to Jesus.

(8) Two verses later, however, the promise is made that 'not a hair of your head will perish' (21.18). The tension between the two statements has been explained in numerous ways: (i) as due to Luke's juxtaposition of different sources,[16] but this still leaves unanswered the question of what sense the statements would have made for Luke; (ii) it has often been suggested that what is meant in 21.18 is in fact spiritual protection,[17] but the context of the statement makes the physical dimension of the promised protection inescapable;[18] (iii) 21.18 has also been understood as stating simply that the disciples 'can never be plucked from the protecting hand of God',[19] but this seems much too general to do justice to the force of the statement.

---

[15] A case could be made against regarding 21.16–19 as part of the 'trials' prediction, since with 21.16 '[f]rom action in the courts the thought turns to betrayal by relatives and general hatred by mankind' (Marshall, *Gospel*, p. 769). Under closer scrutiny, however, such a case becomes unconvincing: (i) Luke changes the statement in 21.16a from third to second person (cf. Mark 13.12; also Matt. 10.21), thus making the subsequent information an integral part of the trial prediction; (ii) as we shall soon note, the terms γονέων καὶ ἀδελφῶν καὶ συγγενῶν καὶ φίλων can for Luke have a broader meaning than close relatives and friends in the strict sense; (iii) the subject matter of 21.16–19 is in any case very closely related to that of 21.12–15.

[16] Fitzmyer, *Luke*, vol. II, p. 1341.

[17] Ellis, *Gospel of Luke*, p. 244; Marshall, *Gospel*, p. 769.

[18] This is also what Luke's closest parallel to this verse (Ac. 27.34b) seems to suggest.

[19] N. Geldenhuys, *Commentary on the Gospel of Luke: The English Text with Introduction, Exposition and Notes*, London: Marshall, Morgan & Scott, 1951, p. 527.

A more fruitful solution may be to take 21.18 as a general and, as it stands, unqualified promise of God's physical protection for the disciples, a promise which nevertheless allows for Luke's already-given qualification that in the case of 'some of you' God may allow otherwise (θανατώσουσιν ἐξ ὑμῶν, 21.16). This reading is amply substantiated by the material in Acts, where in most cases of genuine danger for the disciples 'not a hair of their head' is lost (4.21; 5.17–20; 12.1–11; 16.26; 18.10, 12–6; 19.24–41; 22.29; 23.10, 12–24; 24.23; 27.1–44; 28.3–6), although in other cases (7.57–60; 12.2) God can allow otherwise.

(9) Steadfastness (ὑπομονή) in the face of such trials, rather even than their 'mouth and wisdom', is (paradoxically)[20] the means whereby the disciples are exhorted[21] to secure their lives.

To summarise, the disciples' trials, as foretold by Jesus in the Third Gospel, are occasions on which the disciples' allegiance to Jesus is challenged (viz. they are on trial for his name's sake, 12.8–9; 21.12, 17) – in Jewish and Gentile settings alike (12.11; 21.12) – but which turn out to provide the disciples with the opportunity and responsibility of bearing witness to Jesus (12.8–9, 12; 21.13). Their role in the trials is thus diametrically reversed from 'defendants', on trial on their own account, to 'witnesses', on behalf of Jesus' name. The disciples' witness to Jesus, rather than their personal safety, is the primary intent and result of their 'apologias' (12.11; 21.14), and it is chiefly for this task that Jesus endows them with words and wisdom which cannot be successfully withstood or contradicted by their opponents (21.15). The disciples' safety, although extremely precarious (esp. 21.17), is not something *they* should worry about (12.4, 7) – *God* is in charge of this and he is going to keep them untouched even amidst the sharpest opposition (21.16–18); yet they must also come to terms with the fact that in *some* cases God may choose otherwise for them (21.16b). Either way, steadfastness in their witness to Jesus' name is the required response (21.18).

It remains now to see how the various accounts of the disciples' trials in Acts relate to the picture offered by the trial predictions.

[20] 'Luke deliberately uses language that will sound paradoxical in a context where secular wisdom would suggest that renouncing Christ is what will assure life' (Nolland, *Luke*, vol. III, p. 998).

[21] A B Θ f^{13} 33 et al. have the verb in future indicative form (κτήσεσθε, 'you will gain/secure'), but the more reliable reading (as attested by ℵ D K L W X ΔΨf^1 et al.) is the aorist imperative κτήσασθε.

Peter's trials and existing paradigms for Lukan apologetics
No case for apologias related to Rome

A number of representations of Lukan apologetics (mainly those which view Luke's concerns as in some way related to the Roman state) have not made and are unlikely to make any substantial claim of finding support in Acts 4–5. There is no need, therefore, to dwell too long on these.

First, the widely accepted view that Luke aimed to gain or maintain political freedom for Christianity within the Roman empire by painting a positive picture of the Romans' attitude towards Christian representatives and of Roman justice[22] has made no use of Acts 4–5.[23] Secondly, within the camp of those who believe that Luke was claiming for Christianity the status of *religio licita*, the only attempt at claiming support from Acts 4–5 is to be found in the work of B. S. Easton. He notes in passing that Luke's view of Christianity as part of Judaism is confirmed by the author's continuous use of the Old Testament, aimed to represent Christianity as true Judaism, by the favourable attitude of Gamaliel towards the apostles, and by the attachment of the Jerusalem Christians to the temple (3.1; 5.12, 20, 42).[24] That such items serve to present Christianity as true Judaism few scholars would dispute. The problems lie rather in assuming that Roman officials would have been able and interested to comprehend Luke's subtle theological arguments, such as those resulting from Luke's use of Scriptures (a Jewish/Christian readership would have been in a much better position in this respect). Moreover, whatever areas of continuity between Christianity and Judaism the Romans may have been able to identify, they would have been easily obscured by the much more overt tone of conflict between the two groups. The complaint of the Jewish authorities – the Romans would have noted – was precisely that the leaders of the Christian movement *did not* act and speak in accordance with the tenets of Judaism.

Finally, the situation is similar in the case of Walaskay's assertion that *'[t]hroughout his writings* Luke has carefully, consistently, and consciously presented an *apologia pro imperio* to his church'.[25] There is nothing to substantiate this claim in the story of Peter's trials (or, for that

---

[22] Conzelmann, *Theology*, pp. 141–4; Cadbury, *Making*, pp. 308–14.

[23] Thus, for instance, Conzelmann's review of the evidence of Acts for his position starts only with Acts 10 (Conzelmann, *Theology*, p. 141).

[24] Easton, *Early Christianity*, pp. 47–51.

[25] Walaskay, *Rome*, p. 64; first set of italics mine.

matter, in much else of Luke–Acts), since the empire and its representatives simply do not feature here.[26]

An ecclesiastic apologia?

One apologetic reading of Acts which has come close to claiming support from Luke's story of Peter's trials is that pioneered by Schneckenburger and followed with some modifications by Mattill. According to this interpretation, Luke's parallel presentation of Peter and Paul is designed to be an ecclesiastic defence of Paul or Pauline Christianity or both, within the context of questions about Paul's orthodoxy in certain Christian quarters, by presenting him as essentially equal with Peter, the Jerusalem apostle *par excellence*, whose authority would have been much less disputed for Luke's readers.[27] Peter's and Paul's trials would naturally appear to be part of this parallelism. Yet three aspects deserve special mention. First, despite the abundance of studies on Luke's parallel presentation of Peter and Paul,[28] very little has been made of their parallel trial experiences[29] (certainly the space allocated by Luke to their respective trials seems to provide *prima facie* evidence for such parallelism). Secondly, to the degree to which Peter's and Paul's trials are parallel, they can provide, at best, only one of the more minor ways in which Peter legitimates Paul; of much greater importance in this respect would be other depictions of Peter, such as missionary to the Gentiles or as defender of Paul's mission at the Jerusalem council. Third, such an interpretation can hardly give Peter's trials a distinctive function in Acts – on this reading, Paul's speeches, miracles, and visions do just the same and, indeed, in a more convincing way. Thus, although the potential of Acts 4–5 to provide ecclesiastic legitimation for Paul and the churches he represents is not entirely excluded, this cannot be taken as indicative of the primary function of the passage within Luke's narrative.

[26] Walaskay's case, as noted in the first chapter, is built on those instances in Luke–Acts (most importantly the accounts of Jesus' and Paul's trials) where a positive picture of the Roman authority is allegedly presented (ibid., pp. 25–63).

[27] Mattill, 'Purpose', 110–11, 118.

[28] For a recent and thorough study in this area (as well as further bibliography), see A. C. Clark, 'Parallel Lives: The Relation of Paul to the Apostles in the Lukan Perspective', unpublished PhD dissertation, London: Brunel University, 1996.

[29] So, for instance, Clark allocates whole chapters of his thesis to parallel commisions (ch. 5), parallel miracles (ch. 6), and parallel speeches (ch. 7), but nothing to parallel trials. See also Mattill, 'Purpose', 110–11, where the closest reference to parallel trials comes through the word 'sufferings'.

Peter's trials in recent studies[30]
A literary analysis of the conflict in Acts 4–5

In his literary interpretation of Acts 4–5,[31] R. Tannehill pays specific attention to narrative development and echo effect in Luke's presentation of the conflict between Peter and John and the temple authorities. The relevance of Tannehill's study to our purposes is that it correctly calls attention to issues such as (i) the centrality of witness to Jesus as the Messiah for the conflict of Acts 4–5;[32] (ii) the continuity between Luke's account of Jesus' Jerusalem ministry and passion, the trials of Peter, the trial of Stephen, and (more tentatively expressed) later conflict scenes of Acts;[33] (iii) God's own involvement in and on behalf of the Christian mission.[34] Such observations clearly support the general contention of the present study, namely that there is a fundamental continuity between the various trial narratives of Luke–Acts and that at the centre of this is Luke's preoccupation with the ongoing conflict surrounding the Christian message (centred, of course, on Jesus' Messiahship). Present concerns require, however, a further major step in the investigation, namely the question of how Luke's presentation of this conflict can be seen to function as an apologia for the gospel.

The political dimension of Acts 4–5, 10

Luke's representation of the political stance of the Jerusalem community, as seen by R. Cassidy,[35] is characterised by general acceptance of the Sanhedrin's right to exercise judicial authority, but also by the realisation that this authority can at times be at odds with what is right in the sight of God – the Sanhedrin's attempts to suppress the apostolic proclamation provide an example of this. In such circumstances the apostles show determination to obey God rather than people and in so doing they follow the example of Jesus. Moreover, what characterises their allegiance to God and Jesus is not tentativeness and meekness but boldness.

---

[30] The contribution of commentaries is not noted here; interaction with them, where necessary, will take place as part of discussion of the Lukan text.

[31] Tannehill, *Narrative*, vol. II, pp. 59–79. See also R. C. Tannehill, 'The Composition of Acts 3–5: Narrative Development and Echo Effect', in K. H. Richards (ed.), *SBL 1984 Seminar Papers*, Chico: Scholars Press, 1984, pp. 217–40.

[32] Acts 4–5 is interpreted as the first two parts of a three-stage conflict (with the final and climactic episode to be reached in the story of Stephen), throughout which the efforts of the temple authorities are 'to suppress the witness to Jesus' (Tannehill, *Narrative*, vol. II, p. 65).

[33] Ibid., pp. 68–9.   [34] Ibid., p. 77.   [35] Cassidy, *Society*, pp. 39–50.

The bearing of these observations on the present work is made particularly evident by Cassidy's conclusions about the incompatibility of his findings with interpretations which see Luke engaged in some form of apologia for the church addressed to Rome or for Rome addressed to the church.[36] Instead, Cassidy argues, Luke's emphases could be more adequately captured in the concepts of *allegiance* to Jesus and *witness* before kings and governors, with the latter representing the specific emphasis of the trial accounts.

A socio-scientific analysis of Acts 3–4

Although limited to Peter's first trial, R. Brawley's investigation[37] is of relevance for the study of Acts 4–5 as a whole, not least in view of the evident parallelism between the two trial incidents. Brawley makes use of labelling and deviance theory to analyse the conflict between the Christian protagonists and their opponents, and, more specifically, the role of voices of Scripture in this conflict. His case, built mainly on Acts 4,[38] is that Luke's use of Scripture (4.11, 24–6; cf. Pss. 117.22; 2.1–2; 145.3, 6, LXX) is designed to persuade his readers into the revision of socio-cultural norms. Thus, Luke's hope is that the readers will come to disagree with the Jewish establishment's negative evaluation of Jesus as a deviant (an evaluation supremely expressed in his crucifixion) and accept instead his position 'as a prominent'.

That Brawley's study suggests for Peter's trials an apologetic agenda along the lines described here should need no detailed argumentation. There is a very short distance indeed between talk of 'rehabilitating Jesus' (as used in Brawley's title for his study of Acts 3–4) and an *apologia pro evangelio* expressed in Christological language. However, there is much more to Luke's apologia in Acts 4–5 than his use of Scriptural 'voices' for the rehabilitation of Jesus.

The trial of Peter and John (Acts 4.1–31)

The analysis of this text will concentrate on a number of issues which are likely to throw light on Luke's apologetic presentation of Peter's trials,

---

[36] Ibid., pp. 148–57. Cassidy's term 'ecclesial apologetic' (by which he means an apologia addressed to the church on behalf of Rome) should not be confused with the use of ecclesiastic apologia in this study.

[37] R. L. Brawley, *Text to Text Pours Forth Speech. Voices of Scripture in Luke–Acts*, Indiana University Press, 1995, pp. 91–107.

[38] Three pages (92–5) are allocated to Acts 3 and twelve (95–107) to Acts 4.

such as the participants in the conflict, object(s) of the apologia, issues at stake, apologetic strategies, and, mainly by way of conclusion, the possible function of all these for Luke's intended audience.

The participants in the conflict

Although, as noted in the conflict leading to Jesus' trial, Luke's interest in the participants in the conflict tends to be secondary to his interest in the issues around which the conflict revolves,[39] some attention to the former is a necessary prerequisite for a better understanding of the latter.

On one side of the conflict are Peter and John, with Peter as the most representative figure of the new Christian movement in its Jerusalem setting[40] (John plays no role independently of Peter, apart perhaps from adding to the weight of the Christian representation in the episode). Their portrayal in the trial account is that of messengers of the word who, despite strong opposition, refuse to abandon their proclamation to the people. On the other side stand the representatives of Judaism. The initiative seems to belong primarily to the temple authorities (οἱ ἱερεῖς καὶ ὁ στρατηγὸς τοῦ ἱεροῦ) and Sadducees (4.1), but soon the whole Sanhedrin joins in (4.5–6).[41] Thus, despite Haenchen's contention that '[a]ccording to Luke, it is not Judaism and Christianity which confront each other as enemies, but only Sadducees and Christians',[42] the Jewish representation denoted here is much broader than Sadduceeism (even if this group is among the initiators of the conflict).[43] This is in keeping with Luke's formulation of the accusation (4.2), which, we shall see, is not limited to the issue of the resurrection (which would only have scandalised the Sadducees) but also refers to the teaching 'in the name of Jesus' *per se*.

It seems correct, then, to say that Luke portrays a conflict between the representatives of the new Christian movement and the representatives of Judaism, with the temple authorities and the Sadducees as the initiators

---

[39] I shall argue in the next section that the primary focus of the trial is on 'the word'; it is the word that polarizes the participants in the conflict.

[40] Clark notes that although in Acts 9 Peter begins to act in a personal capacity, in the first eight chapters he is always portrayed as a representative of the apostles (who evidently in turn represent Christianity) ('Parallel Lives', pp. 83–8).

[41] Barrett, *Acts*, vol. I, p. 223.   [42] Haenchen, *Acts*, p. 223.

[43] Contra Haenchen, Barrett takes the apostles' opponents here to be representatives of Judaism as a whole, when he states that '[w]hatever some other parts of the book may suggest . . . Luke makes it clear that Christianity is not Judaism: at least it is not the Judaism of those who officially represent Judaism' (Barrett, *Acts*, vol. I, p. 218).

of the conflict. But this is not the whole picture. There is a third group
which plays an important role in the conflict (albeit often a tacit one) –
ὁ λαός. Although to a certain extent the role of 'the people' overlaps
with that of their leaders (in so far as 'all the people of Israel' are the
indirect addressees of Peter's words, 4.10),[44] there are several important
aspects in which their role is rather distinctive. On the one hand, they play
a passive role, as the ones who are continuously in 'danger' of accepting
the teachings of the Christian 'sect' (4.2, 17). On the other hand, they play
the more active roles of legitimating the Christian movement through their
favourable disposition towards it (4.21b) and, closely related to this, of
providing a role model for the readers in terms of readiness to accept the
Christian message (4.4, 21c).

The implications of these observations are that whatever apologetic
task Luke may be seen to undertake, it must account for the respective roles played by each group represented in the conflict – for the
Christian witnesses' determination to preach the word to ordinary Jews,
for the Jewish leaders' desperate attempts to hinder this process (at the
initiative of temple authorities and Sadducees), and for 'the people' as
those over whose position in regard to the word the two rival groups
clash.

The object of the apologia

What are the immediate precedents of the apostles' trial, what is at
stake in the conflict, and what do these have to say about the object of Luke's apologia? Luke's explanation of the apostles' arrest is
in terms of their prior preaching in connection with the healing of a
lame man (4.2). Barrett's claim that '[i]t is clear from v. 7 that in the
story it is the act rather than the speech of Peter and John that pro-
vokes the authorities to arrest them'[45] could hardly be further from
the truth. No fewer than three times in two verses (through the verbs
[λ]αλούντων, διδάσκειν, and καταγγέλλειν, 4.1–2) Luke stresses
the direct connection between the apostles' *speaking* and their arrest.
Indeed, 4.7 likewise locates the cause of the conflict in the apostles'

---

[44] It is possible, however, that ὑμεῖς ἐσταυρώσατε of 4.10 refers specifically, or at least
primarily, to the ἄρχοντες τοῦ λαοῦ καὶ πρεσβύτεροι (4.8; cf. πᾶσιν ὑμῖν, 4.10), and
not equally to the παντὶ τῷ λαῷ Ἰσραήλ (4.10). In other words, it is not clear whether
the attention of 'all the people' is called so that they all may be held responsible for Jesus'
crucifixion (so J. T. Sanders, *Jews*, p. 239), or in order that they, too, may hear and heed the
solemn words which are being said to the leaders.

[45] Barrett, *Acts*, vol. I, p. 216.

preaching, for it was through the preaching that the healing was ascribed to a 'power' and a 'name' with which the Jewish leadership felt uncomfortable.[46]

Despite the apparently singular character of the authorities' complaint (4.2), a twofold scandal is implied. First, the proclamation is ἐν τῷ 'Ιησοῦ,[47] and attitudes towards this person create divisions within Israel throughout Luke–Acts. Second, in Jesus' name 'the resurrection (which is) from the dead' (τὴν ἀνάστασιν τὴν ἐκ νεκρῶν) is proclaimed, and this is incompatible with the Sadducees' beliefs (it is *Jesus'* resurrection that is most certainly meant (3.15), although an additional resurrection, along the lines of 23.6; 24.15, 21; 26.23, may also at least be alluded to).[48] It is important to note that both Jesus' name and the resurrection feature in Acts, both separately and together, as distinctive marks of the Christian message (the former especially in Acts 3–5; the latter in 23.6; 24.15, 21; 26.23; together in 17.18; 26.8–9). For Luke to state that the cause of the apostles' trial is their proclamation of the resurrection in Jesus' name is to affirm in unmistakable terms that what is at stake in the present conflict is the Christian gospel itself.

It is no surprise then to find that the whole chapter revolves around this 'word'. It is its proclamation that is recalled in the authorities' programmatic question in 4.7b; it is its content *in nuce* that is again unpacked in 4.10–12;[49] it is its being spread among 'the people' that the authorities are trying to prevent in 4.17; it is its further proclamation that the threatened apostles would not give up in 4.20, would envisage through prayer in 4.29, and see accomplished in 4.31, 33; it is its unfailing validity and unstoppable power that, as will be seen in the following section, Luke's apologetic devices defend throughout the trial account. Dunn has effectively summarised the chapter, when referring to the content of 4.5–22 as 'the first formal defense of the new movement's testimony'.[50]

---

[46] 4.7 recalls the 'name' of Jesus in 3.6, 16 and thereby is presented as a challenge to the Christological assertions of Peter's preaching in that context. This is further confirmed by the renewed statement of the connection between the healing and Christology in 4.10–12.

[47] The statement functions similarly to ἐν ποίῳ ὀνόματι in 4.7 (see above).

[48] See, however, Barrett, *Acts*, vol. I, pp. 219–20, who thinks such a reference improbable on grammatical grounds.

[49] 'Peter's reply to the Council's question (4:8–12) contains in effect what is a brief version of the proclamation of Jesus as this appears in chs. 2, 3, 10, and 13' (ibid., p. 217).

[50] J. D. G. Dunn, *The Acts of the Apostles*, Peterborough: Epworth, 1996, p. 49.

Apologetic strategies

Among the strategies which substantiate Luke's apologia for the word, the following seem to have a leading role:

(1)   The characterisation of the witnesses of the word as popular with the people (4.1–2, 4, 21), full of the Holy Spirit (4.8, 31),[51] performers of a good deed (4.9), persuasive albeit ordinary (4.13–14), obeying God rather than humans (4.19–20),[52] bold (4.13, 31), and gaining access to God through prayer (4.24–30).

(2)   The characterisation of the opponents of the word as 'annoyed' (διαπονούμενοι, 4.2), unable to offer credible counter-arguments and therefore resorting to groundless threats (4.14b–18), opposed to God (4.10–11, 19), and belonging to a long tradition of opponents of God's servants (4.25–9).

(3)   The appeal to a number of authorities shared by the apostles, Jewish authorities, and intended readers: (i) appeal to the Scriptures for the rehabilitation of Jesus' 'name' (4.11, 24–6);[53] (ii) appeal to God's direct verdict with regard to Jesus, as manifested in the resurrection (4.10b); (iii) appeal to miracles, such as the lame man's healing and the earthquake (4.31);[54] and (iv) appeal to witnesses for the authentication of the healing miracle – the event is attested by 'all the inhabitants of Jerusalem' (4.16), as well as by the healed man himself, who, being 'more than forty years old, must have been quite capable to attest his healing'.[55]

(4)   The use of logical and theological reasoning, when taking the 'salvation' (σέσωται) of the lame man as a 'sign' (σημεῖον,

---

[51] For the Holy Spirit's role as legitimator of protagonists and speeches in Luke–Acts, see Darr, *Character Building*, p. 52; W. H. Shepherd, *The Narrative Function of the Holy Spirit as a Character in Luke–Acts,* Atlanta: Scholars Press, 1994, p. 39.

[52] Dunn (*Acts*, p. 55) calls attention to Socrates' similar response to his judges – 'I will obey God/the god rather than you' (Plato, *Apology*, 29d) – as well as parallel attitudes in Jewish and Christian writings (Dan. 3.16–18; 2 Macc. 7).

[53] See Brawley's socio-scientific analysis, outlined at p. 140.

[54] That Luke understands miracles as having a legitimating role is made clear by 4.30. Such an understanding of miracles is also attested in Hellenistic and Jewish writings of the period (Squires, *Plan*, pp. 78–102).

[55] Although the primary function of Luke's remark about the man's age is probably to highlight the greatness of the miracle (Marshall, *Acts* (1980), p. 103) and possibly also to justify the feelings of the people (Haenchen, *Acts*, p. 220), it is very probable that the adult age of the man is mentioned to indicate that he was quite capable of testifying for himself to the authenticity of the miracle, in a manner not dissimilar to that in John 9.21.

4.16, 22) of the salvation (σωτηρία) which is now universally
and exclusively available through the name of Jesus (4.10–12).[56]

(5) The subtle refutation of potential objections related to Christianity's relationship to Judaism. Thus, the emphasis on the constant
efforts of the Jewish leadership to prevent 'the people' from accepting the apostolic message may clarify for Luke's readers
why such a large segment of Judaism is still in unbelief – the
people's initial response, Luke contends, was very different (4.4,
21), but the Jewish authorities suppressed it. Also the leading role
which the temple authorities are shown to have played within
the opposition to the new movement explains why Christianity
is no longer attached to the temple, as it originally had been
(Luke 24.53; Ac. 2.46; 3.1).

The trial of Peter and the apostolic group (Acts 5.17–42)

Because of the close similarity between Peter's first and second trials, the
discussion here will largely follow the format of the previous one.

The participants in the conflict

The Christian representation in the conflict is this time even more significant than in the first trial account – it includes the whole apostolic group
(5.18, although this evidently need not mean that literally every apostle
was present). Peter remains, however, their spokesman (5.29). In the opposite camp stand once again the Sadducees, this time accompanying the
high priest, as the instigators of the renewed conflict. Yet, just like the first
time, they soon receive the cooperation of the whole Sanhedrin (5.21b).[57]

Between the two opposing groups again stand the people. They are
the ones among whom and for the benefit of whom 'many signs and
wonders' had been done by the apostles (5.12, 15–16), so that they came
to hold the apostles 'in high honour' (5.13) and great numbers from among
them were accepting the apostolic message (5.14).[58] Thus what stands
at the centre of Luke's presentation in 5.12–16 is the highly successful

[56] For an instructive discussion of salvation (especially as this relates to 'the name' of
Jesus) in Acts 4.8–12, see C. K. Barrett, 'Salvation Proclaimed', *ExpT* 94 (1982), 68–71.

[57] Both συνέδριον and γερουσία should be understood as denoting the Sanhedrin
(Barrett, *Acts*, vol. I, p. 285). Luke's hendiadys, τὸ συνέδριον καὶ πᾶσαν τὴν
γερουσίαν, especially as it is followed by τῶν υἱῶν Ἰσραήλ, is most certainly meant to
highlight the comprehensive representation of the Jewish leadership.

[58] Luke also adds the puzzling information that 'none of the rest dared to join them
[apparently the apostles]'. Are 'the rest' (οἱ λοιποί) to be understood as the Christians

ministry of the apostles among the people, a ministry based in the temple (5.12b), although also overflowing to the streets of Jerusalem (5.15) and even benefiting Jerusalem's surroundings (5.16). In continuity with this, the subsequent narrative portrays the people as those towards whom the Christian teaching is directed but whose contact with this message the Jewish leaders are desperately trying to prevent. So, in 5.20 the apostles are told by the angel to go into the temple and speak to the people while in 5.25 they are found doing just that; in 5.26 the people's good disposition towards the apostles prevents the authorities' use of violence; in 5.28 the apostles are formally accused of having made their message known to all (the people of) Jerusalem; finally, the people are the assumed recipients of the forbidden, yet ongoing, apostolic proclamation in 5.40, 42.

The object of the apologia

With the apostles enjoying a response from the people as described in 5.12–16, it is hardly surprising that the already antagonistic Jewish leadership is 'filled with jealousy' (5.17), so the conflict resumes. The conflict continues to be related to the apostles' teaching of the people in the temple: in the prelude to the apostles' rearrest and official interrogation they are portrayed 'standing in the temple and teaching the people' (5.25). Thus, although Luke does not record the authorities' complaint until late in the narrative (5.28), the readers already know that what sparked off and fuelled the conflict was the escalating influence of the apostles among the people – this influence being exercised (all the more scandalously for the leaders) from the temple premises and spreading throughout Jerusalem and its surroundings. It is only to be expected, therefore, that when the formal accusation is made, the heart of the matter is the influence of the apostles' teaching among the people of Jerusalem: 'We strictly charged you not to teach in this name, yet here you have filled Jerusalem with your teaching and you intend to bring this man's blood upon us' (5.28, RSV). However, in addition to what could already have been inferred from the foregoing narrative, the last sentence in this verse adds a new element to the explanation of the leaders' antagonism towards the

---

other than the apostles (Pesch, *Die Apostelgeschichte*, p. 206) or, more likely, the non-Christians (Haenchen, *Acts*, p. 242; Barrett, *Acts*, vol. I, p. 274)? Also, is κολλᾶσθαι to be taken as commitment in terms of sharing of property (D. R. Schwartz, 'Non-Joining Sympathizers (Acts 5,13–14)', *Bib* 64 (1983), 554)? A detailed discussion of this statement is not possible here, but it certainly cannot be taken to cast doubt on the much clearer subsequent remark about the increasing number of converts (4.14), who evidently must be understood as coming from among the people.

apostolic preaching: it is not simply that the apostles' influence may cause the leaders to fade into comparative insignificance in 'their' own temple and city and among their own people; implicit is also the issue of their inevitable disrepute and guilt, resulting from the apostles' announcement of God's rehabilitation of the one whom the leaders had put to death.

Indications of the actual content of the apostolic teaching are given on several occasions. First, in 5.20 an angel tells them to 'go and stand in the temple and speak to the people all the words of this life', that is, the life which originates from Jesus as ἀρχηγὸς τῆς ζωῆς (3.15).[59] Despite Barrett's evaluation of it as 'doubtful',[60] the existence of a further theological point, indicating that the temple ought to be the place where the gospel is proclaimed,[61] is far from being implausible, especially in view of its second occurrence in 4.25 and of Luke's general interest in Christian proclamation and worship in the Jewish temple and synagogues (throughout the ministries of Jesus, Peter, and Paul). Second, the high priest summarises the apostolic message in Christological terms (viz. teaching ἐπὶ τῷ ὀνόματι τούτῳ) and shows particular offence at the notion of being made to appear (together with the whole council) responsible for Jesus' death (5.28). Third, Peter's more comprehensive summary focuses on Jesus' death at the hands of the Jewish leaders (no indication is given that Peter wants to appease the council), the contrasting verdict of God given in Jesus' resurrection and glorification, and Jesus' divinely appointed position as Leader (ἀρχηγός), Saviour (σωτήρ) and the one through whom forgiveness and salvation are now available to Israel (5.30–1). Fourth, the apostles' ongoing teaching and preaching is said to consist of presenting τὸν χριστὸν Ἰησοῦν (5.42).

In conclusion, if Luke's account of the apostles' trial is to be seen as having an apologetic intent, the primary object of this apologia is undoubtedly the apostolic teaching, with its assertions about Jesus and his significance for Israel. Particular attention within this Christological agenda is given to (i) the relationship between the Christian teaching and the Jewish temple (5.20, 25, 42), capital (5.28), and people (5.12–16, 20, 25) and to (ii) the diametrically opposed ways in which the Jewish leaders and God had dealt with Jesus (5.28, 30–1). How exactly Luke builds his case to deal with these issues is the concern of the following section.

---

[59] Barrett, *Acts*, vol. I, p. 284.   [60] Ibid.

[61] J. Roloff, *Die Apostelgeschichte*, Das Neue Testament Deutsch 5, Göttingen, 1981, p. 102; G. Stählin, *Die Apostelgeschichte*, Das Neue Testament Deutsch 5, Göttingen, 1962, p. 89.

Apologetic strategies

Almost the same apologetic strategies as those in the account of Peter's first trial are also evident here:

(1)   The characterisation of the apostles as faithful to the temple (5.12b, 42), performing miracles (5.12, 15–16), popular with the people (5.13–16, 26), obedient to God rather than humans (5.29), and rejoicing amidst hardships (5.41).

(2)   The characterisation of a supporter (Gamaliel) as 'a Pharisee in the council, a teacher of the law' (thus indicating that not even all Jewish leaders opposed the Christian witness), 'held in honour by all the people' (5.34), reasonable (as shown by his speech), and careful not to oppose God (5.39).

(3)   The characterisation of the apostles' opponents as acting out of jealousy (5.17); incapable of substantiating their case and resorting instead to violence (5.33, cf. 5.18, 40); when violence is not used it is because of fear of the people (5.26); acting in opposition to God (5.29, 30, 39).

(4)   Appeal to undisputed authorities: (i) God is presented as the initiator (and therefore legitimator) of the apostolic teaching of the gospel to the people in the temple (5.19–20) and as the one who entrusted Jesus with the attributes which the Christians ascribe to him (5.30–1); (ii) Gamaliel, a Pharisee of high standing, is brought on the scene to be the one who gives expression to the Christian case for the benefit of his own Jewish peers; (iii) reliable witnesses can be found in the apostles themselves, as the ones who possess first-hand knowledge of the Christian story (5.32a), and in the Holy Spirit, who confirms the apostles' testimony (5.32b).

(5)   Logical and theological reasoning, most evidently present in Gamaliel's speech (5.35–9). In a nutshell, his argument is that experience shows that movements which are not from God do not stand, the corollary of which is that if they do stand they may well be from God and therefore must not be opposed. At the time of the readers' contact with the text the argument must have sounded all the more convincing, for by then enough time had passed to indicate that Christianity and its message do stand and therefore must be from God.

(6)   Refutation of potential objections related to Christianity's relationship to Judaism, along the same lines as in the account of the first Petrine trial.

Conclusion

The present investigation of Peter's trials in Acts started with a brief survey of the already existing models for the interpretation of Luke's apologetic tendencies and attempted to see how these relate to Luke's account of Peter's trials. It revealed not only that these models have made virtually no use of Acts 4–5 in their argumentation but also that it is very hard to see how they *could* adequately explain certain features of these chapters. At the same time, a few recent studies on Acts 3–4 from literary, political, and socio-scientific angles, although not specifically analysing Luke's apologetic tendencies or even the narrative function of the trial accounts, indicated that the way ahead for the understanding of the narratives in question appears to require a focus on Luke's interest in the Christian gospel, whether that interest be represented as a Messianic conflict,[62] or as a conflict over Christian witness,[63] or as the rehabilitation of Jesus.[64]

The representation of Luke's apologetic tendencies in the account of Peter's trials centres on the observation that *the primary thrust of Acts 4–5 is a conflict surrounding the influence of the Christian teaching among 'the (Jewish) people'*, with the Jewish leadership on one side of the conflict and the apostles on the other. Ample evidence has been found that it is the influence of the word among 'the people' that constitutes the bone of contention between the two groups. First, what sparks the conflict which leads to each of the two trial episodes is the apostles' teaching of the people and popularity among them (4.2; 5.12–17). Second, the charges which are brought against the apostles concentrate on the 'power' and the 'name' in which they claim to have performed the healing of the lame man (4.7) – thus using the healing to substantiate their claims about the fulfilment of Israel's hopes in Jesus (3.12–26; cf. 2.22–36) – or, in wording from the second incident, on the fact that the apostles had 'filled Jerusalem' with the teaching 'in this name' (5.28). Third, the outcome of the two incidents is the prayer for and success of the proclamation of the word (4.29, 31; 5.42).

That Luke's concern with the conflict surrounding the apostolic proclamation has a specifically apologetic character (with the content of the proclamation constituting in fact the object of Luke's apologia) becomes clear when the apologetic devices employed by Luke are seen in relation

---

[62] So Tannehill on echoes of the Lukan passion narrative (see above).
[63] So Tannehill on echo effects among various conflict passages in Acts; also Cassidy's emphasis on witness (see above).
[64] So Brawley on voices of Scripture (see above).

to the claims of the apostolic message in Acts 4–5. *In nuce*, the apostles' contention is that Jesus is the one in whom exclusively and universally God is now making available salvation (4.12), life (5.20), repentance and forgiveness (5.31). Various clusters of information in the cotext of the trial function as devices whereby this contention is substantiated and defended. Thus, miraculous events within the Christian community, such as the healing of the lame man and the numerous other healings and exorcisms performed by the apostles in the name of Jesus, are 'signs' of the divine benefits which are now available through him (4.9–12); the inability of all opposition to overthrow the Christian mission, with its claims about Jesus, shows that this work is not of human origin but of God (5.34–9); the sharp contrast between the positive image of the Christian witnesses and their supporters and the negative image of their opponents is a powerful indication of the side on which the readers should be; the validity of the Christian message is confirmed by reliable authorities such as God, the Holy Spirit, Gamaliel, multitudes of (eye-)witnesses, and so forth.

These observations lead to the overall conclusion that this part of Luke's work is designed to function as an *apologia pro evangelio* in relation to Judaism. Christologically, the contention is that Jesus is the one in whom exclusively and universally God is now making available salvation, life, repentance, and forgiveness. Soteriologically, the physical healing in the name of Jesus is the 'sign' that salvation is now offered to everyone through Jesus and through him alone (4.8–12). Ecclesiologically, it is claimed that through the Christian community (as represented by Peter and the apostolic group) Israel's symbols find their correct, albeit somewhat modified, expression. It is through the apostolic teaching and ministry that: (i) *the people* experience God's salvation, in the form of healing and forgiveness (4.9–10, 12; 5.14, 16, 31); (ii) *the temple* (which hosts most of the events of chs. 4–5) receives its proper use, as the locus of prayer, teaching, and healing – even if its function could now be extended to streets or homes (5.15, 42); (iii) *the Scriptures* are adequately interpreted (4.11, 25–6),[65] and *the land* (as embodied in Jerusalem) knows once again 'signs' of divine visitation (4.16, 22, 30; 5.12, 15–16).

Finally, an understanding of Peter's trials in Acts as designed for the confirmation of the Christian *kerygma* is in evident agreement with what has been noted at the beginning of the chapter regarding Jesus' predictions of his disciples' trials. Through the trials of Peter and his apostolic

---

[65] Although within the trial narratives the apostolic use of the Jewish Scriptures is unimpressive, the readers know from Acts 2–3 that the teaching for which the apostles are now on trial is based on the Scriptures.

companions, the Lukan reader has encountered for the first time instances
where the disciples are prosecuted on behalf of 'Jesus' name' and in which
their role is ironically transformed from defendants to 'witnesses', as they
mount their 'apologias' in the interest not of their personal safety, but of
their testimony to Jesus.

6

THE 'TRIAL' OF STEPHEN

Introduction

Despite Luke's explicit reference to Stephen being 'brought before the council' (ἤγαγον εἰς τὸ συνέδριον) and to the activity of (false) μάρτυρες (6.12–14; 7.58), language which is clearly suggestive of a trial setting, the question has been raised whether Stephen's death, according to Acts, may not be better understood as the outcome of a lynching, rather than of a trial.[1] Among the arguments which appear to support this interpretation are the absence of any formal verdict, the emphasis on the anger of Stephen's opponents as immediate precedent to his execution (7.54), the unlikelihood that the Sanhedrin had at the time the authority of capital punishment, and the fact that the Romans are not mentioned as taking any notice of the incident. Yet the overall picture seems to make best sense when understood as a legal trial, which due to the offensive words of the defendant and the escalating anger of his opponents soon succumbed to a more disorderly outburst of violence.[2] With these qualifications, the story can be regarded as belonging to the Lukan trial narratives. As far as the scope of this 'trial' story is concerned, 6.12 and 7.57 seem to be the two limits; yet an adequate understanding of this section inevitably requires some consideration of the slightly larger literary unit, extending at least from the origins of the conflict in 6.9 to Stephen's death in 7.60.

Due to the very limited number of works specifically dealing with the function of Stephen's *trial* (as distinct from his story, or speech)

---

[1] 7.54–58a is usually taken as indicating lynching, while 7.58b–60 is said to denote trial (Barrett, *Acts,* vol. I, p. 380). For a recent discussion on the subject, see T. Seland, *Establishment Violence in Philo and Luke: A Study of Non-Conformity to the Torah and Jewish Vigilante Reactions*, Leiden: E. J. Brill, 1995, pp. 226–7, 238–44. The issue is even more complex when one moves from the narrative level to the historical level (see Seland, *Establishment*, pp. 240–1), but that is beyond the concerns of this study.

[2] Seland, *Establishment*, p. 244.

in Acts, the present chapter will commence with an overview of previous understandings of the function of the Stephen *story*, and at the
same time establish the need for further work in this area. Thus I shall
outline first the way in which this part of Luke's work relates to the
existing interpretations of Lukan apologetics. Second, some attention
will be paid to three monographs which recognise the existence of an
apologetic intent in the Stephen story but do not develop the suggested
apologetic paradigm beyond the limits of the Stephen narrative. Finally,
I shall consider two works which do not indicate the presence of any
apologetic dimension in the Stephen narrative. The next main section
will take a sequential look at the principal parts of the Stephen story.
Because of the complexity of the issues relating to this passage,[3] attention will be limited to a number of specific issues which are directly connected with Luke's presentation of the trial and the apologetic role of this description. These issues will include the participants
in the conflict, the charges, the major themes of the speech, and the
outcome of the trial. A concluding section will bring together the findings and will seek to articulate the kind of apologetic which is thereby
suggested.

---

[3] As early as 1958, M. Simon observed that '[t]here are probably few more vexed
questions in the history of the early Church than those raised by chapters 6 and 7 of
the Acts of the Apostles. Much has already been said and written on the matter, and
there is an amazing diversity of conflicting opinions' (*St Stephen and the Hellenists
in the Primitive Church*, London, New York, and Toronto: Longmans, Green and Co.,
1958, p. 1).
   Among the more detailed and more recent works on this part of Luke's narrative, the
following can be noted: J. Bihler, *Die Stephanusgeschichte im Zusammenhang der Apostelgeschichte*, Münchener Theologische Studien, Munich: Max Hueber Verlag, 1963; Clark,
'Parallel Lives', ch. 8; D. A. deSilva, 'The Stoning of Stephen: Purging and Consolidating an
Endangered Institution', *StudBT* 17 (1989), 165–84; J. Kilgallen, 'The Function of Stephen's
Speech (Acts 7,2–53)', *Bib* 70 (1989), 173–93; J. Kilgallen, *The Stephen Speech. A Literary
and Redactional Study of Acts 7,2–53*, Rome: Biblical Institute Press, 1976; E. Larsson,
'Temple-Criticism and the Jewish Heritage: Some Reflexions on Acts 6–7', *NTS* 39 (1993),
379–95; S. Légasse, *Stephanos. Histoire et discours d'Etienne dans les Actes des Apôtres*,
Lectio Divina 147, Paris: Cerf, 1992; E. Richard, *Acts 6:1–8:4. The Author's Method of
Composition*, SBLDS 41, Missoula, MT: Scholars Press, 1978; Seland, *Establishment*;
Simon, *Stephen*; D. D. Sylva, 'The Meaning and Function of Acts 7:46–50', *JBL* 106
(1987), 261–75; A. Watson, *The Trial of Stephen: The First Christian Martyr*, Athens, GA:
University of Georgia Press, 1996; F. D. Weinert, 'Luke, Stephen, and the Temple in Luke–
Acts', *BTB* 17 (1987), 88–90; R. F. Wolfe, 'Rhetorical Elements in the Speeches of Acts 7
and 17', *JOTT* 6 (1993), 274–83. For a number of works before 1958 see Simon, *Stephen*,
p. 117, n. 1.

The function of Luke's story of Stephen: previous research
The Stephen narrative and existing interpretations of Lukan apologetics

As regards the relationship of Acts 6–7[4] to the available interpretations of Luke's apologetics, the situation is somewhat similar to Acts 4–5 and therefore some brief observations should suffice. Among those who see Luke's work as a political apologetic, Easton is again[5] the only one who, in his substantiation of the *religio licita* interpretation, claims support from Acts 6–7.[6] The purpose of Stephen's account of Jewish history, Easton insists, is to establish Christianity as part of Judaism and therefore as a *religio licita*.[7] While there can be little doubt that the relationship between Judaism and Christianity is one of Luke's major concerns at this juncture, a number of aspects of Stephen's trial in Acts indicate major difficulties with taking any form of political apologetic as the governing concern of this part of Luke's narrative: (1) For the third consecutive time in Luke's narrative, an exponent of Christianity is placed at the centre of sharp social conflict; if the first trial finishes with a warning (4.18, 21; 5.28) and the second one with flogging (5.40), this third trial results in the death of the Christian defendant. Such a picture of the Christian community would hardly have satisfied the Roman concerns that all new movements contribute to the peace and orderliness of the empire.[8] (2) Stephen's intransigence towards the Jewish authorities, most strikingly expressed in 7.51–3, could have easily fed the suspicion that when it comes to matters to do with their beliefs, Christians take little notice of human authorities (presumably Roman included). (3) In addition to the issue of Christianity's political harmlessness, two other major ingredients of a political apologetic – namely, precedents for the Romans' favourable attitude towards Christians and flattering pictures of the Roman justice – are completely absent.

In a different vein, Brawley has sought to align Stephen's story with his assertion that Acts has been written as an ecclesiastic defence of Paul.

---

[4] Due to limitations of space, only the more notable contributions on this part of Luke's work are discussed below. For a broader spectrum of opinions on the matter, but with very little critical evaluation, see M. Scharlemann, *Stephen: A Singular Saint*, Rome: Pontifical Biblical Institute Press, 1968, pp. 3–6.

[5] See chapter 5 for discussion of previous contributions on Peter's trials in Acts.

[6] Note the complete absence of references to the story of Stephen in such classical representations of the political apologetic theory as those of Cadbury (*Making*, pp. 308–14) and Conzelmann (*Theology*, pp. 138–44).

[7] Easton, *Early Christianity*, pp. 46–7.   [8] Cassidy, *Society*, pp. 148–9.

In Brawley's understanding, 'Luke does not allow the Stephen incident to stand on its own as an intrinsically interesting event. Rather, he makes it preparatory for his story of Paul.'[9] Luke is said to establish this significance for the Stephen incident by his mention of Paul's involvement in Stephen's martyrdom (7.58; 22.20) and his subsequent persecution of the Jerusalem church (8.3). That the double mention of Saul in connection with the story of Stephen is in keeping with the prominent role played by Paul in the latter part of Acts is beyond dispute. Yet the specific way in which Brawley views the link between the two characters is problematic in at least two areas. First, the burden of proof is still with him to show that the significance of Stephen in Acts is established in terms of his part in Paul's story. As it stands, his work has only demonstrated that even in the first half of Acts the author makes use of certain opportunities to give glimpses of the character who is to dominate the second half of the book.[10] Second, to the extent to which the story of Stephen can be regarded as contributing to the Lukan portrait of Paul, that particular contribution is a negative, rather than a positive (legitimating), one: it shows Paul as a former persecutor of 'the Way' (9.1, 13, 21; 26.10, 11; esp. 22.4) and, ironically, it is the defence of the Way and its witness, rather than of Paul, that typically provides the immediate context of the later recollections of Saul's deeds.[11]

The Stephen narrative as apologia in its own right

Several authors have viewed the Stephen narrative as having some apologetic function, without developing the proposed apologetic paradigm beyond the limits of this narrative.[12]

According to M. Simon,[13] the Stephen story represents an ecclesiastic rehabilitation of Stephen himself,[14] occasioned by the unpopularity, even within Christian circles, of Stephen's hostile attitude towards the temple.[15] Simon's interpretation can be commended for its ability to account for at least two major features of the narrative: the centrality of Stephen to

---

[9] Brawley, *Luke–Acts*, p. 44.   [10] Ibid., pp. 42–6.

[11] For an analysis of Paul's speeches in Acts 22 and 26, see the relevant sections in the next chapter.

[12] As we shall see, Kilgallen suggests a connection between the apologetic of Acts 6–7 and Luke's broader Christological apologetic, but he does not develop his suggestion at any length.

[13] Simon, *Stephen*.

[14] Kilgallen (*Stephen*, pp. 16–17) lists several other works which suggest (albeit often only in passing) the existence of a Lukan 'vindication' of Stephen.

[15] Simon, *Stephen*, pp. 25–6.

the story and his positive characterisation. Yet certain problems remain. First, our Lukan source (the only available source on Stephen's life) offers little evidence that Stephen was such an unpopular character among his brethren and therefore in need of legitimation. His attitude towards the temple, which according to Simon was the one cause of his unpopularity, is not as radically different from that of other Lukan protagonists as has often been maintained.[16] Second, the fact that at least some of the themes which govern Luke's presentation of Stephen's story (e.g. Israel's rejection of God's messengers; Jesus' resurrection and glorification; the temple) are also present in other trial narratives of Luke–Acts indicates that one is dealing here with certain Lukan concerns which transcend his interest in Stephen as an individual and which reflect, rather, certain broader issues pertaining to the earliest Christian community and having, probably, some contemporary relevance for the author.

One work which comes close to presenting the apologetic tendencies of Stephen's story in this way is that of J. Kilgallen, according to whom, 'Stephen represents a Christian point of apologetics about the temple',[17] that is, 'an explanation of the disappearance of the Temple's importance or necessity'.[18] Kilgallen's study undoubtedly points in the right direction. Yet a number of limitations of special concern to us need to be noted. First, his contention that the temple is portrayed as a misunderstanding of God from its very construction by Solomon[19] is, despite its popularity, in need of revision. Inevitably, therefore, his representation of the temple-related apologetic also needs some modification. Second, his contention that out of the three elements of the Jewish accusation (Jesus, temple, and law) Stephen only gives an adequate answer to the first two[20] is also problematic. The theme of the law, we shall see, functions apologetically in much the same way as the temple theme. Third, Kilgallen's treatment of Luke's apologetics, while offering some useful insights, is secondary to his purposes and therefore lacking any systematic character. Fourth, the same is true of Kilgallen's treatment of Stephen's trial – his primary interest in the speech[21] means that the trial has received only indirect attention.

Finally, a major study on the Stephen narrative has come from the pen of S. Légasse.[22] Despite its overall thoroughness, however, less explicit attention than might have been expected is given to the function

---

[16] See the discussion of the temple theme, below.   [17] Kilgallen, *Stephen*, p. 34.
[18] Ibid., p. 117.   [19] Ibid., pp. 88–9.   [20] Ibid., pp. 117–18.
[21] Note the title of the book: *The Stephen Speech: A Literary and Redactional Study of Acts 7, 2–53*.
[22] Légasse, *Stephanos*.

of the Stephen narrative as a whole (and even less to the trial account in particular). Most of what can be gleaned on this topic comes from his discussion of the function of the speech,[23] which he summarises as 'polémique et enseignement' ('polemics and teaching').[24] Luke's concern, Légasse argues, is not so much to refute the Jewish charges against Stephen but rather to indicate a reversal of roles, through which the accused becomes the accuser: 'l'inversion des rôles est l'instrument d'une revanche contre le tribunal ou plutôt contre ceux qu'il incarne' ('the reversal of roles is the instrument of a revenge against the tribunal or, rather, against those who constitute it').[25] Ultimately, however, Luke's hope is that Stephen's address will give the readers instruction and reassurance: 'il entend instruire et rassurer les chrétiens et, parmi eux, sans aucun doute, ces Juifs qui avaient adhéré à l'Evangile, plus aptes que les autres chrétiens à s'interroger avec angoisse' ('he intends to instruct and reassure the Christians and, together with them, no doubt, the Jews who had accepted the Gospel and who would have been more likely than the other Christians to ask themselves serious questions').[26]

Although Légasse's insights into the apologetic character of the Stephen episode (and especially the trial) are too general to be of much help, his insistence on the reversal of roles between Stephen and his opponents and his understanding of Luke's concerns in terms of instruction and reassurance are certainly correct and worth further investigation.

Non-apologetic interpretations of the Stephen narrative

In a detailed analysis of Acts 6–7, Scharlemann has argued that Luke did not include Stephen's story and speech because of any intention of offering in this way answers to any specific problems of his own day, but rather because of his interest in the history of Christianity[27] – in this case his interest in Stephen's solution to the problem of the Samaritans' relationship to Judaism and Christianity.[28] Two observations, in particular, seem to render this explanation unsatisfactory: its incompatibility with decades of research which has been demonstrating that Luke did

---

[23] Ibid., pp. 92–4. See also his brief discussion of Stephen's role, as 'polémiste et catéchète' (pp. 219–20).

[24] Ibid., p. 92.

[25] Ibid., p. 93. Légasse adds, however, that not all Jews are 'embodied' in the tribunal; a division has been created in Israel, as prophesied by Simeon in Luke 2.34–5, and Stephen himself is a token of the believing part.

[26] Ibid., p. 94. [27] Scharlemann, *Stephen*, pp. 185–8.

[28] Ibid., pp. 52–3, 56, 185.

not write for historical reasons alone, and the high degree of uncertainty regarding the alleged Samaritan background of Stephen's speech.[29]

A more recent work dealing specifically with Stephen's trial is that of A. Watson.[30] According to Watson, Stephen had been proclaiming Jesus' return as political Messiah, who would overthrow the Romans, would change the law of Moses, and would destroy the temple (since God had required a tabernacle, not a temple). Stephen's teaching led to his conflict with the Jewish authorities and eventually to his trial. His only hope of escaping the charge of blasphemy was to state that Jesus was entitled to do such things due to his Messianic status. To stress Jesus' Messiahship, however, was going to scandalise the Romans. To avoid that, Stephen gave his response to the Jews in a language which for the Romans was coded and therefore inaccessible. This, Watson contends, explains why the Romans are not mentioned as becoming involved in the dispute.

By far the biggest difficulty with Watson's approach is that there is very little in the text to substantiate his notions of a political Messiah or Roman domination. The only evidence he brings for their existence is the theme of Israel's exile.[31] To be sure, this theme does have the potential to provide one important ingredient for a message of political liberation, but on its own this is hardly sufficient to indicate the presence of a liberation theme and even less to establish it as the primary meaning of the passage. It is abundantly clear from 7.52–3 that the primary analogy between Jesus and Moses – with the latter being the only political liberator in Stephen's survey of Jewish history – is not their political roles but rather their rejection by the rebellious Jews.

Stephen's trial re-examined
The participants in the conflict

The central character in the conflict of Acts 6–7 is undoubtedly Stephen. Luke's characterisation of him exhibits a significant element of irony. After introducing him as someone whose ministry is 'to serve at tables'

---

[29] Among the many authors who question such a background, see: K. Haacker, 'Samaritan, Samaria', *NIDNTT*, vol. III, pp. 464–6; W. H. Mare, 'Acts 7: Jewish or Samaritan in Character?', *WTJ* 33–4 (1970–2), 1–21; R. Pummer, 'The Samaritan Pentateuch and the New Testament', *NTS* 22 (1975–6), 441–3; E. Richard, 'Acts 7: An Investigation of the Samaritan Evidence', *CBQ* 39 (1977), 190–208. In favour of a Samaritan background, cf. C. H. H. Scobie, 'The Origins and Development of Samaritan Christianity', *NTS* 19 (1972–3), 390–414; A. Spiro, 'Stephen's Samaritan Background', in J. Munck, *The Acts of the Apostles*, revised by W. F. Albright and C. S. Mann, The Anchor Bible 31, New York: Doubleday, 1967, pp. 285–300.

[30] Watson, *Trial of Stephen*. See especially pp. 78–83.   [31] Ibid., pp. 43, 82.

(διακονεῖν τραπέζ αις), so that *others* (viz. the twelve) can perform
the ministry of the word (6.2–4), the activity through which Stephen's
prominence is next established is that of performing wonders and signs
among the people (6.8), disputing (συζητοῦντες,[32] 6.9), and speaking
(ἐλάλει, 6.10; cf. 6.11, 13, 14, and the lengthy speech of 7.2–53), that
is, precisely those activities which up to that point had been the lot of
the apostles.[33] How is this to be explained? Why does he come into
prominence as a minister of the word if his appointment was to a different
type of service? Two observations may help in the approximation of a
solution. First, it would be wrong to infer from Luke's description of
the allocation of different services (of the word and of the tables) to the
two groups (the twelve and the seven respectively) that Luke intends his
readers to understand that from now on the preaching of the word is
exclusively the task of the apostles. True, they have a unique role and
(eye-witness) authority in the proclamation of the word (Ac. 1.2–3, 8,
21–2), and Acts 6.1–6 records the church's recognition of this task, but
this hardly implies the exclusion of others from the task of proclamation.
Second, since Luke is going to deal at some length with Stephen as
a Christian witness, and since he wants his Hellenistic audience to be
favourable to Stephen rather than to the group of Hellenistic Jews who
oppose him, it seems an efficient device of *captatio benevolentiae* that he
should highlight Stephen's charitable activity in the primary interest of
yet another Hellenistic group (6.1).

The second important role in the conflict of Acts 6–7 is played by
a group whom Luke describes as τινες τῶν ἐκ τῆς συναγωγῆς τῆς
λεγομένης Λιβερτίνων καὶ Κυρηναίων καὶ Ἀλεξανδρέων καὶ τῶν
ἀπὸ Κιλικίας καὶ Ἀσίας (6.9). Much discussion has surrounded the
question of how many synagogues are meant, the range of suggestions
covering every possibility from one to five,[34] with one[35] and two[36] being the most widely held alternatives. It is generally accepted, however,
that the groups mentioned here were (probably like Stephen himself)

[32] The term is by implication applicable to Stephen, as well as his adversaries.

[33] In the words of deSilva, 'Stephen, appears thus to have arrogated to himself, or had
been privately commissioned by God to perform, the work of a full apostle. The author
links him to the same charisma which was operative in the apostles from the beginning of
Acts' ('Stoning', 170).

[34] Bruce, *Acts*, p. 187.

[35] Barrett, *Acts*, vol. I, p. 323; Bruce, *Acts*, p. 187; Dunn, *Acts*, p. 86; *The Partings of
the Ways Between Christianity and Judaism and Their Significance for the Character of
Christianity*, London: SCM Press, p. 294, n. 27.

[36] Marshall, *Acts* (1980), p. 129. Barrett (*Acts*, vol. I, p. 323) and Haenchen (*Acts*, p. 271)
also call attention to the twofold syntactical construction of the sentence.

Hellenistic Jews who had returned from the Diaspora to live in Jerusalem.[37] The significance of this is that Stephen is 'opposed by his own sort',[38] from among whom came also the Hellenists of 6.1, whom Stephen's ministry was specifically designed to benefit.

On the same side of the conflict as the non-Christian Hellenists stand also the Jewish leaders (albeit this time the initiative is not theirs), whom Luke identifies first as τοὺς πρεσβυτέρους καὶ τοὺς γραμματεῖς and then, indicating again the comprehensiveness of the Jewish representation, as τὸ συνέδριον (6.12). The 'false witnesses' (μάρτυρας ψευδεῖς) also cooperate with Stephen's opponents (6.13), but no separate role should be sought for them in the narrative, since their attitude and words do not represent their own position as much that of Stephen's initial prosecutors, the Hellenists, in whose service the witnesses are. More important for the Lukan plot is the double reference to 'the people'. The position first ascribed to them (6.8) is in line with their role in the conflict between Peter and the Jewish authorities, a conflict during which the people had been the enthusiastic recipients of the apostolic teaching and ministry (3.11–12; 4.1–2, 21; 5.12–16, 21, 42). Similarly here, the people are those among whom Stephen 'did great wonders and signs' and among whom the word of God had been 'increasing', even to the point that 'a great many of the priests were obedient to the faith' (6.1,7). Their position dramatically changes, however, when they are mentioned the second time (6.12) – so much so that now they head the list of those whom the non-Christian Hellenists had managed to 'stir up' (συνεκίνησαν) and who for the rest of the Stephen narrative are to be regarded as Stephen's opponents. The shift in the people's role is strikingly similar to what we have noted in connection with Jesus' trial: as the conflict in Jerusalem reaches once again its climax,[39] the unbelieving part of Judaism is scandalised by the popularity of the Lukan protagonist among 'the people' and eventually succeeds in manipulating the crowd (or, perhaps more accurately, a significant section of it) into joining the hostile leadership.

---

[37] Barrett, *Acts*, vol. I, p. 324; Dunn, *Acts*, p. 86; C. C. Hill, *Hellenists and Hebrews: Reappraising Divison within the Earliest Church*, Minneapolis: Fortress, 1992, p. 28; Marshall, *Acts* (1980), p. 129.

[38] Barrett, *Acts*, vol. I, p. 324. According to Barrett, '[i]t is perhaps not unnatural that Hellenistic Jews who remained Jews and did not become Christians should be particularly incensed with those of their number who, in their view, betrayed the ancestral faith, and should initiate action against them' (p. 325). In a similar vein, Seland develops at some length the notion of what he regards here as an '*intra-group conflict*' (*Establishment*, p. 246; see also pp. 246–50).

[39] Stephen's trial and martyrdom undoubtedly bring to a climax the Jerusalem conflict of the first half of Acts.

The nature of the conflict: origins and development

Luke's account of the conflict between Stephen and the non-Christian Hellenists is connected with his account of the appointment of the seven by means of two summary statements, found respectively in 6.7 and 6.8. The first one rehearses the already established emphasis on the advance of the word among the people of Jerusalem, as the Christian community placed 'the ministry of the word' at the forefront of its concerns (6.1a, 2b, 4). The second one indicates Stephen's specific role within this enterprise. The significance of this is that, in so far as Stephen is introduced as instrumental in the spreading of the word among the people, his subsequent conflict with the non-Christian Hellenists is inevitably and programmatically introduced as a challenge to the word, of which he is the spokesperson.

As regards the development of the conflict, escalating popularity among the people is met initially by attempts to silence Stephen by reasoning (6.9b), but the opponents fail to bring forward a convincing case and eventually resort to violence. The underlying Lukan message is that there are no convincing objections which can be brought against the word and its spokesperson and that those hostile to them can only resort to rather desperate means, such as trying to 'silence' them by physical violence. The inability of the Hellenists to 'withstand' (ἀντιστῆναι) the 'wisdom' and the 'Spirit' with which Stephen spoke (6.10) recalls Jesus' predictions in Luke 12.11–12 and 21.12–18, in which Jesus had promised the disciples the Holy Spirit (12.12) and wisdom (21.15) so that no adversaries would be able to 'withstand' (ἀντιστῆναι) their 'testimony' (21.13). The present conflict is thus portrayed as belonging to those hostile settings in which the disciples' witness to Jesus is the chief aim and the result of their 'apologias' (Luke 12.11–12; 21.13–15).

The charges

The centrality of the charges against Stephen to Acts 6–7 is indicated by the triple presentation of their content in 6.11–14. Opinions vary as to the number of charges which are meant. Some have maintained the existence of four charges, namely blasphemy against Moses (6.11), blasphemy against God (6.11), speaking against the temple (6.13–14), and speaking against the Mosaic law (6.13–14).[40] Others have argued that three charges are involved, relating respectively to Jesus, the temple, and

---

[40] O'Neill, *Theology*, p. 90; Richard, *Acts 6:1–8:4*, pp. 316–17, 324–5.

the law.[41] The (probably correct) majority view is, however, that there are in fact only two charges – concerning the temple and the law – and that the three statements of the accusation represent a progression from smaller to greater explicitness of these two charges.[42] Essentially, then, the accusation is made by some non-Christian Hellenists against a Christian Hellenist that his association with Jesus[43] has led him to a breach with two major identity markers of the people of God, the temple and the law.

How the readers are to view this accusation is effectively summed up by Luke in his qualification of the witnesses as 'false' (ψευδεῖς), a term inevitably suggestive of the validity of the witnesses' charges as well.[44] Questions have been raised regarding the justification of such a qualification in the light of Jesus' words and actions in the Third Gospel,[45] but such questions can hardly obscure the fact that, in the present context at least, Luke *intends* the charges to be understood as false.[46] The implications of this are rather disastrous – and therefore often glossed over – for any interpretations which maintain a thoroughly negative portrayal of the temple in the Stephen narrative: the author qualifies as *false* the charge that Stephen has spoken against the temple (although, as we shall see later, God's *transcendence* over the temple is a major contention of the speech).

The speech: major themes and their apologetic function

The space allocated by modern research to the study of Stephen's speech is not disproportionate to the length of this discourse.[47] The specific aim

---

[41] So, for example, Kilgallen, 'Function', 185; Kilgallen, *Stephen*, p. 119. He claims, however, that the charges can also be 'capsulized' in one: 'Christ-and-the-Temple' (*Stephen*, p. 35), or 'Jesus' relationship with the Temple and Law' (p. 33; cf. p. 32).

[42] See, among others, Barrett, *Acts*, vol. I, pp. 323–9; Marshall, *Acts* (1980), pp. 128, 132; Sylva, 'Meaning', 17.

[43] Ironically, Stephen is on trial for something that *Jesus* is supposed to have said. For a more detailed discussion of this, see Kilgallen, *Stephen*, pp. 32–3.

[44] Seland, *Establishment*, p. 232.

[45] Barrett usefully summarises the evidence: 'it seems that a strong case can be made for the belief that Jesus did foretell the destruction of the Temple, even if he did not say that he would himself destroy it, and that he did change Mosaic regulations, even if he regarded his changes as fulfilment rather than destruction' (*Acts*, vol. I, p. 329). See also Marshall, *Acts* (1980), p. 128, who believes that Stephen must have said something which was liable to be 'twisted' to imply an attack upon the temple and the law.

[46] See B. Witherington III, *The Acts of the Apostles: A Socio-Rhetorical Commentary*, Grand Rapids: Eerdmans; Carlisle: Paternoster, 1998, pp. 257–8, who argues at some length that 'at every step along the way Luke makes abundantly clear that the witnesses and the testimony are false . . .'

[47] A helpful outline of the various angles from which Stephen's speech had been analysed prior to 1976 can be found in Kilgallen, *Stephen*, pp. 3–26. For a more recent bibliography, see Barrett, *Acts*, vol. I, pp. 333–4.

of the present section is to indicate and elucidate the apologetic function
of a number of themes which previous scholarship has already established
as central to Stephen's speech.[48]

(a) The independence of God

Kilgallen regards the umbrella-concept of 'independence' as '[o]ne of the
most consistently expressed interpretations of Stephen's intended purpose
before the Sanhedrin'.[49] What he means by this term is the claim that God
is not tied down to a temple, a land, a law, or even a nation.[50] According to
this trend of interpretation, Stephen's story of Abraham (7.2–8a), taking
its starting point from God's appearance to Abraham 'when he was in
Mesopotamia', shows that 'God's self-revelation is not confined to the
land of the Jews, still less to the temple'.[51] God's dealings with his people
in Egypt, Midian, and the wilderness, throughout the stories of Joseph
and Moses (7.9–44) provide further and ample evidence for the continuity
of this theme throughout the speech. The climax is, however, reached in
Stephen's criticism of Israel's attempt of 'housing' God in the temple
(7.47–50).

The full apologetic weight of this theme can only be adequately appreciated when the speech is seen in its larger context in Acts. As the gospel

---

[48] The choice of themes here relies partly on Kilgallen's account of 'Past Reflections
on the Speech of Stephen' (*Stephen*, pp. 3–26). The themes of exile and political Messiah,
suggested by Watson, are not included here due to insufficient data in the speech to support
them (see above for a critique of Watson's work). A more important omission is the theme
of Christology. The reason for this is that most of what is said in the speech (directly
and indirectly) is in terms of Jesus' rejection, so it seems sufficient to deal briefly with
Christology under the theme of Israel's rejection of God's messengers. For more detailed
analyses of this theme, see Légasse, *Stephanos*, pp. 88–90; Kilgallen, 'Function', 182–7
and *Stephen*, pp. 21–3.

[49] Kilgallen, *Stephen*, p. 17.

[50] This independence of God, Kilgallen notes, is understood in different ways by different
scholars. Thus, H. H. Wendt expresses it in terms of temple alone, B. Reicke includes also the
land (see also F. F. Bruce, 'Stephen's Apologia', in B. Thompson (ed), *Scripture: Meaning
and Method*, Hull University Press, 1987, pp. 40–3), J. Renié applies it to the law as well,
while D. C. Arichea extends it even further, to Israel (Kilgallen, *Stephen*, pp. 17–19). Two
recent statements of the independence theme with regard to the land have been offered by
D. Ravens and S. Légasse. According to the former, the speech argues that 'God is not
confined to the land of Israel for his revelation, salvation and worship' (D. Ravens, *Luke
and the Restoration of Israel*, JSNTSup 119, Sheffield Academic Press, 1995, p. 60), while
for the latter the whole address creates 'une impression de mouvement, qui s'oppose à l'idée
selon laquelle Dieu aurait confiné, et pour ainsi dire immobilisé, son action à l'intérieur
des frontières du pays d'Israël' ('an impression of movement, which is opposed to the idea
according to which God would have confined, or, in other words, immobilised, his action
within Israel's frontiers') (Légasse, *Stephanos*, p. 78; see also pp. 77–80).

[51] Marshall, *Acts* (1980), p. 135.

moves out into non-Jewish territory (geographically, linguistically, culturally, and ethnically), as part of its journey from Jerusalem towards 'the ends of the earth', one challenge which it persistently has to face is that of preserving its continuity with Israel's salvation history. Stephen's speech represents an important milestone in this journey, not because, with the narrative concerning him, Luke gives up on (the mission to) the Jews,[52] but because it lays down the conceptual foundations for the legitimacy of the gospel's subsequent transcendence of the Jewish boundaries. To make this point clear, Luke places the speech in the context of the 'increase' of the word of God and just before this word moves out from Jerusalem into Samaria and then further afield. To heighten the tone of the challenge for the attention of his 'Hellenistic' (Jewish and non-Jewish) readers Luke reveals its origin with a group of Hellenists who would have been particularly concerned with the preservation of Jewish identity – the Hellenists who had returned to live in Jerusalem.[53] To add weight to the force of the argument for the same readership, Luke has already taken pains to portray Stephen as someone who serves the interests of the Hellenists.

(b) *Israel's rejection of God's messengers*

A second dominant theme of the speech, also of a relatively general character but rather more overt than that of 'independence', is that of Israel's habitual rejection of God's messengers.[54] Apart from the story of Abraham, where the theme is hard to detect, much of the speech, focusing on the lives of Joseph and Moses, abounds with examples of this regrettable side of Israel's history (7.9, 25, 27–9, 35, 39). The theme is brought to a climax in 7.52, first through a rhetorical question (τίνα τῶν προφητῶν οὐκ ἐδίωξαν οἱ πατέρες ὑμῶν;) indicating the universality of this destiny for Israel's prophets, and second through an unsparing statement about the killing of 'the righteous one' and of all those who had prophesied his coming (7.52b).

The apologetic function of this theme should not need much elaboration. The history of Israel, it is argued, puts into perspective the

[52] Pace Kilgallen, *Stephen*, pp. 111–13. Of itself, the fact that the Christian witness is no longer focused on Jerusalem after Acts 7 should no more imply the abandonment of the Jews than, say, the disappearance of Samaria from the Lukan horizon after Acts 8 would indicate the abandonment of the Samaritans. Luke's point is, rather, that God and his word are not static, limited by places and peoples, but free to transcend human entities.

[53] On the 'conservativeness' of Diaspora Judaism, and particularly of the Diaspora Jews who had returned to live in Jerusalem, see Seland, *Establishment*, pp. 248–51.

[54] Among the numerous works discussing this theme, see Kilgallen, 'Function', 187–8, 181–4; Kilgallen, *Stephen*, p. 107; Marshall, *Acts* (1980), p. 132.

contemporary rejection of Jesus and his witnesses (Stephen included) – and, as far as Luke's readers are concerned, the ongoing rejection of the gospel by the majority of their Jewish contemporaries. Rather than raising doubts about the relationship of the Christian protagonists to the historic people of God or about the 'orthodoxy' of the message they proclaim, their rejection should be regarded as confirmation of their belonging to the true prophetic tradition. Moreover, the apologetic force of the rejection theme is greatly enhanced by the subordinated theme of the Holy Spirit's rejection.[55] By condemning someone so full of the Holy Spirit as Stephen (6.3, 10; 7.55), the Jews are not merely rejecting a human agent but once again they re-actualise their habitual resistance to the Holy Spirit.

(c) *Moses and the law*

With the issues of law and temple, one comes to the foci of both God's independence and Jewish rejection in the context of the Stephen narrative. With regard to the law, the question has been raised whether, despite the repeated accusation that Stephen had spoken against Moses and the law (6.11–14), enough is said on this topic for it to be regarded as a theme of the speech. Kilgallen's answer to this is in the negative, as he points out somewhat surprisedly that the speech appears to deal with only the first two elements of what he regards as a triple accusation (focusing on Jesus, the temple, and the law). To the issue of the law, he notes, only two references are made (7.38, 53), both of which are said to be positive statements about the law, but these are considered insufficient to denote a theme. The response to this element of the accusation is said to come much later, in Acts 15.[56]

Kilgallen's analysis at this point is rather intriguing, for two reasons. First, when it comes to the issue of Christology, he is prepared to take this as 'a Theme of the Entire Stephen Episode',[57] although no more than one direct reference to Jesus is made in the whole speech (7.52). Secondly, he is keen to clarify that the accusations of 6.13 and 6.14, about the law and, respectively, 'the customs which Moses delivered to us', are the equivalent of the charge of 6.11, regarding Moses. Should such observations not alert one to the possibility that (i) there may be

---

[55] Kilgallen sees the role of the Holy Spirit in the Stephen narrative as parallel to that in Peter's trial, where it is said to be of a 'psychological' nature, viz. to convince the readers of the Spirit's activity among the Christians and thus of the culpability of the Jewish rejection of the Christian witness (*Stephen*, pp. 114–15). See also Seland, *Establishment*, p. 236.

[56] Kilgallen, *Stephen*, pp. 115–18.   [57] Kilgallen, 'Function', 185; see also 185–7.

much more to the law theme than the direct references to it indicate, and that (ii) in the speech, just as in the accusations, Moses and the law may be part and parcel of the same theme?[58]

When due weight is given to this association between Moses and the law, it becomes inappropriate to speak of a postponing of the answer to the law charge until Acts 15 and also of a distinction being made between the authentic Mosaic traditions and the Jewish interpretations of it.[59] Instead of concentrating on the attitude of Jesus and his followers towards the law, Stephen's approach (and here the apologetic character of the narrative comes again to the fore) consists rather of turning the tables against his opponents – their rejection of Jesus and his witnesses aligns them with their fathers, who have so many times rejected Moses and his words[60] and in so doing have become transgressors of the Mosaic law. Thus, the theme of Moses and the law clarifies for Stephen's hearers and Luke's readers alike that it is the unbelieving Jews, rather than Jesus or Stephen or any other witnesses of the gospel, who are the true opponents of the law.[61]

(d) *The temple*

Taking its starting point from the temple charge in 6.13–14, the theme of the temple is developed first somewhat indirectly in the speech, through the emphasis on 'Israel's liturgical defection':[62] God's intention for Abraham's offspring was that they shall 'worship [him] in this place' (7.7b),[63] but they soon distorted their worship of the true God into worship of idols (7.40–3). The temple section (7.44–50) comes then as a second example of Israel's corrupted worship.

The majority of modern research on this closing section of the speech has tended to regard it as radically critical of the temple. According to this position, the particle δέ of 7.47 denotes a contrast between the acceptable 'tent of witness' (σκηνὴ τοῦ μαρτυρίου, 7.44), and probably also David's intended 'tabernacle' (σκήνωμα, 7.46), and Solomon's unacceptable 'house made with hands' (οἶκος, 7.47, 49; χειροποιήτοις,

---

[58] So Légasse, who names one theme of the speech 'Moise et la Loi' (*Stephanos*, p. 80).

[59] *Pace* Marshall, *Acts* (1980), p. 130, who claims that '[t]he *customs* [of 6.14] are no doubt the oral traditions giving the scribal interpretation of the law'. Cf. Barrett, *Acts*, vol. I, pp. 328–9.

[60] By far the greatest part of the rejection theme (see above) consists of references to Moses.

[61] Légasse, *Stephanos*, pp. 81–2.   [62] Kilgallen, *Stephen*, p. 107.

[63] Kilgallen regards this verse as the central point of the Abraham story (ibid., p. 42).

7.48).[64] More recently, however, several works have argued that such a thoroughly negative reading of the portrayal of the temple is unwarranted by the text.[65] Among the observations which seem to lead to such a corrective, the following can be noted: (1) The δέ of 7.47 need not be regarded *ipso facto* as introducing a contrast; it is perfectly plausible to take it as introducing a new element in a series.[66] Moreover, even if a contrast *is* meant, it need not necessarily be between σκήνωμα and οἶκος; it is at least equally possible (although scholarship seems to have been surprisingly silent about this) to view it as a contrast of activities, indicating a progression from the smaller to the greater. '[David] *asked leave to find* a habitation ... but it was Solomon who *built* a house for him' ([Δαυίδ] ᾐτήσατο εὑρεῖν σκήνωμα ... Σολομῶν δὲ οἰκοδόμησεν αὐτῷ οἶκον). (2) There is no reason to take σκήνωμα as referring only to the tent and not to the temple as well.[67] (3) It is also possible that χειροποιήτοις be understood as referring to the tent, as well as the temple.[68] (4) There are good reasons to believe that 'although in Acts 7:49, 50 Luke uses a citation from Isaiah, the whole of Acts 7:46–50 is designed by Luke to refer to the tradition of the dedication of the first temple (1 Kgs. 8:14–30; 2 Chr. 6:3–21)',[69] which points *not to temple-criticism but to God's transcendence over it.*[70]

It would surely be wrong to infer from such observations that all forms of criticism of the temple are excluded – the subsequent section of the speech (7.51–3) would in this case become (even more) inexplicable. One item in particular is hard to understand in any other way but as a sharp accusation relating to the temple: Luke's use of χειροποίητος. The term has often been taken to imply that the temple itself is portrayed as an idol[71] – the resemblance of the term to the description of the idol in 7.41 (καὶ ἐμοσχο**ποίησαν** ... καὶ εὐφραίνοντο ἐν τοῖς ἔργοις **τῶν χειρῶν** αὐτῶν) would certainly support this association. Yet some qualification of this charge seems necessary in the light of the discussion above. The problem is not with what the temple *was* initially, when David thought about it and Solomon built it; the problem is with what it *has become* – the epitome of Israel's attempt to limit God. It is in

---

[64] See Sylva's bibliography on the 'rejection thesis' ('Meaning', 261–2, n. 4).

[65] So, for example, Hill, *Hellenists*, pp. 69–81; Larsson, 'Temple-Criticism'; Légasse, *Stephanos*, pp. 82–8; Sylva, 'Meaning'.

[66] Kilgallen, *Stephen*, p. 89 (although for Kilgallen this observation only exonerates Solomon, not the temple); Larsson, 'Temple-Criticism', 390–1; Sylva, 'Meaning', 264–5.

[67] Sylva, 'Meaning', 264.   [68] Larsson, 'Temple-Criticism', 391.

[69] Sylva, 'Meaning', 265.   [70] Ibid., 265–7.

[71] So, for example, Dunn, *Partings*, p. 67.

such circumstances that the temple can be thought of as an idol. A brief reminder of the themes noted above may help to substantiate and clarify this point.

In the language of the independence theme, it is when the temple is used as a means of limiting God's independence that it becomes 'a house made with hands', having a function not dissimilar to that of Israel's idols in the desert (7.40–3). It is not only the independence theme, however, with which my suggested reading of the temple material ties in. A close parallel can be noted with the apologetic function of the law theme. According to the speech, just as it was not Jesus or his followers who opposed the law, but rather the unbelieving Jews, so also the charge that Jesus would destroy the temple is false, for it is not him, but the same rebellious Jews who, through their attempts to limit God and his activity to this building, have turned it into an idol and thus ensured God's judgement upon it. As for the actual meaning of Israel's limitation of God to the temple, the temple section is not sufficient on its own to provide an answer. Yet its location between two major rejection accounts – Moses, the antitype of the eschatological prophet (7.37), and the prophet, the Righteous One, himself (7.52) – suggests that a connection is intended between the temple's degradation and Jesus' rejection. In the broader context of Luke–Acts this connection becomes clearer: the temple's decadence was most notably re-actualised when the Jewish leadership denied Jesus and his witnesses the right to reform the temple to its true *raison d'être*: 'a house of prayer' (Luke 19.46; cf. 20.2; Ac. 4.1–2; 5.20, 25, 28).

In conclusion, when the major themes of Stephen's address are correctly evaluated in relation to each other and to the larger Lukan narrative, the apologetic significance of the resulting picture is unmistakable. The speech legitimates the incipient Christian movement at the point of its climactic rejection by the representatives of Judaism and its imminent transcendence of Jewish boundaries: it assures the readers that such transcendence is rooted in the nature of God himself (a God whose 'independence' cannot be restricted by such categories as temple, law, and land) and is occasioned by the climactic re-actualisation of Israel's habitual rejection of God's servants in the current rejection of Jesus and his heralds by the Jewish leadership. Thus, ironically, it is not those who, through allegiance to Jesus, *transcend* the Jewish symbols who are the true enemies of these symbols, but those who wish to *limit* God's independence to them and in so doing give these symbols an idolatrous function.

The outcome of the trial

As in the case of Luke's story of Jesus, the conflict which Stephen's trial represents finds its final outcome only beyond the boundaries of the trial account. Stephen was brought to trial as a representative of the word and facing the charge that his allegiance to Jesus had led him – and was likely to lead the Jerusalemites, among whom he had been so influential (6.7–8) – to a breach with two fundamental pillars of the people of God: the law and the temple.[72] The greatest part of the trial narrative was then taken up with unpacking the position which the readers should adopt on the matter. Nevertheless, the jury is still out, for the reader is still awaiting the verdict – a verdict which from a judicial point of view never comes. Instead, Luke narrates the outcome of the trial in a way which lets the events speak the verdict for themselves. It is, therefore, my contention in what follows that Luke indicates this verdict through his apologetic presentation of the trial outcome.

(a) *Immediate outcome: the word is confirmed*

(i) *The executioners' case defeated through their victory.* Few theoretical arguments against the legitimacy of the accusations of 6.11–14 could have matched the rhetorical force of Luke's characterisation of the executioners. At a *prima facie* reading, they appear to have achieved a major victory against the Christian message, as for the first time in Acts they have succeeded in eradicating one of its influential witnesses. It is precisely in so doing, however, that from the perspective of the Lukan readers their cause has lost even further ground. They are described as 'enraged' and 'grinding their teeth' (7.54), 'crying out with a loud voice', 'stopping their ears', and 'rushing together' (7.57), and finally 'casting Stephen out of the city and stoning him' (7.58, 59). As already noted in connection with other similar passages,[73] such descriptions inform the reader that, due to their inability to produce credible accusations, the opponents consistently have to resort to noise, anger, and violence; their weapon is heat, not light.

(ii) *Stephen's case substantiated through his defeat.* In sharp contrast to his executioners, Stephen's cause is proved right precisely through his

---

[72] Ibid., pp. 23–35.

[73] For example, the decision of the Jewish leaders to kill Jesus when they realised they could not defeat him with words (Luke 20.26, 40); their repetitive, unconvincing, and loud accusations at Jesus' trial (Luke 23.10, 17, 20, 23); their threats (4.21), rage (5.33), and chastisement (5.40) of the apostles once their arguments were defeated (4.14; 5.35–9); their prosecution of Stephen when proved unable to 'withstand the wisdom and the spirit with which he spoke' (5.10).

apparent defeat. Just as in the case of Jesus' conflict with the authorities, Stephen's case is ultimately vindicated by God. The martyr's fullness of the Holy Spirit (7.55a), his vision of God's glory, of the heaven opened, and of Jesus, the Son of man, standing at God's right hand (7.55b–56), and his death in close communion with God through prayer (7.59–60) are all powerful testimony before the reader to God's vindication of Stephen and his cause.[74] Luke's account of Jesus' baptism (Luke 3.21–2) provides an interesting parallel: the subject is praying, the heaven is opened, association with the Holy Spirit is noted, and God's (audible or visible) presence is noted. If the parallelism is to be extended to God's statement in the matter, his explicit approval of Jesus ('You are my beloved Son; with you I am well pleased') has its inescapable counterpart in God's implicit approval of Stephen.

(iii) *Jesus' vindication confirmed through his disciple's death.* As noted in the section dealing with the accusations against Stephen, the root cause of his alleged break with the people of God was his allegiance to Jesus – the accusations against him were ultimately accusations against Jesus (6.14). It is hardly surprising then to find that the vindication of Stephen also turns out to be a (confirmation of the) vindication of Jesus. Twice in two consecutive verses the text speaks of Jesus 'standing at the right hand of God' (7.55–6). While the significance of the 'standing' position (as distinct from 'sitting'; cf. Ps. 110.1, Ac. 2.34) is hard to determine with certainty,[75] this cannot obscure the Christological apologetic of the sentence. The last (and only) time the Lukan reader will have met a strikingly similar statement was in Peter's Pentecost address. There, too, Jesus' presence at the right hand of God had been mentioned – also twice within the space of two verses (2.33–4) – and the conclusion to which the observation was meant to lead[76] was on that occasion made explicit by Luke: the house of Israel was to 'know assuredly that God has made him both Lord and Christ, this Jesus whom you crucified' (2.36). In view of this, whatever else the recurrence of the sentence in the Stephen episode may also mean, one message could not have been missed by the attentive reader: that Jesus' exalted status at the right hand of God, of which Peter had *spoken* at Pentecost (thus asserting his vindication against his opponents), was now *eye-witnessed* by Stephen. Two other textual details seem then to bring further emphasis to this Christological apologetic.

---

[74] Barrett quotes with approval Weiser's claim that both Stephen's vision and his fullness of the Spirit indicate that 'Gott is auf seiten des Stephanus, nicht seiner Gegner' ('God is on the side of Stephen, not his opponent') (Barrett, *Acts*, vol. I, p. 383).

[75] Barrett (*Luke*, vol. I, pp. 384–5) lists no fewer than eleven suggested interpretations.

[76] Note the causal οὖν at the beginning of the sentence.

First, Stephen's reference to Jesus as 'the Son of man' may be a way of drawing attention to him as 'the One who suffered and was vindicated by God (Lk. 9:22)'.[77] Second, the fact that the dying martyr commits his spirit to Jesus (7.59), in much the same way as Jesus had committed his spirit to the Father (Luke 23.46), is yet another acknowledgement and confirmation of Jesus' exalted (and therefore vindicated) status.

(b) *Further consequences: the word defies opposition*

(i) *A villain announcing a hero.* The account of Stephen's death brings on the scene for the first time the one who is to dominate so heavily the second half of Acts. Both through his involvement in and consent to Stephen's trial and death (7.58; 8.1) and through his subsequent persecution of the church (8.3), Saul is portrayed as a vehement opponent of the word. No change in his attitude is yet anticipated. However, it is precisely through this negative portrayal that Luke skilfully prepares the reader for a better appreciation of a dominant theme in Acts: such is the power of the Christian witness that it cannot be destroyed by opposition; indeed, it is even able to turn the sharpest enemy into the most enthusiastic ally (9.1–16, 21–2; 22.4–8, 14–15; etc.).

(ii) *Persecution turned into mission.* Side by side with the story of Saul runs the story of the Christian community. The 'great persecution' (διωγμὸς μέγας, 8.1) which started 'on that day' (ἐν ἐκείνῃ τῇ ἡμέρᾳ) of Stephen's trial and martyrdom is the most widespread threat to the Christian community which the Lukan reader has encountered so far – until now only a few leaders have tasted opposition, but this time the 'church in Jerusalem' as a whole is persecuted and scattered,[78] 'house after house' is invaded, and 'men and women' are imprisoned (8.1b, 3). Yet the outcome of all this is that 'those who were scattered *went about preaching the word* ' (8.4), and the subsequent story of Philip's mission is only an example of this outcome. The extent of the mission resulting from the Stephen incident is not even limited to Judaea and Samaria, as 8.1 and Philip's mission might lead one to infer. Several chapters later, the reader is informed that 'those who were scattered because of the persecution

---

[77] Marshall, *Acts* (1980), p. 149.

[78] πλὴν τῶν ἀποστόλων (8.1) indicates a notable exception. Doubts have often been expressed whether this would have been historically possible, and the generally adopted solution is to take the persecution as affecting only one segment of the Jerusalem church (viz. Stephen's Hellenistic group). At a narrative level, however, one finds in the apostles' remaining in Jerusalem a significant hint that Luke *does not* irrevocably give up on Jerusalem or the Jews with the event of Stephen's death (contra, e.g., Kilgallen, *Stephen*, pp. 111–13).

that arose over Stephen travelled as far as Phoenicia and Cyprus and Antioch, speaking the word . . .' (11.19). However, it is not *geographical* boundaries alone that this mission comes to cross; Luke also attributes to it the beginnings of an *ethnic* transition, as he explains that although the scattered Christians spoke the word 'to none except the Jews', there were 'some of them, men of Cyprus and Cyrene, who on coming to Antioch spoke to the Hellenists/Greeks[79] also' (11.20).

Thus, Stephen's trial is portrayed in remarkable resonance with Jesus' prediction of the disciples' trials, according to which the primary goal and the promised result of their apologias would not be their personal safety but the witness to Jesus.[80] Stephen is dead, the church is scattered, but the word is preached throughout Judaea and Samaria, reaching out into Phoenicia, Cyprus, and Antioch, and Paul is visible at the horizon to take it from Antioch even further afield (13.1–3).

Conclusion

The present chapter started with a brief survey of previous suggestions regarding the function of the Stephen story. The findings of this survey can be summarised as follows: (1) Previous interpretations of Lukan apologetics have not been able to account adequately for this part of Luke's writing. (2) Several major works on Acts 6–7 have spoken of some kind of apologetic intent behind this part of Luke's work, whether this apologia be in terms of an ecclesiastic defence of Stephen,[81] or a Christian explanation of the temple's disappearance,[82] or a more general polemic against Judaism.[83] Yet since the notions of both trial and apologia have been only secondary to the concerns of these works, their insights in these areas, although often highlighting important aspects of Stephen's story, have not been developed sufficiently and are often in need of revision. (3) The situation is even less satisfactory with the non-apologetic interpretations of Luke's intentions in Acts 6–7: of the two works examined, Scharlemann's suggestion of historical reasons alone runs counter to decades of Lukan research, and Watson's detection of a coded political language suffers from insufficient textual support.

---

[79] The contrast with 'the Jews' requires that τοὺς Ἑλληνιστάς here (as supported by most MSS) refer to Greek-speaking Gentiles (Barrett, *Luke*, vol. I, p. 550), or at least a Greek-speaking mixed population (B. M. Metzger, *A Textual Commentary on the Greek New Testament*, second edition, Stuttgart: Deutsche Bibelgesellschaft, 1994, pp. 340–2).

[80] See my discussion of the origins and development of the Stephanic conflict, where I noted the close resemblance between 6.10 and Jesus' predictions in Luke 12.12 and 21.15.

[81] See Simon's contribution above.   [82] See Kilgallen's contribution above.

[83] See Légasse's contribution above.

Instead, several indicators have been found that *Luke deliberately portrays the story of Stephen's trial as inseparable from the larger story of the word*. First, the immediate narrative precedent of the trial account is Luke's repeated emphasis on the 'increase' of the word through its growing popularity among the people of Jerusalem (6.1, 7) and on the special priority the church gave to the ministry of the word (6.2, 4). Second, although initially appointed 'to serve at tables', Stephen is soon revealed as heavily instrumental in the witness and defence of the word (6.8–10). Third, the ultimate outcome of Stephen's trial is the further expansion of the word through the preaching of the scattered Christian community (8.2, 4; 11.19–20) and through the subsequent ministry of Paul, who is now for the first time introduced to the reader.

Within the broader story of the word, the specific location of Stephen's trial is defined by the narrative context of the incident. Retrospectively, Stephen's trial and subsequent martyrdom represent the culmination of the Jerusalem conflict between the representatives and the opponents of the word. Prospectively, the incident inaugurates the gospel's transcendence of Jewish symbols – geographically, linguistically, and ethnically. Geographically, the church which until now has stayed in Jerusalem spreads as a result of Stephen's execution further into Judaea, Samaria, Phoenicia, Cyprus, Antioch and eventually (through Saul, to whom the readers are now being introduced) throughout the Gentile world. Linguistically, the reader learns for the first time of a 'Hellenistic' branch of Christianity. Ethnically, glimpses are offered (again through Saul's presence and the scattered Christian community) of the Gentiles' forthcoming inclusion into the people of God.[84] At the same time, however, important indications are provided of Christianity's rootedness in Judaism. Contrary to frequent scholarly claims that, with the Stephen incident, Luke officially gives up on Jerusalem and the Jews, even when the whole church is scattered, the apostles – representatives of 'the Hebrews' – stay in Jerusalem.

It is hardly surprising, in view of this, that Luke's apologetic at this point is also centred on the topics of Judaism's rejection of the Way and the Christian transcendence of Jewish identity-markers. The four Stephanic themes discussed above have all pointed to an apologetic related to these

---

[84] See S. G. Wilson, who disagrees with J. C. O'Neill and F. Overbeck in taking the *content* of Stephen's speech as 'a prefigurement of the Gentile mission', but agrees with Dibelius that in terms of its *position*, the Stephen-narrative is the inauguration of Acts 6–12, which narrates the progress of the gospel into the Gentile world (*The Gentiles and the Gentile Mission in Luke–Acts*, Cambridge University Press, 1973, pp. 135–6). See also Ravens, *Luke*, pp. 67–8.

two major issues. Thus, the theme of Israel's rejection of God's messengers legitimates Jesus and his followers *versus* their rejection by the
Jewish leadership, while the remaining three themes (God's independence; Moses and the law; and the temple) contend that it is not those
who through allegiance to Jesus *transcend* the Jewish symbols that are
parting ways with the people of God, but that this charge is instead applicable to those who seek to *limit* God to such categories and so run the
danger of idolatry. A vivid *résumé* of this counter-offensive apologetic
comes at the beginning of Stephen's *peroratio*,[85] when Stephen applies
to his audience the term ἀπερίτμητοι (7.51). If forfeiting the status of
people of God is the charge, Stephen seems to imply, then the unbelieving
Jews, rather than Jesus and his witnesses, are guilty of it.

---

[85] For divisions of Stephen's speech according to the criteria of ancient rhetoric,
see Légasse, *Stephanos*, pp. 19–20; Seland, *Establishment*, 233–5; Wolfe, 'Rhetorical
Elements', pp. 278–80.

7

THE TRIALS OF PAUL

Introduction

With Luke's account of Paul's trials, one reaches the apex of Lukan apologetics. A telling indication of this is Luke's use of the ἀπολογία word group: out of a total of ten occurrences (Luke 12.11; 21.14; Ac. 19.33; 22.1; 24.10; 25.8, 16; 26.1, 2, 24), the first two are found on Jesus' lips as he predicts the disciples' trials, the third refers to Alexander's would-be defence in Ephesus, in an incident in which the main 'offender' is Paul, and all the remaining seven are directly associated with Paul's defence speeches in the context of his trials. Lukan scholarship, we shall shortly see, also bears witness to the importance of Paul's trials for Luke's apologetics – with a few exceptions, most studies on this part of Acts recognise here the existence of some form of apologetic agenda.

It is important first to pay some attention to the main interpretations of the intended function of these trial accounts.[1] I shall note first a few works which have either denied or simply bypassed the existence of any apologetic tendencies in this part of Luke's work. Next, due to their large number and diversity, I shall group the apologetic readings of Paul's trials into several major categories and try to assess both their positive contributions and their limitations. Finally, this survey of previous research will provide the basis for my own investigation of the apologetic orientation of the narrative.

---

[1] It is not my intention here to deal with the more general issue of Luke's *Paulusbild*. For that, see: C. Burchard, *Der dreizehnte Zeuge. Traditions- und kompositionsgeschichtliche Untersuchungen zu Lukas' Darstellung der Frühzeit des Paulus*, FRLANT 103, Göttingen: Vandenhoeck & Ruprecht, 1970; Clark, 'Parallel Lives', pp. 9–21; K. Lönig, *Die Saulustradition in der Apostelgeschichte*, Neutestamentliche Abhandlungen 112, Münster: Aschendorff, 1973, pp. 1–12; M.-E. Rosenblatt, *Paul the Accused. His Portrait in the Acts of the Apostles*, Collegeville, MN: Liturgical, 1995; V. Stolle, *Der Zeuge als Angeklagter. Untersuchungen zum Paulusbild des Lukas*, BWANT 102, Stuttgart: W. Kohlhammer, 1973.

The function of Paul's trials in Acts: previous research
Non-apologetic readings of Paul's trials
(a) *A mimetic purpose*

Two relatively recent studies, dealing with aspects of Luke's presentation of Paul's encounters with various opponents, have argued at some length that Luke's primary aim in this part of his work is to present Paul to the Christian readers as a model of commitment and witness, in the context of political opposition to the Christian movement.[2]

One important merit of these works is their search for some form of continuity among a wide range of Pauline conflicts in Acts.[3] This is an important antidote to the all too familiar tendency to investigate Paul's conflicts solely in terms of his dealings either with the Jews[4] or with the Romans[5] (the 'pagans' of Philippi, Athens, or Ephesus being typically left out of the dominant picture). Also, it should be granted that a mimetic intent may indeed be at work in the narratives in question – undoubtedly Luke would have expected his readers to learn a good deal from so great a Christian witness as Paul. Yet it is very doubtful that Luke's desire to provide his readers with a model of commitment and witness for the times when they too may be in situations of conflict can be taken as the author's *governing* interest throughout these narratives, since such a reading fails to account satisfactorily for some of the most prominent features of Paul's conflicts in Acts. Paul the Pharisee, Paul the Roman citizen, Paul the persecutor, his miraculous encounter with the risen Christ, his controversial role in the Gentile mission, all become superfluous repetitions and of little value for the author's case, since they relate to Paul's personal identity or experiences and could not have been imitated by the readers. Luke could have achieved his mimetic goal in far fewer words, or would have been better off elaborating on different aspects of the conflict (e.g. the extent of the physical abuse which Paul was willing to defy for the sake of his Lord).

It appears, therefore, that to the extent to which one is to attribute to Paul's trials in Acts a mimetic aim, this aim needs to be defined in such a way as to do justice to the recurring themes of the narratives. M. Dibelius' brief suggestion appears to be a step in the right direction:

---

[2] Cassidy, *Society*, esp. pp. 159–62; Rosenblatt, *Paul*, esp. pp. 94–7.

[3] Both Cassidy and Rosenblatt construct their case on the basis of all the major Pauline conflict scenes in Acts (Cassidy, *Society*, chs. 5–8 and p. 162; Rosenblatt, *Paul*, chs. 2–4).

[4] See the interpretations concentrating on the relationship between Paul and Judaism (chapter 1).

[5] See the interpretations emphasising Luke's political apologetic (chapter 1).

when, in the five trial scenes examined here [22:30–23:10; 24:1–23; 24:24–5; 25:6–12; 26:1–32], Paul always says the same thing in his defence, it is because the author wants thereby to commend to the Christians of his day the use of such themes in their own defence ...

So, within the framework of Paul's trial, Luke *presents Christian belief with an apologetic purpose*, and it is only because of this purpose that his description of the trial is so elaborate.[6]

It remains to be explained, however, how Christians of Luke's day could have used in their own apologias the themes of Paul's defence, so many of which seem to have a specifically Pauline referent.

(b) *An evangelistic purpose*

J. C. Lentz's analysis of *Luke's Portrait of Paul*[7] takes Luke's account of Paul's trials (especially Acts 16 and 22, where Paul appeals to his Roman citizenship) as evidence that the author intends to present his hero as a man of high social status (citizen of Tarsus, Roman citizen, and strict Pharisee) and of virtue (of good birth and heritage, upright, well educated, pious, wealthy). Such an idealistic picture of Paul is in Lentz's assessment 'quite frankly, too good to be true'.[8] Yet Luke chose to portray Paul in this way because he wanted his readers to recognise in him the ideal Graeco-Roman man and thus be more inclined to take Christianity seriously.

Whatever position one may take with regard to the historicity of Luke's portrayal of Paul,[9] or with respect to Lentz's insistence that Luke's *Paulusbild* would have been at home in an 'evangelistic' but not in a 'defensive' work,[10] Lentz's study has made subsequent scholarship aware that any attempt at making sense of Paul's trial in Acts should be able to account for a Paul who is simultaneously a Hellenist, a Roman, a Jew, and a man of virtue.

---

[6] Dibelius, *Studies*, p. 213; italics mine.

[7] SNTSMS 77, Cambridge University Press, 1993.

[8] Lentz, *Portrait*, p. 171.

[9] See, for instance, B. Rapske's contention that, contrary to Lentz's claim, Paul's triple status need not be regarded as a Lukan creation: while it is true that such a multiple identity would have often created tension for Paul, such tension may well be the key to understanding Paul's harsh treatment in Acts, rather than the basis for discarding Luke's historical reliability (B. Rapske, *The Book of Acts and Paul in Roman Custody, BAFCS*, vol. III, Grand Rapids: Eerdmans; Carlisle: Paternoster, 1994, esp. pp. 71–112; B. Rapske, 'Luke's Portrait of Paul, by John Clayton Lentz Jr', book review, *EvQ* 66 (1994), 347–53).

[10] Lentz, *Portrait*, p. 171.

Apologetic readings of Paul's trials

(a) *An apologia for Paul*[11]

(i) *An apologia regarding Paul's relationship to Judaism.* According to one of the most popular interpretations of Paul's trials in Acts, Luke's primary aim here is to defend Paul against widespread Jewish criticism, occasioned by his teaching in the Diaspora and by his acceptance of the Gentiles into the people of God, without requiring of them full observance of the law.[12]

Jervell's explanation can be commended for its ability to make sense of several important emphases in this part of the narrative, such as Paul the faithful Jew and devout Pharisee, tried for his commitment to the hope of Israel, without having transgressed against the Jewish law, nation, or temple. Also, the sheer amount of space taken up with anti-Pauline accusations and pro-Pauline speeches makes inescapable the conclusion that one of the functions of the trial narratives was to defend Paul. Yet to say that this defence is relevant only for Paul himself and not for Christianity[13] is to introduce an artificial divorce between the messenger and the movement whose exponent he is – Paul is neither more nor less a representative of Christianity than Peter, Stephen, and Philip had also been at earlier points in the story.

An even more important limitation of this position, however, is that while it successfully explains *some* of the material Luke includes in his story of Paul's trials, there are still large amounts of material and important emphases which are made redundant, namely, trials such as those in Philippi, Athens, or Ephesus, in which Jews do not feature at all, charges related to Rome or Caesar, the repeated exculpation of Paul by Roman officials, Luke's emphasis on Paul's social status, and so forth. To note

[11] I shall not rehearse here Mattill's particularly problematic thesis, which takes Luke's interest in Paul's trials as indicative that the whole of Acts was designed to help Paul at his forthcoming trial in Rome (see for this chapter 1).

[12] Jervell, 'Teacher'; Jervell, 'Defender'; Jervell, 'Paul in the Acts'; Jervell, *Unknown.* Among the works which have followed largely in Jervell's footsteps, the following can be noted: Brawley, *Luke–Acts,* chs. 3–5; C. Gempf, 'Historical and Literary Appropriateness in the Mission Speeches of Paul in Acts', unpublished PhD dissertation, University of Aberdeen, 1989, ch. 6, pp. 341–71; W. R. Long, 'The Trial of Paul in the Book of Acts: Historical, Literary, and Theological Considerations', unpublished PhD dissertation, Brown University, 1982, chs. 4–5; W. R. Long, 'The Paulusbild in the Trial of Paul in Acts', in K. H. Richards (ed.), *Society of Biblical Literature 1983 Seminar Papers,* Chico, CA: Scholars Press, 1983, pp. 87–105.

[13] The biographical character of Paul's speeches (a feature not paralleled in any other speeches in Acts) is for Jervell the supreme indication that Luke's apologia in this part of Acts is concerned with Paul himself and not (as Dibelius had argued) with Paul as a representative or model of Christianity – Paul is no exchangeable figure for Luke (Jervell, 'Teacher', 154–5, 161).

this limitation does not mean, of course, to exclude the defence of Paul from the author's intentions. It merely warns against taking such an aim as the controlling agenda of the narrative.[14]

One final difficulty with the interpretation of Jervell *et alii* is that it leaves one wondering how Paul's relationship to Judaism could have been helped by the rehearsal of his endless conflicts with the Jews.

(ii) *A Hellenistically oriented apologia regarding Paul's innocence.* In an often quoted article, G. Miles and G. Trompf have argued that Luke's account of Paul's sea voyage and shipwreck at the end of Acts is of one piece with the story of Paul's trials and represents the climax of Luke's defence of Paul's innocence.[15] These authors call attention to a passage from the Athenian orator Antiphon (*c.* 480–411 BC),[16] in which the safe journeying of an alleged malefactor and of his companions is referred to as forensic evidence of his innocence. Antiphon's writing is taken as indicative of the fact that 'the failures of the gods to visit disaster upon an individual and his associates during a sea voyage would be regarded by a representative cross-section of Athenians as a legitimate, indeed, even as an especially persuasive, evidence of religious purity'.[17] When Paul's sea voyage is viewed against this background, the article contends, it is revealed as the climax of Luke's case for Paul's innocence.

A few years later, Miles and Trompf's study was developed, with minor modifications, by D. Landouceur,[18] who brings to light additional evidence from Hellenistic literature in support of the central thesis of Miles and Trompf.

The work of Miles, Trompf, and Landouceur is of significance to our concerns inasmuch as it shows that for a Hellenistic reader, at least, the story of Paul's travel and shipwreck in the last two chapters of Acts can be legitimately regarded, at the level of narrative function, as part of Paul's 'trials' in Acts – in certain respects perhaps even as their culmination.

---

[14] While it is entirely plausible to conceive of several unrelated Lukan agendas, and thus of the possibility that no single paradigm will be able to account satisfactorily for everything that Luke has to say in relation to Paul's trials, the quest for a dominant goal must not be dismissed *a priori*.

[15] G. B. Miles and G. Trompf, 'Luke and Antiphon: The Theology of Acts 27–28 in the Light of Pagan Beliefs about Divine Retribution, Pollution, and Shipwreck', *HTR* 69 (1976), 259–67.

[16] Antiphon, Περὶ τοῦ Ἡρώδου φόνου, pp. 10–11, as referred to in Miles and Trompf, 'Luke and Antiphon', 261–2.

[17] Miles and Trompf, 'Luke and Antiphon', 264.

[18] D. Landouceur, 'Hellenistic Preconceptions of Shipwreck and Pollution as a Context for Acts 27–28', *HTR* 73 (1980), 435–49.

What these authors could not aim to do, however, on the basis of such a limited part of Paul's 'trials' in Acts, is to work out in more detail the role of this defence of Paul's innocence in Luke's overall apologetic agenda, or what specific reasons are likely to have led Luke to such a defence. These are issues which need to be borne in mind in our own analysis of Paul's trials.

(iii) *An ecclesiastic apologia related to Paul's ordeals.* In his own analysis of Paul's voyage and shipwreck in Acts 27–8,[19] B. Rapske agrees with Miles, Trompf, and Landouceur that this section of Luke's work is part of the author's defence of Paul, but deems it 'quite un-likely that Luke would adopt and argue Paul's innocence from a pagan perspective'.[20] Instead, Rapske argues, Luke was concerned with the fact that his predominantly Christian readers might have developed mixed feelings about Paul, as they have been reading about the many conflicts and hardships which had come his way.[21] Accordingly, in the story of Paul's voyage, rather than relying on pagan preconceptions of divine ret-ribution and pollution, Luke 'furnishes his readers in the record of a divine assurance at Acts 27:23f. the hermeneutical tool by which known Pauline difficulties – storm, the threat of summary execution, the shipwreck, and the snakebite – may be accurately deciphered'.[22]

Rapske's understanding of Luke's apologia for Paul is developed more fully in his monograph on *Paul in Roman Custody*,[23] which argues that the object of Luke's story of Paul's trials and custody was aimed to defend Paul the missionary against the stigma associated with his custody.[24]

Despite the thoroughness of Rapske's work, it remains doubtful whether he has done sufficient justice to the Lukan text. Regarding his criticism of Miles, Trompf, and Landouceur, the burden of proof is still with him to show why the same author who was happy to employ aspects of pagan philosophy in the service of his apologetic agenda in, say, Acts 17.28 was not happy to do something similar in Acts 27–8. As for his own hypothesis, suffice it to note that nothing of significance in the narrative conflict of the second half of Acts (e.g. accusations, defence speeches, summaries) suggests that the stigma of Paul's hardships and custody was the author's primary concern.

[19] B. Rapske, 'Acts, Travel and Shipwreck', in D. W. J. Gill and C. Gempf (eds.), *The Book of Acts in Its Graeco-Roman Setting*, BAFCS, vol. II, Grand Rapids: Eerdmans; Carlisle: Paternoster, 1994, pp. 1–47.

[20] Ibid., 44.   [21] Ibid., 46.   [22] Ibid.   [23] Rapske, *Acts and Paul.*
[24] Ibid., pp. 313–422.

(b) *An* apologia pro ecclesia *addressed to the Roman state*

One of the most thorough examinations of Paul's trials in Acts has come from the pen of H. W. Tajra.[25] As in the case of Rapske, however, Tajra's work is of limited significance for the present study, since its focus is not theology or apologetic but (judicial) history: its announced goal is to show that 'Luke has given a *legally realistic* account of Paul's judicial history in Acts.'[26] Yet in the concluding part of his study, Tajra pays some attention to the way Luke has constructed his account of Paul's trial and to the apologetic aims revealed by this construction. His comments there are of significance to us, not least because they represent a recent statement of the centuries-long interpretation of Paul's trials in Acts as an *apologia pro ecclesia*.[27]

According to Tajra, Paul's legal history in Acts is said to revolve around his Roman citizenship and his appeal to Rome.[28] Accordingly, a Rome-related apologetic is suggested, based on: (i) the positive opinions of Roman magistrates; (ii) the positive portrayal of the Roman authorities and justice (in contrast to the way the Jews are represented); and (iii) the basic tolerance which Christianity enjoys from Rome.[29]

Despite their overall popularity, such interpretations of Paul's trials in Acts have been subjected to detailed criticism in recent years. Cassidy's critique is perhaps the most comprehensive available to date.[30] His observations, although meant to gather all relevant material in Acts, are built mainly on the account of Paul's trials.[31] Contrary to the claims of those who see here a political apologetic, Cassidy's contention is that (i) Paul is not presented as law-abiding and harmless but as always being at the centre of controversy; (ii) his attitude towards his Roman citizenship and his cooperation with Roman officials are qualified by his higher commitment to his Lord; (iii) Luke's portrayal of the Roman system is not particularly

---

[25] H. W. Tajra, *The Trial of St Paul: A Judicial Exegesis of the Second Half of the Acts of the Apostles*, WUNT 2, Reihe 35, Tübingen: J. C. B. Mohr, 1989. See also H. W. Tajra, *The Martyrdom of St Paul: Historical and Judicial Contexts, Traditions, and Legends*, Tübingen: J. C. B. Mohr, 1994, pp. 33–6.

[26] Tajra, *Trial*, p. 2; see also Tajra, *Martyrdom*, p. 33.

[27] See the review of this interpretation in chapter 1.

[28] Tajra, *Trial*, p. 197; see also Tajra, *Martyrdom*, p. 36.

[29] Tajra, *Trial*, p. 199. In addition to this apologia addressed to Rome, Tajra considers that 'Luke's marked pro-Roman stance is meant to counterbalance certain anti-Roman tendencies present in the Church in the wake of the savage Neronian persecution' (ibid.). I shall discuss this possibility next, in connection with Walaskay's work.

[30] Cassidy, *Society*, pp. 148–55.

[31] For his observations relating to the trials of Jesus and Peter, see pp. 31 (n.13), 139–40 above.

favourable – Paul suffers a great deal as a result of the Romans' failure to implement justice.

Cassidy's objections are valuable reminders that significant parts of Paul's trials in Acts cannot easily be aligned with a political apologetic[32] and that, consequently, one should be hesitant to take such an apologetic as Luke's controlling agenda in this part of his work. This need for reticence becomes even more acute when one takes into account the vast amounts of material in Paul's trials which would have been largely irrelevant to a political apologia. The legitimation of Paul in relation to Judaism, the emphasis on his Christophany and divine commissioning, and the Christological character of Paul's defences would be only some of the more striking redundancies. Yet recognising that an *apologia pro ecclesia* cannot account for *all* aspects of Paul's trials must not obscure the fact that Luke does show a remarkable interest in Rome, its laws, and its representatives, and that in so doing one of his (probably secondary) aims is that his readers realise that Paul is not against the state nor the state against Paul.

(c) *A socio-political apologia addressed to the Graeco-Roman world*

According to a doctoral dissertation by R. K. Mackenzie,[33] the whole of Acts is concerned with a 'socio-political' apologetic[34] addressed to the Graeco-Roman world.[35] This apologetic is said to come to the fore in

---

[32] It is interesting to note that even Tajra, in his more recent monograph, recognises the existence of such material, albeit attributing it to Luke's carelessness: 'Luke's lenitive writing does not always succeed in obscuring how conflictual Paul's relationship to the Roman State really was' (*Martyrdom*, p. 36).

[33] R. K. Mackenzie, 'Character-Description and Socio-Political Apologetic in the Acts of the Apostles', unpublished PhD dissertation, Edinburgh, 1984.

[34] When spelled out in more detail, this apologetic is said to include social, economic, political, and cultural-artistic dimensions (Mackenzie, 'Character-Description', pp. 207–8).

[35] A similar position to that of Mackenzie has been advanced by A. J. Malherbe, in an article focusing on Acts 26.26 ('"Not in a Corner": Early Christian Apologetic in Acts 26:26', *SC* 5 (1985–6), 193–210). According to Malherbe, Luke is writing a social apologia for Christianity, dealing with the widespread charge that Christians were uneducated and socially insignificant (p. 196) and not philosophical in any sense (p. 197). 'It is particularly in the person of Paul', Malherbe claims, 'that Luke provides a paradigm of the educated Christian preacher' (p. 197). The specific way Luke is said to achieve this is by portraying Paul in the conventions used for moral philosophers. The evidence offered in support of this includes the portrayal of Paul in Athens and in Miletus, but concentrates on Acts 26, especially verse 26: 'οὐ γάρ ἐστιν ἐν γωνίᾳ πεπραγμένον τοῦτο'. The multiple occurrences of 'in a corner' in philosophical polemic suggest that Luke 'is presenting Paul as speaking in the manner of a philosopher and . . . this presentation is part of his apologetic program' (p. 202). Additional support for this reading of Acts 26 is finally found in Festus'

Acts 21–6, which comprises two major sections (21.39–25.12 and 25.13–26.32), each of them displaying the rhetorical features of an apology.[36] The second and more prominent of these, corresponding to Paul's final defence before Agrippa, is regarded as the summation of all the major apologetic themes of Acts.[37]

It is generally accepted, although not necessarily due to Mackenzie's work, that Acts 21–6 is particularly reminiscent of ancient apologias[38] and that Paul's defence before Agrippa represents the climax of the whole section.[39] What is perhaps Mackenzie's most notable contribution is his exploration in considerable detail of the wide range of apologetic themes in Acts 21–6, and the way these might have been received by Luke's Graeco-Roman readers. What needs, however, to be borne in mind, for the purposes of the present study, is that Mackenzie's work is not on Paul's *trials* but on his '*character-description*'. It is hardly surprising, then, to find that the trial scenes are not even identified, that important sections of Paul's trials play no part in Mackenzie's investigation (e.g. all trial scenes prior to Acts 21), and that his findings are not linked in any systematic way to the central elements of the trial accounts, such as charges, defences, the identity of the prosecutors, and so on. Yet Mackenzie's work remains a powerful reminder that no study of Luke's aims can afford to overlook the richness of apologetic themes and devices present in this part of Acts.

(d) *An* apologia pro imperio

Walaskay's study of Paul's trials[40] begins with a brief analysis of Paul's own use of the term 'apology'. He finds that Philippians 1.7, 16 are the only instances where Paul uses the term in a legal context and that according to the apostle's words here he is in prison 'for a defence of the gospel'.[41] As he turns to Acts, Walaskay finds Luke to be a faithful Paulinist as regards the content of Paul's apologia: 'Luke has skilfully woven thematic threads supplied by Paul into his own tapestry of the

words to Paul, 'your great learning has driven you mad' (26.24), in Paul's 'boldness' (26.26), and in the debate regarding Agrippa's 'conversion' (26.28–9) (pp. 206–10). In summary, 'Luke has Paul, like the moral philosophers, claim divine guidance (26.16–17, 22), deny that his activity has been confined to a corner (26.26), speak fearlessly to rulers (26.26), and offer himself as an example to all (26.29). Luke's apologetic aim in this scene, to present Christianity in Paul's person as philosophical, would seem to be clear' (p. 206).

[36] Mackenzie, 'Character-Description', pp. 153–79.   [37] Ibid., pp. 179–99.

[38] So, for example, Gempf, 'Historical', pp. 341–71; Jervell, 'Teacher'; Long, 'Trial', pp. 159–256.

[39] See especially R. F. O'Toole, *The Christological Climax of Paul's Defence (Ac 22:1–26:32)*, Analecta Biblica 78, Rome: Biblical Institute Press, 1978, *passim*.

[40] Walaskay, *Rome*, pp. 50–63.   [41] Ibid., p. 51.

apostle's trial: Paul is on trial not to defend himself against any specious charges, but to bear witness to the gospel (Acts 25:18–19).'[42] The four major Pauline hearings recorded by Luke (21.27–23.30; 24.1–27; 25.6–12; 25.13–26.32), with their unanimous emphasis on Paul's belief in the resurrection of the dead (23.6; 24.15, 21; 25.19; 26.6–8, 23), are said to substantiate such a reading.[43]

What intrigues Walaskay is the fact that Luke has placed such material in the context of a Roman trial: 'Luke has rightly reported Paul's message, but forced it into a courtroom context that makes little sense.'[44] To be sure, Walaskay believes he knows why Luke was prepared for such artificiality – it was the price he needed to pay in order to build his *apologia pro imperio*. He wants the church to realise that the Roman state was the instrument through which God protected the gospel (in the person of Paul) and brought it to the heart of the empire.[45]

Quite apart from the challenges posed to Walaskay's interpretation by the text itself,[46] one cannot help suspecting that Walaskay has created a problem in the Lukan text only in order to find a basis for his own solution. Even a cursory reading of the various trial accounts reveals that although Paul's gospel is always at the centre of the trial conflict (as will be seen later in more detail), Paul's references to his religious commitments never sound 'forced' in the contexts in which they occur. To use Walaskay's own example, the centrality of Paul's belief in the resurrection of the dead to his trials is meaningful both when the addressees are Jews and when they are Romans: to the former it shows the defendant's commitment to Israel's hopes, to the latter it indicates that his 'guilt' relates not to socio-political misconduct but to Jewish religious controversies.

What is perhaps even more disappointing in Walaskay's study is the fact that he has made far too little of his otherwise important observation that the legal history of the Lukan Paul, like that of the 'real' Paul, is bound up with his defence of the gospel. When the story of Paul's trials is read as an *apologia pro evangelio* (rather than *apologia pro imperio*), it becomes evident that the defence of the gospel and the trial settings are by no means at odds with one another but work interdependently to yield the

---

[42] Ibid.; see also pp. 52, 58.   [43] Ibid., pp. 53–8.   [44] Ibid., p. 58.
[45] Ibid., pp. 58–63.
[46] It is not clear how impressed the readers would have been with Rome's protection of Paul, once they had learnt of the magistrates' repeated failure to release him (not to mention the significance of Paul's death at their hands, of which the readers may have known independently of Acts). Nor is it clear that the state has brought Paul to Rome – the initiative belongs to Paul (25.10–11) and in the final sea journey it is due to him that the Romans arrive safely at the shore, rather than the reverse (27.10–11, 21–4, 31–6; contra Walaskay, ibid., pp. 59–62).

author's intended result: only together can they depict the confirmation of the gospel through trials.

(e) *A Christological apologia*

One final work which deserves attention here is that of R. O'Toole, on Acts 26.[47] According to O'Toole's analysis, Paul's speech here stands as the Christological climax of the whole of Acts 22.1–26.32,[48] the main purpose of Acts 26 being 'to defend the Christian belief in a resurrection of the dead realized in Christ'.[49]

O'Toole has done much to make Lukan scholarship aware of the strategic place of Acts 26 in the structure of the last section of Acts. More importantly, he has demonstrated that all readings of this section solely or primarily in terms of a (socio-)political apologetic have inevitably turned a blind eye to the thoroughly Christological character of the narrative, and thus to the author's special concern with the defence of the Christian beliefs. Yet for all its importance, O'Toole's study needs to be recognised for what it is – an analysis of *Acts 26*. While this chapter may indeed encapsulate the essence of Luke's apologia to *Judaism*, the same cannot be said regarding the apologetic tendencies encountered in those trial accounts where the scenario is primarily Hellenistic or Roman. If the defence of Christian beliefs is taken to be Luke's primary concern not only in Acts 26 but throughout the account of Paul's trials, this needs to be demonstrated systematically for all the relevant passages. Finally, one important question which O'Toole's study on Acts 26 has not satisfactorily addressed is why Luke would have Paul argue at so much length in favour of the resurrection of the dead before an audience which, largely speaking, would have had no difficulties accepting this belief.[50] I shall return to this issue in due course.

---

[47] O'Toole, *Christological.*

[48] Among the features of Acts 26 which establish its climactic position, O'Toole mentions the importance of Agrippa II (the most important political figure Paul encounters in Acts), the special attention given to the resurrection, the parallels with Luke 23.1–25, and the structure of the passage (*Christological*, p. 156).

[49] Ibid., p. 160. O'Toole does not exclude, however, the existence of other secondary aims, such as the presentation of Paul as a model for Christians, or finding a place for Christianity within Judaism and the empire (pp. 159–60).

[50] On one occasion, at least, O'Toole points in the right direction: 'The belief in a resurrection of the dead serves as a springboard to introduce two other beliefs not so digestible to the Pharisees: Jesus is the Christ and the Christ had to suffer, die, and rise from the dead' (ibid., p. 121). Unfortunately he never develops this observation at any length in relation to Luke's choice of material in the speech.

Concluding observations and present approach

As a first observation resulting from this review, attention must be called to the sheer variety of representations of Luke's aims in the chapters dealing with Paul's trials and to the clear dominance of the apologetic representations of these aims. Virtually without exception, the lines of interpretation listed above have rightly highlighted (if at times exaggerated or even misrepresented) features of Paul's trial narrative. Thus, Luke's elaborate, repetitive, and often biographical presentation of Paul's defence, the emphasis on Paul's socio-religious status, moral virtues, Jewish faithfulness and political harmlessness, the predominantly favourable treatment of Paul by various Roman officials, the numerous themes in which a Graeco-Roman apologetic can be detected, and the centrality of Christian belief (especially in the resurrection) to the Pauline defence are all aspects of Paul's trials in Acts which have correctly been brought to light by Lukan research.

Despite this variety of interpretations, however, no sufficiently comprehensive analysis of the function of Paul's trials in Acts seems to have been offered. More precisely, insufficient efforts have been made (a) to assess if and how the proposed interpretations are able to account for the various features of Paul's trials brought to light by other studies and (b) to demonstrate the plausibility of these interpretations in relation to all the relevant trial narratives in Acts. To recall only some of the more significant examples: the mimetic interpretations have not been able to account for the biographical elements of Paul's trials; those who see Luke writing for a Graeco-Roman audience have done little to explain Luke's interest in Paul's faithfulness to Judaism; conversely, those emphasising the Jewish apologetic offer inadequate explanations of Luke's interest in Paul's relations to Romans; and the fact that most authors limit their investigations of Paul's trials to Acts 21–6, or fragments of it, leaving out Paul's mission trials and (perhaps less surprisingly) Acts 27–8.

In the light of these observations, the intention in the remaining part of this chapter is to show that a reading of Paul's trials in Acts as an *apologia pro evangelio* is able to account for the diversity of Lukan emphases already noted, and to demonstrate this in relation to all of the Pauline trials in Acts.[51] Specific attention will be paid in the study of Paul's trials

---

[51] Due to the familiar disputes about what can and cannot be regarded as 'trial' in Luke's story, it should be remembered that the present use of 'trial' is not restricted to its judicial meaning, but denotes any incident in which a Lukan protagonist is in a situation of conflict with judicial or quasi-judicial authorities, charges are brought against the defendant, and a defence is offered on his behalf.

to the two main parts of any trial – the charges and the defence. It is, however, to be expected that the discussion of these two elements will often involve discussions of other related issues, such as the precedents leading to the trial scenes, the characterisation of the major participants in the conflict, the outcome of the trials, and suchlike.

Paul's trials re-examined
Summary statements on Paul's trials
(a) *Christ's interpretation of Paul's trials (9.15–16; 23.11)*

Immediately after his Christophany, Saul is introduced by the risen Christ[52] to Ananias as 'a chosen instrument of mine to carry my name before the Gentiles and kings and the sons of Israel; for I will show him how much he must suffer for the sake of my name' (9.15–16). That Paul's trials are specifically (albeit not exclusively) on the author's mind at this point is indicated (i) by the close parallel with Jesus' prediction of the disciples' trials in Luke 21.12–13;[53] (ii) by the act of bearing witness[54] in the context of suffering, which within Luke–Acts almost always denotes trial settings; and, most importantly, (iii) by the fact that the only other instances in which Acts speaks of Paul meeting 'kings' are found in the context of his trials (viz. the trial before Agrippa II and the awaited trial before Caesar). According to Acts 9.15–16, then, the purpose of Paul's trials is that witness will be borne to Jesus' name. As for the addressees of this witness, three groups are specifically mentioned: 'the Gentiles and kings and the sons of Israel'. It can be expected, then, that to the degree to which Paul's witness during his trials in Acts has an apologetic dimension, his apologia may appear particularly fitting for such groups.

Following his trials in Jerusalem (Acts 21.27–23.10), Paul receives a vision which is aimed to encourage and prepare him for the hardships ahead (23.11).[55] What is of interest to us is the fact that although trials are almost everything the reader knows of Paul's time in Jerusalem, and a trial is also what Paul awaits in Rome (25.10–12), the author summarises Paul's experiences in both Jerusalem and Rome in terms of his witness to (the things about) Christ: ὡς γὰρ **διεμαρτύρω τὰ περὶ ἐμοῦ** εἰς

---

[52] For the identification of 'the Lord' in 9.15 with the risen Christ, see 9.5.

[53] The parallelism includes references to sufferings, bearing testimony, being 'before (ἐπί/ἐνώπιον) kings', doing such things for the sake of Jesus' name.

[54] 'Carrying Jesus' name' should be understood as equivalent to 'bearing witness to Jesus' name' (Conzelmann, *Acts*, p. 72; Marshall, *Acts* (1980), pp. 171–2).

[55] Note especially the use of θάρσει.

Ἰερουσαλήμ, οὕτω σε δεῖ καὶ εἰς Ῥώμην **μαρτυρῆσαι** (23.11). Thus, although the passage elaborates even less than 9.15–6 on the significance of Paul's trials, it is nonetheless important for our purposes in that it reaffirms witness to Jesus as the essence of Paul's trials.

(b) Paul's understanding of his trials (20.22–4)

It is common knowledge in Lukan scholarship that, with the completion of his third missionary journey, 'Paul the missionary' gives way to 'Paul the defendant'. The distinction becomes blurred, however, when due weight is given to two observations – that Paul the missionary is often on trial and that Paul the defendant remains a missionary. Both observations are conveniently summarised in Paul's farewell address to the Ephesian elders (20.18–35).[56] As he reflects upon his past service, 'from the first day that [he] set foot in Asia' (20.18), he finds it characterised by humility, tears, and 'trials (πειρασμῶν) which befell [him] through the plots of the Jews' (20.19). Behind all these, the driving force was his determination to 'declare' (ἀναγγεῖλαι), 'teach' (διδάξαι), and 'testify' (διαμαρτυρόμενος) to an audience which, the text underlines, included both Jews and Greeks (20.20–1). Turning to his forthcoming departure to Jerusalem and beyond (where his trials will come to the fore), Paul admits his uncertainties (20.22); what he is certain of, nevertheless, is the fact that sufferings are ahead (20.23) and that the goal towards which he must press on through all these is the accomplishment (τελειώσω) of the 'race' (δρόμον) and the 'ministry' (διακονίαν) entrusted to him, namely 'to witness to the gospel of the grace of God' (διαμαρτύρασθαιτὸ εὐαγγέλιον τῆς χάριτος τοῦ θεοῦ, 20.24).

Thus, Paul's view of his trials, past and future, is that they are a means whereby testimony is being brought to the gospel.

Paul's mission trials[57]
(a) Philippi (16.16–40)

The first scene in Acts which may be identified as a Pauline trial is located in Philippi.[58] That the episode is not intended to portray a regular trial is explicitly stated in 16.37, as Paul complains of being beaten 'without

---

[56] For more detail, see the analysis of the trial scenes below.

[57] I refer to these as 'mission trials' because they take place during Paul's 'missionary journeys'.

[58] For other works which include this episode among Paul's trials, albeit not elaborating on the reasons for doing so, see Rapske, *Acts and Paul*, pp. 115–34; Tajra, *Trial*, pp. 3–29.

trial' (ἀκατακρίτους).[59] Yet the logic of the complaint itself assumes that since punishment has been administered, a trial *ought* to have taken place. To be sure, several elements of the story do in fact point to a trial episode: the *duoviri*[60] (στρατηγοί) become involved in the conflict (16.19–20), charges are brought (16.20–1), a city crowd is present (16.22),[61] and custody is administered (16.23). The important missing component (explaining Paul's complaint in 16.37) is the proper weighing of the evidence before reaching a verdict. At the narrative level, however, that is precisely the readers' role. It is before them that ultimately Luke presents Paul's case 'on trial'.

The charge is that Paul and Silas are causing social disturbance (ἐκταράσσουσιν ἡμῶν πόλιν) by advocating un-Roman customs: καταγγέλλουσιν ἔθη ἃ οὐκ ἔξεστιν ἡμῖν παραδέχεσθαι οὐδὲ ποιεῖν Ῥωμαίοις οὖσιν (16.20–1). What exactly are these 'customs' advocated by the two missionaries?[62] The only indication of any influence being exercised by Paul and his companion(s) in the city is that they had spoken to a group of women (16.13–14), but nothing explicit is said about the content of their address. What the text does say is that the Lord 'opened the heart' of one woman to what Paul had said and that she was subsequently baptised, together with her household (16.14–15). The reader has thus implicitly learnt that the content of Paul's words was the message of the gospel. This is later confirmed by the words of a slave girl with a spirit of divination, who refers to the missionaries' activity as the proclamation of 'the way of salvation' (ὁδὸν σωτηρίας, 16.17), and by Paul's dialogue with the jailer (16.30–2). The resulting charge is, then, that the gospel which Paul proclaims causes social unrest and is incompatible with Roman identity.

In response to this charge, Luke's apologia takes several forms. First, Paul's encounter with the slave girl reveals that in Christianity the Roman

[59] Louw and Nida's definition of the term is: 'pertaining to not having gone through a judicial hearing, with the implication of not having been condemned' (*GELNT*, vol. I, 56.19, p. 554).

[60] Sherwin-White, *Roman Society*, p. 93; Tajra, *Trial*, pp. 10–11.

[61] On taking the crowd here as a trial ingredient, see Rapske, *Acts and Paul*, p. 121.

[62] Following van Unnik, Rapske suggests that 'to a Jew the term designates the impossibility of Roman military service, the requirements of Sabbath observance, food regulations and sending offerings to Jerusalem, recourse to special legal jurisdiction and, in general, a life according to the Jewish law' (Rapske, ibid., p. 118). To these Rapske adds monotheism and circumcision (p. 118). Haenchen correctly points out that 'Paul certainly did not preach circumcision', but goes on to say that 'it could have been, for example, the custom of the φίλημα ἅγιον at the Lord's Supper which gave the semblance of an immoral oriental cult' (*Acts*, p. 496, n. 6). While some of these proposals are legitimate historical speculations, they suffer from insufficient textual support.

world[63] is faced with a religion which is both confirmed by[64] and superior to[65] pagan practices. Second, the invalidity of the charge is indicated by the selfish material interests which motivate it (16.19a). Third, the validity of the Christian message is also evident in its ability to overcome opposition (shaking the prison open and converting the jailer) and in the fact that those who proclaim it are men of prayer (16.13, 16, 25).[66] Fourth, there is nothing inherently un-Roman about the Christian message – three Romans (Paul, Silas, and the jailer) in this incident alone have no difficulties in accepting it. Rather, it is their opponents who are breaking Roman law by beating and jailing two uncondemned Roman citizens (16.37) – a mistake which will soon cause the magistrates to fear and apologise (16.38–9). Fifth, those responsible for the social unrest in Philippi are, once again, not those who proclaim the word but those who oppose it.[67] Finally, in addition to this elaborate Roman-related apologia, a Jewish-oriented one may also be present in Luke's emphatic specification that Paul and Silas are accused and suffer *as Jews*[68] (οὗτοι οἱ ἄνθρωποι ἐκταράσσουσιν ἡμῶν τὴν πόλιν, Ἰουδαῖοι ὑπάρχοντες, 16.20), a detail which acquires additional force in view of the Jewish long-standing opposition to divination (Lev. 19.31; 20.27).

(b) *Thessalonica (17.1–9)*

It may seem particularly inappropriate to include the Thessalonian episode among Paul's trials in Acts since Paul is not even present when the actual 'trial' takes place (17.6–9).[69] Yet there is no question that what is being judged here 'before the politarchs' is *Paul's* case and that 'Jason and some of the brethren' are only his substitutes (17.6).

The content of the charges is fundamentally the same as at Philippi. It is again alleged that the proclamation of the Christian message leads to social disruption (οἱ τὴν οἰκουμένην ἀναστατώσαντες οὗτοι, 17.6)[70]

---

[63] Note Luke's explicit reference to the Roman context in which the events take place (16.12; see Rapske, *Acts and Paul*, p. 116).

[64] 16.17. The fact that someone with supernatural abilities declares publicly the tenets of the missionaries' message inevitably amounts to a confirmation of this message.

[65] 16.18. The superiority of Christianity is implicit in the fact that the spirit of divination is cast out 'in the name of Jesus'.

[66] Throughout Luke's two volumes, prayer plays a legitimating role.

[67] Note the indications of violence in 16.19b, 22–3.

[68] Note the emphatic position of this identification in the sentence.

[69] Once again, Tajra includes the incident in his discussion of Paul's trials, but without offering any justification for doing so (*Trial*, pp. 30–44).

[70] Although the accusation does not make explicit in what way Paul and Silas had 'turned the world upside down', the foregoing story of Paul's missions (not least the Philippian

and implies political disloyalty to Rome (οὗτοι πάντες ἀπέναντι τῶν δογμάτων Καίσαρος πράσσουσιν, βασιλέα ἕτερον λέγοντες εἶναι 'Ιησοῦν, 17.7).[71] The one significant difference is that this time the accusations come from Jewish lips (17.5).

Luke's refutation of these charges is packed with irony: the charge of social disturbance is introduced by an avalanche of terminology indicating the prosecutors' own social misbehaviour (17.5–6), while the political concern with Caesar's decrees and kingship hardly looks appropriate coming from a Jewish group. Additionally, both charges are undermined by the jealousy which motivates them (17.5a).

The refutation of the social and political allegations against the Christian proclamation does not, however, exhaust the apologetic emphases of the trial account. An apologetic related to Judaism is also identifiable in Luke's specification (a) that Paul entered the Jewish synagogue 'according to [his] custom' (κατὰ . . . τὸ εἰωθός); (b) that his proclamation was grounded in the Jewish Scriptures; (c) that according to these Scriptures the Christ had to suffer and rise from the dead; and (d) that this Christ is Jesus whom he proclaims (17.2–3).[72] Moreover, the emphatic presentation of Paul's proclamation as based on argument,[73] the examples of both Jews[74] and God-fearing Greeks who were persuaded (ἐπείσθησαν) by Paul's message (17.4), and the singling out among them of the 'prominent women' (γυναικῶν τε τῶν πρώτων οὐκ ὀλίγαι, 17.4; cf. 17.12)[75] suggest that the readers (perhaps especially those of the more educated and upper class) are also encouraged to appreciate the 'persuasiveness' of the Christian message.[76]

---

incident) points to the proclamation of the word as the typical way in which they had 'offended' socially.

[71] The participle λέγοντες indicates that the latter half of the sentence explains the sense in which the missionaries 'act' (πράσσουσιν) against Caesar's decrees: their crime is what they 'say' about Jesus.

[72] On Paul's logic here, see Witherington, *Acts*, p. 505.

[73] No fewer than three terms within the space of two verses point in this direction: διελέξατο, διανοίγων, and παρατιθέμενος (17.2–3). For a detailed discussion of the 'intellectual element' in Paul's method of preaching here, see D. W. Kemmler, *Faith and Human Reason: A Study of Paul's Method of Preaching as Illustrated by 1–2 Thessalonians and Acts 17, 2–4*, Leiden: E. J. Brill, 1975, pp. 11–143; cf. Witherington, *Acts*, pp. 504–6.

[74] The referent of τινες ἐξ αὐτῶν in 17.4a can only be τῶν 'Ιουδαίων of 17.1b.

[75] Commenting on Luke's reference to these women, Haenchen writes: 'Luke likes to mention conversions from the upper classes' (*Acts*, p. 507).

[76] This reading of the Thessalonian trial is also supported by Luke's account of Paul's mission in Beroea (17.10–14). The contrast between the Thessalonians and the Beroeans in terms of their respective openness to the word and examination of its reliability (17.11; cf. 17.13) indicates that this had always been the focus of the Thessalonian account. The significance of this for the apologetic character of the Thessalonian account is to be found

(c) Athens (17.16–34)

Lukan scholarship has long debated whether Luke's words in 17.19–20 should be regarded as denoting a trial. Arguments on both sides of the debate have abounded, but little agreement has been reached.[77] Regardless of the position which one reaches on the judicial matters, it remains clear that the author has once again cast his story in a trial form: charges are brought (17.18–19); Paul is 'taken hold of' (ἐπιλαβόμενοι... αὐτοῦ) and 'led' (ἤγαγον) to the place of interrogation (17.19), where a formal response is offered (17.22–31).

The charges against Paul relate to the 'strangeness' of the message which he proclaims.[78] Luke's identification of this message as 'Jesus and the resurrection' (17.18) – two hallmarks of the Lukan gospel – informs the reader that what is once again 'on trial' is the essence of Christian belief, this time specifically challenged in terms of its relevance to the educated Greek.

In response to this challenge, Luke's apologia asserts (i) that the Athenians' idols are indicative of their search for God (17.22–3; cf. 17.16); (ii) that idolatry is the wrong answer, since God, as Creator and Lord, needs no human temples (17.24–5); (iii) that, instead, it is the people who need God and are dependent on him (17.26–7); (iv) that since people are God's offspring they should not worship material things (17.28–9); and (v) that they should, rather, turn towards the man whom God attested by raising him from the dead.[79] Thus, far from being irrelevant to the educated Greeks, the man Jesus and his resurrection – representing the core of the Christian faith – provide precisely the answer for which they had been searching.

It must not be overlooked, however, that as Paul presents his case for Christianity *versus* paganism, a subtle apologia related to Judaism is concomitantly taking shape. Except for the concluding part, the whole

firstly in the implicit assertion that the Jews of Thessalonica who reject the word do so not because they have good reasons for their attitude but because, unlike the Beroean Jews, they are not willing to enquire about its validity. Secondly, relating to the social charge against Paul and Silas, further confirmation is given that the prosecutors are more guilty of social disruption than the defendants (17.13).

[77] For a thorough examination of the evidence, see B. Gärtner, *The Areopagus Speech and Natural Revelation*, Uppsala: Gleerup, 1955, pp. 52–65. Gärtner's personal position is that there is 'reason for supposing that the Areopagus speech and its narrative framework are part of an informal interrogation by the education commission of the Areopagus court' (p. 64).

[78] ξένων δαιμονίων δοκεῖ καταγγελεὺς εἶναι (17.18); ξενίζοντα γάρ τινα εἰσφέρεις εἰς τὰς ἀκοὰς ἡμῶν (17.20).

[79] For this five-part division of Paul's speech (i.e. introduction, three main sections, and conclusion), see, among others, Dibelius, *Studies*, p. 27; Marshall, *Acts* (1980), p. 282.

speech is a defence of monotheism. This inevitably makes Paul speak not only as a Christian but also as a Jew, reminding the reader of the common ground between Judaism and Christianity and that together with 'all people everywhere' the Jews too are 'commanded' to come to terms with the 'strange' concepts of Jesus and his resurrection.

(d) *Corinth (18.12–17)*

Corinth is the first city where Paul is found in an explicitly judicial setting: the term 'tribunal' (βῆμα) is used twice to define the location of the incident (18.12, 17), while the judge is identified as Gallio, the proconsul (ἀνθύπατος) of Achaia (18.12). On the other hand, Gallio's words – κριτὴς ἐγὼ τούτων οὐ βούλομαι εἶναι (18.15) – would seem to indicate that a fully fledged trial does not in fact take place. Ironically, however, it is precisely in the proconsul's refusal 'to be a judge' that the reader discovers that in a fundamental sense the trial has already been under way and that the verdict has just been issued – Gallio has understood that there was no question of ἀδίκημά τι ἢ ῥᾳδιούργημα πονηρόν in the defendant (18.14).

The charge which the Jews bring against Paul is that παρὰ τὸν νόμον ἀναπείθει οὗτος τοὺς ἀνθρώπους σέβεσθαι τὸν θεόν (18.13). The words need to be understood in the context of Paul's earlier conflict with the Jews in Corinth (18.6), due to his 'persuasion' of Jews and Greeks in the synagogue and his preaching to the Jews 'that the Christ is Jesus' (18.4–5). The specific contention is, thus, that the Christian message is incompatible with 'the law'. Commentators lament the difficulty of deciding whether the Jewish or the Roman law is meant,[80] but perhaps more attention should be given to the possibility that Luke deliberately intends the term to be open to both interpretations, thereby indicating the duplicity of Paul's prosecutors.[81] Thus, on the one hand, the origins of the controversy (18.4–6), together with the significant impact of the gospel in Corinth (18.8–11), provide the readers with grounds to infer that the true motives of the Jews relate to the relationship between Paul's teaching and *their* law. On the other hand, the unqualified use of the term may be understood as a Jewish attempt to cause the proconsul to suspect Paul of promoting socio-political misconduct, that is, some infringement of

[80] So, for instance, Bruce, *Acts*, p. 396; Haenchen, *Acts*, p. 536; Marshall, *Acts* (1980), pp. 297–8.

[81] Witherington notes this as a possibility and points out as a parallel the equally ambiguous use of 'people' (denoting Jews, Gentiles, or both?) in the same verse (*Acts*, p. 552).

the *Roman* law.[82] On this reading, Gallio's response in 18.14–15 astutely uncovers the duplicity of which the Jews' use of νόμος smacks, stating at the same time that at the level at which he is willing (and, from the reader's point of view, competent) to make a judgement – socio-political matters – there is no case against Paul.

Once again, then, Luke has narrated an incident which is intended to show that there is no inherent incompatibility between the Christian message (particularly in its Christological form in which the readers had last encountered it, 18.5) and the Roman system. At the same time, as has been noted, the accusation against Paul comes from Jews, and its real, if somewhat concealed, thrust is the relationship between Paul's gospel and the Jewish law. Although no explicit apologia is offered in response to this charge – Paul does not get a chance to present one (18.14a) and Gallio refuses to judge such matters (18.15) – Luke has built an all the more efficient apologia by informing the readers that Paul's proclamation enjoyed God's direct approval (18.9–10) and by providing them with a precedent of a believing Jew in no less a figure than the ruler of the synagogue in Corinth (if not two such rulers).[83]

(e) *Ephesus (19.23–41)*

In many respects the Ephesian episode resembles the incident in Thessalonica. Paul is again not physically present at the 'trial' (19.30–1; cf. 17.6–9) and yet it is abundantly clear that the main character in the development of the conflict, as well as the explicit target of the accusation (19.26), is Paul and his mission. To this extent, then, the reader is dealing with a Pauline trial, with Gaius and Aristarchus (19.29) and perhaps Alexander (19.33) featuring in the narrative as Pauline substitutes.

Once again, indications exist that the author does not intend to portray a regular trial – for that, the clerk explains, proper proceedings are available and they ought to be followed (19.38–9). At the same time, several major elements of a trial story are present in the passage and support the inclusion of the passage among Luke's 'trial' narratives: the presence of a crowd (19.29–41) and of the city clerk (19.35) is recorded, accusations are brought (19.25–7), and a defence speech is offered (19.35–40).

---

[82] A similar situation has been noted in the trials of Jesus, where the true religious motives of Jesus' prosecutors, as revealed at the Sanhedrin hearing, are turned into socio-political accusations in order to impress the Roman governor.

[83] Sosthenes (18.17) could be a second example (Bruce, *Acts*, p. 397; Marshall, *Acts* (1980), p. 299); see however Haenchen, *Acts*, p. 536, n. 5.

The accusation is that 'not only at Ephesus but almost throughout all Asia this Paul has persuaded and turned away a considerable company of people, saying that gods made with hands are not gods' and that Paul's success is specifically detrimental to those involved in idol trading and to Artemis' fame (19.25–7). The readers already know that what the Ephesians and 'all the residents of Asia' had heard from Paul was 'the word of the Lord' (19.10; cf. 19.20),[84] in specifically Christological terms (19.13, 17). What the readers are now witnessing, therefore, is an open confrontation between Paul's gospel and pagan idolatry. The superiority of the former is established in at least three ways: (1) *Ideologically*, the prosecutors' reference to Paul's preaching, according to which 'gods made with hands are not gods', is an effective reminder of Paul's preaching in Athens,[85] through which the foolishness of idolatry has been exposed in the light of the gospel. Against this background, the Ephesians' passion for (19.28, 34) and confidence in (19.35–6) the Artemis cult acquire a subtle tone of irony. (2) The *motives* behind the pagan opposition to the gospel are less than commendable (19.24–5). (3) *Socio-politically*, it is not those who proclaim the gospel but those who oppose it who are 'in danger of being charged with rioting', as the clerk himself observes (19.40).

Paul's custody trials
(a) *Jerusalem (21.27–23.11)*

With Paul's arrival in Jerusalem,[86] the reader encounters the first elaborate statement of the Jewish charges against Paul.[87] The accusation is addressed to the 'men of Israel' and reads: οὗτός ἐστιν ὁ ἄνθρωπος ὁ κατὰ τοῦ λαοῦ καὶ τοῦ νόμου καὶ τοῦ τόπου τούτου πάντας πανταχῇ διδάσκων, ἔτι τε καὶ Ἕλληνας εἰσήγαγεν εἰς τὸ ἱερὸν καὶ κεκοίνωκεν τὸν ἅγιον τόπον τοῦτον (21.28). At stake is, thus, the relation between Paul's teaching and the 'people', the 'law', and 'this holy place' (the last sentence being part of the temple charge).[88] Coming from 'the Jews of Asia' (21.27),[89] the accusation reminds the readers

---

[84] Kistemaker, *Acts*, p. 697.

[85] Haenchen, *Acts*, p. 572; Kistemaker, *Acts*, p. 697; Witherington, *Acts*, p. 591.

[86] I refer to Paul's trials in Jerusalem, Caesarea and Rome as 'custody trials' because throughout their course Paul is in custody.

[87] The accusation in Thessalonica (17.6–7), regarding the socio-political threat inherent in Paul's message, can hardly be regarded as the Jews' most representative concern, while the one in Corinth (18.13) is relatively cryptic and unelaborated.

[88] On the similarity between this episode and the Stephen story, see Tannehill, *Narrative*, vol. II, p. 273.

[89] It is probable that Ephesus itself is meant, since the Jews recognise Trophimus of Ephesus (Haenchen, *Acts*, p. 615; Marshall, *Acts* (1980), p. 347; J. R. W. Stott, *The Message*

specifically of Paul's successful ministry in that region, summarised by Luke in 19.10: 'all the residents of Asia heard the word of the Lord, both Jews and Greeks'. The inference is that this teaching of 'the word of the Lord' has been taken by the unbelieving Jews[90] as a fundamental breach with the hallmarks of God's people – the nation, the law, and the temple.[91]

Paul's speech in 22.1–21 is an ἀπολογία (22.1) related to this accusation. His address to the Jerusalemites as 'brethren and fathers' (22.1); his emphatic self-identification as a Jew (22.3); his reference to his former education 'according to the strict manner of the law of our fathers' (22.3), to his post-conversion association with Ananias ('a devout man according to the law, well spoken of by all the Jews who lived there [in Damascus]', 22.12), and to his prayer 'in the temple' (22.17) are only some of the more evident features of the speech designed to demonstrate that Paul sees no incompatibility between his teaching and his Jewish identity. It is hardly surprising, in view of such material, that Jervell (and his followers) finds here and in Paul's other 'apologetic speeches' in Acts the basis for his claim that this part of Luke's work is intended as a defence of Paul's faithfulness to Judaism.[92] Moreover, the biographical character of most of the speech, as we have seen, is taken by Jervell as indicative that Luke's apologia here relates to Paul and to him alone: Dibelius is wrong to think that Luke intends to provide Christians with material for their own apologias and the advocates of the political apologetic are equally mistaken to think that Luke is fashioning a defence of Christianity as a whole.[93]

Although Jervell is undoubtedly correct to call attention to the biographical character of the speeches, on closer scrutiny it is doubtful that even his explanation of this feature strictly in terms of a Jewish defence of Paul has done full justice to the text. Notwithstanding the existence of *some* elements of the speech (such as those noted in the last paragraph) which could be satisfactorily explained in this way, large parts of the 'biographical' material in the speech point beyond such a goal. The detailed narration of Paul's *former* persecution of the church (22.4–5, 19–20),[94]

---

of Acts. To the Ends of the Earth, The Bible Speaks Today, Leicester: Inter-Varsity Press, 1990, p. 343; Witherington, *Acts*, p. 652), but the text does not state this explicitly (Dunn, *Acts*, p. 288).

[90] See, for example, 19.9.

[91] This is in keeping with the accusation about which the Christians in Jerusalem had already warned Paul: 'that you teach all the Jews who are among the Gentiles to forsake Moses, telling them not to circumcise their children or observe the customs' (21.21).

[92] See the discussion of Jervell's thesis, pp. 178–9.

[93] Jervell, 'Teacher', esp. pp. 154–5, 161–3.

[94] The fact that Paul was prepared to be so zealous for Judaism *before* his conversion does not guarantee his Jewish orthodoxy in the present.

of his direct encounter with the risen Christ (22.6–11), and of his double commissioning as a witness to Jesus (22.14–15 and 22.18–21) indicate a Lukan concern which clearly transcends the person of Paul. Their focus is not merely the *messenger* but also (and perhaps more importantly) the *message* which he proclaims and represents. On this view, Paul is portrayed as a zealous Jew, entertaining no positive thought for the Way (22.3–5, 19–20), but who is so persuasively confronted with the reality of what his persecutees proclaim (Jesus is truly risen and glorified; 22.6–11), that he is left with no alternative but to yield to this truth and become its witness (22.12–16). As for his proclamation of this message among the Gentiles, this is due to the Jews' failure to accept it (22.17–20)[95] and to Christ's direct commission for Paul (22.21; cf. 22.15).

Thus Luke's account of Paul's trial in Jerusalem builds an apologia to Judaism which on the one hand refutes the accusation that Paul's gospel entails a breach with the distinctives of God's people, and on the other hand puts forward a persuasive case for the validity of the Christological claims of this gospel.

Outside Paul's address, the apologia related to Judaism is supplemented with an apologia related to the Roman world. Paul's knowledge of Greek – combined, evidently, with the unrest which his arrival in Jerusalem had created – is enough to raise for Lysias the suspicion that Paul may be a well-known Egyptian insurrectionist.[96] The suspicion is quickly eliminated by a Paul who takes pride in the respectability of his status: he is both a Jew and a citizen of 'no mean city', Tarsus. Following Paul's speech, the readers learn that it is Paul's Roman citizenship that not only saves him from scourging but sets him in a position which even overshadows the tribune.[97] Finally, in Lysias' report to Felix (23.26–30) the reader finds a summary of Paul's trial in Jerusalem from a Roman perspective – Paul enjoys the protection of the state representatives by virtue of his Roman citizenship (23.27), and his religious views,[98] although controversial within Jewish circles, involve 'nothing deserving death or imprisonment' from a Roman viewpoint (23.29). The readers have thus found

[95] 17.19–20 adds emphasis to the Jewish refusal to accept the gospel: Paul implies that they ought to pay attention at least because it is he, the former vehement persecutor of this message, that now proclaims it.

[96] Josephus, *Jewish War*, 2.261–3; *Antiquities*, 20.169–72. For οὐκ ἄρασὺ εἶ ὁ Αἰγύπτιος; (21.38) the translation 'are you, then, not the Egyptian' (adopted by NIV, RSV, Conzelmann, *Acts*, p. 182; Marshall, *Acts* (1980), p. 352) is to be preferred to 'then you are not the Egyptian' (so Haenchen, *Acts*, 619; Johnson, *Acts*, p. 383).

[97] Paul is portrayed as superior to Lysias in two ways: (i) Lysias has *bought* his Roman citizenship while Paul was *born* into it (22.28); (ii) it is Lysias who ends up being fearful, rather than Paul (22.29).

[98] See περὶ ζητημάτων τοῦ νόμου αὐτῶν (23.29).

in Paul proof that there is no inherent incompatibility between being a Christian and being a Roman. Moreover, they could learn from Lysias' experience that yielding too easily to anti-Christian accusations such as those advanced by the Jews can be both embarrassing (mistaking a respectable citizen for an insurrectionist) and legally dangerous (scourging an unconvicted Roman citizen).

The second part of Paul's trial in Jerusalem – his hearing before the Jewish council – fits easily with the kind of apologia related to Judaism which we have noted in the first part. It is intriguing that Luke should introduce this second hearing as aimed at enabling Lysias to appreciate better 'the real reason why the Jews accused [Paul]' (γνῶναι τὸ ἀσφαλές, τὸ τί κατηγορεῖται ὑπὸ τῶν 'Ιουδαίων, 22.30; cf. 23.28) and then provide no further information on the Jewish accusations. The answer is probably to be sought in the fact that this time it is Paul himself, rather than his opponents, who states the real issue of contention between him and the Jews. He does so when he declares: περὶ ἐλπίδος καὶ ἀναστάσεως νεκρῶν κρίνομαι (23.6).[99] For readers who have already learnt so many times that the core of the Christian message is the claim that the hopes of Israel have been fulfilled in someone who has been attested by God through resurrection, there can be no doubt that in effect the 'real reason' for Paul's trial is the Christian message, in Lukan terms.[100]

If the issue which is at stake in Paul's trial is the gospel, it is not surprising that the apologetic devices of the narrative are also geared in this direction. First, Luke indicates that it is not Paul but those who disagree with his interpretation of the hope of Israel that act against the Jewish law: Paul has 'lived before God in all good conscience' (23.1), while his opponents make pronouncements 'contrary to the law' (23.3). Second, not all Jews find Paul's interpretation of the hope of Israel problematic: by describing Paul's faith as centring on 'the resurrection of the dead', rather than on the more contentious claim of *Jesus'* resurrection, Luke is able to set Paul in substantial agreement with a trustworthy branch of Judaism – the Pharisees.[101] His agreement with them is additionally emphasised by Paul's self-identification as 'a Pharisee, a son of Pharisees'

---

[99] It is this declaration, together with the accusation at 21.28, that later justifies Lysias in formally describing the Jewish charge as relating to 'questions of their law' (23.29).

[100] Commenting on Paul's declaration of his resurrection belief, Dunn writes that for Luke this is 'one of the primary identity markers, if not the decisive identity of the new sect' (*Acts*, p. 305; see also p. xix).

[101] In the words of Marshall, '[w]hat Paul was now [in 23.6] in effect claiming was that one could be a Christian, while accepting the Pharisaic point of view, or more precisely, that Pharisaic Judaism found its fulfilment in Christianity' (Marshall, *Acts* (1980), p. 364).

(23.6)[102] and by the Pharisees' own recognition of Paul's innocence and of the possibility that he may have been the recipient of some special revelation (23.9).

(b) Caesarea (24.1–26.32)

(i) *Before Antonius Felix (24.1–27)*. Following a Jewish plot against Paul in Jerusalem, the defendant is transferred by Lysias to Caesarea (23.12–24, 30a), so that his prosecutors can also present their case before Felix (23.30b). The letter which accompanies the defendant (23.26–30) is meant to familiarise Felix with Paul's case. In it Lysias states that the accusations against Paul are of a religious nature (relating to the Jewish law) and that, from the Roman perspective, they comprise 'nothing deserving death or imprisonment' (23.29).

The charges are soon heard live by Felix, as they are stated by the specially appointed orator Tertullus (24.1),[103] and backed by the Jewish elite (24.9; cf. 24.1). According to Tertullus' words, Paul is λοιμὸν καὶ κινοῦντα στάσεις πᾶσιν τοῖς Ἰουδαίοις τοῖς κατὰ τὴν οἰκουμένην πρωτοστάτην τε τῆς τῶν Ναζωραίων αἱρέσεως, ὅς καὶ τὸ ἱερὸν ἐπείρασεν βεβηλῶσαι (24.5–6). The charge regards Paul's relationship to Judaism, in so far as his influence is said to have been exercised among Jews and the temple represents their supreme national and religious symbol. At the same time, however, it is assumed that terms such as λοιμός ('troublemaker'), στάσις ('rebellion'), and πρωτοστάτης ('ringleader')[104] will sound just as suspicious to Roman ears. Put briefly, the charge states that Paul, acting as a representative of the Christian movement, poses a national and religious threat to the Jews and a socio-political danger to Romans.[105]

---

[102] See Dunn, *Acts*, p. 305, on taking these words as an apologetic device. To the question of the legitimacy of Paul's self-identification in this way, Haenchen (*Acts*, pp. 642–3) answers in the negative, while Marshall (*Acts* (1980), p. 365), following R. P. C. Hanson (*The Acts of the Apostles*, Oxford University Press, 1967, p. 221) answers in the affirmative.

[103] For a detailed examination of Tertullus' and Paul's speeches in Acts 24–6 against the background of forensic proceedings and rhetorical conventions, see B. W. Winter, 'Official Proceedings and the Forensic Speeches in Acts 24–26', in B. W. Winter and A. D. Clarke (eds.), *The Book of Acts in Its Ancient Literary Setting, BAFCS*, vol. I, Grand Rapids: Eerdmans; Carlisle: Paternoster, 1993, pp. 305–36.

[104] For this translation of the three terms, see *GELNT*, vol. I, 22.6, p. 243; 39.34, p. 497; 87.52, p. 739, respectively.

[105] For more detail on the character and seriousness of the charge(s), see Rapske, *Acts and Paul*, pp. 160–2; Witherington, *Acts*, pp. 707–8; B. W. Winter, 'The Importance of the *Captatio Benevolentiae* in the Speeches of Tertullus and Paul in Acts 24:1–21', *JTS* 42 (1991), 518–21.

Responding to Tertullus' accusation, Paul's defence begins (after the short introduction of 24.10b) by flatly denying that during his short stay in Jerusalem (24.11) he has caused any public disruption 'either in the temple or in the synagogues, or in the city' (24.12)[106] – the prosecutors simply cannot prove such accusations (24.13).[107] The true substance of the conflict, Paul explains, is Paul's worship of God κατὰ τὴν ὁδὸν ἣν λέγουσιν αἵρεσιν (24.14), a worship which centres on belief in the 'resurrection of both the just and the unjust' (24.15).[108] Once this is regarded as the *raison d'être* of Paul's trial, the two participial clauses preceding the resurrection pronouncement, as well as the indicative one following it, function as Paul's Jewish-related apologetic for the worship and the (resurrection) belief of his Christian 'sect': his worship according to this sect involves believing everything written in the Jewish Scriptures (24.14b); his resurrection belief, in its general form, is shared with the Jewish prosecutors themselves (24.15a), with the implication that the more specific claim of Jesus' resurrection (which the readers know to be the actual point of contention) should come as no surprise; and in all this[109] – worship and belief – the defendant strives to keep a clear conscience before God and people.

The second half of Paul's address (24.17–21)[110] is, from the point of view of its apologetic function, a close rehearsal of the arguments of the first half. Once again Paul speaks of himself as someone who is neither a national/religious threat to the Jews (his behaviour, according to 24.17–18a, is thoroughly Jewish), nor a socio-political discomfort to Romans (he was found 'without any crowd or tumult' and even now nobody can produce a credible case against him; 24.18b–19). The one issue for which he truly is on trial is his belief in the resurrection of the dead (24.21).

According to the contents of the speech, then, Paul's self-exculpation in terms of his relationship both to Judaism and to the imperial order

[106] Undoubtedly, the readers will still remember that Paul's arrival in Jerusalem did cause a significant public disruption, but Luke will soon explain that it is not Paul but the Asian Jews who were responsible for this (24.18–19). As for the specific charge that he tried to defile the temple but his prosecutors had seized him (24.6), Acts 21 tells a rather different story (Witherington, *Acts*, p. 708; Rapske, *Acts and Paul*, p. 162).

[107] Witherington, *Acts*, pp. 710–11.

[108] Paul's worship is also qualified by belief in 'everything laid down by the law or written in the prophets', 24.14b. This qualification, however, is not meant to explain the cause of the conflict, in the way in which the resurrection belief does (cf. 24.21), but rather to legitimate the latter.

[109] ἐν τούτῳ (24.16) should probably be understood as referring to everything that Paul 'admits' in 24.14–15.

[110] Both the summary-statement form of 24.16 and the change of tense between 24.16 and 24.17 (from the present ἀσκῶ to the aorist παρεγενόμην) indicate that with 24.17 a new section of the speech begins.

appears to be secondary and subordinated to his apologia for the beliefs which he, as a worshipper of God 'according to the Way', holds. It is for these beliefs, rather than for any allegations of misconduct, that he is ultimately on trial. Further confirmation for this reading comes from 24.22–7, where the outcome of Paul's trial before Felix is described. The formal verdict is postponed by Felix until Lysias' arrival (which for the reader never happens), although a verdict of innocence is implicit in the order of lightened custody (24.23).[111] A greater Lukan concern – indicated especially by the fact that it relates to material which seems irrelevant to the trial proceedings – is Felix's attitude to the movement to which Paul belongs and the faith which he proclaims. Felix is portrayed as someone who had already manifested a good deal of interest in 'the Way' (hence his 'accurate knowledge' of it; 24.22a) and who is willing to hear Paul 'speak about faith in Christ Jesus' (24.24). The fact that for the time being he chooses to stay away from Paul's message is explained by Luke as relating to Felix's discomfort, as he hears of justice, self-control, and future judgement, rather than to any negative view of Paul's message.

To summarise, Luke is at pains to indicate that the substance of Paul's trial before Felix is his Christian belief and the type of worship implied thereby, that this belief is in harmony with the Jewish Scriptures and aspirations, that any socio-political accusations against it are based on misrepresentations of events, and that even a Roman governor is prepared to give it serious thought (although his personal shortcomings cause him temporarily to stay away from it).

(ii) *Before Porcius Festus and Agrippa II (25.1–26.32).* The replacement of Antonius Felix by Porcius Festus (24.27) provides the Jews in Jerusalem with the occasion to resume their case against Paul (25.1– 2). Their intentions are frustrated inasmuch as they fail to obtain Paul's transfer to Jerusalem (25.3–5; cf. 23.9); what they do get is a new trial of Paul in Caesarea.

This time there is no account of the actual content of the charges; Luke states only that they were 'many and serious' (πολλὰ καὶ βαρέα) and that the Jews 'were unable to prove' (οὐκ ἴσχυον ἀποδεῖξαι) them (25.7). Paul's 'apologia'[112] before Festus is almost equally sketchy. The defendant simply states, with no elaboration, his innocence in relation to both Judaism and Rome: οὔτε εἰς τὸν νόμον τῶν Ἰουδαίων οὔτε εἰς τὸ

---

[111] The fact that Paul is not released raises questions about Felix's character, not Paul's innocence.

[112] ἀπολογουμένου (25.8).

ἱερὸν οὔτε εἰς Καίσαρά τι ἥμαρτον (25.8). It is out of this conviction that, as a last resort, Paul appeals to Caesar (25.10–12).

A few verses later, as Festus lays Paul's case before Agrippa, it again becomes apparent that Luke makes positive efforts to show that the real issue in Paul's trials is nothing which, from the Roman perspective at least, could be qualified as 'evil'; rather, at the centre of the conflict stands a religious dispute, focusing on Paul's beliefs about Jesus and particularly about his resurrection (25.17–19).[113] Once Paul's trial before Agrippa has commenced, Festus familiarises the audience with the Jews' request, according to which Paul should be put to death, and with his personal inability to find in Paul anything that would match such a petition. It remains now for Agrippa, as someone 'especially familiar with all the customs and controversies of the Jews' (26.3), to judge the situation and hopefully enable Festus to present Caesar with a meaningful report of the charges against Paul (25.25–7).[114]

At Agrippa's invitation, Paul offers his 'apologia' (26.1).[115] The first section of the speech (26.4–8) is replete with material which would seem to denote a special Lukan concern with Paul's relationship to Judaism, along the lines suggested by Jervell. Paul is heard making statements such as 'my nation', 'our religion', 'I have lived as a Pharisee', 'I stand here on trial for hope in the promise made by God to our fathers, to which our twelve tribes hope to attain, as they earnestly worship night and day.' What else could all this portray if not Paul the Jew? The difficulty arises when after making 'Paul the Jew' the hermeneutical key of the speech, one discovers that no further 'doors' in the passage will be easily unlocked: the story of Paul's conversion from an opponent of Jesus to a witness for him, occupying much of the speech (26.9–18), is, frankly, disproportionately long (especially when told for the third time) for the little which it could contribute to the establishment of Paul's Jewishness;[116] the elaborate Christology, pervading virtually the whole speech,[117] could have only a secondary contribution at best; even the grounding of this Christology in the Jewish Scriptures (26.22–3) is no more a defence of *Paul* the Jew than we have seen it at earlier stages to be a defence of the Jewishness of

---

[113] Marshall correctly notes that 'by this stage the question of Paul's alleged desecration of the temple has quite disappeared from sight, and the topic of the resurrection (23.6; 24.21) has replaced it' (*Acts* (1980), p. 388).

[114] It is Festus' need for help in finding any form of criminal charge that ought perhaps to be regarded as his most persuasive declaration of Paul's innocence.

[115] For a detailed account of alternative interpretations of Acts 26, both as a whole and in parts, see O'Toole, *Christological*, pp. 1–12.

[116] O'Toole is correct to see a Christological focus throughout 26.9–19 (ibid., pp. 44–85).

[117] Ibid., esp. p. 159.

Jesus, Peter, or Stephen (it is not 'biographical' enough to be a *peculiarly Pauline* defence); the reactions of both Festus and Agrippa (26.24, 28) would seem to miss the major point – neither of them concludes that Paul is truly a Jew (the former admires Paul's learning and the latter discusses the possibility of becoming a Christian); nor do Paul's replies point them in the 'right' direction – the former is encouraged to accept the truthfulness of Paul's foregoing statements (26.25–6)[118] and the latter (together with 'all who are listening') is prayed for to become a Christian (26.29).

In the light of such observations, it becomes extremely difficult to accept Paul's faithfulness to Judaism as the dominant emphasis of Acts 26. A different understanding of the chapter is needed. O'Toole points in the right direction when he concludes his study of Acts 26 with the remark: 'The trial concerns itself more with the belief that God raises the dead than with Paul himself.'[119] What O'Toole's interpretation does not do, as I have already noted, is to address adequately the question of why Luke would have his protagonist take so much trouble to persuade a Jewish prosecution and judge about a doctrine which all Jews, apart from the Sadducees, happily accepted: belief in the resurrection of the dead.

Two observations may help to solve the difficulty. First, according to Festus' explanation of Paul's case to Agrippa, the essence of the conflict in which Paul is now involved regards, specifically, 'one Jesus, who was dead, but whom Paul asserted to be alive' (25.19). Second, the Lukan reader has already learnt by now that hope in the resurrection of the dead is a hallmark of faithful Judaism, and that the realisation of this hope in Jesus' resurrection is the Christian proclamation *in nuce*. Such information provides the reader of Acts 26 with reasons to see in Paul's defence of the resurrection of the dead an attempt to highlight the confirmation of the whole gospel which Paul now represents and proclaims.

Luke's choice of material in Acts 26 supports such a reading. It is first emphasised that Paul's present position implies no abandonment of his long-standing commitment to Jewish aspirations – indeed, it is precisely because of these (or, as the readers can infer, because he believes they have *already* materialised) that he is now on trial (26.4–8). Next, as regards

---

[118] Truthfulness in the sense that they are based on verifiable facts – the king himself is surely familiar with them, since they were not 'done in a corner'. The possibility that through this last remark Luke 'is presenting Paul as speaking in the manner of a philosopher' (Malherbe, 'Not in a Corner', p. 202) is not excluded, but the primary function of the statement is defined by Paul himself, as he claims to speak ἀληθείας καὶ σωφροσύνης ῥήματα. 'With *alêtheias*, Luke has in mind the truth of the Christian message' (O'Toole, *Christological*, p. 149).

[119] O'Toole, *Christological*, p. 157.

'the name of Jesus of Nazareth' (in which these aspirations have allegedly been fulfilled), Paul too used to vehemently oppose it and all those
who identified with it (26.5–12). Nevertheless, his dramatic meeting with
Jesus (now glorified) has forced him to realise that he had been 'kicking
against the goads', and has turned him into a servant of and witness to the
things which he has come to know and which he is yet to know about this
Jesus (26.12–16). An essential part of the commission which he received
from Christ on that occasion was that these things should also be preached
to the Gentiles, so that they too may be forgiven (26.17–18). While
controversial to a large segment of Judaism, the Gentile-oriented shape
of this commission is fully in keeping with Israel's deutero-Isaianic vocation of bringing the light of God's salvation to the Gentiles (Isa. 42.6;
49.6; 60.1–3; cf. Luke 2.32; Ac. 9.15; 13.47; 22.21; 28.28).[120] Thus,
Paul's proclamation, to Jews and Gentiles alike, was the result of his obedience to this scripturally grounded 'heavenly vision' (26.19–20). Nevertheless, the Jews set themselves against this proclamation (especially
against its spreading among the Gentiles)[121] when they attempted to kill
Paul (26.21), but, ironically, a diametrically opposed verdict on Paul's
gospel[122] has been pronounced by the highest Jewish authorities: God,[123]
the prophets, and Moses (26.22).[124] Finally, it is the turn of Festus and
Agrippa to give their verdict in relation to Paul's proclamation.[125] Festus
regards it as 'madness' (μανίαν),[126] although he is compelled to admit
that it is based on Paul's 'great learning' (τὰ πολλά ... γράμματα); Paul
counters this pronouncement with the claim that his statements are 'true
and reasonable' (ἀληθείας καὶ σωφροσύνης) and based on public facts
(26.24–6). In contrast to Festus, Agrippa finds Paul's arguments 'almost
persuading' (ἐν ὀλίγῳ με πείθεις) him to become a Christian (26.28).[127]

[120] Marshall, *Acts* (1980), pp. 396–7; Turner, *Power*, p. 301; Witherington, *Acts*, p. 744.

[121] ἕνεκα τούτων looks back upon Paul's entire missionary proclamation (26.20a), but
especially upon his mission among the Gentiles (26.20b). See, for example, Bruce, *Acts*,
p. 503; Haenchen, *Acts*, p. 687.

[122] 26.23 is clearly a nutshell statement of the whole gospel, in Lukan terms. Conzelmann
(*Acts*, p. 211) refers to it as 'a concluding summary of the essence of faith'.

[123] For the legitimating function of the divine help enjoyed by Paul, see Rapske, *Acts
and Paul*, pp. 393–422.

[124] On Luke's apologetic use of the Old Testament, see Dupont, 'Apologetic', in *Salvation*, pp. 129–59.

[125] That the statements of Festus and Agrippa refer to Paul's Christian proclamation is
indicated both by their content (as we shall see) and by their position, immediately following
Paul's summary of the gospel in 26.23.

[126] ' "Madness" describes Christianity and its major belief in a resurrection of the dead
realised in a suffering Christ' (O'Toole, *Christological*, p. 148).

[127] It is not clear from Agrippa's words whether he is actually beginning to be persuaded
(so, e.g. AV), or, perhaps more likely, he is simply recognising that Paul's arguments (and

Which of the two judges makes the more credible pronouncement is abundantly clear – it is Agrippa, not Felix, who is competent to evaluate the true substance of Paul's trial (25.20a; 26.3), and who is also familiar with the public facts and authoritative prophets on which Paul bases his claims (26.26–7). At this point the intention of the Lukan Paul becomes explicit: that not only Agrippa but all those who have listened will become like him (26.29), that is, people who have been faced with the truthfulness of the Christian message[128] and are therefore prepared to accept it as such. As for the judicial side of Paul's trial, Luke returns to it only in the last three verses. All those present readily agree on Paul's innocence – if he is still not set free, it is (this time) because he had appealed to Caesar – an appeal which, for the Lukan reader, serves to fulfil the will of God, according to which 'it is necessary' for Paul to bear witness to Christ in Rome as well (23.11).

To conclude, the account of Paul's trials before Festus and Agrippa provides ample evidence that the primary focus of the conflict in this part of Acts is not Paul's alleged guilt in relation to either Judaism or Rome, but his Christological assertions about Jesus, with specific focus on the claim of Jesus' resurrection, as the one assertion on which the reliability of the whole Christian message hinges (25.18–19). Such a belief is difficult to stomach both for Jews such as Paul's prosecutors (26.8), and for Romans such as Festus (26.24). Correspondingly, Luke's apologia addresses both groups. He tries to persuade Jews (and those familiar with their beliefs) of their need to come to terms with the fact that the Christian message is far from incompatible with Jewish tradition (26.4–8); that nothing other than Paul's genuine encounter with the resurrected and glorified Christ could have turned a vehement opponent of Jesus into a witness for him (26.9–20); that Jewish efforts to stop the spread of this message (26.21) are misguided, since God, Moses, and the prophets have spoken in its favour (26.22–3), and that the proclamation of this message not only to Jews but also to Gentiles is based both on the direct command of the risen Christ (26.17–18) and on the testimony of Moses and the prophets (26.23). If a competent contemporary opinion on the matter is needed, attention ought to be paid to king Agrippa, as someone well familiarised both with the Jewish tradition and with Christian claims (25.20a; 26.3,

especially the direct question of 26.27) are strongly urging him in this direction. What commentators are generally agreed on is that Agrippa's remark is no mocking sarcasm but is meant to be taken seriously (not least because otherwise it would be completely dissonant with the climactic nature of the Christology of Acts 26). For more detail on the dominant interpretations of 26.28, see Marshall, *Acts* (1980), p. 400, n. 1; O'Toole, *Christological*, pp. 141–5.

[128] That is, just as Paul was on his journey to Damascus.

26–7), and who after hearing Paul's rehearsal of the relevant data finds himself being pushed (perhaps rather faster than he would like) towards becoming a Christian.

On the other hand, Luke hopes to persuade the Romans that there is nothing in the Christian message or behaviour that they need to worry about. Paul and his sect are no opponents of social order or of Caesar (25.8, 11, 18, 25–7; 26.31–2). As for the credibility of the Christian message in religious matters, to which the real controversies with Judaism are related, although some Romans may, like Festus, find that certain aspects of this message (such as Jesus' resurrection[129] or Paul's Christophany and commissioning) sound like 'madness', they cannot dismiss it light-heartedly, since people of 'great learning',[130] like Paul, are happy to identify with it, while someone of no lower a social status than 'king' Agrippa (himself in the service of Rome) finds its claims persuasive.

(c) *Rome, at last (27.1–28.31)*

With the unanimous declaration of Paul's innocence by the distinguished jury in Caesarea (26.30–2), the judicial tone of Luke's narrative comes to an abrupt end. A number of observations favour, however, the inclusion of Acts 27–8 in Luke's account of Paul's 'trials'. First, the Christophanic assurance that Paul has to 'testify' in Rome in the same way as he has done in Jerusalem (23.11), together with the defendant's appeal to Caesar (25.10–12, 21, 25–7; 26.32), alert the reader to the fact that the resolution of the Pauline trials cannot be expected before Paul reaches Rome. Second, despite its apparently non-judicial tone, the story of Paul's journey to Rome (27.1–28.16) has been regarded by numerous scholars as having serious import for the issue of Paul's innocence.[131] Third, Paul's encounter with the Roman Jews (28.17–31) focuses largely on the same issues and requires of him the same kind of defence as the ones encountered by the reader in Acts 21–6.[132]

---

[129] Luke has thus had Jews, Greeks (17.18–19), and now a Roman, encountering difficulties with the Christian belief in Jesus' resurrection.

[130] For this translation of πολλά γράμματα see Bruce, *Acts*, p. 505; Marshall, *Acts* (1980), p. 24. Other possible but less probable meanings are listed in Witherington, *Acts*, pp. 748–9.

[131] See above the works of Miles and Trompf, Landouceur, and Rapske on pp. 179–80.

[132] *Pace* O'Toole (*Christological*, p. 15), who 'distinguishes' between Paul's defence in 22.1–26.32 and 28.17–28. For other authors who include Paul's Roman experience in their study of Paul's trials (albeit for partially different reasons from the ones outlined here), see Rapske, *Acts and Paul*, pp. 173–91; Tajra, *Trial*, pp. 172–96.

Before the two major sections of this last part of Acts (27.1–28.16 and 28.17–31) are discussed separately, an important common denominator between them must be highlighted. In addition to the chains of Paul, which, literarily (although not literally), bind together most of the last eight chapters of Acts,[133] the last two of these chapters are also united by their common focus on Rome – the destination of the voyage in 27.1–28.16 and the location of the events in 28.17–31. It can be expected, therefore, that the apologetic character of these chapters may reflect this unity.

(i) *On 'trial' before the court of nature (27.1–28.16).* There is no need to dwell too long on an observation which has become common knowledge in Lukan scholarship, namely that Paul's sea journey and his stay at Malta serve further to confirm his innocence. In addition to works which have made this observation the specific object of their explorations,[134] commentators often speak of such a theme with equal confidence.[135] In particular, the comment of the Maltese (28.4) concerning Paul, places the existence of this theme beyond dispute. One point which perhaps still deserves special emphasis is the finality of this verdict of innocence for Luke's story of Paul, with regard both to its comprehensiveness (establishing Paul's innocence in a general form and thereby addressing *all* charges) and to its competence (there can be no higher authority to judge Paul than the one who controls nature – not even Caesar). God himself has now ratified the verdict that Paul had done 'nothing to deserve death' (23.29; 25.25; 26.31).

In addition to the theme of Paul's innocence, a second theme, which has received only scant attention in Lukan studies,[136] seems just as much to permeate this part of Acts–*Paul's competence to assist people in experiencing divine salvation.* A brief survey of Acts 27.1–28.16 should help in tracing this theme. After introducing the main characters and briefly narrating the first and comparatively less adventurous part of the

---

[133] This is not to say that Paul is actually in chains throughout this section, but simply that he is a prisoner.

[134] So, again, the works of Miles and Trompf, Landouceur, and Rapske.

[135] So, for example, Dunn, *Acts*, p. 343.

[136] See, for instance, Haenchen's unelaborated observation that Paul is 'the focal point of the action: he, the prisoner, saves them all!' (*Acts*, p. 709). Walaskay also shows some awareness of such a theme, but misrepresents it by insisting that in Luke's view the Romans 'save' Paul and the gospel (*Rome*, p. 60). On the contrary, as will be seen, the Roman centurion's failure to take Paul's advice puts their lives at risk in the first place and it is Paul who repeatedly instructs them on how they can be 'saved'. It is only in response to Paul's tireless contribution that on one occasion the centurion 'saves' Paul (27.43); even this time, however, all the other prisoners are 'saved' because of Paul.

journey (27.1–8), Luke shows Paul warning his companions of the life-threatening dangers ahead (27.9–10). The Roman centurion, however, disregards Paul's advice (27.11–12) and thereby puts everyone's life in great danger (27.13–20). Paul blames his companions for not heeding his warnings (27.21), but invites them to share in his hope,[137] according to which, the God whom he 'worships' and in whom he 'has faith' is able to save their lives[138] (27.22–6). A short travel report follows (27.27–9) and Paul is again found instructing the Roman centurion and soldiers as to the way their lives can be 'saved' (σωθῆναι, 27.31). This time his words are heeded and appropriate action is taken (27.32). Immediately after this, Paul takes further care to secure their lives by 'urging' (παρακαλέω) them all to eat (27.33).[139] Before they do so, Paul gives thanks to God 'in the presence of all', thereby recognising, according to common Judaeo-Christian practice, the food as a gift from God (27.33–5). Once again, then, Paul has led his companions to benefit from the provision which God has made in order to 'save' their lives. Once they have all eaten (27.36–8) and a new day has come, everyone's life is again endangered (27.39–41). The prisoners in particular are at great risk, but the centurion's concern for Paul[140] enables them all to stay alive (27.42–3). Finally, the chapter ends with a summary statement of everyone's 'salvation': καὶ οὕτως ἐγένετο πάντας διασωθῆναι ἐπὶ τὴν γῆν (27.44).

The theme continues, although in a different form, in the account of Paul's stay in Malta (28.1–10). The story of Paul's unexpected survival after being bitten by the viper, and the subsequent recognition of his innocence, is accompanied by the account of how he helped Publius' father and 'the rest of the people on the island who had diseases' to experience physical healing – a well-known Lukan facet of 'salvation'.[141]

To summarise, as Paul draws near to Rome, with the final goal of bearing testimony to Jesus (23.11), he does so as someone who has

---

[137] Twice they are told to 'take heart'. Paul exhorts them 'in effect to share his *faith* that what God promised to him would come to pass' (Marshall, *Acts* (1980), pp. 410–11).

[138] Note especially Paul's assurance: 'there will be no loss of life among you' (27.22).

[139] That their lives were at serious risk is implicit in the information that they had not eaten for fourteen days (27.33).

[140] The centurion had already shown kindness to Paul in Sidon (27.3), but this time he takes deliberate measures to save Paul's life.

[141] On Luke's understanding of the relationship between physical healing and 'salvation', see M. D. Hamm, 'This Sign of Healing, Acts 3.1–10. A Study in Lukan Theology', unpublished PhD dissertation, Saint Louis University, 1975, especially pp. 263–74, 278.

That it is God who ultimately does the healing, while Paul only mediates it, is implicit in Luke's reference to Paul's prayer, before the healing of Publius' father (28.8; note the aorist form of προσευξάμενος, indicating temporal priority).

been 'tried' by God himself (on sea and land) and found not only innocent but also competent to assist others in experiencing divine salvation.

(ii) *On 'trial' before the Roman Jews (28.17–31).* For all the literary ingenuity of Luke's characterisation of Paul in 27.1–28.16, the passage does not provide sufficient information as to the precise role of this characterisation. The Lukan narrative prior to Acts 27 should already have led the reader some way towards the answer; yet it is up to Luke's presentation of Paul's activity in Rome (28.17–31) to provide the more conclusive explanation.

After a brief description of Paul's reception by the Christian community in Rome (28.15) and the mild conditions of his custody (28.16), the author narrates the first major episode involving Paul in Rome – his meeting, at his own initiative, with the Jewish leaders there, and the apologetic address which he volunteers to give (28.17–20). The address begins with a firm statement of his innocence in relation to the Jewish nation and customs (28.17). His declaration is then backed up with the observation that the Romans had not found him guilty of the Jewish charges (28.18), that his appeal to Caesar implied no betrayal of his nation (the Jewish protest against the Roman verdict 'compelled' him to do so) and that he is presently in custody precisely 'because of the hope of Israel'.

It may, however, come as a surprise to readers who regard the defence of Paul in relation to Judaism as Luke's governing concern in this part of Acts that once such a defence has been narrated, special care is (once again) taken to place it in a secondary position to (and, as we shall see, in the service of) a different type of apologia. Having listened to Paul's personal defence, the Jewish leaders reply that this is *not* their concern (28.21). Rather, they prefer to hear his views on the αἵρεσις to which he belongs and which, they are well aware, πανταχοῦ ἀντιλέγεται (28.22). What follows is an alternation of Pauline and editorial material through which the new apologia is fashioned (28.23–31). That Paul's personal apologia (28.17–20) is meant to be regarded as in some way secondary to this latter apologia is indicated not only by the Jews' comment in 28.21–3 but also by the respective amount of space which is allocated to each of them (three verses to the former, nine to the latter) and by the difference in the formality and proportions of the episodes which encompass them (the former is offered at Paul's initiative and only the leaders are present; for the latter the Jews appoint a day, come 'in great numbers', and Paul speaks 'from morning till evening').

The arguments of 28.23–31 are: (i) Paul's testimony about the Kingdom of God and Jesus (denoting major loci of the sect's beliefs) is based on the Jewish Scriptures (28.23b); (ii) the validity of this testimony was recognised by part of Paul's Jewish audience – those who were 'persuaded' (ἐπείθοντο, 28.24a); (iii) the fact that some did *not* believe is no surprise – Isaiah had predicted it (28.24b–27); (iv) it is, at least partly, because[142] of the unbelief of some of the Jews (past and present) that God's salvation has now been offered to the Gentiles (28.28); (v) despite Paul's personal limitations resulting from his custody, his message – the same one of which he had set out to persuade his audience in 28.23[143] – continues 'boldly and unhindered' (28.31),[144] thereby enjoying the vindication for which the incipient Christian 'sect' had prayed (4.29).[145]

A parallelism between the arguments of 28.17–20 and 28.23–31 seems apparent:

Paul's innocence in relation to Judaism	*The gospel's validity in relation to Judaism*
Paul's innocence is declared in relation to two major Jewish identity-markers: the nation and the customs (28.17)	the validity of the gospel is declared in relation to two major Jewish authorities: the law of Moses and the prophets (28.23)
specific attention is given to the appeal to Caesar (28.19)	specific attention is given to the turning towards the Gentiles (28.28)
the appeal happened because the Jews refused to accept Paul's innocence (28.19a)	the turning happened because the Jews refused to believe the Christian testimony (28.25–7)
another reason for the appeal was that the Romans seemed more open to recognise Paul's innocence (28.18)	another reason for the turning was that the Gentiles are more open: they will listen (28.28b)

---

[142] Note the use of οὖν in 28.28.

[143] In both 28.23 and 28.31 Paul's message has the same major components: the Kingdom of God and Jesus.

[144] It is hard to miss a note of irony in the fact that Acts ends with Paul in chains, facing a gloomy future, while his message continues to go out 'unhindered' (ἀκωλύτως). See D. Mealand, 'Acts 28.30–31 and Its Hellenistic Greek Vocabulary', *NTS* 36 (1990), 583–97 (esp. p. 595); Witherington, *Acts*, pp. 815–16.

[145] The same words describe the Christian proclamation here (μετὰ πάσης παρρησίας) and in 4.29 (μετὰ παρρησίας πάσης).

Tajra notes, with a good degree of justification, that '[t]he appeal to Caesar is the central event on which Luke's whole account of Paul's legal history turns'.[146] In the light of the parallelism noted here, the centrality of Paul's appeal to the Lukan narrative is to be explained not simply in terms of its significance for *Paul's* relationship to Rome and Judaism,[147] but also, and perhaps more importantly, as due to the way Paul's story serves to illustrate the analogous position of *the gospel* in relation to Rome and Judaism: just as Paul goes to Rome, thereby exercising his right as a Roman citizen, yet without betraying his Jewish identity, the Christian message which Paul proclaims makes its own 'appeal' to the Roman world (and thus to the world at large) but does so in a way which is fully harmonious with the aspirations of its Jewish origins.

Finally, alongside the elaborate Jewish-related apologia with which Acts ends, some elements of a Roman-oriented case may also be noted. Thus, despite its general form, the implicit contention of 27.1–28.16, according to which Paul had done 'nothing deserving death', specifically recalls the Roman declarations of Paul's innocence of a capital charge in 23.29; 25.25; 26.30–1. Moreover, Julius' repeated kindness to Paul (27.3, 43), the mention of the prisoner's lightened custody in Rome (28.16, 30–1), and the reminder of Paul's earlier exculpations by the Romans (28.18) can easily be regarded as continuations of the already-noted motif, emphasising that there is no inherent enmity between Paul and Rome. If such material is to be related to what we have seen to be Luke's primary concern in Acts 28 (the validity of what Paul's 'sect' believes), its ultimate function appears to provide the basis for Paul's confidence (and Luke's hope) that the Gentiles will be more receptive to the Christian message than the Jews; indeed, that they 'will listen'. The author hopes that, following the example of the Roman centurion and of the Maltese, more Gentiles will come to receive from the followers of the Christian sect guidance and assistance for appropriating divine salvation.

The suggested reading of the last two chapters of Acts may now be summarised. Paul approaches Rome as someone who, through his 'nature trials', has been vindicated as having done 'nothing to deserve death' and who is competent to help others experience divine salvation (27.1–28.16). The significance of such a characterisation of Paul becomes explicit only after his arrival in Rome. The theme of Paul's innocence (one of the two major themes of 27.1–28.16 and the thrust of 28.17–20) makes not merely

---

[146] Tajra defines its significance exclusively in such terms (*Trial*, p. 197).
[147] So Tajra, ibid.

a personal statement about Paul, but serves to illustrate and substantiate Luke's more dominant apologia (implicit in the second theme of 27.1–28.16 and explicit in 28.23–31) for the message which Paul has come to proclaim in Rome: his innocence is a sign that his message can truly lead people to salvation. It is only after Paul's personal innocence and the trustworthiness of his witness have been established that the success of the gospel in Rome can be envisaged (28.30–1).

It is hoped that a reading of Acts 27–8 along these lines can also throw some light on the long-debated issue of why Acts ends where it does and in the way it does.[148] First, if one is to regard Luke as primarily interested in informing the readers about the *spread* of the gospel, it is surprising that Luke says so little about Paul's actual preaching and so much about the apologetic defences both preceding and following it. Also, Acts 28 could hardly be regarded as the arrival of the gospel at Rome, once the readers have been informed that a Christian community already existed there (28.14–15). Second, if Luke's governing interest is the political stance of Paul or Christianity in relation to Rome,[149] it is difficult to see why Luke fails to narrate Paul's trial in Rome (assuming it had taken place)[150] and why there is no political defence of Paul in Acts 28. Third, if at the top of Luke's agenda is Paul's personal innocence in relation to Judaism,[151] why does Paul's personal defence occupy only a secondary position in Acts 28? If, however, Luke's primary concern is the *defence and confirmation* of the gospel during its transition from the belief of an obscure Jewish sect to a faith which hopes to make some impact within the Roman empire, the ending of Acts appears to be less baffling: the Lukan narrative ends with a 'trial' and confirmation of the gospel in the empire's capital and with specific reference to a matter in which the gospel was particularly open to criticism – its rejection by a large number of Jews, who should have been the first group to accept it.

---

[148] For some helpful discussions of this issue, see W. F. Brosend II, 'The Means of Absent Ends', in B. Witherington III (ed.), *History, Literature, and Society in the Book of Acts*, Cambridge University Press, 1996, pp. 348–62; J. Dupont, 'La conclusion des Actes et son rapport à l'ensemble de l'ouvrage de Luc', in J. Kremer (ed.), *Les Actes des Apôtres*, Leuven University Press, 1979, pp. 359–404; H. J. Hauser, *Strukturen der Abschlusserzählung der Apostelgeschichte (Apg. 28, 16–31)*, Rome: Pontifical Institute Press, 1979; D. Marguerat, ' "Et quand nous sommes entrés dans Rome": l'énigme de la fin du livre des Actes (28, 16–31)', *RHPR* 73 (1993), 1–21; Witherington, *Acts*, pp. 807–33.

[149] See the readings of Acts as an *apologia pro ecclesia* or *apologia pro imperio*.

[150] Contemporary Lukan scholarship is virtually unanimous that Acts was written after Paul's trial (Sterling, *Historiography*, pp. 329–30). Kistemaker, *Acts*, pp. 21–4, is one of the few exceptions.

[151] As suggested by Jervell *et alii*. See also Brawley, *Luke–Acts*, pp. 69–83.

Conclusion: the trial of the gospel

The review of previous research on the function of Paul's trials in Acts at the beginning of this chapter has revealed the need for a unifying paradigm in this area, one which is able to account for the great diversity of Pauline trials in Acts and in particular for the numerous features of the Lukan story which have been brought to light by previous works in this field. After discussing the trial accounts separately, it is now possible to conclude that *the Pauline trials in Acts, for all their specificity, share in one overarching trial story – the trial of the gospel.*

(a) *The defendant.* At an explicit level the defendant is, evidently, Paul. Yet much of the material which is included as part of Paul's trials transcends what could have been of judicial relevance to his case (most notably, perhaps, the rehearsal at great length of Paul's conversion story and of its Christological implications). Instead, efforts have been made, both through the general contents of the charges and defences and through more explicit devices (e.g., 23.6b; 24.14, 21; 25.19; 26.6, 27–8; 28.21–2) to shift the reader's attention from matters relating to Paul's personal guilt to issues which encapsulate the beliefs of his 'sect'. In this respect, then, *the defendant is ultimately the gospel itself.*

(b) *The prosecution and the defence.* Broadly speaking, both the prosecution and the defence focus on how the Christian witness relates to three major groups: Jews, pagans,[152] and Romans. In relation to Judaism, the *charges* are mainly that the Christian proclamation amounts to an inevitable breach with the hallmarks of God's people – the nation, the temple, and the law. The *apologia* includes: (i) Paul's persistent self-identification as a Jew, even to the point of coming under attack due to his Jewish beliefs (e.g. his anti-divination stance in Philippi and monotheistic campaigns in Athens and Ephesus), and his insistence that he is on trial for Israel's resurrection hope (as in Jerusalem, Caesarea, and Rome); (ii) the repeated reference to the notable agreement between the beliefs of Pharisees and Christians; (iii) the rootedness of the Christian message in the Jewish Scriptures; (iv) the examples of Jews who believed (e.g. in Thessalonica and Rome), with special notice being taken of such key figures as the ruler(s) of the synagogue in Corinth; (v) the Isaianic legitimation of the Christian witness in relation to the (Roman) Jews who failed to accept it; (vi) the divine approval of the Christian witness (indicated through visions, prison rescues, travelling protection); (vii) the

---

[152] For lack of a better word, the term 'pagans' is used to denote those Lukan characters who neither subscribe to Judaeo-Christian monotheism nor are explicitly associated with the Roman system.

specific legitimation of the Gentile mission, as based on Jesus' deutero-Isaianic representation of Israel's vocation (22.21; 26.17–18) and on a poorer receptivity among Jews than among Gentiles (28.25–8).[153]

In relation to paganism, the *charges* are that the Christian gospel is 'strange' (Athens) and that it brings pagan religions into disrepute (Ephesus). The *defence* argues (i) that pagan practices (such as the Philippian girl's divination) are powerless when confronted with the Christian message; (ii) that idolatry is a misguided answer to the human search for God (Athens); (iii) that, far from being irrelevant to the educated pagan, the Christian message provides the correct answer to this search – it is through this message that the 'unknown god' can now be known (Athens); (iv) that those who promote idolatry may often do so not out of conviction but out of hidden and selfish reasons (Ephesus).

In relation to Rome and those who identify with its system, the *charges* are that the Christian witness is generally incompatible with Roman identity (Philippi) and specifically conducive to social unrest and political disloyalty (Thessalonica, Corinth, Caesarea). Just as in the case of Jesus' Roman trial, the refutation of the charges hardly ever takes the form of explicit argumentation; Luke seems to believe that facts and people are better defenders of his protagonists than elaborate arguments. Thus, the *apologia* associated with the Roman-related charges includes: (i) the repeated references to how unimpressed Roman magistrates have been by the arguments of the prosecution (note especially 28.18); (ii) the corollary of this in the stories of two Romans (Lysias and Julius) who, under the influence of others, failed to give Paul sufficient credit and soon found this

---

[153] A definition of the readership which would have been served by Luke's Jewish-related material may be attempted. The following characteristics seem to define it: (a) readers who did not identify themselves with non-Christian Judaism (note Luke's unsparing polemic against Paul's Jewish opponents); (b) readers who had some knowledge of and sympathy for the Jewish heritage (note Luke's effort to stress Paul's commitment to Jewish hopes and the Jewish Scriptures); (c) readers who would have had questions about Paul's faithfulness to his Jewish tradition (note the accusations and defences related to Paul's Jewishness). Non-Christian Jews would not have met the first criterion and possibly not the third either (in relation to the third criterion, it is not clear how many non-Christian Jews at the time of Luke's writing would have manifested a great interest in Paul). It seems more probable, then, that to the extent to which Paul's trials in Acts were intended as a Jewish-related apologia for Paul, they were targeted at a Christian readership which was questioning or being questioned about Paul's attitude to the Jewish faith. If one elaborated on the make-up of this readership, the following groups would be possible candidates: Jewish(-minded) Christians, who through their conversion to Christianity had parted ways with the majority Judaism; Gentile Christians, worshipping alongside Jewish Christians and thereby being exposed to the latter's theology and concerns, or Gentile Christians interested in the Christian origins and the salvation-historical questions these origins posed; Gentiles or God-fearers living in areas inhabited by Jews and thus exposed to Jewish objections.

to be an embarrassing and dangerous choice; (iii) the characterisation of the opponents of the Christian witness as the actual troublemakers (as in Philippi, Thessalonica, Corinth, Ephesus, Jerusalem) and typically guided by dubious motives (e.g. jealousy, greed); (iv) the examples of Romans who had no difficulty in embracing the gospel (Paul himself, Silas, the Philippian jailer) or who at least gave it a serious hearing (Felix, Agrippa); (v) the plethora of Roman officials with whom Paul, a mere 'prisoner for the gospel', converses at ease and from whom he so often enjoys protection and favours; (vi) the challenge which is implicit in Paul's confidence that 'the Gentiles' will be more receptive than the Jews (28.28).

In addition to the apologetic devices relating specifically to one of these three groups, a more general apologia for the gospel is evident in Luke's presentation of (i) the social status of some believers (Paul, the 'leading women' of Thessalonica, the Areopagite in Athens, the synagogue ruler(s) in Corinth); (ii) the ability of the gospel to overcome opposition; (iii) Paul's transformation from an opponent of Jesus into a witness for him (explainable, according to Luke, only by the reality of Paul's encounter with the glorified Christ); (iv) the plausible character of the gospel, indicated by Paul's typical 'persuasion' of his hearers, his characterisation as a man of 'great learning', his insistence that his proclamation is 'true and reasonable' and that the facts behind it are of a public domain (26.24–6).

Such a multifaceted representation of the prosecution and defence in Paul's trials, I suggest, establishes the cohesion between emphases which have customarily been studied at the neglect, if not exclusion, of each other. According to the above reading, the variety of emphases simultaneously present in the Lukan narrative is indicative of the plurality of angles from which the author seeks to establish the validity of the gospel, and of the diversity of devices which he is prepared to employ for this goal. Thus[154] it is possible to speak with Cassidy of a Lukan interest in Paul's allegiance and witness to the gospel without denying (as he in effect does) that Tajra or Mackenzie may legitimately speak of a socio-political apologetic for Paul and the movement he represents,[155] and without dismissing altogether Walaskay's observations about Luke's predominantly positive portrayal of the Romans' attitude towards the Christian message;[156] it is

---

[154] For references to the authors mentioned in this paragraph, see the survey of their works in the first section of the present chapter.

[155] Cassidy, *Society*, pp. 145–55.

[156] Ibid., pp. 156–7. Walaskay may be wrong in representing this portrayal as a deliberate Lukan *apologia pro imperio*, but he can hardly be faulted for insisting that such an emphasis exists. In the present scheme, its primary role is to highlight positive precedents for the Romans' attitude to the gospel and its representatives.

also possible to speak with Lentz of an 'evangelistic tone' of the Lukan narrative, without having to deny the author's simultaneous efforts to 'defend' his case against criticism; it is feasible to speak (with Dibelius and Haenchen) of the Lukan Paul travelling from Jerusalem to Rome as a representative of the gospel (and not merely as an individual), without thereby inferring that the author gives up on the Jews;[157] it is reasonable to conceive (with Miles, Trompf, and Landouceur) of Luke as willing to employ Hellenistic conventions in the service of his apologetic, without (like Rapske) viewing such a practice as incompatible with his emphasis on Paul's Judaeo-Christian commitment; it is important to speak with Jervell, Gempf, Long, and many others, of a Lukan apologetic related to Judaism, without forgetting that the picture is only complete when the Roman and pagan dimensions are also added.

(c) *The witness.*[158] Regarding the gospel itself as the primary defendant in Paul's trials and viewing both the prosecution and the defence as centred on it inevitably raise the question of Paul's own role in his Lukan trials. The answer is explicitly given in each of the three summary statements discussed earlier in the chapter. Immediately after Paul's encounter with Christ, the Lord informs Ananias that the new convert is a chosen instrument 'to carry my name' (a Lukan equivalent, as has been noted, of 'bearing witness to Christ') 'before the Gentiles and kings and the sons of Israel' (9.15). Again, as Paul approaches the final and most formal phase of his trials, he tells the Ephesian elders that his role, as entrusted to him by the risen Christ, is 'to bear witness to the gospel' (διαμαρτύρασθαι τὸ εὐαγγέλιον, 20.24). Finally, the same role of 'witness' is twice ascribed to Paul in the course of his Christophanic vision in Jerusalem: ὡς γὰρ **διεμαρτύρω** τὰ περὶ ἐμοῦ εἰς Ἰερουσαλήμ, οὕτω σε δεῖ καὶ εἰς Ῥώμην **μαρτυρῆσαι** (23.11). Paul's role, then, is to be a 'witness' for the gospel – someone who is called upon to vouch for it. Moreover, 'the Gentiles and kings and the sons of Israel', before whom he is called to bear witness, appear to correspond fairly closely (although not as exact equivalents) to the three groups to which Luke's apologia for the gospel specifically relates: the 'pagans', those identifying with the Roman system, and the Jews, respectively.

Nevertheless, Paul is not for Luke yet another witness for the gospel, who merely happens to be the one vouching for it before the mentioned groups. Paul has a unique role in the economy of Luke's apologia for the

---

[157] *Pace* Brawley, *Luke–Acts*, especially p. 28.

[158] For a similar approach to the one taken in this section, see Stolle, *Zeuge*, especially pp. 140–7.

gospel. First, as the Christian world-missionary *par excellence*, responsible more than anyone else for the development of Christianity from a
Jewish sect into a religion which is beginning to acquire a voice in the empire, Paul is the ideal person through whose 'mission trials', in particular,
a case can be made for the gospel in relation to the pagan world. Luke's
contention in this respect is that the gospel has been 'tried' in relation to
the pagan world, and the verdict is that there is nothing that ought to keep
the gospel from being accepted in such environments; indeed, it provides
precisely the answer for which the pagan world had been searching.[159]
Second, as someone enjoying the privilege of Roman citizenship and yet
having a legal history which would put many a sympathiser of the Roman
system on alert, Paul provides Luke with a convenient means for asserting
on the one hand that allegiance to the gospel is not inherently incompatible with Roman identity (Paul can be committed to the gospel while
remaining a Roman citizen) and on the other hand that when Romans
are faced with socio-political accusations against Christianity, they ought
to remember that such accusations are typically motivated by dubious
reasons (as in Philippi) or by disputes which are irrelevant to Romans (as
discovered by Lysias and Festus) and that under closer Roman scrutiny
the accusations have never held water. Third, both through his special part
in the spread of the gospel beyond Jewish boundaries and through his appeal for justice to Caesar, Paul is the epitome of a Christianity which,
due to its theological, ethnical, and cultural transition beyond its Jewish
origins, is susceptible to the accusation of discontinuity with the people
of God. Once again, then, Paul provides Luke with an ideal vehicle for a
defence of the gospel, this time in relation to a group which could have
been expected to be the first to embrace it and which is instead (at least
for Luke) the one most commonly responsible for its bad press.

It is hardly surprising, in the light of such observations, that Luke is
prepared to allocate so much space to Paul and his trials, or that Lukan
scholarship finds it so difficult to define to what degree the latter half of
Acts is a defence of Christianity and to what degree a defence of Paul.[160]
To a large extent, we have seen, Luke defends the gospel precisely by
defending Paul.

[159] The fact that at times Paul's 'success' is limited (most notably, perhaps, 17.32–4;
contrast, however, 19.10, 17–20) in no way jeopardises the gospel's case in relation to
paganism. Conzelmann points out, in connection with 17.32, that '[t]he mocking is the
foil for the superiority of the θεῖος ἀνήρ, "divine man"' (*Acts*, p. 146), while Haenchen,
commenting on 17.33, correctly observes that '[n]ot he [Paul] but the audience has failed'
(*Acts*, p. 526).

[160] See the explicit or implicit disputes over this issue in the survey of scholarship at the
beginning of the present chapter.

When one looks at Paul's trials in Acts in the way suggested here, it becomes clear that 'the Paul of Acts' and 'the Paul of the epistles' have at least one major thing in common – the legal history of both of them is centred in τῇ ἀπολογίᾳ καὶ βεβαιώσει τοῦ εὐαγγελίου ('the defence and confirmation of the gospel'; Phil. 1.7; cf. 1.16).

8

CONCLUSIONS

In the introductory chapter, the need was established for a thorough examination of the function of Luke's trial narratives. It was noted that apologetics has been the only context within which the question of authorial intent had been raised in relation to the trial material of Luke–Acts as a whole. Notwithstanding the success which some of the available apologetic interpretations of Luke's trial narratives have had in highlighting and explaining some textual traits and emphases, the conclusion was reached that these interpretations have not been able satisfactorily to explain Luke's trial material in its entirety and complexity. On the other hand, a growing trend in Lukan scholarship seemed to suggest a more promising direction for the interpretation of Luke's apologetics, along the lines of what I have named for convenience an *apologia pro evangelio*: a deliberate attempt on the author's part to assure his readers about the reliability and relevance of the Christian message. Accordingly, the rest of the study has been concerned with exploring the viability of such an apologetic reading of Luke's trial material. The details of Luke's individual trial narratives have been discussed in the course of the foregoing chapters and the results have been summarised at the end of each chapter. It remains now first to draw together the threads of the investigation and so to attempt a description of the overall picture of Luke's trial material. Second, I shall indicate certain implications of the findings for other areas of Lukan study. Third, I shall suggest some related areas in which further research would seem profitable.

The apologetic function of Luke's trial narratives: a synopsis

Luke is undoubtedly writing at a time when the Christian movement has travelled a long way from its rather obscure beginnings in Galilee. Indeed, the story of Acts is itself sufficient to indicate that Luke is aware of a church which is beginning to take the empire for its new home. The chronological, geographical, and cultural gap between Luke's Christian contemporaries and the events on which the gospel story is built provides the author of Luke–Acts with the occasion for writing a detailed and carefully researched account of these matters (Luke 1.1–4). Yet the author is not satisfied with establishing the historical grounds for the Christian faith. Equally important is its theological basis. That is to say, Luke wishes to provide his readers (and those whom the readers will influence) with assurance not only about what has come to pass, but also about the significance of these historical events. One of the specific ways in which Luke builds towards his goal is by portraying the judicial or quasi-judicial encounters between major figures in the Christian movement and the opponents of the Way as 'trials' of the gospel itself, special attention being paid to some key or controversial episodes of the Christian story, episodes with which these figures were particularly associated. Accordingly, *the overall function of Luke's trial narratives is an* apologia pro evangelio, *in the form of a trial and confirmation of the gospel and with particular reference to strategic episodes in the unfolding of the Christian story.*

The first in the series of episodes is *the story of Jesus, with its Christo-logical implications.* According to part one of this investigation, the trial of Jesus serves formally to test and confirm the (sometimes direct but more often indirect) Christological contention of the foregoing Gospel narrative – that *Jesus is the divinely appointed agent for the restoration of Israel.* The plot of the Third Gospel in general and the passion predictions in particular prepare the reader for such an understanding of the trial nar-rative (chapter 2). The actual account of Jesus' trial strongly supports this reading (chapter 3). The Sanhedrin trial tests and confirms the Gospel's Christological case specifically in relation to Judaism: the readers ought to be able to avoid repeating the Sanhedrin's misjudgement and instead to recognise that sufficient evidence exists for regarding Jesus as Israel's Messiah. The misjudgement of the Jewish leaders who prosecuted Jesus is partially explained and condoned by the fact that for them the decisive event of Jesus' glorification had not taken place; but this is an excuse which Luke's contemporaries cannot invoke. Jesus' Roman trial, on the other hand, while continuing the case for Jesus' Messianic identity, seeks also to clear the air between such a belief and the sensitivities of those who identify with the Roman system. Jesus' Messiahship, the narrative contends, need not be taken as intrinsically incompatible with the existent socio-political order. Finally, the issue of Jesus' Messianic identity, and particularly God's disclosed position on this matter, seems to be Luke's dominant concern in the post-trial section of the passion narrative, as well as in the passages of the resurrection narratives and of Acts where reference is made to Jesus' trial (chapter 4).

A second gospel episode under Luke's scrutiny, narrated in the opening chapters of Acts, is *the establishment of the Christian community under the banner of allegiance to Jesus.* In relation to this episode, the trials of Peter and his apostolic companions (chapter 5) serve to test and confirm the claim that *it is in the name of Jesus and through the ministry of his followers that God is now visiting and restoring his people.* Luke's case takes several forms: (1) Christologically, the 'signs and wonders' (4.30; 5.12) performed in the 'name' of Jesus are evidence that it is through his mediation that God is now manifesting his presence. (2) Soteriologically, the availability of physical healing is the 'sign' that salvation is being offered through Jesus and through him alone (4.8–12). (3) Ecclesiologically, it is through the life and ministry of the apostolic church that Israel's symbols (the people, the temple, the Scriptures, and the land) find their appropriate, albeit 'updated', expression. Third, a new important phase in the progress of the gospel story is reached with the Stephen narrative: *the culmination of the Jerusalem conflict between Jesus' followers and the Jewish leadership as well as the beginning of a theological and cultural transition within the Christian movement.* Against this backdrop, the trial of Stephen (chapter 6) serves to test and confirm the claim that *the gospel's rejection by the Jewish leadership and its gradual reorientation towards new territory poses salvation-historical questions not about the church but about its opponents.* Christologically, the Scriptures legitimate Jesus, whom the Jewish leadership has rejected, by placing him in the line of those who save their people and yet are rejected by them (e.g. Joseph and Moses), or, more generally, by aligning him with the prophetic tradition which both prefigured and announced him (7.52). Ecclesiologically, it is not those who, through allegiance to Jesus, transcend the Jewish symbols that forfeit the status of God's people, but those who limit God to these symbols and in so doing run the risk of idolatry.

Finally, with the story of Paul, *the church of Acts is beginning to discover and live out its identity and mission in an imperial setting.* Accordingly, the lengthy accounts of Paul's trials (chapter 7) test and confirm the contention that *the Christian gospel has a legitimate place within the Gentile world and, more specifically, within the Roman empire.* An *apologia pro evangelio* is therefore presented in relation to three groups of particular interest to Luke and his cause. In relation to *Judaism*, the author continues to address the issue of Christology (typically encapsulated in the notion of Jesus' resurrection), bringing into discussion an additional major ecclesiological concern – the legitimacy of the Gentile mission. Thus, Christologically, the narrator's case *in nuce* is that the belief in Jesus' resurrection, on which (according to Luke, at least) the church's Christology hinges, is (i) in line with Jewish hopes and to a significant extent shared by Pharisaic Judaism and (ii) strongly supported by Paul's Christophany and his radical transformation as a result. Regarding the Gentile mission, Luke's case is that this initiative is specifically legitimated by Isaiah's characterisation of God's Servant as a light to the Gentiles and that it has been prompted by the risen Christ and by Jewish unbelief. In relation to *paganism*, it is argued that the Christian message alone is able to reveal the One who would otherwise remain 'an unknown god' and that paganism's religious alternative, idolatry, is unreasonable and often promoted by selfish concerns. In relation to those who identify with *Rome*, Paul's trials continue the case of Jesus' Roman trial by showing that the gospel is not intrinsically incompatible with the imperial socio-political order and that a good number of Roman citizens are already regarding it with favour, if not (as Paul himself) positively accepting it. In short, the legal history of the Lukan Paul, like that of the 'Paul of the epistles' is bound up with ἡ ἀπολογία (καὶ βεβαίωσις) τοῦ εὐαγγελίου (Phil. 1.7, 16).

Implications for other areas of Lukan study
The nature of Luke's task

Since the dawn of modern critical research, Lukan scholarship has been at pains to understand correctly the nature of Luke's enterprise. The debate has most commonly been in terms of Luke the historian *versus* Luke the theologian. Thus, F. C. Baur and most exponents of the *Tendenzkritik* in Tübingen at the beginning of the nineteenth century have argued that Luke's work originated around the middle of the second century and dealt with ecclesiastic problems of that period. The corollary of this was that Luke could not be regarded as a reliable historian of the apostolic era.[1] Yet not everyone even within the Tübingen school shared Baur's views about Luke the historian: a much more positive view of Luke's historical reliability was advocated, for instance, in M. Schneckenburger's study on the purpose of Acts.[2] The portrait of Luke the historian came even more into prominence at the beginning of the twentieth century, through the work of W. M. Ramsay, which aimed to show the close correspondence

---

[1] See Gasque, *History*, pp. 21–54, for the views of F. C. Baur and his disciples within the Tübingen school.

[2] Schneckenburger, *Zweck*; see Gasque, *History*, pp. 32–9.

between Luke's historical data and the (then) recent archaeological discoveries.[3]

The debate continued into the second half of the century. The *redaktionsgeschichtliche* study of Luke–Acts, inaugurated by Conzelmann[4] and carried out in detail in Haenchen's influential commentary on Acts,[5] has led to an unprecedented appreciation of Luke as a theologian, at the expense of his significance as a historian. Responding to this tendency, Marshall produced a monograph on *Luke: Historian and Theologian*, in which a simultaneous appreciation of the writer's historical and theological agendas is explicitly advocated. Yet when seeking a term to describe Luke's enterprise *in toto*, Marshall chooses the word 'evangelist', which in his opinion 'includes both of the others'.[6] 'The title of evangelist which we are suggesting for him', Marshall explains, 'is meant to indicate that his concern was to present the Christian message in such a way as *to promote and confirm faith in Jesus Christ.*'[7]

Our findings in relation to Luke's trial narratives fit well with such a definition of Luke's task. Yet as regards Marshall's choice of a *term* which would correctly describe this task, it is less certain that 'evangelist' is the ideal one. No doubt, the term is appropriate in so far as the story which Luke narrates comprises the Christian gospel (in the same way in which this is true for Matthew, Mark, and John). But this is precisely where a first limitation of this term for our purposes is revealed: appropriate as it may be, the term 'evangelist' is not specific enough to set the author apart from other exponents of the Gospel tradition. Second, apart from its usage in connection with the Gospel tradition, the term has come to be typically associated with *acquainting* a certain audience with the story of the gospel, with a view to their *acceptance* of it. By contrast, Luke specifically mentions the fact that his addressees had already been acquainted with (parts of) the gospel story (Luke 1.4), and undoubtedly many of them had already accepted it.

Luke's aim, at least as declared in the Gospel preface and as revealed in the trial narratives, is to lead his audience to assurance about the content of the Christian message. In view of such a task, the description which appears most accurately to set Luke apart from the other 'evangelists'

---

[3] W. M. Ramsay, *The Bearing of Recent Discovery on the Trustworthiness of the New Testament*, London: Hodder & Stoughton, 1920; see W. W. Gasque, *Sir William M. Ramsay: Archaeologist and New Testament Scholar*, Grand Rapids, 1966.

[4] Conzelmann, *Theology*.   [5] Haenchen, *Acts*.   [6] Marshall, *Historian*, p. 18.

[7] Ibid., p. 19; italics mine.

is his endeavour as an 'apologist for the gospel'.[8] My contention at this juncture is, therefore, that a more adequate place ought to be given in New Testament scholarship to the notion of apologetic among the various descriptions of Luke's task. He is not merely a historian, or a theologian, or an evangelist, or even a combination of these. He is also, and perhaps (I venture to suggest more tentatively) primarily, an apologist, albeit an apologist whose tool is not philosophy (as customary in subsequent Christian eras), but history (as he narrates *what* has come to pass) and theology (as he explains *the significance* of these events).

To be sure, the recognition of apologetic dimensions in Luke's work is no novelty. The discussion (in chapter 1) of previous research in this area has indicated the long-standing use of apologetic terminology in connection with Luke's task. Nevertheless, due to the too narrow definition of the object of Luke's apologetic (typically focusing on Christianity's political innocence or on Paul and his Gentile mission), the applicability of apologetic terminology to Luke–Acts has come to be either dismissed altogether[9] or effectively restricted to relatively small sections of Luke's narrative.[10] When a broader representation of Luke's apologetic agenda has been suggested,[11] this has commonly been done rather indirectly and unsystematically, often as a by-product of the study of other aspects of Luke–Acts. What the findings of the present study suggest is that Luke–Acts as a whole may be better understood when seen as an *apologia pro evangelio*.

The death and glorification of Jesus in Luke–Acts

The present contention about the way in which the Lukan narrative might be better understood when Luke's apologetic task is adequately defined can be tentatively illustrated by a few observations related to the death of Jesus in Luke–Acts and its implications for Lukan Christology and soteriology. Many a Lukan scholar has been baffled by how little Luke appears to say about the soteriological significance of Jesus' death: he has often been understood as having replaced the *theologia crucis* with a *theologia*

---

[8] Suggesting such a distinction between Luke and the other 'evangelists' by no means denies the existence of apologetic material in the other Gospels. It simply means that Luke's declared goal in Luke 1.1–4 (as well as the above discussion of the trial narratives) suggests a level of apologetic self-consciousness on the author's part which may not be paralleled in the other Gospels, and that the story of Acts, with its ecclesiological and soteriological dimensions, brings Luke's apologetic to a unique level of complexity.

[9] Most notably in the works of Cassidy.

[10] Usually to Jesus' and Paul's Roman trials.

[11] By works such as those noted in the last section of the review of research in chapter 1.

gloriae.[12] To explain this situation in terms of Luke's ignorance of the *theologia crucis* or disagreement with it is difficult because on at least two occasions (Luke 22.19–20[13] and Ac. 20.28) Luke gives positive expression to such a theology. One has to reckon, therefore, with the fact that although the author knew of it and accepted it, he chose not stress it. Why?[14] In view of our findings, the answer appears to be that Luke, as an apologist for the gospel, is primarily concerned with the *that* (and perhaps the *for whom*) rather than with the *how*, of salvation. That is to say, he is at pains to assure his audience *that* Jesus is indeed the one through whom salvation is made available (*for everyone*, Gentiles included), rather than to elaborate on *how* Jesus makes this salvation possible. In the words of Strauss (who, from a rather different angle of Lukan research, arrives at strikingly similar observations about Jesus' death and glorification in Luke–Acts),[15] 'the emphasis falls on the fact *that* salvation has arrived in the person and work of Jesus rather than on the theological basis upon which Jesus saves'.[16] And again: 'It is the apologetic and christological significance of the cross rather than its atoning value which is Luke's primary concern.'[17]

It is no surprise, in the light of such observations, that Luke should elaborate more on Jesus' glorification than on his death,[18] or that, what the author does stress in relation to Jesus' death is two strongly apologetic points: (i) that the event is according to the plan of God,[19] and (ii) that Jesus dies as δίκαιος.[20]

Suggestions for further related research

Due to the large textual scope of the present investigation (comprising all Lukan trial narratives) and in view of the limitations of space, it has

[12] For relevant bibliography, see Doble, *Paradox*, p. 3, n. 1; Strauss, *Davidic*, p. 352, n. 1.

[13] On the authenticity of 22.19b–20, see Green, *Death*, pp. 35–41; Jeremias, *Eucharistic*, pp. 139–59; Marshall, *Gospel*, pp. 799–807; J. Jeremias, *Last Supper and Lord's Supper*, Grand Rapids: Eerdmans, 1980, pp. 36–8; Metzger, *Textual Commentary*, pp. 148–50; H. Schürmann, 'Lk 22, 19b–20 als ursprüngliche Textüberlieferung', *Bib* 32 (1951), 364–92, 522–41.

[14] For a brief account of major explanations, see Doble, *Paradox*, pp. 4–8.

[15] Strauss, *Davidic*, pp. 344–53.   [16] Ibid., p. 352.   [17] Ibid., p. 353.

[18] On the importance of Jesus' glorification for Luke's Christological apologetic, see the discussion of the references to Jesus' trial in the context of Luke's resurrection narratives and in Acts (chapter 4): it is Jesus' resurrection-exaltation that vindicates his Messianic role (which includes the distribution of salvation).

[19] Doble, *Paradox*, p. 4; Strauss, *Davidic*, pp. 352–3. See also my discussion of the Lukan predictions of Jesus' passion (chapter 2).

[20] On the apologetic function of δίκαιος , see the discussion at Luke 23.47. See also Doble, *Paradox*, especially. pp. 226–7.

226   *The Trial of the Gospel*

mostly been neccessary to limit the discussion of Luke's trial narratives to internal evidence, in the case of Acts, and to Synoptic evidence, in the case of the Gospel. Of the external evidence which might have thrown additional light on the subject matter, two areas, in particular, are worth mentioning at this stage as potential directions for further research.

The first such area regards the relationship between Luke's use of the trial motif in the service of his *apologia pro evangelio* and the close association of trial settings with persuasion devices in the ancient Graeco-Roman world. It is well known that rhetoric was a central component of the educational systems of the Hellenistic and Roman world[21] (so much so that philosophers of the second century BC saw the need to give open expression to their concern about the threat which the increasing popularity of rhetoric posed to their own discipline).[22] The significance of this for the purposes of the present study is that Luke can be expected to have been aware of rhetorical conventions, and that he would have been likely to expect that at least some of his readers/hearers would appreciate them – indeed, Lukan research has often demonstrated Luke's use of rhetorical devices.[23] More important, even, for our specific concerns is the fact that from its very origins and well into the Christian Era, rhetoric was closely associated with trials. It was the trial settings of the fifth to fourth centuries BC and, more specifically, the challenge which they posed for the litigants to persuade a usually large jury, that gave birth to the art of oratory,[24] and it is 'judicial oratory' that was going to remain the most prominent of the three types of ancient oratory (the other two being 'deliberative' and 'epideictic').[25] Such a close association between trial settings and persuasion devices seems to cohere with – and therefore also potentially to confirm – my contention that Luke has employed the trial motif as a leading device in his apologetic enterprise. It remains, however, outside the goal here to explore in more detail the

[21] G. Kennedy, *The Art of Persuasion in Greece*, Princeton University Press, 1963, pp. 3, 270–1; G. Kennedy, *The Art of Rhetoric in the Roman World: 300 B.C.–A.D. 300*, Princeton University Press, 1972, p. 428 (referring specifically to the first century CE).

[22] Kennedy, *Art of Persuasion*, pp. 321–30; G. Kennedy, *Classical Rhetoric and Its Christian and Secular Tradition from Ancient to Modern Times*, London: Croom Helm, 1980, pp. 89–90.

[23] See especially P. E. Satterthwaite, 'Acts Against the Background of Classical Rhetoric', in Winter and Clarke (eds.), *Book of Acts*, pp. 337–79.

[24] Kennedy, *Art of Persuasion*, pp. 26–7; 126–7.

[25] Kennedy, *Art of Rhetoric*, pp. 7–23. 'The law courts were always the primary scene of ancient oratory and the arena for which rhetorical education offered preparation' (ibid., p. 434). On the centrality of judicial oratory to the 'technical rhetoric' (or 'the rhetoric of the handbooks'), see Kennedy, *Classical*, pp. 21–2.

implications of these observations for one's understanding of Luke's trial motif.[26]

A second related area which appears to invite further investigation is the function of trial stories in ancient literary compositions. More specifically, the question is whether there is any extant evidence of trial narratives being used as apologetic devices, and, if so, what light this evidence throws on the function of Luke's own trial narratives. As a preliminary answer, attention may be called to Plato's and Xenophon's well-known writings on the trial of Socrates (both of them known as *Apology*, or *Defence*), to which one may also add the beginning section of Xenophon's *Memorabilia* (Book I, i–ii, consisting of a lengthy critique of the two major charges brought against Socrates at his trial: impiety and corruption of the young). In all these works, aspects of Socrates' trial are narrated with the indubitable purpose of defending (and presumably promoting) the great master's convictions and way of life – a purpose not dissimilar to what we have seen in relation to Luke's depiction of his own protagonists' trials.

---

[26] Some research has already been done on smaller segments of Luke's trial material (e.g. Winter, 'Official').

BIBLIOGRAPHY

Aberle, M. V., 'Exegetische Studien. 2. Über den Zweck der Apostelgeschichte', *TQ* 37 (1855), 173–236.

Alexander, L., 'Luke's Preface in the Context of Greek Preface-Writing', *NovT* 28 (1986), 48–74.

The Preface to Luke's Gospel: Literary Convention and Social Context in Luke 1.1–4 and Acts 1.1, SNTSMS 78, Cambridge University Press, 1993.

'The Acts of the Apostles as an Apologetic Text', in M. Edwards, M. Goodman, and S. Price (eds.), *Apologetics in the Roman Empire: Pagans, Jews, and Christians*, Oxford University Press, 1999, pp. 15–43.

Bachmann, M., *Jerusalem und der Tempel: Die geographischtheologischen Elemente in der lukanische Sicht des judischen Kultzentrums*, Stuttgart: Kohlhammer, 1980.

Bammel, E., 'Erwartungen zur Eschatologie Jesu', *TU* 88 (1964), 3–32.

Bammel, E. (ed.), *The Trial of Jesus – Cambridge Studies in honour of C. F. D. Moule*, SBT 2:13, London: SCM Press, 1970.

Bammel, E. and Moule, C. F. D. (eds.), *Jesus and the Politics of His Day*, Cambridge University Press, 1984.

Barr, A., 'The Use and Disposal of the Marcan Source in Luke's Passion Narrative', *ExpT* 55 (1943–4), 227–31.

Barrett, C. K., *Luke the Historian in Recent Study*, London: Epworth, 1961.

'Salvation Proclaimed', *ExpT* 94 (1982), 68–71.

'Faith and Eschatology in Acts 3', in E. Grässer and O. Merk (eds.), *Glaube und Eschatologie: Festschrift für Werner Georg Kümmel zum 80. Geburtstag*, Tübingen: J. C. B. Mohr, 1985, pp. 1–17.

The Acts of the Apostles, vol. I, ICC, Edinburgh: T. & T. Clark, 1994.

Bayer, H. F., *Jesus' Predictions of Vindication and Resurrection: The Provenance, Meaning and Correlation of the Synoptic Predictions*, WUNT 2:20, Tübingen: J. C. B. Mohr, 1986.

Bennett, W. J., 'The Son of Man Must . . .', *NovT* 17 (1975), 113–29.

Bihler, J., *Die Stephanusgeschichte im Zusammenhang der Apostelgeschichte*, Münchener Theologische Studien, Munich: Max Hueber Verlag, 1963.

Black, M., 'Paul and Roman Law in Acts', *RQ* 24 (1981), 209–18.

Blinzler, J., 'Die Niedermetzelung von Galiläer durch Pilatus', *NovT* 2 (1958), 24–49.

The Trial of Jesus, Cork: Mercier Press, 1959 (originally published in German as *Der Prozess Jesu* by Verlag Friedrich Pustet of Regensburg, 1959).

228

'Passionsgeschehen und Passionsbericht des Lukasevangeliums', *BK* 24 (1969), 1–4.

Bock, D. L., 'The Son of Man Seated at God's Right Hand and the Debate over Jesus' "Blasphemy"', in Green and Turner (eds.), *Jesus of Nazareth*, pp. 181–91.

Luke, Baker Exegetical Commentary on the New Testament 3, 2 vols., Grand Rapids: Baker, 1994/1996.

Brandon, S. G. F., *The Trial of Jesus*, London: B. T. Batsford, 1968.

Brawley, R. L., *Luke–Acts and the Jews: Conflict, Apology, and Conciliation*, SBLMS 33, Atlanta: Scholars Press, 1987.

Centering on God: Method and Message in Luke–Acts, Louisville: Westminster/John Knox, 1990.

Text to Text Pours Forth Speech. Voices of Scripture in Luke–Acts, Indiana University Press, 1995.

Brooks, P., *Reading for the Plot: Design and Interpretation in Narrative*, New York: Knopf, 1984.

Brosend II, W. F., 'The Means of Absent Ends', in B. Witherington III (ed.), *History, Literature, and Society in the Book of Acts*, Cambridge University Press, 1996, pp. 348–62.

Brown, C. (ed.), *New International Dictionary of New Testament Theology*, 4 vols., revised edition, Carlisle: Paternoster, 1992.

Brown, R. E., *The Birth of the Messiah: A Commentary on the Infancy Narratives in the Gospels of Matthew and Luke*, new updated edition, London: Geoffrey Chapman, 1993.

The Death of the Messiah, 2 vols., London: Geoffrey Chapman, 1994.

Bruce, F. F., *The Apostolic Defense of the Gospel: Christian Apologetics in the New Testament*, London: Inter-Varsity Fellowship, 1959.

'Stephen's Apologia', in B. Thompson (ed.), *Scripture: Meaning and Method. Essays Presented to Antony Tyrrell Hanson for his Seventieth Birthday*, Hull University Press, 1987, pp. 37–50.

The Book of Acts, revised edition, Grand Rapids: Eerdmans, 1988.

The Acts of the Apostles: The Greek Text with Introduction and Commentary, third revised and enlarged edition, Leicester: Apollos, 1990.

Büchele, A., *Der Tod Jesu im Lukasevangelium. Eine redaktionsgeschichtliche Untersuchung zu Lk 23*, Frankfurter Theologische Studien 26, Frankfurt: Josef Knecht, 1978.

Buck, E., 'The Function of the Pericope "Jesus Before Herod" in the Passion Narrative of Luke', in W. Haubeck and M. Bachmann (eds.), *Wort in der Zeit: Neutestamentliche Studien. Festgabe für Karl Heinrich Rengstorf zum 75. Geburtstag*, Leiden: E. J. Brill, 1980, pp. 165–78.

Buckwalter, H. D., *The Character and Purpose of Luke's Christology*, SNTSMS 89, Cambridge University Press, 1996.

Bultmann, R., *History of the Synoptic Tradition*, translated by J. Marsh, Oxford: Basil Blackwell, 1963.

Burchard, C., *Der dreizehnte Zeuge. Traditions- und kompositionsgeschichtliche Untersuchungen zu Lukas' Darstellung der Frühzeit des Paulus*, FRLANT 103, Göttingen: Vandenhoeck & Ruprecht, 1970.

Busse, U., *Das Nazareth-Manifest Jesu: Eine Einführung in das lukanische Jesusbild nach Lk 4.16–30*, Stuttgart: Katholisches Bibelwerk, 1978.

Cadbury, H. J., 'Commentary on the Preface of Luke', in Foakes-Jackson and Lake (eds.), *Beginnings*, vol. II, 1922, pp. 489–510.

The Making of Luke–Acts, London: SPCK, 1968 (originally published New York: Macmillan, 1927).

Caird, G. B., *The Gospel of St Luke*, London: A. & C. Black, 1968.

Calvin, J., *Commentary upon the Acts of the Apostles*, ed. H. Beveridge, 2 vols., Grand Rapids: Eerdmans, 1949.

Carroll, J. T., *Response to the End of History: Eschatology and Situation in Luke–Acts*, Atlanta: Scholars Press, 1988.

'Luke's Crucifixion Scene', in Sylva (ed.), *Reimaging*, pp. 108–24, 194–203.

Cassidy, R. J., *Jesus, Politics, and Society: A Study of Luke's Gospel*, Maryknoll, NY: Orbis, 1978.

'Luke's Audience, the Chief Priests, and the Motive for Jesus' Death', in Cassidy and Sharper, *Political Issues*, pp. 146–62.

Society and Politics in the Acts of the Apostles, Maryknoll, NY: Orbis, 1987.

Cassidy, R. J. and Sharper, Philip J. (eds.), *Political Issues in Luke–Acts*, Maryknoll, NY: Orbis, 1983.

Catchpole, D. R., *The Trial of Jesus: A Study in the Gospels and Jewish Historiography from 1770 to the Present Day*, Leiden: E. J. Brill, 1971.

Chavel, C. B., 'The Releasing of a Prisoner on the Eve of Passover in Ancient Jerusalem', *JBL* 60 (1941), 273–8.

Clark, A. C., 'Parallel Lives: The Relation of Paul to the Apostles in the Lukan Perspective', unpublished PhD dissertation, London: Brunel University, 1996.

Clark, D. K., *Dialogical Apologetics: A Person-Centered Approach to Christian Apologetics*, Grand Rapids: Baker, 1993.

Clark, D. K. and Geisler, N. L., *Apologetics in the New Age: A Christian Critique of Pantheism*, Grand Rapids: Baker, 1990.

Coleridge, M., *The Birth of the Lukan Narrative: Narrative as Christology in Luke 1–2*, JSNTSup 88, Sheffield: JSOT, 1993.

Conzelmann, H., *The Theology of St Luke*, London: Faber and Faber, 1960.

'Geschichte, Geschichtsbild und Geschichtsdarstellung bei Lukas', *TLZ* 85 (1960), 214–50.

Acts of the Apostles, translated by J. Limburg *et alii*, Philadelphia: Fortress, 1987 (original German: 1972).

Creed, J. M., *The Gospel according to St Luke: The Greek Text, with Introduction, Notes, and Indices*, London: Macmillan, 1930.

Culpepper, R. A., *Anatomy of the Fourth Gospel: A Study of Literary Design*, NT Foundations and Facets, Philadelphia: Fortress, 1983.

Danker, F. W., *Jesus and the New Age. A Commentary on Luke's Gospel*, revised edition, Philadelphia: Fortress, 1988.

Darr, J. A., *On Character Building: The Reader and the Rhetoric of Characterization in Luke–Acts*, Louisville: Westminster/John Knox, 1992.

deSilva, David A., 'The Stoning of Stephen: Purging and Consolidating an Endangered Institution', *StudBT* 17 (1989), 165–84.

Dibelius, M., 'Herodes und Pilatus', *ZNW* 16 (1915), 113–26.

'Das historische Problem der Leidensgeschichte', *ZNW* 30 (1931), 193–201.

From Tradition to Gospel, translated from German (1919, 1933) by B. L. Woolf, London: Nicholson & Watson, 1934.

Studies in the Acts of the Apostles, ed. H. Greeven, translated from German by Mary Ling, London: SCM Press, 1956.

Dietrich, W., *Das Petrusbild der Lukanischen Schriften*, ed. K. H. Rengstorf and L. Rost, Stuttgart, Berlin, Cologne, and Mainz: W. Kohlhammer, 1972.

Dillon, R. J., *From Eye-Witnesses to Ministers of the Word: Tradition and Composition in Luke 24*, Rome: Biblical Institute Press, 1978.

Dipple, E., *Plot*, London: Methuen, 1970.

Doble, P., 'The Son of Man Saying in Stephen's Witnessing: Acts 6.8–8.2', *NTS* 31 (1985), 68–84.

The Paradox of Salvation: Luke's Theology of the Cross, SNTSMS 87, Cambridge University Press, 1996.

Dulles, A., *A History of Apologetics*, London: Hutchinson, 1971.

Duncan, G. S., *St Paul's Ephesian Ministry: A Reconstruction (With Special Reference to the Ephesian Origin of the Imprisonment Epistles)*, New York: Charles Scribner's Sons, 1930.

Dunn, J. D. G., *The Partings of the Ways Between Christianity and Judaism and Their Significance for the Character of Christianity*, London: SCM Press, 1991.

The Acts of the Apostles, Peterborough: Epworth, 1996.

Dupont, J., *The Sources of the Book of Acts: The Present Position*, London: Darton, Longman, & Todd, 1964.

'Apologetic Use of the Old Testament in the Speeches of Acts', in J. Dupont, *The Salvation of the Gentiles: Studies in the Acts of the Apostles*, New York: Paulist Press, 1979, pp. 129–59.

'La conclusion des Actes et son rapport à l'ensemble de l'ouvrage de Luc', in J. Kremer (ed.), *Les Actes des Apôtres*, Leuven University Press, 1979, pp. 359–404.

Etudes sur les Actes des Apôtres, Paris: Cerf, 1984.

Dyrness, W., *Christian Apologetics in a World Community*, Wheaton: Inter-Varsity Press. 1983.

Easton, B. S., *The Gospel according to St Luke*, New York: Scribner, 1926.

The Purpose of Acts, London, 1936, reprinted as *Early Christianity: The Purpose of Acts and Other Papers*, ed. F. C. Grant, London: SPCK, 1955.

Edwards, R. A., *Matthew's Story of Jesus*, Philadelphia: Fortress, 1985.

Ellis, E. E., *The Gospel of Luke*, The New Century Bible Commentary, revised edition, Grand Rapids: Eerdmans; London: Marshall, Morgan & Scott, 1974.

Ernst, J., *Das Evangelium nach Lukas: übersetzt und erklärt*, Regensburg: Pustet, 1977.

Esler, P. F., *Community and Gospel in Luke–Acts: The Social and Political Motivations of Lucan Theology*, Cambridge University Press, 1987.

Evans, C. A., 'Prophecy and Polemic: Jews in Luke's Scriptural Apologetic', in C. A. Evans and J. A. Sanders (eds.), *Luke and Scripture: The Function of Sacred Tradition in Luke–Acts*, Minneapolis: Fortress, 1993, pp. 171–211.

Evans, C. F., *Resurrection and the New Testament*, SBT 2:12, London: SCM Press, 1970.

Saint Luke, London: SCM Press, 1990.

Farmer, W. R., 'A "Skeleton in the Closet" of Gospel Research', *BR* 9 (1961), 18–42.

The Synoptic Problem: A Critical Analysis, Macon, GA: Mercer University, 1976.

'Modern Developments of Griesbach's Hypothesis', *NTS* 23 (1976–7), 275–95.

Fascher, E., 'Theologische Beobachtungen zu δεῖ im A.T.', *ZNW* 45 (1954), 244–52.

Fearghail, F. Ó., *The Introduction to Luke–Acts: A Study of the Role of Lk 1,1–4,44 in the Composition of Luke's Two-Volume Work*, Analecta Biblica 126, Roma: Editrice Pontificio Istituto Biblico, 1991.

Filson, F. V., *Three Crucial Decades*, Richmond, VA: John Knox, 1963.

Fitzmyer, J. A., 'The Priority of Mark and the "Q" Source in Luke', in D. G. Miller (ed.), *Jesus and Man's Hope*, 2 vols., Pittsburg: Perspective Books, Pittsburg Theological Seminary, 1970, vol. I, pp. 131–70.

The Gospel According to Luke, 2 vols. (I–IX and X–XXIV), New York: Doubleday, 1981.

Flender, H., *St Luke, Theologian of Redemptive History*, London: SPCK, 1967.

Foakes-Jackson, F. J. and Lake, K. (eds.), *The Beginnings of Christianity*, Part 1: *The Acts of the Apostles*, 5 vols., London: Macmillan, 1920–33 (reprinted Grand Rapids: Baker, 1979).

Franklin, E., *Christ the Lord: A Study in the Purpose and Theology of Luke–Acts*, London: SPCK, 1965.

Freedman, D. N. *et alii* (eds.), *The Anchor Bible Dictionary*, 6 vols., New York: Doubleday, 1992.

Frein, B. C., 'Narrative Predictions, Old Testament Prophecies and Luke's Sense of Fulfilment', *NTS* 40 (1994), 22–37.

Fuller, D. P., *Easter Faith and History*, London: Tyndale Press, 1968.

Fuller, R. H., *The Foundations of New Testament Christology*, London: Lutterworth, 1965.

Garrett, S. R., *The Demise of the Devil: Magic and the Demonic in Luke–Acts*, Minneapolis: Fortress, 1989.

Gärtner, B., *The Areopagus Speech and Natural Revelation*, Acta Seminarii Neotestamentici Upsaliensis 21, Uppsala: Gleerup, 1955.

Gasque, W. W., *A History of the Interpretation of the Acts of the Apostles*, Peabody, MA: Hendrickson, 1989.

Sir William M. Ramsay: Archaeologist and New Testament Scholar, Grand Rapids, 1966.

Geisler, N. L., *Christian Apologetics*, Grand Rapids: Baker, 1978.

Geldenhuys, N., *Commentary on the Gospel of Luke: The English Text with Introduction, Exposition and Notes*, London: Marshall, Morgan & Scott, 1951.

Gempf, C., 'Historical and Literary Appropriateness in the Mission Speeches of Paul in Acts', unpublished PhD dissertation, University of Aberdeen, 1989.

Gerhardsson, B., *The Testing of God's Son*, Lund: Gleerup, 1966.

Giblin, C. H., *The Destruction of Jerusalem According to Luke's Gospel*, Analecta Biblica 107, Rome: The Pontifical Biblical Institute, 1985.

Gibson, J. B., *The Temptation of Jesus in Early Christianity*, Sheffield: JSOT, 1995.

Goulder, M. D., *Luke, a New Paradigm*, 2 vols., JSNTSup 20, Sheffield: JSOT, 1989.

A Tale of Two Missions, London: SCM Press, 1994.

Gourges, M., *A la droite de Dieu. Résurrection de Jésus et actualisation du psaume 110:1 dans le Nouveau Testament*, Paris: Gabalda, 1978.

Green, J. B., *The Death of Jesus: Tradition and Interpretation in the Passion Narrative*, WUNT 2:33, Tübingen: J. C. B. Mohr, 1988.

'The Death of Jesus, God's Servant,' in Sylva (ed.), *Reimaging*, pp. 1–28, 170–3.

'The Demise of the Temple as "Culture Center" in Luke–Acts: An Exploration of the Rending of the Temple Veil', *RB* 101 (1994), 495–515.

The Theology of the Gospel of Luke, Cambridge University Press, 1995.

Green, J. B. and Turner, M. M. B. (eds.), *Jesus of Nazareth, Lord and Christ. Essays on the Historical Jesus and New Testament Christology*, Grand Rapids: Eerdmans; Carlisle: Paternoster, 1994.

Griesbach, J. J., '*Commentatio qua Marci evangelium totum e Matthaei et Lucae commentariis decerptum esse monstratur*', Jena, 1789–90; reprinted in J. P. Gabler (ed.), *J. J. Griesbachii Opuscula Academica*, Jena, 1825, pp. 358–425; translated by B. Orchard in B. Orchard and T. R. W. Longstaff (eds.), *J. J. Griesbach: Synoptic and Text-Critical Studies 1770–1776*, Cambridge University Press, 1978, pp. 103–35.

Griffiths, P. J., *An Apology for Apologetics: A Study in the Logic of Interreligious Dialogue*, Maryknoll, NY: Orbis, 1991.

Grundmann, W., *Das Evangelium nach Lukas*, Theologischer Handkommentar zum Neuen Testament 3, second edition, Berlin: Evangelische Verlagsanstalt, 1961.

'δεῖ', *TDNT*, vol. II, pp. 21–5.

Gutbrod, W., 'νόμος', *TDNT*, vol. IV, pp. 1036–91.

Haacker, K., 'Samaritan, Samaria', *NIDNTT*, vol. III, pp. 449–67.

Haenchen, E., 'Judentum und Christentum in der Apostelgeschichte', *ZNW* 54 (1963), 155–87.

'The Book of Acts as Source Material for the History of Early Christianity', in L. E. Keck and J. L. Martyn (eds.), *Studies in Luke–Acts*, London: SPCK, 1966.

The Acts of the Apostles, Oxford: Basil Blackwell, 1971.

Hamm, M. D., 'This Sign of Healing, Acts 3:1–10. A Study in Lukan Theology', unpublished PhD dissertation, Saint Louis University, 1975.

Hanson, R. P. C., *The Acts of the Apostles*, Oxford University Press, 1967.

Harvey, A. E., *Jesus on Trial: A Study in the Fourth Gospel*, London: SPCK, 1976.

Hauser, H. J., *Strukturen der Abschlusserzählung der Apostelgeschichte (Apg. 28, 16–31)*, Rome: Pontifical Institute Press, 1979.

Hay, D. M., *Glory at the Right Hand: Psalm 110 in Early Christianity*, Nashville: Abingdon, 1973.

Heil, J. P., 'Reader-Response and the Irony of Jesus before the Sanhedrin in Luke 22:66–71', *CBQ* 51 (1989), 271–84.

'Reader-Response and the Irony of the Trial of Jesus in Luke 23:1–25', *ScEsp* 43 (1991), 175–86.

Hengel, M., 'Zwischen Jesus und Paulus', *ZTK* 72 (1975), 151–206.

Heumann, C. A., 'Dissertatio de Theophilo cui Lucas Historiam Sacram Inscripsit', *BHPT*, classis IV, Bremen, 1720, pp. 483–505.

Hickling, C., 'The Emmaus Story and its Sequel', in S. Barton and G. Stanton (eds.), *Resurrection: Essays in Honour of Leslie Houlden*, London: SPCK, 1994, pp. 21–33.

Hill, C. C., *Hellenists and Hebrews: Reappraising Division within the Earliest Church*, Minneapolis: Fortress, 1992.

Hoehner, H. W., 'Why Did Pilate Hand Jesus over to Antipas?', in Bammel (ed.), *Trial*, pp. 84–90.

Herod Antipas, SNTSMS 17, Cambridge University Press, 1972.

Houlden, J. L., 'The Purpose of Luke', *JSNT* 21 (1984), 53–65.

Jeremias, J., *The Eucharistic Words of Jesus*, third edition, London: SCM Press, 1966.

Last Supper and Lord's Supper, Grand Rapids: Eerdmans, 1980.

Jervell, J., *Luke and the People of God: A New Look at Luke–Acts*, Minneapolis, Minnesota: Augsburg, 1972.

'James: The Defender of Paul', in Jervell, *Luke*, pp. 185–207.

'Paul: The Teacher of Israel: The Apologetic Speeches of Paul in Acts', in Jervell, *Luke*, pp. 153–83 (previously published in German as 'Paulus – Der Lehrer Israels. Zu den apologetischen Paulusreden in der Apostelgeschichte', *NovT* 10 (1968), pp. 164–190).

'Paul in the Acts of the Apostles: Tradition, History, Theology', in J. Kremer (ed.), *Les Actes des Apôtres*, BETL 48, Gembloux: J. Duculot; Leuven University Press, 1979, pp. 297–306; also in Jervell, *Unknown*, pp. 68–76.

The Unknown Paul: Essays on Luke–Acts and Early Christian History, Minneapolis: Augsburg Publishing House, 1984.

Johnson, L. T., *The Writings of the New Testament*, London: SCM Press, 1986.

The Gospel of Luke, Collegeville, MN: Liturgical, 1991.

'Luke–Acts, Book of', in *ABD*, vol. IV, pp. 403–20.

Johnson, M. D., *The Purpose of the Biblical Genealogies, With Special Reference to the Setting of the Genealogies of Jesus*, SNTSMS 8, second edition, Cambridge University Press, 1988.

Johnson, S. E., *The Griesbach Hypothesis and Redaction Criticism*, Atlanta: Scholars Press, 1990.

Joüon, P., 'Luke 23,11: ἐσθῆτα λαμπράν', *RSR* 26 (1936), 80–5.

Karris, R. J., *What Are They Saying about Luke and Acts: A Theology of the Faithful God*, New York: Paulist Press, 1979.

'Missionary Communities: A New Paradigm for the Study of Luke–Acts', *CBQ* 41 (1979), 80–97.

Luke: Artist and Theologian. Luke's Passion Account as Literature, New York: Paulist Press, 1985.

'Luke 23:47 and the Lucan View of Jesus' Death', *JBL* 105 (1986), 65–74; reprinted in Sylva (ed.), *Reimaging*, pp. 68–78, 187–9.

Kee, H. C., *Good News to the Ends of the Earth*, London: SCM Press, 1990.

Kemmler, D. W., *Faith and Human Reason: A Study of Paul's Method of Preaching as Illustrated by 1–2 Thessalonians and Acts 17, 2–4*, Leiden: E. J. Brill, 1975.

Kennedy, G., *The Art of Persuasion in Greece*, Princeton University Press, 1963.

The Art of Rhetoric in the Roman World: 300 B.C.–A.D. 300, Princeton University Press, 1972.

Classical Rhetoric and Its Christian and Secular Tradition from Ancient to Modern Times, London: Croom Helm, 1980.

Kilgallen, J., *The Stephen Speech. A Literary and Redactional Study of Acts 7,2–53*, Rome: Biblical Institute Press, 1976.

'The Function of Stephen's Speech (Acts 7,2–53)', *Bib* 70 (1989), 173–93.

Kilpatrick, G. D., 'A Theme of the Lucan Passion Story and Luke xxiii. 47', *JTS* 43 (1942), 65–74.

Kimball, C. A., *Jesus' Exposition of the Old Testament in Luke's Gospel*, Sheffield: JSOT, 1994.

Kingsbury, J. D., *Conflict in Luke: Jesus, Authorities, Disciples*, Minneapolis: Fortress, 1991.

'The Plot of Luke's Story of Jesus', *Int* 48 (1994), 369–78.

Kinman, B., *Jesus' Entry into Jerusalem in the Context of Lukan Theology and the Politics of His Day*, Leiden: E. J. Brill, 1995.

Kistemaker, S. J., *Exposition of the Acts of the Apostles*, New Testament Commentary, Grand Rapids: Baker, 1990.

Kittel, G. and Friedrich, K. (eds.), *Theological Dictionary of the New Testament*, 9 vols., Grand Rapids: Eerdmans, 1964–76.

Klostermann, E., *Das Lukasevangelium*, Handbuch zum Neuen Testament 5, third edition, Tübingen: J. C. B. Mohr, 1975.

Kreeft, P. and Tacelli, R. K., *Handbook of Christian Apologetics*, Downers Grove, IL: Inter-Varsity Press, 1994.

Kümmel, W. G., 'Current Theological Accusations against Luke', *ANQ* 16 (1975), 131–45.

Kurz, W. S., *Reading Luke–Acts: Dynamics of Biblical Narrative*, Louisville: Westminster/John Knox, 1993.

Landouceur, D., 'Hellenistic Preconceptions of Shipwreck and Pollution as a Context for Acts 27–28', *HTR* 73 (1980), 435–49.

Larsson, E., 'Temple-Criticism and the Jewish Heritage: Some Reflexions on Acts 6–7', *NTS* 39 (1993), 379–95.

Laurentin, R., *The Truth of Christmas. Beyond the Myths. The Gospels of the Infancy of Christ*, translated from French by M. J. Wrenn *et alii*, Petersham, MA: St Bede's, 1982.

Légasse, S., 'L'apologétique à l'égard de Rome dans le procès de Paul. Actes 21,27–26,32', in J. Delorme and J. Duplacy (eds.), *La parole de grâce*, Paris: Recherches de science Religieuse, 1981, pp. 249–55.

Stephanos. Histoire et discours d'Etienne dans les Actes des Apôtres, Lectio Divina 147, Paris: Cerf, 1992.

The Trial of Jesus, London: SCM Press, 1997 (original French by Paris: Cerf, 1994).

Lentz, J. C., *Luke's Portrait of Paul*, SNTSMS 77, Cambridge University Press, 1993.

Lightfoot, R. H., *History and Interpretation in the Gospels*, London: Hodder & Stoughton, 1935.

Lindars, B., *New Testament Apologetic: The Doctrinal Significance of the Old Testament Quotations*, London: SCM Press, 1961.

Lohse, E., 'συνέδριον', *TDNT*, vol. VII, pp. 860–71.

Loisy, A., *L'Evangile selon Luc*, Paris: E. Nourry, 1924, reprinted Frankfurt: Minerva, 1971.

Long, W. R., 'The Trial of Paul in the Book of Acts: Historical, Literary, and Theological Considerations', unpublished PhD dissertation, Brown University, 1982.

'The Paulusbild in the Trial of Paul in Acts', in K. H. Richards (ed.), *Society of Biblical Literature 1983 Seminar Papers*, Chico, CA: Scholars Press, 1983, pp. 87–105.

Lönig, K., *Die Saulustradition in der Apostelgeschichte*, Neutestamentliche Abhandlungen 112, Münster: Aschendorff, 1973.

Louw, J. P. and Nida, E. A. (eds.), *Greek–English Lexicon of the New Testament, Based on Semantic Domains*, New York: UBS, 1988.

Mackenzie, R. K., 'Character-Description and Socio-Political Apologetic in the Acts of the Apostles', unpublished PhD dissertation, Edinburgh, 1984.

Maddox, R., *The Purpose of Luke–Acts*, ed. J. Riches, Edinburgh: T. & T. Clark, 1982.

Malherbe, A. J., 'The Apologetic Theology of the Preaching Peter', *RQ* 13 (1970), 205–23.

'"Not in a Corner": Early Christian Apologetic in Acts 26:26', *SC* 5 (1985/6), 193–210.

Malina, B. J. and Neyrey, J. H., 'Conflict in Luke–Acts: Labelling and Deviance Theory', in J. H. Neyrey (ed.), *The Social World of Luke–Acts: Models for Interpretation*, Peabody: Hendrickson, 1991, pp. 97–122.

Mare, W. H., 'Acts 7: Jewish or Samaritan in Character?', *WTJ* 33–4 (1970–2), 1–21.

Marguerat, D., '"Et quand nous sommes entrés dans Rome"': l'énigme de la fin du livre des Actes (28, 16–31)', *RHPR* 73 (1993), 1–21.

'Juifs et chrétiens selon Luc–Actes. Surmonter le conflit des lectures', *Bib* 75 (1994), 126–46.

Marshall, I. H., 'The Resurrection of Jesus in Luke', *TynB* 24 (1973), 55–68.

The Gospel of Luke: A Commentary on the Greek Text, NIGTC 3, Exeter: Paternoster, 1978.

The Acts of the Apostles: An Introduction and Commentary, TNTC, Leicester: Inter-Varsity Press; Grand Rapids: Eerdmans, 1980.

Last Supper and Lord's Supper, Grand Rapids: Eerdmans, 1980.

'Luke and his "Gospel"', in P. Stuhlmacher (ed.), *Das Evangelium und die Evangelien*, Tübingen: J. C. B. Mohr, 1983, pp. 289–308.

Luke–Historian and Theologian, third edition, Exeter: Paternoster, 1988.

The Acts of the Apostles, New Testament Guides, Sheffield: JSOT, 1992.

'Acts and the "Former Treatise"', in B. W. Winter and A. D. Clarke (eds.), *The Book of Acts*, pp. 163–82.

Matera, F. J., 'The Death of Jesus according to Luke: A Question of Sources', *CBQ* 47 (1985), 469–85.

Passion Narratives and Gospel Theologies: Interpreting the Synoptics Through Their Passion Stories, New York and Mahwah: Paulist Press, 1986.

'The Plot of Matthew's Gospel,' *CBQ* 49 (1987), 235–40.

'Luke 22:66–71: Jesus Before the Πρεσβυτέριον', in Neirynck (ed.), *L'Evangile*, pp. 517–33.

'Luke 23:1–25: Jesus Before Pilate, Herod, and Israel', in Neirynck (ed.), *L'Evangile*, pp. 535–51.

Responsibility for the Death of Jesus according to the Acts of the Apostles', *JSNT* 39 (1990), 77–93.

Mattill, A. J., 'The Purpose of Acts: Schneckenburger Reconsidered', in W. W. Gasque and R. P. Martin (eds.), *Apostolic History and the Gospel: Biblical and Historical Essays Presented to F. F. Bruce*, Exeter: Paternoster, 1970, pp. 108–22.

'*Naherwartung, Fernerwartung* and the Purpose of Luke–Acts: Weymouth Reconsidered', *CBQ* 34 (1972), 276–93.

'The Jesus–Paul Parallels and the Purpose of Luke–Acts: H. H. Evans Reconsidered', *NovT* 17 (1975), 15–46.

'The Date and Purpose of Luke–Acts: Rackham Reconsidered', *CBQ* 40 (1978), 335–50.

McDonald, J. I. H, *The Resurrection: Narrative and Belief*, London: SPCK, 1989.

McGrath, A., *Bridge-Building: Effective Christian Apologetics*, Leicester: Inter-Varsity Press, 1992.

Mealand, D., 'Acts 28.30–31 and Its Hellenistic Greek Vocabulary', *NTS* 36 (1990), 583–97.

Merritt, R. L., 'Jesus, Barabbas, and the Paschal Pardon', *JBL* 104 (1985), 57–68.

Metzger, B. M., *A Textual Commentary on the Greek New Testament*, second edition, Stuttgart: Deutsche Bibelgesellschaft, 1994.

Miles, G. B. and Trompf, G., 'Luke and Antiphon: The Theology of Acts 27–28 in the Light of Pagan Beliefs about Divine Retribution, Pollution, and Shipwreck', *HTR* 69 (1976), 259–67.

Moessner, D. P., *Lord of the Banquet: The Literary and Theological Significance of the Lukan Travel Narrative*, Minneapolis: Fortress, 1989.

Mommsen, T., *Römisches Strafrecht*, Leipzig, 1899.

Moxnes, H., *The Economy of the Kingdom: Social Conflict and Economic Relations in Luke's Gospel*, Philadelphia: Fortress, 1988.

Murphy, J. J., 'Early Christianity as a "Persuasive Campaign": Evidence from the Acts of the Apostles and the Letters of Paul', in S. E. Porter and T. H. Olbricht (eds.), *Rhetoric and the New Testament: Essays from the 1992 Heidelberg Conference*, Sheffield Academic Press, 1993.

Neirynck F. (ed.), *L'Evangile de Luc*, revised and enlarged edition of *L'Evangile de Luc. Problèmes littéraires et théologiques*, BETL 32, Leuven University Press, 1989.

Neirynck, F. and Friedrichsen, T. A., 'Note on Luke 9,22. A Response to M. D. Goulder', in Neirynck (ed.), *L'Evangile*, pp. 393–8.

Neyrey, J. H., 'Jesus' Address to the Women of Jerusalem (Luke 23:27–31) – A Prophetic Judgment Oracle', *NTS* 29 (1983), 74–86.

'The Forensic Defence Speech and Paul's Trial Speeches in Acts 22–26: Form and Function', in C. H. Talbert (ed.), *Luke–Acts: New Perspectives from the Society of Biblical Literature Seminar*, New York: Crossroad, 1984, pp. 210–24.

The Passion According to Luke: A Redaction Study of Luke's Soteriology, New York: Paulist Press, 1985.

The Resurrection Stories, Wilmington, DE: M. Glazier, 1987.

Nolland, J., *Luke*, 3 vols. (Luke 1–9:20; 9:21–18:34; 18:35–24:53), Word Biblical Commentary 35 A, B, C; Dallas, TX: Word, 1989 (vol. I), 1993 (vols. II–III).

O'Neill, J. C., *The Theology of Acts in Its Historical Setting*, London: SPCK, 1970.

O'Toole, R. F., *Acts 26, The Christological Climax of Paul's Defense (Ac 22:1–26:32)*, Analecta Biblica 78, Rome: Biblical Institute Press, 1978.

Parsons, M. C. and Pervo, R. I., *Rethinking the Unity of Luke and Acts*, Minneapolis: Fortress, 1993.

Pattison, S. E., 'A Study of the Apologetic Function of the Summaries of Acts', unpublished PhD dissertation, Emory University, 1990.

Pervo, R. I., *Luke's Story of Paul*, Minneapolis: Fortress, 1990.

Pesch, R., *Die Apostelgeschichte*, Evangelisch-Katholischer Kommentar zum Neuen Testament 5:1–2, Zürich and Neukirchen-Vluyn: Benzinger, 1986, 1990.

Plevnik, J., 'The Origin of Easter Faith according to Luke', *Bib* 61 (1980), 492–508.

'The Eyewitnesses of the Risen Jesus in Luke 24', *CBQ* 49 (1987), 90–103.

'Son of Man Seated at the Right Hand of God: Luke 22,69 in Lucan Christology', *Bib* 72 (1991), 331–47.

Plooij, D., 'The Work of St Luke', *Exp* 8:8 (1914), 511–23.

'Again: The Work of St Luke', *Exp* 8:13 (1917), 108–24.

Plummer, A., *A Critical and Exegetical Commentary on the Gospel according to St Luke*, ICC, Edinburgh: T. & T. Clark; New York: Scribner, 1896.

Pummer, R., 'The Samaritan Pentateuch and the New Testament', *NTS* 22 (1975–6), 441–3.

Ramsay, W. M., *The Bearing of Recent Discovery on the Trustworthiness of the New Testament*, London: Hodder & Stoughton, 1920.

Rapske, B., *The Book of Acts and Paul in Roman Custody*, BAFCS, vol. III, Grand Rapids: Eerdmans; Carlisle: Paternoster, 1994.

'Acts, Travel and Shipwreck', in David W. J. Gill and Conrad Gempf (eds.), *The Book of Acts in Its Graeco-Roman Setting*, BAFCS, vol. II, Grand Rapids: Eerdmans; Carlisle: Paternoster, 1994, pp. 1–47.

'Luke's Portrait of Paul, by John Clayton Lentz Jr', book review, *EvQ* 66 (1994), 347–53.

Ravens, D., *Luke and the Restoration of Israel*, JSNTSup 119, Sheffield Academic Press, 1995.

Rehkopf, F., *Die lukanische Sonderquelle: Ihr Umfang und Sprachgebrauch*, WUNT 5, Tübingen: J. C. B. Mohr, 1959.

Rengstorf, K. H., *Das Evangelium nach Lukas*, ninth edition, Göttingen: Vandenhoeck & Ruprecht, 1962.

Resseguie, J. L., 'Interpretation of Luke's Central Section (Luke 9:51–19:44) since 1856', *StudBT* 5 (1975), 3–36.

Richard, E., 'Acts 7: An Investigation of the Samaritan Evidence', *CBQ* 39 (1977), 190–208.

Acts 6:1–8:4. The Author's Method of Composition, SBLDS 41, Missoula, MT: Scholars Press, 1978.

Richardson, Alan, *Christian Apologetics*, London: SCM Press, 1947.

Robinson, J. A. T., *Twelve New Testament Studies*, SBT 34, London: SCM Press, 1962.

Roloff, J., *Die Apostelgeschichte*, Das Neue Testament Deutsch 5, Göttingen, 1981.

Rosenblatt, M.-E., *Paul the Accused. His Portrait in the Acts of the Apostles*, Collegeville, MN: Liturgical, 1995.

Samain, E., 'Le discours-programme de Jésus à la synagogue de Nazareth. Luc 4,16–30', *Foi et Vie* 11 (1971), 25–43.

Sanders, E. P., *Jesus and Judaism*, London: SCM Press, 1985.
    Judaism: Practice and Belief 63BCE–66CE, London: SCM Press, 1992.
Sanders, J. T., *The Jews in Luke–Acts*, London: SCM Press, 1987.
Satterthwaite, P. E., 'Acts Against the Background of Classical Rhetoric', in
    Winter and Clarke (eds.), *Book of Acts*, pp. 337–79.
Scharlemann, M., *Stephen: A Singular Saint*, Rome: Pontifical Biblical Institute
    Press, 1968.
Schmid, J., *Das Evangelium nach Lukas*, third edition, Regensburg: Pustet,
    1955.
Schmidt, D., 'Luke's "Innocent" Jesus: A Scriptural Apologetic', in Cassidy and
    Scharper (eds.), *Political Issues*, pp. 111–21.
Schneckenburger, M., *Über den Zweck der Apostelgeschichte*, Bern, 1841.
Schneider, G., *Die Passion Jesu nach den drei ältern Evangelien*, Munich: Kösel,
    1973.
    Das Evangelium nach Lukas, 2 vols., Gütersloh: G. Mohn; Würzburg: Echter,
    1977.
    'Der Zweck des lukanischen Doppelwerkes', *BZ* 21 (1977), 45–66.
    Die Apostelgeschichte, Herders Theologischer Kommentar zum Neuen Testa-
    ment, 2 vols., Freiburg: Herder, 1980/2.
    'The Political Charge against Jesus (Luke 23:2)', in Bammel and Moule (eds.),
    Jesus, pp. 403–14.
Schramm, T., *Der Markus-Stoff bei Lukas*, Cambridge University Press, 1971.
Schubert, P., 'The Final Cycle of Speeches in the Book of Acts', *JBL* 87 (1968),
    1–16.
Schürer, E., *The History of the Jewish People in the Age of Jesus Christ (175
    B.C.–A.D. 135)*, revised and edited by G. Vermes et al., 3 vols., Edinburgh:
    T. & T. Clark, 1973–87.
Schürmann, H., 'Lk 22, 19b–20 als ursprüngliche Textüberlieferung', *Bib* 32
    (1951), 364–92, 522–41.
    Der Paschamahlbericht, Münster im Westphalia: Aschendorff, 1953.
    Der Einsetzungsbericht, Münster im Westphalia: Aschendorff, 1955.
    Jesu Abschiedsrede, Münster im Westphalia: Aschendorff, 1957.
Schwartz, D. R., 'Non-Joining Sympathizers (Acts 5,13–14)', *Bib* 64 (1983),
    550–5.
Schweizer, E., 'Zur Frage der Quellenbenutzung durch Lukas', in his *Neues Tes-
    tament und Christologie im Werden*, Göttingen: Vandenhoeck & Ruprecht,
    1982, pp. 33–85.
    The Good News according to Luke, translated from German by D. E. Green,
    London: SPCK, 1984.
Scobie, C. H. H., 'The Origins and Development of Samaritan Christianity', *NTS*
    19 (1972–3), 390–414.
Seland, T., *Establishment Violence in Philo and Luke: A Study of Non-Conformity
    to the Torah and Jewish Vigilante Reactions*, Leiden: E. J. Brill, 1995.
Senior, D., *The Passion of Jesus in the Gospel of Luke*, Collegeville, MN:
    Liturgical, 1989.
Shepherd, W. H., *The Narrative Function of the Holy Spirit as a Character in
    Luke–Acts*, Atlanta: Scholars Press, 1994.
Sherwin-White, A. N., *Roman Society and Roman Law in the New Testament*,
    Oxford: Clarendon, 1965.

The Trial of Jesus. Historicity and Chronology in the Gospels, London: SPCK, 1965.

Shin, G. K., *Die Ausrufung des endgültigen Jubeljahres durch Jesus in Nazareth: Eine historisch-kritische Studie zu Lk 4,16–30*, Bern: Lang, 1989.

Silberman, L. H., 'Paul's Viper. Acts 28:3–6', *Forum* 8:3–4 (1992), 247–53.

Simon, M., *St Stephen and the Hellenists in the Primitive Church*, London, New York, and Toronto: Longmans, Green and Co., 1958.

Sloyan, G. S., *Jesus on Trial*, Philadelphia: Fortress, 1973.

Smith, T. V., *Petrine Controversies in Early Christianity: Attitudes towards Peter in Christian Writings of the First Two Centuries*, WUNT 2:15, Tübingen: J. C. B. Mohr, 1985.

Soards, M. L., *The Passion According to Luke: The Special Material of Luke 22*, Sheffield Academic Press, 1987.

'Tradition, Composition, and Theology in Jesus' Speech to the "Daughters of Jerusalem" (Luke 23:26–32)', *Bib* 68 (1987), 221–44.

Spencer, F. S., *Acts*, Sheffield Academic Press, 1997.

Spiro, A., 'Stephen's Samaritan Background', in J. Munck, *The Acts of the Apostles*, revised by W. F. Albright and C. S. Mann, The Anchor Bible 31, New York: Doubleday, 1967, pp. 285–300.

Squires, J. T., *The Plan of God in Luke–Acts*, Cambridge University Press, 1993.

Stählin, G., *Die Apostelgeschichte*, Das Neue Testament Deutsch 5, Göttingen, 1962.

Sterling, G. E., *Historiography and Self-Definition: Josephos, Luke–Acts and Apologetic Historiography*, Leiden: E. J. Brill, 1992.

Still, J. I., *St Paul on Trial*, London: SCM Press, 1923.

Stolle, V., *Der Zeuge als Angeklagter. Untersuchungen zum Paulusbild des Lukas*, BWANT 102, Stuttgart: W. Kohlhammer, 1973.

Stott, J. R. W., *The Message of Acts. To the Ends of the Earth*, The Bible Speaks Today, Leicester: Inter-Varsity Press, 1990.

Strauss, M. L., *The Davidic Messiah in Luke–Acts: The Promise and its Fulfilment in Lukan Christology*, Sheffield Academic Press, 1995.

Streeter, B. H., *The Four Gospels: A Study of Origins*, London: Macmillan, 1924.

Summers, R., *Commentary on Luke*, Waco, TX: Word, 1972.

Sylva, D. D., 'The Temple Curtain and Jesus' Death in the Gospel of Luke', *JBL* 105 (1986), 239–50.

'The Meaning and Function of Acts 7:46–50', *JBL* 106 (1987), 261–75.

Sylva, D. D. (ed.), *Reimaging the Death of the Lukan Jesus*, Bonner Biblische Beiträge 73, Frankfurt-am-Main: Hain, 1990.

Tajra, H. W., *The Trial of St Paul: A Judicial Exegesis of the Second Half of the Acts of the Apostles*, WUNT 2, Reihe 35, Tübingen: J. C. B. Mohr, 1989.

The Martyrdom of St Paul: Historical and Judicial Contexts, Traditions, and Legends, Tübingen: J. C. B. Mohr, 1994.

Talbert, C. H., *Luke and the Gnostics: An Examination of the Lucan Purpose*, Nashville: Abingdon, 1966.

Literary Patterns, Theological Themes, and the Genre of Luke–Acts, Missoula: Scholars Press, 1974.

Reading Luke: A Literary and Theological Commentary on the Third Gospel, New York: Crossroad, 1984.

Tannehill, R. C., 'The Composition of Acts 3–5: Narrative Development and Echo Effect', in K. H. Richards (ed.), *SBL 1984 Seminar Papers*, Chico: Scholars Press, 1984, pp. 217–40.

'Israel in Luke–Acts: A Tragic Story', *JBL* 104 (1985), 69–85.

The Narrative Unity of Luke–Acts: A Literary Interpretation, 2 vols. Minneapolis: Fortress, 1986, 1990.

'The Narrator's Strategy in the Scenes of Paul's Defense. Acts 21:27–26:32', *Forum* 8:3–4 (1992), 255–69.

Taylor, V., *Behind the Third Gospel: A Study of the Proto-Luke Hypothesis*, Oxford: Clarendon, 1926.

The Passion Narrative of St Luke: A Critical and Historical Investigation, ed. O. E. Evans, Cambridge University Press, 1972.

Thayer, J. H., *Greek–English Lexicon of the New Testament*, Grand Rapids: Zondervan, n.d.

Tiede, D. L., ' "Fighting against God": Luke's Interpretation of Jewish Rejection of the Messiah Jesus', in C. A. Evans and D. A. Hagner (eds.), *Anti-Semitism and Early Christianity: Issues of Faith and Polemic*, Minneapolis: Fortress, 1993, pp. 102–12.

Trites, A. A., 'The Importance of Legal Scenes and Language in the Book of Acts', *NovT* 16 (1974), 278–84.

Trocmé, E., *Le 'Livre des Actes' et l'histoire*, Paris: Presses Universitaires de France, 1957.

Tuckett, C. M., *The Revival of the Griesbach Hypothesis*, SNTSMS 44, Cambridge University Press, 1983.

Turner, M. M. B., *Power from on High: The Spirit in Israel's Restoration and Witness in Luke–Acts*, Sheffield Academic Press, 1996.

'Acts 3 and the Christology of Luke–Acts', in 'Acts', unpublished collection of papers for Open Theological College, n.d., pp. OTC3/1–OTC3/17. Used with permission.

Twelftree, G., *Christ Triumphant: Exorcism Then and Now*, London: Hodder & Stoughton, 1985.

Tyson, J. B., 'The Lucan Version of the Trial of Jesus', *NovT* 3 (1959), 249–58.

'Jesus and Herod Antipas', *JBL* 79 (1960), 239–46.

'Conflict as a Literary Theme in the Gospel of Luke', in W. R. Farmer (ed.), *New Synoptic Studies: The Cambridge Gospel Conference and Beyond*, Macon, GA: Mercer, 1983, pp. 303–27.

The Death of Jesus in Luke–Acts, Columbia, SC: University of South Carolina Press, 1986.

Tyson, J. B. (ed.), *Luke–Acts and the Jewish People. Eight Critical Perspectives*, Minneapolis: Augsburg, 1988.

Van den Sandt, H., 'Acts 28:28: No Salvation for the People of Israel? An Answer in the Perspective of the LXX', *ETL* 70 (1994), 341–58.

Van Unnik, W. C., 'The "Book of Acts": The Confirmation of the Gospel', *NovT* 4 (1960), 26–59.

'Once More St Luke's Prologue', *Neot* 7 (1973), 7–26.

'Eléments artistiques dans l'évangile de Luc', in Neirynck (ed.), *L'Evangile*, pp. 39–50.

Veltmann, F., 'The Defense Speeches of Paul in Acts', in C. H. Talbert (ed.), *Perspectives on Luke–Acts*, Edinburgh: T. & T. Clark, 1978, pp. 243–84.

Via, E. J., 'According to Luke, Who Put Jesus to Death?', in Cassidy and Scharper (eds.), *Political Issues*, pp. 122–40.

Vine, V. E., 'The Purpose and Date of Acts', *ExpT* 96 (1984), 45–8.

Walaskay, P. W., 'The Trial and Death of Jesus in the Gospel of Luke', *JBL* 94 (1975), 81–93.

    'And so we came to Rome': The Political Perspective of St Luke, Cambridge University Press, 1983.

Watson, A., *The Trial of Jesus*, Athens, GA: University of Georgia Press, 1995.

    The Trial of Stephen: The First Christian Martyr, Athens, GA: University of Georgia Press, 1996.

Weatherly, J. A., *Jewish Responsibility for the Death of Jesus in Luke–Acts*, JSNTSup 106, Sheffield Academic Press, 1994.

Weinert, F. D., 'The Meaning of the Temple in Luke–Acts', *BTB* 11 (1981), 85–9.

    'Luke, Stephen, and the Temple in Luke–Acts', *BTB* 17 (1987), 88–90.

Weiser, A., *Die Apostelgeschichte*, 2 vols., Gütersloh: Gütersloher Verlagshaus Mohn, 1981, 1985.

Weiss, J., *Über die Absicht und den literarischen Charakter der Apostelgeschichte*, Marburg and Göttingen, 1897.

Wilson, S. G., *The Gentiles and the Gentile Mission in Luke–Acts*, Cambridge University Press, 1973.

    'The Jews and the Death of Jesus in Acts', in P. Richardson and D. Granskou (eds.), *Anti-Judaism in Early Christianity*, Studies in Christianity and Judaism 2, Waterloo, Ontario: Wilfrid Laurier University Press, 1986, pp. 155–64.

Wink, W., *John the Baptist in the Gospel Tradition*, Cambridge University Press, 1968.

Winter, B. W., 'The Importance of the *Captatio Benevolentiae* in the Speeches of Tertullus and Paul in Acts 24:1–21', *JTS* 42 (1991), 504–31.

    'Official Proceedings and the Forensic Speeches in Acts 24–26', in Winter and Clarke (eds.), *Book of Acts*, pp. 305–36.

Winter, B. W. and Clarke, A. D. (eds.), *The Book of Acts in Its Ancient Literary Setting*, *BAFCS*, vol. I, Grand Rapids: Eerdmans; Carlisle: Paternoster, 1993.

Winter, P., 'The Treatment of His Sources by the Third Evangelist in Luke XXI–XXIV', *ST* 8 (1955), 138–72.

    'Luke XXII 66b–71', *ST* 9 (1956), 112–15.

    On the Trial of Jesus, second edition, revised by T. A. Burkill and G. Vermes, Berlin: Walter de Gruyter, 1974.

Witherington III, B., *The Acts of the Apostles: A Socio-Rhetorical Commentary*, Grand Rapids: Eerdmans; Carlisle: Paternoster, 1998.

Wolfe, R. F., 'Rhetorical Elements in the Speeches of Acts 7 and 17', *JOTT* 6 (1993), 274–83.

Wright, N. T., *Christian Origins and the Question of God*, vol. I: *The New Testament and the People of God*, London: SPCK, 1992.

    Christian Origins and the Question of God, vol. II: *Jesus and the Victory of God*, London: SPCK, 1996.

Zeller, E., *The Contents and Origin of the Acts of the Apostles Critically Investigated by Dr Edward Zeller*, London: Williams and Norgate, 1876 (original German edition, 1854).

INDEX OF BIBLICAL PASSAGES

INDEX OF SUBJECTS